LAW AND RELIGION:
NEW HORIZONS

The new series *Law and Religion Studies* is published by the European Consortium for Church and State Research, a group of scholars from the member states of the European Union. Top level monographs and other publications are envisaged. They cover problems concerning law and religion, in Europe or elsewhere, with a specific focus on comparative and international dimensions.

The Editorial Committee
N. Doe
J.M. Gonzalez del Valle
F. Messner
Ch. Papastathis
R. Torfs

LAW AND RELIGION STUDIES

7

LAW AND RELIGION: NEW HORIZONS

Editors:

Norman Doe
Russell Sandberg

PEETERS

LEUVEN – PARIS – WALPOLE, MA

2010

A catalogue record for this book is available from the Library of Congress

© 2010 Uitgeverij Peeters, Bondgenotenlaan 153, B-3000 Leuven (Belgium)

D/2010/0602/69
ISBN 978-90-429-2159-7

TABLE OF CONTENTS

LIST OF CONTRIBUTORS

ANTHONY BRADNEY

Anthony Bradney is presently Professor of Law at Keele University and has previously been Professor of Law at the Universities of Sheffield and Leicester. His previous publications include *Religions, Rights and Laws* (Leicester, Leicester University Press, 1993), *Living Without Law: An Ethnography of Dispute Avoidance and Resolution in the Religious Society of Friends* (with Fiona Cownie) (Aldershot, Ashgate, 2000) and *Conversations, Chances and Choices: The Liberal Law School in the Twenty-First Century* (London, Hart, 2003). His latest book *Law and Faith in a Secular Age* was published by Routledge in 2009.

REBECCA CATTO

After completing her BA at the University of Oxford, Rebecca Catto did her masters degree in the Anthropology and Sociology of Religion at King's College London. She is currently completing her doctorate in Sociology at the University of Exeter, supervised by Professor Grace Davie, researching the phenomenon of non-western Christian missionaries currently working in Britain as a field of mission. Her interest in blending the sociological and legal in the study of religion has burgeoned since being commissioned to produce, with Grace Davie, the report on State/religion relations in Great Britain for a collection entitled *State and Religion in Europe* funded by the Turkish Religious Foundation Centre for Islamic Studies. The findings were presented at a Symposium on State and Religion in Europe in Istanbul in December 2006, and the resulting book was recently published in Turkish with an English translation to follow.

RICHARD CLARKE

In 2008 Richard Clarke graduated from the University of Warwick with an LLM with distinction in Human Rights Law. He previously studied law at Cardiff University where he took Law and Religion as an elective subject. He holds a Lord Justice Holker Scholarship from Gray's Inn and intends to practise as a barrister in the near future. He is a member of the British Humanist Association.

FRANK CRANMER

Frank Cranmer is a graduate of the Cardiff masters degree in canon law. A Fellow of St Chad's College, Durham and an honorary Research

Fellow in the Centre for Law and Religion at Cardiff Law School, he has recently become Secretary of the Churches' Legislation Advisory Service. Recent publications include articles for *Public Law* and the *Ecclesiastical Law Journal*, on Quaker trusteeship, (with Scot Peterson) on clergy employment, (with Tom Heffer) on the interpretation of scripture and Anglican canon law and (with Anna Harlow and Norman Doe) on Bishops in the House of Lords. He is also the parliamentary and synod editor of the *Ecclesiastical Law Journal*. He is a contributor to a study of Church and State to be published by Palgrave Macmillan.

NORMAN DOE

Norman Doe is a Professor and the Director of the Centre for Law and Religion, Cardiff Law School. He studied law at Cardiff, a masters degree in theology at Oxford, and, for his doctorate, at Cambridge. He is an associate professor at the University of Paris, a member of the European Consortium for Church and State Research, and is author of *Fundamental Authority in Late Medieval English Law* (Cambridge, Cambridge University Press 1990), *The Legal Framework of the Church of England* (Oxford, Clarendon Press, 1996), *Canon law in the Anglican Communion* (Oxford, Clarendon Press, 1998), and *The Law of the Church in Wales* (Cardiff, University of Wales Press, 2002). He is editor of *Essays in Canon Law* (Cardiff, University of Wales Press, 1992) and *The Portrayal of Religion in Europe: Media and Arts* (Leuven, Peeters, 2004), and co-editor, with Mark Hill and Robert Ombres OP, of *English Canon Law* (Cardiff, University of Wales Press, 1998), with J Conn and J Fox, *Initiation, Membership and Authority in Anglican and Roman Catholic Canon Law* (Rome, 2005) and with R Puza, *Religion and Law in Dialogue: Covenantal and Non-Covenantal Cooperation between State and Church in Europe* (Leuven, Peeters, 2006). His latest book is *An Anglican Covenant: Theological and Legal Considerations for a Global Debate* (London, Canterbury Press, 2008). He is a member of the general committee of the Ecclesiastical Law Society and was a member of the Lambeth Commission (2004).

DAVID HARTE

David Harte is Senior Lecturer in Law at Newcastle Law School, Newcastle University. He is also a trained barrister and is Deputy Chancellor for the Diocese of Durham. He is book review editor of the *Ecclesiastical Law Journal* and has contributed to a number of publications on ecclesiastical law and other aspects of law and religion, including contributing chapters to *Law and Religion* edited by Richard O'Dair and Andrew Lewis (Oxford, Oxford University Press, 2001), *Christian Perspectives on the Limits of Law*, edited by Paul Beaumont (London, Paternoster, 2002) and *Religious Liberty and Human Rights*, edited by Mark Hill (Cardiff, University of Wales Press, 2002).

MARK HILL

Mark Hill is a practising barrister and Honorary Professor of Law at Cardiff University at its Centre for Law and Religion. His publications include *Ecclesiastical Law* (Third edition, Oxford, Oxford University Press, 2007) and he is editor of *Religious Liberty and Human Rights* (Cardiff, University of Wales Press, 2002) and the *Ecclesiastical Law Journal* (published by Cambridge University Press). He is a Recorder of the Crown Court, and Chancellor of the Dioceses of Chichester and Europe. He regularly lectures in the United Kingdom and abroad on matters concerning the law of Church and State.

DAVID LAMBERT

David Lambert is a Solicitor. Until his retirement, he was a lawyer in the Government Legal Service attached to the Welsh Office and was the chief legal adviser from 1990-1999. He was the legal adviser to the Presiding Officer of the newly established National Assembly for Wales from 2000-2004. He is now a Research Fellow in Public Law at Cardiff Law School. He has been the Legal Registrar of the Diocese of Llandaff since 1986.

PETER LUXTON

Peter Luxton is Professor of Law at Cardiff University. He has written widely on charity law, and is author of *The Law of Charities* (Oxford, Oxford University Press, 2001), and *Charity Fund-raising and the Public Interest* (Aldershot, Avebury, 1990). He is a member of the Charity Law Association, and has chaired two of their working parties. He has spoken on charity law at many international conferences, most recently at Heidelberg in July 2006. He was also an invited delegate to the Charity Law Association's Public Benefit Conference held in Methodist Central Hall, Westminster, in May 2007.

JAVIER OLIVA

Dr Javier Oliva studied law at the University of Cadiz, where he obtained his first degree, LLM and PhD. After finishing his first degree, he became a lecturer at the University of Cadiz (1996-2000) and a Research Fellow at the Centre for Law and Religion at Cardiff University (2001-2004). Javier was appointed lecturer at the University of Wales Bangor in 2004 where he is currently Head of Public Law as well as the Course Leader of Law with Modern Languages. He is also a Research Associate at the Centre for Law and Religion at Cardiff University and he is teaching on a part-time basis at University College London (UCL). Furthermore, he is the Convenor of the SLS Public Law Section and Book Review Editor of *Law and Justice*.

AUGUR PEARCE

Dr Augur Pearce has taught Law and Religion at Cardiff University since 2002 and authored a number of articles in the constitutional and ecclesiastical fields, usually from an historical perspective. Recent articles have appeared in the *Journal of Church and State, Journal of Manx Studies* and *Common Law World Review*. Earlier he contributed to the *Ecclesiastical Law Journal* and *Celebrating Christian Marriage*, edited by Adrian Thatcher (London, Continuum, 2002). Ecclesiastical and charity law were among his specialist areas during twelve years' private legal practice in Westminster, and his doctoral thesis at Cambridge concerned the contrasting development of the church-nation relationship in the legal systems of England and pre-revolutionary Prussia. He is a Director of the United Reformed Church Trust and commencing a study of the rules and polity of mainstream non-episcopal Protestantism in England and Wales.

ALEXANDRA PIMOR

Alexandra Pimor is lecturer in (Public & EU) Law at LJMU School of Law; she obtained an LLB (Hons) in English & French Laws with French at the University of Liverpool School of Law; and is currently undergoing doctoral studies on 'Law, Religion and the Future of the European Union' at Bristol Law School under the supervision of Dr J Rivers and Dr P Syrpis. Alex is the co-author (with Professor C Lyon) of *Physical Interventions & the Law* (BILD 2005) – other publications include 'The Interpretation and Protection of Article 9 ECHR: Overview of the Denbigh High School (UK) case' (2006) 28(3-4) *Journal for Social Welfare and Family Law* 323-334.

PAULINE ROBERTS

Pauline Roberts is a lecturer at Cardiff Law School. Having qualified as a solicitor and worked in private practice, she now teaches and researches in the area of Employment Law and Discrimination and the Law. Recent publications include 'From Monitoring to Mainstreaming: Changing Workplace Culture through the Positive Duty to Promote Race Equality' (*Contemporary Issues in Law*, 2006/2007). She has also published co-authored research (with Lucy Vickers) on harassment at work as discrimination in the *International Journal of Discrimination and the Law*.

RUSSELL SANDBERG

Russell Sandberg is a lecturer at Cardiff Law School and an Associate of both the Centre for Law and Religion and the Centre for the Study of Islam in the UK, Cardiff University. After graduating from the Law School with First Class Honours in July 2005, he commenced doctoral study at Cardiff University examining the relationship between religion, law and society. He has written widely on religion and human rights, discrimination law, religious dress and Church-State relations for a wide range of journals including *Public Law*, *Law Quarterly Review*, *Cambridge Law Journal*, *Modern Law Review* and the *Ecclesiastical Law Journal*.

CHARLOTTE SMITH

Charlotte Smith attained her doctorate from King's College London in 2003 for a thesis entitled 'Assessing the Impact of Establishment on Reforms to Clergy Discipline, c. 1840-1883'. She has been Lecturer in Law at the University of Reading since September 2002. Her publications include articles for *Public Law*, *Northern Ireland Legal Quarterly* and *Legal History*, as well as chapters in the books *Landmark Cases in the Law of Restitution*, edited by C Mitchell and P Mitchell (London, Hart, 2006) and *Law and Religion in Theoretical and Historical Context*, edited by P Cane, C Evans, and Z Robinson (Cambridge, Cambridge University Press, forthcoming).

LIST OF MAIN ABBREVIATIONS

CLJ   Cambridge Law Journal

CL&PR   Charity Law and Practice Review

Crim LR   Criminal Law Review

Ecc LJ   Ecclesiastical Law Journal

EHRLR   European Human Rights Law Review

Ent LR   Entertainment Law Review

LQR   Law Quarterly Review

MLR   Modern Law Review

PL   Public Law

INTRODUCTION

Norman Doe and Russell Sandberg

Law and Religion in England and Wales

In contrast to North American and many continental European countries, the study of the interaction between law and religion has been a neglected area in Law Schools in England and Wales. The Reformation ban on the teaching of Canon Law at the Universities, the perceived secularisation of society and the piecemeal and subtle way in which English law regulated religion meant that the study of law and religion was largely ignored. This changed in the last quarter of the twentieth century with the formation of the Ecclesiastical Law Society in 1987, the introduction of a master's degree in Canon Law at Cardiff University in 1991 and the advent of a distinct academic literature. There are now specialist journals of repute dedicated to this subject, distinct research clusters and academics that exclusively specialise in the area.

This process was accelerated by the sheer number of legal developments affecting religion. There has been a step change: the passive accommodation provided by the common law has been superseded by the active protection of religious liberty as a positive right[1]. The Human Rights Act 1998 incorporated the right to freedom of thought, conscience and religion under Article 9 of the European Convention on Human Rights into domestic law. The Employment Equality (Religion or Belief) Regulations 2003 and the Equality Act 2006 now outlaw discrimination on grounds of religion or belief in relation to employment and the provision of goods and services. Further, in addition to numerous laws on education and immigration, major legislative developments include the Anti–Terrorism, Crime and Security Act 2001, the Divorce (Religious Marriages) Act 2002, the Civil Partnership Act 2004, the Racial and Religious Hatred Act 2006, the Charities Act 2006 and the Criminal Justice and Immigration Act 2008. These developments have been followed by a tide of case law applying and interpreting the effect of the new laws, including an

---

[1] M Hill and R Sandberg, 'Is Nothing Sacred? Clashing Symbols in a Secular World' [2007] *P L* 488 at 490.

unprecedented number of decisions by the highest court of the land, the House of Lords.

These major changes, often the result of international pressures, occur at a time in which the place of religion in the public sphere has attracted great attention and debate. They also occur against a general legal framework which is characterised by a number of complexities, ambiguities, and, sometimes, contradictions; it is a system with both the identification of a Church with the State (in England) and of separation of Church and State (as in Wales), it is a system where some religious organisations have statutory recognition while the courts generally view religious organisations as voluntary associations and are traditionally reluctant to intervene in religious matters. This move towards, and now beyond, toleration has been more pragmatic than philosophical.

Given this legal and societal background, it is unsurprising that the study of law and religion in law schools in England and Wales has now progressed from the embryonic stage. The high placing of questions of religious liberty on the political and media agendas has engaged, and led to the development of, a distinct academic community. It is also not surprising given the pace and quantity of this transformation, that most of that academic attention has focussed upon specific changes. By contrast, little attention has been paid to the collective effect of the jurisprudential evolution or the question of the ambit and scope of law and religion as an academic discipline.

Law and Religion: New Horizons seeks to redress this imbalance. This collection has its origins in a 'Law and Religion' Stream held at the Socio-Legal Studies Association Annual Conference 2007 at Canterbury[2]. The papers presented at that event and the ensuing discussions indicated a number of innovative research questions, concepts and methods. It is a pleasure to collect those contributions in the chapters that follow, together with a number of invited papers inspired by the events of Canterbury. This collection seeks to reflect upon the changing legal regulation of religion in England and Wales by reference to recent developments in numerous areas of law, including human rights law, constitutional law, criminal law, discrimination law, charity law and European Union law. It also looks at underlying trends, how the law affects specific religious groups and the state of scholarship in this field. The conclusion extrapolates the cumulative effects of the legal developments discussed and

---

[2] For a report, see R Sandberg, 'Socio-Legal Studies Association: Law and Religion Stream' (2007) 9 *Ecc LJ* 320.

reflects upon how the scholarship in this field may develop further. It is intended that this collection will help to set the agenda for future research in the field.

Defining Law and Religion

Given this collection's focus upon both the substantive law and the scholarly study of that law, it seems appropriate to reflect briefly at the outset about what we conceive of as 'law and religion'. For us, to study law and religion is to study both:

(i) The 'external' national and international laws affecting religious individuals and collectives; which may be styled 'religion law'; and

(ii) The 'internal' laws or other regulatory instruments created by religious collectives themselves, which may be styled 'religious law'.

'Religion law' and 'religious law' are two complimentary and overlapping entities[3]. The distinction is made to stress their interconnected state and to allow closer analysis to be paid to the proper ambit of the discipline. Many works on religion law routinely exclude the study of religious law and many studies on religious law fail to place it within the wider environment of State law on religion and society. This seems misguided, especially given the establishment of the Church of England. The prime question for most law and religion academics in England and Wales is how law does and does not (or should and should not) accommodate religious difference. We submit that the word 'law' in this question should be interpreted to include both the laws that apply to religious groups and also the laws created by those religious groups. It includes the study of how State law accommodates religious difference manifest in religious law. The study of law and religion is actually the study of *laws* and *religions*.

This categorization allows greater scrutiny to be given to the ambit of the study of both 'religion law' and 'religious law'. 'Religion law' may be considered as analogous to family law: rather than corresponding to a certain legal action, like tort law, it relates to an entity that has meaning outside the legal domain, is impacted upon by a number of different areas of law, is seen largely as a 'problem' to be tackled and has a goal the achievement of which is increasingly seen as an universal human

---

[3] See further R Sandberg, 'Church-State Relations in Europe: From Legal Models to an Interdisciplinary Approach' (2008) 1(3) *Journal of Religion in Europe* 329.

right[4]. Religion law may be defined as the part of (national and international) law concerned with the recognition and regulation of certain religious relationships and the implications of such recognition[5]. 'Religious law' is understood here to encompass the various forms of regulatory instruments of religious organisations, communities and traditions. Its comparative study seeks in part to expose the extent to which visions, problems and possible solutions are shared[6]; its approach is 'irrepressibly interdisciplinary', smuggling understandings across the frontiers of several disciplines[7], most notably history and theology. The enterprise may thus be seen as an exercise of both scholarly and practical worth.

The work of the late Harold Berman provides a reminder that to study the interaction between law and religion is to study a broad canvas. In his introduction to *The Interaction of Law and Religion*, based on his 1971 Lowell Lectures on Theology, he noted that some listeners 'were concerned that more emphasis was not placed on the conflicts between law and religion'[8]. Although it is understandable and valuable that much work in law schools in England and Wales seems to focus on such conflicts, it is important that the study of law and religion extends further than this. This book seeks to examine those conflicts in their wider context, exploring not only new developments but also new concepts, approaches and questions. We hope that the essays that follow will provide the catalyst for further research for those interested in going behind the headlines to understand more fully the relationship between law and religion and its new horizons.

May 2008

---

[4] Compare, G Douglas, *An Introduction to Family Law* (Second edition, Oxford, Clarendon Press, 2004) 3.

[5] Ibid.

[6] N Doe, *The Legal Framework of the Church of England* (Oxford, Clarendon Press, 1996) 2.

[7] A Huxley, *Religion, Law and Tradition: Comparative Studies in Religious Law* (London, Routledge, 2002) 5.

[8] H J Berman, *The Interaction of Law and Religion* (London, Bloomsbury Press, 1974) 11.

ENGLAND'S LAW OF RELIGION –
THE HISTORY OF A DISCIPLINE

Augur Pearce

Introduction

This chapter traces the emergence of a law of religion in England and Wales, separate from ecclesiastical law (in the sense of the law governing the national church). A recent aspect of the story has been the dawn of a new field of scholarship: recognising the coherence of legal issues affecting religion, but yet standing back from the story of any one tradition. From a virtually monocredal English society before the Reformation, in which the law regarding religion was studied primarily by writers within the tradition of the English Church and loyal to its sources of authority, we have moved today to a pluralism in which each tradition still has specialists in its 'internal' rules, but there is scope for writers of all faiths and none to consider how society relates to the phenomenon of religion through the medium of the law. The question will be raised, at the close of the story, how widely this scope is so far being realised.

I. The Reformation and Dissent

One consequence of England's sixteenth-century breach with Rome was to replace the medieval distinction between recognised sources of the law touching religion[1] by a legal monism, according to which the same authority lay behind all the law of the land, religion being no exception[2]. A by-product of this changed official thinking was the coming into being of significant groups of the population who sought leave to differ: to recognise in their own readings of Scripture (or in the papacy)

[1] That is, the allocation of temporal causes to princes and spiritual causes to priests (and ultimately the papacy).

[2] See the preamble to the Ecclesiastical Licences Act 1533; also the frequent implications in Tudor statutes that clerical legislation had been a usurpation of royal power and the statement in the Ecclesiastical Appeals Act 1532, s.1, that episcopal courts operate 'within the King's jurisdiction and authority'. The contrary view underlying the Continental canon law was surely a major motivation for its suppression as an academic discipline by the Vicegerent's university visitation instructions of 1535.

an authority against which decrees of Crown and parliament could be measured and found wanting.

Such leave was not granted. To acknowledge a jurisdiction on English soil derived from Rome was soon declared treason[3] – partly because, at least until the repulsion of the Armada, there was a real possibility of establishing that jurisdiction by force. Protestant Dissent might pose a less critical threat but was nonetheless a challenge to lawful authority that could not be allowed to pass unchecked. In 1592 unlawful assembly 'under colour or pretence of religion' became punishable with banishment even for those who were not 'popish recusants'[4]. Non-domestic worship alternative to the official provision would remain criminal in some cases for 250 years, which naturally inhibited the courts from recognising any structure designed to oversee or support such practices[5].

Yet a lack of official status for church institutions had never inhibited scholars from writing about them. On the Continent canonical literature continued to flourish. John Calvin, most prolific on institutional questions amongst the protestant Reformers, was widely read and admired in England; the *Discipline Ecclésiastique* was adopted by the Reformed Synod of Paris in 1559 and Knox's *First Book of Discipline* became the provisional basis of the Scots Reformation in the following year. By the 1570s the Cambridge scholars Cartwright and Travers were expounding a scheme of Presbyterian church government for English use.

The dwindling Roman Catholic population aside, there was as yet no serious religious dissent from any branch of the law aside from that of public worship and preaching. Catholics, of course, also had issues with the law of marriage: impediments such as precontract and holy orders were contentious, as was the dispensing power, and from 1670 (if not before) there would be legislative dissolutions of marriage, effective in England but not in the eyes of Rome[6].

It has been questioned how far the dualism of the medieval law on religion was in fact ended at the Reformation. The research of Richard Helmholz has shown that in the eyes of the bishops and their officials

---

[3] Stat 23 Eliz I c1 (1580).

[4] Stat 35 Eliz I c1 (1592).

[5] A 1623 attempt by Pope Urban VIII to place resident Vicars Apostolic in England ended with the flight of the last appointee in 1631 to avoid arrest.

[6] The opinion of half the House of Lords in *R v Millis* (1844) 10 Cl & Fin 534 that marriage at common law required an episcopally ordained officiant, with the result that many unions of Irish Presbyterians were void (as would English Dissenters' marriages have been before 1753) caused consternation at the time and retrospective validation by statutes such as 5 & 6 Vict c.113.

who presided over ecclesiastical courts in the late Tudor and Stuart periods, the canon law of western Christendom was still an authoritative source, not merely to the extent that it had been somehow 'received' on English soil. Litigants invoked it and episcopal judges deferred to it; foreign canonical writers were cited with approval even if they had written in Catholic territories after the English Reformation[7]. In the courts of Westminster Hall, however, this approach was increasingly deplored. It was after all irreconcilable with parliament's clear declaration in the preamble to the Ecclesiastical Licences Act 1533, which explained the binding effect of rules of external origin exclusively in terms of reception 'not as to the laws of any foreign prince or prelate, but [by the English] at their own free liberty', and with Coke CJ's characterisation of such rules as 'the *King's* ecclesiastical law'[8].

Vaughan CJ set the future course with his comment in 1667 that:

> If the canon law be made part of the law of this land, then is it as much the law of the land, and as well, *and by the same authority*, as any other part of the law of the land. And if it be not made the law of the land, then hath it no more effect than a law of Utopia[9].

II. The Law of Religion at and after the Revolution

1. The Unity of the Law and the Development of Alternative Religious Rules

From the period of the Glorious Revolution onward, even episcopal judges tended to recognise that the law was one, albeit jurisdiction as to its enforcement remained divided[10]. There was by then a new categorisation possible, though, into law of general application and law made by and for the clergy; since the claim of archbishops and provincial convocations (encouraged by some earlier sovereigns, including Elizabeth I)

---

[7] R Helmholz, *Canon Law and the Law of England* (London, Hambledon Press, 1987).

[8] *Caudrey's case* (1591) 5 Co Rep 1a (italics supplied).

[9] *Edes v Bishop of Oxford* (1667) Vaughan 18 (italics supplied). See also *Bishop of Exeter v Marshall* (1868) LR 3 HL 17 and the exposition of Lord Blackburn in *Mackonochie v Lord Penzance* (1881) 6 App Cas 424, 446.

[10] The statement to this effect by Uthwatt J. in *A.-G. v Dean & Chapter of Ripon* [1945] Ch 239, 245 was nothing new. However it was not just the law as a whole, but ecclesiastical law whose enforcement was divided. As well as its supervisory jurisdiction over episcopal tribunals generally, the King's Bench enjoyed original jurisdiction in some ecclesiastical suits such as *quare impedit*, and was able to step in with its own remedies when the episcopal courts could not, or no longer, punish an ecclesiastical offence adequately – such as blasphemy in *R v Taylor* (1676) 1 Vent 293.

to legislate in religious matters with general effect was finally refuted by
the post-revolutionary courts[11]. Clerical canons could supplement the law
of the land, imposing additional expectations upon the ordained, and all
courts would take note of and enforce such expectations; but they could
neither contradict the general law[12], nor restrict the religious rights and
freedoms of laymen.

Although it could therefore be argued that Civil War and Revolution
together had restored the unity of the law of religion as declared in the
Tudor preamble, rejecting the endeavours of Elizabeth and Charles I to
exempt religious lawmaking from the need for popular consent through
parliament, yet their aftermath also raised afresh the issue of the customs
and usages of alternative religion. The Civil War and the exile of Charles II
had allowed Dissenting Protestantism a temporary respite from the penal
legislation. In 1642 the Lords and Commons had summoned an advisory
Assembly of Divines to Westminster, which left a lasting legacy to the
Presbyterian tradition[13]. The relaxation of restrictions allowed other
groups to surface, including the oldest tradition – that of the Independent
congregations – and consult on matters relevant to their common identity. Particular Baptist representatives agreed a statement of their position
in the First London Confession of 1644; paedobaptist Congregational-
ists did the same in the Savoy Declaration of 1658. Oliver Cromwell
also indicated that he would not object to the settlement of Jewish families within the kingdom, and the first congregation (of largely Hispanic
origin) opened the Creechurch Lane synagogue in 1657.

The return to constitutional government in 1660 led the newly-surfaced
traditions back underground for a time. The later Stuarts' unparliamentary
Declarations of Indulgence allowed *de facto* appearance of some Dissenting protestant congregations in purpose-built meeting-houses, but were
withdrawn again in the face of parliamentary protest. Directions to the
Attorney-General to halt prosecutions by *nolle prosequi*[14] prevented interference with the earliest synagogues. The seemingly propitious conditions

---

[11] *Middleton v Crofts* (1736) 2 Atk 650; affirmed in *Bishop of Exeter v Marshall*
(1868) LR 3 HL 17.

[12] Submission of the Clergy Act 1533, s3.

[13] Travers' 1587 *Book of Discipline* was influential in the preparation of the new *Form
of Presbyteral Church Government*. The *Confession of Faith, Directory of Public Worship*
and two Catechisms were also products of the Assembly. Only the *Directory*, however,
acquired such force as the Houses could give it; and in 1650 the Rump of the Commons
purported to repeal the Act of Uniformity 1559 altogether, allowing liberty of worship in
all of England's churches.

[14] Order in Council of 13th November 1685.

moved Pope Innocent XI to re-establish the Apostolic Vicariate of England in 1685 under James II's personal protection. Yet whatever the factual toleration, the law continued to acknowledge one religion only. Trusts for otherwise charitable purposes still contravened public policy if they supported an unlawful Dissenting Protestant ministry[15]; the presence of the papal appointee (Leyburn) in England remained illegal, and he was imprisoned in Newgate immediately after King James's abdication; and as Lord Hardwicke observed years later, the toleration of protestant Dissent in 1689 only 'renders those religions lawful, which is not the case of the Jewish religion, that is not taken notice of by any law, but is merely connived at by the legislature'[16].

The organisation of alternative religion on the eve of the Toleration Act, therefore, was already the subject of rules and scholarship – the Talmud, Mishnah and *Corpus Juris Canonici*, together with the writings of Calvin, the protestant documents of the 'interregnum' and a growing expository literature – but a clear distinction had to be drawn between such rules (binding only so far as individuals acted on them in conscience, or with the support of unconstitutional royal power) and the law of the land in religious matters. So far as the latter was concerned, there was still only ecclesiastical law.

To the continental lawyer today, especially in Roman Catholic territories, the linguistically equivalent expression (*diritto ecclesiastico, droit ecclésiastique, &c.*) means 'the law of the state regulating religion' and is contrasted with the 'law of the church' or 'canon law'. In protestant England at the Glorious Revolution, such connotations were simply not possible: there was but one English Church, the kingdom considered in its spiritual character[17]. The rules governing English worship and doctrine, pastoral care and offices of oversight, marriage and decedent estates, religious assets and the supporting fiscal framework, were no more and no less than a branch of the wider law of the land.

Part of that branch, too, were the rules which penalised misconduct in the moral and religious sphere; and among those rules, the general

---

[15] *A-G. v Baxter* (1684) 1 Vern 248.

[16] *Da Costa v. Da Paz* (1736) Ambl 228.

[17] 'When we oppose the Church therefore and the Commonwealth in a Christian society, we mean by the Commonwealth that society with relation unto all the public affairs thereof, only the matter of true religion excepted. By the Church that same society with only reference unto the matter of true religion without any other affairs besides.' – R Hooker, *Of the Laws of Ecclesiastical Polity*, Book VIII, (London 1648; reprinted in the Folger Library Edition, Cambridge Mass. & Binghamton NY) 326.

obligation to attend Sunday and festival services in the parish church[18] and the penalising of alternative assemblies. When it came, toleration – the statutory framework which lifted such penalties on condition, with mechanisms put in place to ensure that those conditions were observed – was equally in its turn a facet of ecclesiastical law.

Conclusions of ecclesiastical law did, of course, have repercussions in other legal fields and *vice versa* during the so-called 'long eighteenth century' that followed. The descent of land might still turn upon the validity of a marriage, or attempted alienation of land be invalidated by its consecration. A commercial deadline might defer to an ecclesiastical festival[19], a person be restricted in his commercial dealings as a cleric[20] or excluded altogether from commerce as an excommunicate[21]. Succession to the Crown now entailed the duty to receive holy communion by the official rite[22], while deprivation of a bishopric entailed forfeiture of a parliamentary seat[23]. In such instances public ecclesiastical law produced an effect in private law, or the political and ecclesiastical branches of public law affected each other.

2. *Private Law in the Religious Field and the First Religious Exemptions*

Yet toleration brought with it the seeds of something new. The individuals whose worship became lawful in 1689 had already been assembling extra-legally for over a century. They had their own concepts of the church, their own ideas of orthodoxy and authority, initiation, ministry and matrimony. Their conduct implied agreement on these points, at least within local groups, and such agreement formed part of the understanding on which their preachers were called and paid. When they acquired land for their meeting-houses and manses, funds to train their ministers or support Sabbath schools, believing donors or subscribers' nominees declared trusts, earmarking these assets for the advancement of religion or education in accordance with their tenets. Most such trusts were considered to benefit society in general, once freed from the charge

---

[18] e.g. Act of Uniformity 1551, s 1.

[19] e.g. Banking Act 1800 (Bills of exchange not due on Good Friday, supplementing the common law protection of Sundays and Christmas Day).

[20] e.g. Pluralities Act 1838, s.29 (giving general effect to earlier canonical provisions).

[21] This became infrequent after the Ecclesiastical Courts Act 1813 replaced excommunication by imprisonment as the sanction for contempt of episcopal courts.

[22] Act of Settlement 1700, s 3.

[23] *Bishop of St David's v Lucy* (1699) Carth 484.

of supporting illegal conventicles[24], and could therefore enjoy the law's favour as expressed through the special privileges of charity.

As a consequence of toleration, therefore, religion became a concern of branches of the law of England other than public ecclesiastical law. Ecclesiastical law might lift the ban on the worship of General Baptists, Roman Catholics, Unitarians or Jews, provided certain conditions were met (and from the mid-nineteenth century the last such conditions were swept away)[25]; but it would not indicate how Dissenting groups were to worship, nor choose between congregational meeting, eldership and episcopacy as their proper form of internal government. These were private matters, for Dissenters to resolve between themselves; and insofar as their resolution required legal enforcement to give it permanence, such enforcement would naturally take place on the private law basis of trust or contract.

It would hardly be meaningful to speak of a 'law of religion' outside ecclesiastical law if individual and voluntary religion were treated in every respect identically to other lawful activity. Even the favouring of religion by charity law merely treated its advancement as worthy – and there were other worthy activities. But an exemption *peculiar to religion* from what the law would otherwise require was something else. Here – in the Toleration Act's provision for 'scrupulous consciences' to which the normal usages of Christian England were unacceptable – one can see the dawn of the law of religion as a distinct legal field.

The Act modified obligations imposed by local government and jury law and supplemented the criminal law to protect Dissenting worship from disturbance. A 'declaration before God and the world' as an alternative to an oath of allegiance sworn 'by Almighty God', foreshadowed later concessions in official oath taking and in the law of evidence. The first recognition of collective religion could be seen in the Act's reference to a Quaker's *bona fides* being certified by other members of 'the congregation to which he belongs'[26].

---

[24] The report of *A-G. v Baxter* (1684) 1 Vern 248, above, notes the reversal of the decision in 1689 in the light of the new law.

[25] The principal statutes were the Toleration Act 1689, Roman Catholic Relief Act 1791, Unitarian Relief Act 1813 and Religious Disabilities Act 1846.

[26] Toleration Act 1689, s7, allowed qualifying Dissenters chosen for certain parish offices which entailed religious oaths or ecclesiastical duties to perform such offices by a suitable deputy. S 11 allowed qualifying Dissenting preachers exemption from such parochial offices and from jury service. S 13 allowed the 'declaration before God', s 14 contained the concept of 'belonging' and s 18 imposed binding over or a fine for disturbing lawful congregations or 'misusing' their preachers. Even before the Act, judges had

In 1753 Lord Hardwicke recognised that Quakers and Jews could not be expected in conscience to contract their marriages in the context of a parish church solemnisation which, under his Clandestine Marriages Act, would henceforth be required of everybody else. Whether this gave any more positive legislative recognition to Quaker and Jewish usage is doubtful: the Act merely said that the law on marriages within those communities would not change. Quaker practice was not unduly problematic, since it already involved words of mutual consent and was Christian marriage *per verba de praesenti* such as the law had generally recognised before the Act[27]. Jewish marriage was also consensual and so arguably satisfied 'the King's ecclesiastical law', though the bridal couple's intention to follow religious custom could be helpful in pinpointing the precise moment in the ceremony at which they intended their consent to take effect[28].

It was of course still possible to treat these as isolated instances, falling under the branch of law – public or private – which they modified. They were hardly enough to give rise to a separate or wider legal discipline of 'the law of religion'. But by the nineteenth century such a separate discipline was becoming familiar to quite a number of continental jurisdictions.

III. At Home and Abroad – the French Revolution to the Great War

1. Concordats and Constitutions

In France the violently anticlerical nature of the 1798 Revolution repudiated any desire to consider the canon law part of the law of the land. The calendar reform set an example of secularisation reaching further than any modern constitution. Bonaparte's developed religious policy, by contrast, envisaged close co-operation between national and Roman

---

reacted to the reappearance of Jews in England by adjusting the court calendar to relieve Jewish litigants from disadvantage: *Barker v Warren* (1677) 2 Mod 271. In *Lindo v Unsworth* (1811) 2 Camp 602 Lord Ellenborough attributed to the intercultural character of the law merchant a deferment (from Yom Kippur) of the day on which a Jewish businessman was required to report the dishonour of a bill of exchange.

[27] Unless the opinions to the contrary in *R v Millis* (1844) 10 Cl & Fin 534, above, were correct.

[28] Only an interpretation such as this – presaging the 'parties' choice' approach to registered building marriages in the Marriage Act 1836 – seems to justify the concern of Scott Ch with Jewish custom in *Lindo v Belisario* (1795) 1 Hagg Con 216. Ironically, though, it was also the 1836 Act which made compliance with Jewish usage a factor in the validity of marriages between Jews.

Catholic organs; but it hinged upon a Concordat, a device enabling those supreme in governmental and ecclesiastical spheres to agree and concede as co-ordinate authorities. Concordat provisions were not canon law since they did not emanate from ecclesiastical authorities alone. They could, strictly speaking, be classified as treaty law, thanks to the international legal personality of the Roman See which (rather than any national episcopate) was the government's bargaining partner. But these were treaties with a difference, having greater immediate domestic effect than most other treaties of the time.

Concordats' popularity during the century overlapped with another legal trend, the fashion for written constitutions. A constitution might guarantee freedom of conscience or church autonomy, identify a national church or mandate the separation of church and state; but if it did any of these things, and above all if it provided for minority religious traditions or groups in a way analogous to its provision for the dominant religion, it gave the country in question a species of law 'about' religion distinct from the rules 'of' any one tradition. Both constitutions and concordats provided key provisions upon which any study of the legal relations of church and state could build.

The Protestant countries in which this development was most pronounced were those strongly affected by the revolutionary movement of the mid-century. The change was striking in Prussia in 1848, where King Frederick William IV, a religious conservative with a high view of the church, granted a constitution associating a new bicameral *Landtag* with the King in general legislation but guaranteeing both 'the protestant and the Catholic church' the right to independent ordering of their own affairs[29]. In the case of Protestantism this meant that while lawmaking competence would remain with the King (the supreme bishop) and organs of his making, the *Landtag* would play no part. As an *Oberkirchenrat* was split off and given autonomy from the Ministry of Spiritual Affairs, commentators spoke of the laws of the State and the protestant church, which had hitherto walked in tandem, parting company.

Only a few decades previously, Prussian writers had still spoken of a branch of the general law relating to the Protestant (or Catholic) *Kirchwesen*, perhaps best roughly translated 'ecclesiastical matters'. The mindshift involved for Protestants in speaking of 'law of the

---

[29] *Verfassungs-Urkunde für den Preußischen Staat*, 5th December 1848, Arts 12 and 60. The Dutch constitution of 1848 also paved the way for a significant measure of church-state separation.

church', *Kirchenrecht*, as something distinct from that general law was considerable; though it had been foreshadowed in the way the Treaty of Westphalia had spoken of Protestant or Catholic communities in particular parts of the Holy Roman Empire having rights to exercise 'their own' religion[30].

Prussia did not entirely embrace the concept of a secular state at this time: following a revision, the Spiritual Affairs Ministry was still required to operate on a Christian basis[31]. But denominational neutrality was henceforth expected of it. The law it administered was (alongside the constitutional guarantee) considered *Staatskirchenrecht*, rules of the State/church relationship, in our terminology 'law of religion'. Protestant *Kirchenrecht* would originate with the King, advised by the *Oberkirchenrat* and later acting with a representative General Synod.

2. English Continuity, with Concessions to Dissent

History explains why England failed to replicate these Continental developments. The Armada's failure had sealed the principle of national autonomy: geographical separation from the Continent allowed indigenous Catholicism to be ignored more consistently than in the Hohenzollern dominions. Democratic institutions in England had preceded rather than followed toleration, and the convention of the King being advised by a responsible minister had emerged before (not, as in Prussia, alongside) notions that government should stand back from the spiritual sphere. In early nineteenth century England judicious concession to a wider franchise prevented revolution – hence, probably, any codified constitution. Gradual concession to Dissenting (including Roman Catholic) interests then avoided the root issue – the law's inherited concept of 'one church' identical with the commonwealth – by relieving its more burdensome symptoms one by one.

In a way this approach delayed the emergence of a fully-fledged law of religion; since it was merely as the King's subjects, not as adherents of a particular creed, that Dissenters enjoyed the nineteenth century concessions. Very few of the new arrangements *required* Dissenting status

---

[30] *Instrumentum Pacis Osnabrugense* 24.10.1648, especially Arts V, VII, in H H Hofmann (ed) *Quellen zum Verfassungsorganismus des Heiligen Römischen Reichs deutscher Nation 1495-1815* (Darmstadt 1976) 170.

[31] *Verfassungs-Urkunde für den Preußischen Staat*, 5th December 1850, Art 14. The 1850 constitution replaced that of 1848 but the provisions already mentioned remained in substance unaltered.

– as a rule the law, including the ecclesiastical law, was modified with general effect; so that conformists were just as free as Dissenters to marry in a register office, matriculate at Oxford without doctrinal subscription[32] or decline the payment of a church rate[33].

The recognition of *organised* Dissent remained half-hearted. Statutory functions were assigned in 1836 to the Recording Clerk of the Society of Friends and the President of the London Committee of Deputies of British Jews, in relation to the marriage privileges of those communities[34]. It remained clear, however, that it was normally to individuals, not communities, that conscientious freedoms were allowed: registered building marriages were to follow such form and ceremony as *the bridal couple* might see fit to adopt[35]; grants in aid of the education of the poor were made to trustees of voluntary religious initiatives, not to hierarchies[36]; any alternative rite used at a churchyard burial would be at the option of the person paying or responsible for the event, and authority to officiate would equally flow from the organiser[37].

Positive provision for alternative religion was nevertheless increasing. Acts directed specifically to the private law affecting religion, while touching neither ecclesiastical law nor other voluntary activity, were passed in 1844 and 1850[38]. New burial arrangements followed[39], and in 1852 registration of Dissenting places of worship was placed on a new

[32] Oxford University Act 1854.

[33] Compulsory Church Rate Abolition Act 1880.

[34] Marriage (Registration) Act 1836, s 30.

[35] Marriage Act 1836, s 20.

[36] Parliamentary grants had been made in support of trusts to educate the poor since 1833; but although these initiatives were mainly religious, Education Committee policy did not make reference to that fact until 1839, when a right to withdraw from religious education was recommended. However from 1862 this became a grant condition.

[37] Burial Laws Amendment Act 1880, s 6. Under the Marriage Act 1898 it was also for the trustees of registered buildings to authorise individuals to attend and validate any solemnisation in lieu of a registrar; the additional modern requirement of the pastor's agreement in Roman Catholic buildings was of later origin.

[38] The Nonconformist Trusts Acts 1844 allowed chapels used for worship in accordance with consistent doctrinal tenets for a stated time to be deemed held upon trust for such use; thereby permitting continued Unitarian use of chapels where Unitarian theology had first been taught in the days of its illegality before 1813. The Appointment of Trustees Act 1850 allowed for automatic vesting of religious charity property in the trustees' successors.

[39] The Cemeteries Clauses Act 1847, whose provisions were designed to be incorporated into the Private Bills promoted by commercial cemetery companies, required companies to have parts of their cemeteries consecrated, but s 35 envisaged companies setting apart other parts for the burial of Dissenters (thus allowing, for example, dedicated Jewish burial portions) – a provision carried over to Burial Board cemeteries in the Burial Act 1852.

footing. This was now a process independent of the ecclesiastical law of worship: registration with the Registrar-General to secure privileges was a far cry from notification to the archdeacon as a condition of legality[40]. The kingdom's first mosque appears, incidentally, to have opened after this reform, meaning Muslims never had to contend with the earlier restrictions[41].

3. Voluntarism in the Church of England

The second half of the nineteenth century, extending to the First World War, was the era of the sometimes bitter challenges to the ecclesiastical authority of Crown and parliament by 'high church' conformists to the Church of England. While parliament by and large stood firm in the face of Anglo-Catholic liturgical illegalities, the bishops' approach was more nuanced; and a side-product of the conflict over doctrine and worship was the episcopal encouragement given to voluntary initiatives involving parish clergy and active laypeople from the 1860s onwards. The first parochial church councils, diocesan conferences and even lay 'Houses' for northern and southern England came into being without any basis in ecclesiastical law, but rather the same basis – voluntary compact – as underlay church synods in certain self-governing colonies overseas or the presbyteries, assemblies and episcopal hierarchies of protestant and Catholic Dissent at home. Money was given and charitable trusts created to support these novel structures, and from 1903 there was an identifiable lay 'membership' of the movement in the form of a 'church electoral roll'.

With its most active adherents entangled in such a structure, the question could reasonably be posed whether the Church of England remained the religious establishment of the realm[42] or had become a religious association essentially like any other, albeit with undeniable privileges and constraints.

---

[40] The notification requirement in Toleration Act 1689, s 19 was modified by 15 & 16 Vic c.36 (1852) to substitute the Registrar-General for ecclesiastical officers, by which time notification was already a prerequisite for marriage registration and rating exemption. The modern law is the Places of Worship Registration Act 1855.

[41] There seem to be several claimants to the title of Britain's first mosque: the statement above refers to the theory that it opened in Cathays, Cardiff in 1860, on the site that is now the Al-Manar Islamic Cultural Centre: see <http://www.bbc.co.uk/religion/religions/islam/history/uk_1.shtml>.

[42] This expression was coined, with reference to the Church of England in pre-independence New Hampshire, by Storey J in the Supreme Court of the United States: *Town of Pawlet v Clark* (1810) 13 US 292, 325.

High churchmen now believed that it had always been the latter[43]. They used the term 'establishment' not in the literal sense of the word which gained meaning from the qualifying words 'by law' – so that the official or Church of England ministry was 'established by law' while that of Primitive Methodism was 'established by voluntary compact' – but in a technical sense to mean the singling out and privileging of a pre-existent body.

One test that might have solved this was whether the Church of England could claim to have its 'own' rules, like the protestant *Kirchenrecht* of post-1848 Prussia. This was the claim of high churchmen, stepping into a scholarly vacuum created by the effective demise of Doctors' Commons[44]. These included clerical authors like Edward Wood who had published a defence of the 'regal power of the church' relying largely upon Continental canonical sources[45]. The clergy convocations, active since the 1850s, had also been prolific in passing resolutions, many directed towards the laity as much as their ordained brethren. In 1857 Parliament had taken the unprecedented step of allowing parish ministers an exemption from their duty on conscientious grounds where a parishioner, judicially divorced on grounds of his own adultery, desired solemnisation of a fresh marriage in his parish church[46]; and in some quarters it was argued that the minister's decision to officiate or not should be made in obedience to convocation policy. Was there accordingly a 'Church of England law of marriage' separate from the law of the land?

That question was answered in the negative by the House of Lords in 1912. Another matrimonial statute, the Deceased Wife's Sister's Marriage Act 1907, had legalised certain unions to which affinity would previously have been an impediment. This Act too contained a conscience clause – wider this time, and favouring the clerical conscience even at the expense of a parishioner's rights – but a minister had gone beyond the Act and refused communion to a parishioner so married, justifying his otherwise unlawful refusal by the parishioner's breach of 'the church's

---

[43] See the analysis of the high churchman Phillimore J in *Marshall v Graham* [1907] 2 KB 112, 126.

[44] The civilians of Doctors' Commons, whose ecclesiastical specialism had been tempered by realism through actual practice in courts where statute and the writ of prohibition were perforce respected, became a dying breed after the transfer of probate and matrimonial jurisdictions in 1857 ended their lucrative monopoly of these fields.

[45] *The Regal Power of the Church, or the Fundamentals of the Canon Law – A Dissertation*, 1888, repr. 1948 with an introduction by E W Kemp.

[46] Matrimonial Causes Act 1857, s 57.

law'. Even the Act's 'civil contract' language could not, however, 'make duality in marriage'[47].

The ecclesiastical law of marriage thus remained a product of the establishment of religion, necessarily consistent with the general law of the land however clergy might dislike it. But, equally clearly, the 1903 constitution of the new representative structures was a matter of private contract between those clerics who chose to participate and the laity on the church electoral roll; they could vary such rules as they pleased without parliament's involvement. The convocation resolutions, too, were quite unenforceable (except indirectly upon such ministers as were vulnerable to episcopal displeasure): they were not canons, and would not have bound laypeople if they were. A significant body of conformists, however, did regard them as morally binding and could perhaps be argued to have accepted them.

On the eve of the Great War, therefore, there were seemingly two faces of the Church of England: the national establishment governed by public ecclesiastical law and the voluntary structures built up in the past half-century to support and reinvigorate it. To high churchmen and Dissenters alike, there was no distinction – neither acknowledged that there could be a religious branch of government in a Christian nation – but many moderate conformists, the liberals and broad churchmen (in a temporary and uneasy alliance with evangelicals) had no problem with the ecclesiastical *status quo* and viewed the voluntary structures with suspicion. The two viewpoints were symbolised by titles in the literature of the period: Thomas Lacey's 1903 *Book of Church Law* suggested the existence of a 'church law' that could be contrasted with 'law of the state', while the 1910 contribution of an ecclesiastical law title to the new series Halsbury's *Laws of England* witnessed to the older view of official religion as a branch of the law of the land[48].

4. The Education Controversy

The early nineteenth century's voluntary initiatives in the education of the poor were, by 1870, no longer sufficient. Rate-funded 'board schools' were established to offer elementary education where it was lacking, but under strong Dissenting pressure were directed to offer only

---

[47] *Thompson v Dibdin* [1912] AC 533, especially *per* Lord Ashbourne at 543.

[48] The title was contributed in the 1st Edition by Thomas Tristram, a noted ecclesiastical judge.

undenominational Christian religious instruction[49]. The changing popular concept of the Church of England was further underlined by this development. Christian instruction by school boards – or later, local education authorities – was clearly a national religious provision, an addition to the 'religious establishment of the realm'. It was not based on the Book of Common Prayer, but after all it was not supposed to be worship. It was not based on the Articles of Religion, but those had only ever been a *ministerial* doctrinal standard. It was not controlled by bishops, but neither was religion in the royal peculiars. In short the undenominational character of religious instruction was no bar to it being considered, on the older view, an aspect of the Church of England.

It was, however, never perceived in this light. In the eyes of high churchmen and Dissenters alike, the Church of England *was* a denomination, for good or ill. High churchmen contrasted undenominational Christianity with the dogmas, liturgical outlook and ecclesiology they wished to impart to children. They found board schools' provision unsatisfactory, particularly when those schools' academic achievements outshone schools connected with their own National Society. But the funding of religious voluntary schools from rates, which they won (with Roman Catholic backing) from the Balfour government in 1902, proved violently controversial. Even Catholic schools had been receiving central government grants since 1848, but that had seemed more remote and so less painful to Protestants than a local tax.

5. The Law and the Unbeliever

The new century's rivalry between Christian traditions accompanied an accelerated drift of sections of English society to agnosticism or atheism. Some now found it preferable for there to be no religious instruction of children at public expense, no Christian symbolism in state ceremonial, no favouring of religious purposes in charity law. The law remained unfriendly toward campaigners. They might exercise individual rights of conscience, such as affirming instead of swearing oaths, and 'a conscientious objection to the undertaking of combatant service' was recognised during the War without requiring it to be religiously-based[50]. But the

---

[49] Elementary Education Act 1870, s 14 (the so-called 'Cowper-Temple clause'), which did not specify 'Christian' but was universally so understood.

[50] Military Service Act 1916, s 2. However as late as *Hynds v Spillers-French Baking Ltd* [1974] IRLR 281, 28 a statutory reference to 'grounds of conscience' was held to imply at least a broadly religious belief.

furtherance of a non-religious philosophy of life, or endeavours to persuade others of religion's demerits, were not charitable purposes[51], and
the limited company was the only device that could give permanence and
legal personality to secularist institutions. The House of Lords' 1917
decision on the legality of anti-religious purposes contains *dicta* to which
too much weight has sometimes been given. Lord Sumner dismissed as
'rhetoric' the claim that 'Christianity is part of the law of England', but
this was in the context of the law of blasphemy: his *ratio* was that only
vilification (not mere denial) of Christian tenets would pose such a threat
to society as to be criminal[52].

IV. The Middle Twentieth Century

1. Protestant Episcopalian Developments

By 1920 the tension between public and voluntary aspects of the
Church of England had been resolved in Wales. The religious establishment had been abolished in the principality and ecclesiastical law no
longer existed as law. Former conformists wishing to continue Cranme-
rian worship voluntarily under a Protestant episcopate had constituted
themselves a 'Church in Wales', Parliament helping this off the ground
with a deemed contract (consisting of the rules of English public ecclesiastical law) until they saw fit to change it[53]. The corollary was a division
of public religious assets: the religious buildings, land and endowments
to which tithe, church rate, Crown and parliamentary grants had contributed so much in the past were partially reallocated to other public purposes. The remainder were ceded to the new voluntary body, subject to
an obligation to provide public burial space in Welsh churchyards[54].

---

[51] *Re South Place Ethical Society* [1980] 3 All ER 1565.

[52] *Bowman v Secular Society* [1917] AC 406, 464. The House was not reflecting on
such matters as the existence of a Christian provision established by law, the legal Calendar or the coronation oath.

[53] Welsh Church Act 1914, s 3(2). This statutory provision argued against the existence of a distinct 'law of the church' in England; had Welsh conformists been bound by
free submission to such a distinct 'law' – as Dissenters were to their rules – before the
support of public law was withdrawn, they would have been equally bound afterwards, so
no 'deemed contract' would have been necessary.

[54] Welsh Church Act 1914. By an afterthought, enshrined in the Welsh Church (Temporalities) Act 1919, s 6, the law of marriage was left unchanged by the Act, although the
general abolition of ecclesiastical law meant there would be no parish churches in which
to marry, nor ecclesiastical officers to solemnise or grant licences, save the premises and
officers of the voluntary association.

In England a compromise had been reached but the tension between understandings of the national church would continue. The Assembly at the apex of the voluntary structure was empowered to frame draft legislative measures concerning the Church of England, which could acquire the force and effect of Acts of Parliament after Lords, Commons and the King had given approval through an expedited process[55]. There was no distinction in this procedure corresponding to that between Public and Private Bills, so rules and organs of the voluntary structure and of the public establishment were equally liable to alteration by the new process, and considerable blurring of the two – including significant transfer of the powers of public authorities to voluntary organs – was to result. As parliament tended after this date to approve ecclesiastical measures with very few exceptions (contentious every time), the Church Assembly was popularly taken to be the author of the new legislation and the notion of 'law of the church' gained wider currency.

Space forbids further examination here of the two faces of the Church of England or the implications that arise if they remain distinguishable today. What is indisputable is that the Welsh Church Acts and English 'Enabling Act' between them provided new contexts in which the views of Protestant episcopalians, both clerics and active laity, could be formulated and expressed even when these differed from the national conscience as expressed through parliament. Maybe Wales no longer had Dissenters, there being no religious establishment to dissent from; but on the other hand many active worshippers in the Church of England now dissented from aspects of the law; whether the official liturgy in the 1920s, divorce in the 1930s or sexual preference in the 2000s.

2. Parliament Assisting Voluntary Religion

Protestant episcopalians aside, ecumenism provided the main field of development of the law of religion at the turn of the twentieth century, with recourse to a new legal vehicle. Co-operation between five Ashkenazi synagogues had been facilitated by a Private Act as early as 1870[56]. The reunion of two strands of Methodism followed this example in 1907[57], after ruinous litigation in Scotland[58] had shown the perils of seeking to

---

[55] Church of England Assembly (Powers) Act 1919.
[56] United Synagogues Act 1870.
[57] United Methodist Church Act 1907.
[58] *General Assembly of the Free Church of Scotland v Lord Overtoun* [1904] AC 515.

unite bodies (with assets held on trust to promote incompatible doctrines) by mere resolution of the voluntary governing organs. Asserting 'spiritual independence' from parliamentary control, many voluntary bodies were careful to seek only protection against legal challenge to a union, variation of trusts to give it effect and possibly legal personality for a representative trustee body. The junior partners in the second statutory Methodist reunion did seek to protect a hard-won doctrinal compromise against majority alteration by anchoring its terms in the Act; but this only embarrassed their successors when further contemplated ecumenical steps necessitated flexibility on those very doctrines[59].

Ecumenism was also beginning to go beyond denominational boundaries. A Cambridgeshire experiment in the 1920s persuaded several nonconformist bodies and Church of England diocesan organs that their representatives could work together with the local authority in creating a syllabus acceptable to all for the nondenominational religious education required in authority-provided schools. The Education Act 1944 confirmed this 'partial voluntarisation' of state religious education by requiring an 'agreed syllabus' in all county schools[60]. Passed when the popular drift away from regular Sunday worship was becoming evident, this Act also required collective worship in all state-maintained schools; although parental rights of withdrawal were given in each case.

Later in the century a joint approach to government by voluntary Christian bodies (including the Church Assembly) secured a Public Act to facilitate the sharing of church buildings, suspending both denominational trusts and impeding provisions of ecclesiastical law while a sharing agreement remained in place[61].

3. The Road to International Intervention

Until the mid-twentieth century, England had always considered the law of religion a strictly domestic matter. Independence from Continental interference in the kingdom's religious affairs had been a key achievement of the Reformation era[62], and even the Union with Scotland had taken

---

[59] Methodist Church Union Act 1929 and *Barker v O'Gorman* [1971] 1 Ch 215. Freedom to change doctrinal tenets internally was restored by the Methodist Church Act 1976.

[60] Education Act 1944, s25, and see W Kay and L Francis, *Religion in Education* (Leominster, Gracewing Publications, 1997) 27.

[61] Sharing of Church Buildings Act 1969.

[62] Ecclesiastical Appeals Act 1532, preamble.

place on the condition that neither kingdom's religious settlement would be affected[63]. What England claimed for itself, it allowed also to other sovereign powers, respecting the Lutheranism of Sweden, the Catholicism of Venice or the loyalty of the Ottoman Empire to Islam. Though the country had expressed shock at perceived persecution abroad, such as the revocation of the French Edict of Nantes or the fate of respectable Catholics during the 'Terror', its response had been either diplomatic or military: it had not appealed to *law* as a basis for intervention and did not accept a need to justify its own religious settlement in any external forum[64]. The militant atheism of the Russian Revolution, however, began to create a new climate, although no immediate prospect of intervention there existed[65].

The Hitler government's interference in the affairs of the German churches and its persecution of the Jews – though the latter were viewed more as a racial than as a religious group by their persecutors – fuelled, alongside wartime massacres elsewhere, an international consensus that religious freedom, with other fundamental rights, needed security in more than domestic law alone. Western Europe and the Americas had by 1945 a long tradition of domestic religious tolerance and at least some legal concession to religious scruples. The world community, through the United Nations, was prepared to accept a formal statement of the principle of religious liberty in the General Assembly's 1948 'Universal Declaration of Human Rights'[66], although the right to *change* a religion once acquired was and remains controversial, and it should be noted that communist China was not an Organisation member at the time.

The Declaration could not as such affect the law of religion in England. It was a statement of principle designed for a hugely diverse global audience. But the member states of the Council of Europe agreed to make its main principles practically enforceable through a regional Convention that could be interpreted in accordance with European consensus and applied by a European supranational judicial structure. The 1950 European Convention for the Protection of Human Rights

---

[63] Stat. 6 Ann c.8 (1706); Act of Union with Scotland 1706, Art 25(3).

[64] These remarks, and indeed this chapter, focus upon England and Wales proper. It is not denied that a different position might prevail in England's ceded colonies, for example in Quebec where a qualified guarantee of the free exercise of (Roman Catholic) religion was given in Art 14 of the 1713 Treaty of Utrecht.

[65] Art 22 of the League of Nations Covenant provided for freedom of conscience and religion in the mandated territories, but the Soviet Union was barred from membership of the League.

[66] Art 18.

and Fundamental Freedoms (ECHR), ratified for the United Kingdom in 1951 and made enforceable against the government by individual petition to the Strasbourg institutions from 1966, was designed to have this effect.

Prior to the advent of individual petitions to Strasbourg, the law of religion remained fairly static. In common with other treaties, England's domestic courts took note of the ECHR only through the canon of statutory interpretation that – where statute was ambiguous – parliament could not intend to legislate inconsistently with the Crown's international commitments. Strasbourg could award 'just satisfaction' damages, but the 'high contracting parties' did not commonly take each other to court for religious violations.

4. Developments in Ecclesiastical Law

Ecclesiastical law, on the other hand, was changing fast, thanks to the virtually unchallenged influence of the Church Assembly (later 'General Synod') over new legislation. The compromise of 1919 had been fully reflected in the Second (Hansell/Macmorran) Edition of *Halsbury's Laws*, which appeared in 1933 and treated ancient institutions and provisions alongside the Assembly and its work. Continued deadlock over parliamentary control of the official liturgy and the credibility of the courts in theologically sensitive cases had been the subject of two Archbishops' Commission reports between the Wars[67]. New generations of high church canonical scholars were emerging, historically and theologically aware but more alive to constitutional realities than their nineteenth century predecessors, typified by names like Kenneth Kirk, N.P. Williams, John Bullard, Robert Mortimer and Eric Kemp.

In 1939 Bullard finally secured the project for which he had long pressed, a wholesale revision of the clerical canons of 1603-05; and although, partly thanks to another War, it took thirty years before the last resulting canons were promulged, a number of significant compromises had emerged by the project's close. First, the principle that canons cannot bind laypeople with the same force as they bind clergy had finally been accepted by high churchmen[68]. Secondly, agreement had been

---

[67] The Lang Report of 1926 and the more moderate, and ultimately more influential, Cecil Report of 1935.

[68] In the foreword to the Garbett Report (*The Canon Law of the Church of England – Report of the Archbishops' Commission*, London 1947).

reached on a two-track system of ministerial discipline which allowed sufficient episcopal involvement at the first instance hearing of theologically sensitive cases to satisfy the high church interest (though the final appeal would remain dominated by common law judges)[69]. Thirdly, a provisional solution to the liturgical question – experimental authorisation of alternatives[70] – and the beginning of a new debate on ministerial doctrinal standards and subscription had focussed attention on new possible devices to increase the Church Assembly's autonomous action in these fields[71].

V. The 1960s to the Present

1. The Challenge of English Religious Pluralism

Canonical revision and the liturgical revision that followed called for another major revision of what was by now the only contemporary and comprehensive ecclesiastical law text, the title in *Halsbury's Laws* which would appear in a fourth (Phillips/Bursell) edition in 1975. Mortimer, Kemp and Garth Moore had meanwhile fanned the embers of academic interest with published historical lectures and an introductory textbook[72]. But by the time Moore's work appeared the law of religion field was at last showing serious potential, not only to break away from ecclesiastical law but actually to overtake it in importance, thanks to the vindication of ECHR rights and the awakening – at last – to a significant non-Judaeo-Christian presence within England and Wales.

Aside perhaps from the Quakers, there had never been real objection on the part of alternative Christian groups to aspects of the English legal framework beyond the law of worship and supporting levies, public functions exercised by the established clergy and the religious content of compulsory education. Exemptions from oaths and military service had met Quaker demands, and England's Christian majority were left united in accepting both the religious symbolism of parliamentary prayers and the coronation rite, the much clearer implication of national Christianity in

---

[69] Ecclesiastical Jurisdiction Measure 1963.

[70] Alternative and Other Services Measure 1965.

[71] Realised in the Church of England (Worship and Doctrine) Measure 1974.

[72] R Mortimer, *Western Canon Law* (London, A & C Black, 1953); E Kemp, *Counsel and Consent – Aspects of the Government of the Church as exemplified in the History of the English Provincial Synods* (London, SPCK, 1961); E G Moore, *Introduction to English Canon Law* (First edition, Oxford, Oxford University Press, 1967).

the coronation oath to 'maintain the laws of God and the true profession of the Gospel'[73], and the practical indicators like military church parades, the place of Christianity in prison law[74], the religious festivals in the legal Calendar[75] and the parliamentary seats of the lords spiritual. The basis of English marriage law remained 'marriage as understood in Christendom', even though marriages by Jewish usage might have legal effect[76]. When debates on what became the Marriage Act 1937 displayed a substantial religious content and the promoter A P Herbert concluded by calling it 'a truly Christian Bill', there were criticisms from religious hardliners and from believers in a secular state, but none who seriously suggested England should recognise any alternative religious basis[77].

Challenges might have been posed to such a blatantly Christian legal system by the drift of the indigenous population to agnosticism or atheism, but despite the fall in churchgoing the majority retained their sense of Christian identity, as shown by over 77% of English respondents to the 2001 Census question 'what is your religion?'[78]. The real challenge therefore came from significant post-war expansion of the non-Christian population through migration and the birth rate. The Race Relations Act 1965, restricting discriminatory treatment on racial grounds, could be used to protect religiously-motivated behaviour if the religious group concerned happened to be virtually coterminous with an ethnic group[79]. But the climate began to change seriously once direct Convention applications began to achieve judgments against the United Kingdom and its neighbours for legal provisions or administrative practice that failed – with what Strasbourg institutions considered insufficient justification – to secure the rights to manifest one's religion, to religiously-motivated self-expression, or to state education following parental convictions[80].

---

[73] Coronation Oath Act 1688.

[74] Prison Act 1952 s 7(4).

[75] Calendar (New Style) Act 1750.

[76] *Hyde v Hyde* (1866) LR 1 P & D 130.

[77] The debate on this and earlier matrimonial legislation is analysed in A Pearce, 'The Christian Claims of the English Law of Marriage' in A Thatcher (ed), *Celebrating Christian Marriage* (Edinburgh, Continuum/T & T Clark, 2001).

[78] <http://www.statistics.gov.uk/census2001/>.

[79] e.g. *Mandla v. Dowell Lee* [1983] 2 AC 548 (Sikhs; the other major group to which this applied were the Jews).

[80] Arts 9 and 10 ECHR and Art 2 of Protocol 1 are the free-standing Convention provisions most likely to be raised in support of a claim by a religious believer as such. Discrimination in securing Convention rights (Art 14) may also be raised.

2. Human Rights Law and Modern Law of Religion Disputes

From the late sixties onwards values began to clash in earnest. In the succeeding decades public safety and school uniform policies were invoked against religious expectations regarding dress, beards and symbolic weaponry; animal welfare considerations clashed with religious purity rules; teachings on the sanctity of life brought medical advances and the 'woman's right to choose' into question; child protection campaigners encountered the biblical precept to use the rod; faith communities' spiritual discipline had to adjust to the requirements of natural justice and employment protection, while health precautions threatened sacred animals and one person's religious message risked becoming another person's 'hate crime'. Education became a live issue again, the call for faith-based schooling now going beyond the issues of religious instruction and worship to school meals, sex education and the proximity of boys and girls. Here, as in relation to the historic law of marriage formation or blasphemy, there was scope for claims of Article 14 discrimination. New insights on gender and sexual orientation, both in society in general and among a minority of active believers, sparked off arguably the most lively controversies of all.

With the right of individual petition from 1966 came a new concept of the litigation lawyer's role. The lawyer might now have to challenge the law head-on – instead of the traditional role of advising how to act within it or to find a way round it. But conversely a lawyer might have to defend the law. Laws come into being to serve an end which at least some people desire; and there is always an argument that an impugned rule is worth retaining. There are values behind the law, sometimes as strongly held as the religious convictions opposed to them. The Human Rights Act 1998, requiring domestic courts to give direct effect to Convention rights or indicate incompatibilities with statute, made disputes in this area easily litigable and spawned a vast increase in dedicated law of religion literature. Also particularly significant was the 1979 decision that, although a religious association such as a church, being neither a natural nor a legal person, cannot have human rights of its own, churches could apply to Strasbourg on behalf of their members or co-religionists in order to vindicate those individuals' right to manifest their religion collectively[81].

---

[81] *X and Church of Scientology v Sweden* (1979) 16 DR 68.

International judicial fora have a commonly harmonising effect. This is true of the Strasbourg institutions just as it is of the House of Lords, which must be considered international in the present context, given the role of judges from the very different Scots tradition in determining appeals relating to the Church of England, despite the exclusion of national religion from the scope of the Anglo-Scottish union. Yet the nations of Europe know perhaps greater diversity of historical experience in the religious field than in any other.

Catholic and Orthodox reservation of spiritual decision-making to the ordained contrasts with the emancipation of the laity in territories of the protestant Reformation; English and Scandinavian legal monism stood out alongside the principled church-state separations of the nineteenth century[82]; the pressure for internal autonomy of religious bodies became far greater in post-Hitler Germany, which had experienced hostile state control, than in countries where a gentlemanly restraint had always prevailed. The association of a particular religion with national identity in Poland or Greece was an understandable, if dangerous, legacy of periods unique to those countries, where religious groups had kept national spirit alive under alien régimes. The European Union recognised at the time of the 1997 Amsterdam Treaty that member states' religious constitutions were best left well alone[83]. Strasbourg too has held back in this area, taking seriously the 'margin of appreciation' allowed to national courts in interpreting Convention rights[84].

It would be an impossible task even to sketch the modern law of religion in the space available: other contributions to this work illustrate the variety and complexity of the field. The examples opening this section will be familiar to most readers, many from notorious litigation since the 1998 Act. Just as many Continental law of religion texts begin with the religious freedom guarantees of their national constitutions, so directly-enforceable Convention rights lie at the heart of many modern English treatments of law and religion issues. This chapter hopefully reminds students of this country's law of religion that it did not begin *ex nihilo* in 1998. Many older religio-legal institutions remain in being, often with a

---

[82] And the Articles Declaratory appended to the Church of Scotland Act 1921.

[83] Declaration 11 attached to the Treaty: 'The European Union will respect and does not prejudice the status under national law of churches and religious associations or communities in the Member States.'

[84] There have of course been criticisms of this approach, as in C Evans, *Freedom of Religion under the European Convention on Human Rights* (Oxford, Oxford University Press, 2002).

specifically Christian flavour, some never tested at Strasbourg and others already found to be within the ECHR's margin of appreciation[85].

3. United Against the World?

Although its effect may be limited by the distinction between actions directly manifesting and those merely motivated by religion[86], by restriction of rights for legitimate goals, and by the national margin of appreciation (as well as by the continuing supremacy of English statute), it is incontestable that the Human Rights Act has radically reversed the approach of English law toward the religious conscience. Religious scruples about a legal requirement had formerly to be put respectfully to government or legislature in seeking concessions: even in the heyday of Dissenting representation, their spokesmen never commanded a majority of the House of Commons, any more than lords spiritual in the post-Reformation House of Lords. If the concession was not granted, the believer had to comply with the law regardless of his scruples: the alternatives were to forego a conditionally-offered benefit, risk prosecution, or leave the country. A lack of legal provision was usually something believers had to remedy by private initiative, relying not on any guaranteed right but on the fact that the common law allows everything that is not prohibited.

Since the Act, religious conviction resembles a sword as much as a shield. One has a right to do what one's religious conviction requires, and if restrictions are made through the law then the lawmaker is put on the defensive, bound to justify the restriction as necessary 'in a democratic society'[87] to secure specific goals. The problem is, however, that English society, while still acknowledging a majority Christian identity, no longer shares the views common to many active believers on certain key issues. Laws are frequently made not for merely administrative or utilitarian goals but from a national morality which, if Christian, is certainly not denominationally so[88].

---

[85] See for instance the decisions in *Darby v. Sweden* (1990) 13 EHRR 774 recognising that what Strasbourg calls a 'state church' system is not incompatible with ECHR Arts 9 or 14, or in *Choudhury v United Kingdom* (1991) 12 HRLJ 172 dismissing a challenge to the exclusive protection of Christianity by the English law of blasphemy.

[86] *Arrowsmith v United Kingdom* (1978) 3 EHRR 218.

[87] Which, according to the Strasbourg court in *Kokkinakis v Greece* (1993) EHRR 397, is a religiously plural society.

[88] Non-discrimination, animal welfare and stewardship of the national heritage are all examples of legal fields where common values lie behind legislation but difficulties have been posed to particular religious groups.

In organised religious groups, while grassroots opinion is usually divided, it is not now uncommon for a conciliar or episcopal hierarchy (or the teachers and leaders of non-Christian faiths), supported by a majority of active laypeople, to dissent strongly and vocally from a national decision expressed in parliament. This raises two ongoing issues: how far is it right to grant exemptions (and is religion truly so different from all other strong conviction?), and how far should society protect individual believers who share the national consensus, but thereby fall foul of their own hierarchy and its discipline?[89]

England's law of religion today, then, is a field open to many who have no background in ecclesiastical law. The latter remains a flourishing discipline, thanks to new publications and the advent of a learned society[90]; but the more the Church of England is portrayed as one religious body among many, the less the law of religion seems concerned with its 'internal' affairs. Consequently the law of religion has potential to be the common concern not only of ecumenically co-operating Christians, nor even of inter-faith alliances, but of those defending the claims of collective religion, individual religion, no religion *and* 'the rights and freedoms of others', each of which the ECHR recognises as worthy of defence.

In closing, a note of caution may be appropriate relating to this very last point. There is perhaps a danger of England's law of religion becoming, as ecclesiastical law once was, an academic discipline of the like-minded. When the collective freedom of believers clashes either with regulation by the general law, or with the claims of an individual dissident, lawyers are involved on both sides. The 'cab-rank rule' of the English Bar generally secures that practitioner expertise of a high order is available both to the religious hierarchy concerned and its opponents.

---

[89] These questions are raised with particular force when society funds a voluntary religious group to perform some public function on its behalf (see *Quality and Equality: Human Rights, Public Services and Religious Organisations*, British Humanist Association 2007), and in relation to organs of the Church of England, given what has been observed above about its dual public and voluntary character. In *Parochial Church Council of Aston Cantlow v Wallbank* [2003] UKHL 37 the House of Lords held an organ of the 'voluntary face' immune to human rights claims, following a Strasbourg decision regarding Greece and treating a 'spiritual' *raison d'être* as necessarily non-governmental; but whether, especially in the light of the coronation oath, all public religious institutions are equally remote from the goals of English government must remain an open question.

[90] The Ecclesiastical Law Society was founded by Graham Routledge in 1987. The leading modern treatment of the main points of ecclesiastical law and representative Church of England structures is M Hill, *Ecclesiastical Law* (Third edition, Oxford, Oxford University Press, 2007). A taught Master's degree course has also existed at Cardiff University since 1991.

But are the academic networks that resource legal practice, inspire new writing and facilitate professional development equally open to all? 'Freedom to manifest religion' is a principle which can unite legal scholars from many religious traditions, while the disparate reasons to qualify such manifestation seem at first glance to call at different times for experts in anything from family law to the Prison Rules. But if such experts lack familiarity with the concepts and arguments underlying the law's relationship to religion, they will inevitably be disadvantaged and the academic world in part to blame.

Of course it is open to one or more organised religions to stage and finance their own discussions of the law, specifically for loyal adherents, if necessary with retained advisers. A religious venue, accompanying prayer and the assumption that religious teaching must prevail are all appropriate to such occasions. But confessionally-neutral academic institutions lend themselves better to networks and conferences that encourage wider participation, allowing an expertise in the law of religion to spread equally among the non-religious. Publications with contributions on both sides of a debate[91], and balanced gatherings, open to the possibility that the law may be right and religious views wrong, could do much for the integrity of this discipline and minimise any risk of it moving to the fringes of English legal scholarship.

---

[91] An example from the United States with contributions from legal and other disciplines is L D Wardle and ors, (eds) *Marriage and Same-Sex Unions – A Debate* (Westport CT, Praeger Publishers 2003).

ESTABLISHMENT AND HUMAN RIGHTS IN THE ENGLISH CONSTITUTION: HAPPY BED-FELLOWS OR UNEASY ALLIES?

Charlotte Smith

Introduction

Given that human rights are the creation of international law it may seem odd here to discuss them in the context of the constitutional arrangements of one part of the United Kingdom. Establishment, however, in any of the many forms in which it arises, is a distinctly local phenomenon. The form it takes in any particular State is the product of a range of political, social and historical factors which are unique to the experiences of that State[1]. As such, only limited success can be expected from any attempt to discuss both it, and its relationship to other bodies of law, as an abstract concept.

The aim of this chapter, then, is to examine Establishment as it exists in England, and to consider the extent to which it can happily co-exist with human rights law as codified in the European Convention on Human rights and incorporated into domestic law by the Human Rights Act 1998[2].

Defining the Key Concepts

Establishment

Establishment is a legal arrangement according to which a church or several churches are given a different and privileged position by the State as against other religious organisations[3]. In return for this constitutional position the church or churches will accept some degree of State influence or control over certain aspects of their affairs.

---

[1] On this see J Martinez-Torron, 'Religious Liberty in European Jurisprudence' in M Hill (ed), *Religious Liberty and Human Rights* (Cardiff, University of Wales Press, 2002) 99.

[2] For a more general look at this question see R Ahdar and I Leigh, *Religious Freedom in the Liberal State* (Oxford, Oxford University Press, 2005) chapters three and five.

[3] P Edge, 'Reorienting the Establishment Debate: From the Illusory Norm to Equality of Respect' (1998) 27 *Anglo-Am L Rev* 265 at 271.

Establishment is not, however, simply a legal entity; it is also a political concept. It is the result of political choices and historical factors and will share the characteristics of the law and constitution by which it is given a concrete form[4]. Thus Establishment consists both in the state of law, and of a web of theory and sentiment which have grown up in support of the state of the law and interacted with its development in the course of history[5]. Given this, any consideration of whether Establishment and human rights can happily co-exist must consider not only the law, but also its ideological underpinnings and social and historical context.

As Ahdar and Leigh note, Establishment can be found in both 'weak' and 'strong' varieties, judged according to the degree of privilege conferred upon the church and the level of State influence or control over its affairs[6]. Similarly, it may take a variety of forms, including the formal, the informal, symbolic and substantive. Varying levels of weak Establishment might be found in the formal and symbolic appeal to God or a particular church in a documentary constitution together, perhaps, with some form of formal State recognition and provision for a church. Equally, an informal and substantive variety of Establishment might be said to exist in various types of State support and funding for one or more churches[7].

Establishment results in the development of a network of ties and relationships between the Established church and the organs of the State; and between the Established church and the citizens of that State. The assumption is that the State takes an interest in the affairs of the church, and accords it a special constitutional position, because that church will minister to the nation as a whole. Establishment will, in consequence, result in a more or less close integration between Church, State and nation (meaning the citizens of the state).

Turning to Establishment in its distinctively English form we can see an Establishment which, like the common law and the organic constitution in which it is embedded, is in a constant state of change and evolution. That Establishment has historically been embodied in a close relationship between the Church of England, the organs of government

---

[4] See M H Ogilvie, 'What is a Church by Law Established?' (1990) 28 *Osgoode Hall LJ*. 179 at 195-6.

[5] See P M H Bell, *Disestablishment in Ireland and Wales* (London, SPCK, 1969), Introduction.

[6] Ahdar and Leigh, *Religious Freedom in the Liberal State* 80.

[7] Ibid, chapters three and five.

and the people of England. That historical picture, however, is increasingly characterised by dis-integration, albeit with significant remnants of the old relationships.

While integration remains in the power of Parliament to veto Church Measures, and the role of the Prime Minister in appointing senior clergy[8], the creation in the twentieth century of the Church Assembly, and the increase in its powers and reformulation as the General Synod, granted novel levels of autonomy to the Church. It marked an increasing divergence from the norm of integration of Church and State in central government and administration. Similarly, the replacement of the old parish vestry by parochial church councils composed solely of active conformists signalled the death of integrated local government and administration[9]. Further, while parishioners (defined by reference to their place of residence) retain legal rights in respect of their parish church, the removal, in the nineteenth century, of civil disabilities from those not in conformity with the Church of England evidenced the acknowledgment of a clear distinction between the Church of England and the nation of England[10]. Thus what remains of Establishment in England seems to fit into Adhar and Leigh's classification of a weak version of that constitutional arrangement. State control and influence over the Church of England have been increasingly attenuated and what remains in no way impinges upon the freedom of citizens to hold and practice other faiths or beliefs.

Human Rights

At a general level the discussion of human rights entered into here refers to the framework of human rights which individuals enjoy against State bodies as a matter of international and domestic law. In the English context this means human rights as implemented in the form of the European Convention of Human Rights, and in the decisions of the Commission and the jurisprudence of the European Court of Human Rights.

---

[8] For a discussion of the powers of the Crown and Parliament in respect of the Church of England see V Bogdanor, *The Monarchy in the Constitution* (Oxford, Oxford University Press, 1995) chapter 9.

[9] Civil functions were removed from the vestry (in which all parishioners could vote) by the Local Government Act 1894, s6. Its ecclesiastical functions were transferred to the parochial church council by the Parochial Church Councils (Powers) Measure 1921.

[10] For a general introduction to the history of Establishment see K Medhurst and G Moyser, *The Church and Politics in a Secular Age* (Oxford, Clarendon Press, 1988) chapters one and two.

It refers also to the incorporation of those rights and that jurisprudence as mandated under the Human Rights Act 1998.

In relation to English Establishment the two most obviously relevant Articles of the Convention are Articles 9 and 14. Article 9 states:

1. Everyone has the right to freedom of thought, conscience and religion; this right includes freedom to change his religion or belief and freedom, either alone or in community with others and in public or private, to manifest his religion or belief, in worship, teaching, practice and observance.
2. Freedom to manifest one's religion or beliefs shall be subject only to such limitations as are prescribed by law and are necessary in a democratic society in the interests of public safety, for the protection of public order, health or morals, or for the protection of the rights and freedoms of others.

Article 14 reinforces Article 9(1), stating:

> The enjoyment of the rights and freedoms set forth in this Convention shall be secured without discrimination on any ground such as sex, race, colour, language, religion, political or other opinion, national or social origin, association with a national minority, property, birth or other status.

The legal form given to freedom of religion, and to protection from discrimination on the grounds of religion in the enjoyment of a Convention right, are obviously relevant to a consideration of the legal compatibility of Establishment and human rights. However, as stated above, Establishment is as much a political and historical concept as it is a legal one. Given this, any consideration of their ability to co-exist must also consider the compatibility of their ideological underpinnings. This must necessarily take us beyond an examination of the legal scope of Articles 9 and 14.

Preliminary Reflections on the Relationship

English Establishment and the European Convention on Human Rights

Taking first Article 9 it seems that there is probably no conflict between religious liberty and English Establishment. The weak Establishment of the Church of England does not, as was noted above, dictate what individuals must believe or how they should worship (or not). It makes provision for a national church but does not require all citizens to conform to it, nor does it restrict their freedom to hold and practice other beliefs or none[11]. The only possible caveat to this statement concerns the religious liberty of the Church of England.

It is at least conceivable that Establishment, entailing as it does some degree of State influence over the church, might result in the restriction of the religious liberty of the Established church. In the English context legislation such as the Church Assembly (Powers) Act 1919 and the Church of England (Worship and Doctrine) Measure 1974 has granted the Church of England quite an extensive measure of independent action and freedom from State interference in its administration and government. Similarly, the conventions and procedures regulating the process by which the Prime Minister appoints senior clergy safeguard the voice and autonomy of the Church. The liberty of the Church from State intervention is not, however, inviolable[12]. Parliament retains, and from time to time exercises, the right to veto Measures put forward by the General Synod. So, too, the Prime Minister retains and exercises the right to choose between the two candidates put forward by the Church's Ecclesiastical Appointments Commission, and may indeed reject them both[13].

While the Prime Minister is a public authority under section 6 of the Human Rights Act 1998, and must as such act in a manner consistent with Convention Rights[14], no such limitation is placed upon the actions of Parliament. The Human Rights Act preserves the unlimited legal sovereignty of Parliament, and thus expressly excludes it from the duty imposed upon public authorities under section 6(3)[15].

Despite the apparent liberty of Parliament to restrict the Church's religious freedom, it seems probable that the Church of England will enjoy a considerable measure of religious liberty. Though Parliament is not bound to act in accordance with Convention rights there is a strong political imperative for it to do so. Further, though not itself bound by the Human Rights Act, Parliament indicated, at first glance at least, a high level of respect for freedom of religion through the inclusion of section 13 of that Act. That section, which applies equally to the Established and voluntary churches, requires special consideration to

---

[11] See Ahdar and Leigh, *Religious Freedom in the Liberal State* chapter five.

[12] See Mark Hill's contribution to this volume.

[13] See K Medhurst, "The Church of England: a Progress Report" (1999) *Parliamentary Affairs*, 275-290.

[14] Unless prevented from doing so by primary legislation.

[15] See J Rivers, 'From Toleration to Pluralism: the UK Human Rights Act' in R J Ahdar (ed), *Law and Religion* (Aldershot, Ashgate, 2000) 133-62.

be given to the effect of any court decision upon the religious liberty of religious organisations[16].

The religious freedom of the Church of England is further safeguarded by three additional provisions of the Human Rights Act 1998. Firstly, section 21 of that Act accords Church of England Measures the status of primary legislation, meaning that they cannot be declared invalid by the courts if they are found to breach a Convention right. Secondly, section 10(6) provides that Measures which have been found to be incompatible with the Convention cannot be amended by a government minister. Only the General Synod has the power to amend a Measure which has been found to be in breach of human rights. Finally, section 6(6) provides that the decision not to bring amending legislation to Parliament cannot be subject to judicial review, meaning that the General Synod cannot legally be compelled to amend incompatible Measures.

It appears then that Article 9 has been accommodated within the English constitution in a way which is legally unproblematic for Establishment. Neither does it appear that Article 14 is problematic. That Article requires non-discrimination on the grounds of religion in respect of the enjoyment of Convention rights. It does not prevent discrimination unless a Convention right is actively engaged. Consequently privileges which arise as a result of Establishment, but which do not impinge upon the religious liberty of non-members, do not engage Article 14[17]. It is possible, however, that in the developing human rights law of the European Union the right to non-discrimination may be interpreted and applied more widely, thus giving rise to the possibility of conflict[18].

Culture Clashes

Setting aside the specifics of the legal position, it appears that more general and pervasive differences of legal culture may be productive of difficulty in attempts to reconcile Establishment and human rights. At the most basic level the organic, common law and incrementally developed (and developing) English constitution within which Establishment has

[16] On this see J Rivers, 'Religious Liberty as a Collective Right' in R O'Dair and A Lewis (ed) *Law and Religion* (Oxford, Oxford University Press, 2001) 227 and P Cumper, 'The Protection of Religious Rights Under Section 13 of the Human Rights Act 1998' [2000] *PL* 254.

[17] On this point see *Choudhury* v *UK* Appl. No. 17439/90 (1991) 12 HRLJ 172.

[18] See European Charter for Fundamental Rights Article 21 concerning equality and Council Directive 2000/78/EC establishing a general framework for equal treatment (including in matters of religion) in employment and occupation. See also Pauline Roberts' contribution to the current volume.

developed contrast starkly with the codification of rights embodied in the European Convention, and with the civil law traditions of the majority of the signatory States. So, too, the scattered, constantly evolving and non-documentary English constitution renders consistent reform and development problematic. Further, the very notion of substantive human *rights* as embodied in the Convention is foreign to the English constitution. Prior to the implementation of the Human Rights Act England adopted a constitutionalist approach, and thus focussed upon freedom within the law rather than substantive rights[19].

Undoubtedly the organic and dynamic creature which is the English constitution can adapt, but this is not to say that the process of adaptation will always be without difficulty, nor that previously essential constitutional features will not be discarded. Neither does it guarantee that the process of adaptation will always be consistent and coherent.

In relation to Establishment itself, human rights might also pose a challenge in terms of cultural assimilation. While the human rights now domesticated through the Human Rights Act are largely the product of international law-making, Establishment operates only as a domestic relationship between Church and State and is inward-facing. Further, Establishment in England has throughout much of its history been an expression of national identity and sovereignty. Part of its function or justification has been to exclude the influence of foreign powers, and to reinforce and foster the idea of the nation State[20].

Even simple differences in terminology may cause unforeseen difficulties. In the context of English Establishment one particular problem which has arisen has concerned the distinction between governmental and non-governmental bodies under Article 34 of the Convention, and the corresponding definition of who or what is a public authority under section 6 of the Human Rights Act 1998. The terminology of Article 34 is alien to English administrative law jurisprudence and contrasts even with the language of the Act which gives effect to it in domestic law. This, combined with ahistorical appeals to precedent which reflects a historical High Church Anglican desire to distance the Church of England from the State[21], led the majority in the House of Lords in a recent

---

[19] As seen in *Entick* v *Carrington* (1765) 19 State Tr 1029 and *Malone* v *Metropolitan Police Commissioner* [1979] Ch 344.

[20] See e.g. S T Coleridge, *On the Constitution of Church and State According to the Idea of Each* (Third edition, London, William Pickering, 1869).

[21] Chiefly a dictum by Phillimore J, a proponent of extreme High Church views, in *Marshall* v *Graham/Bell* v *Graham* [1907] 2 KB 112 at 126.

decision[22] to retreat from the possibility of Church of England bodies having a public face and role in respect of its religious mission. As will be discussed below, this challenges a fundamental premise upon which Establishment rests[23].

A Closer Examination of the Relationship

The analysis engaged in so far has suggested that the version of Establishment seen in England is unlikely to be problematic in terms of Article 9, and at present remains unproblematic in respect of Article 14. It further suggests that, though the Human Rights Act 1998 seems to have made a reasonable job of accommodating both Establishment and human rights in law, problems may still arise as a result of the very different histories and approaches of the Convention and the English Constitution.

The Jurisprudence of the European Convention

An analysis of European jurisprudence provides little illumination on the question of how to accommodate both Establishment and human rights in a coherent manner. There have been very few decisions on Article 9, and even fewer on the question of Establishment. As Ahdar and Leigh have commented '[w]hen one turns to international law there is an enigmatic and perhaps discrete silence on the establishment question.'[24] In the little jurisprudence which exists in this area the approach taken has been characterised as one of pragmatism rather than of theoretical coherence, and of reticence in considering something which is viewed as being essentially a matter of political choice in individual States[25].

Both the Court and the Commission have consistently upheld the legality of the varieties of Establishment found within Europe, and have

---

[22] *Aston Cantlow and Wilmcote with Billesley Parochial Church Council v Wallbank and Another* [2003] UKHL 37. See citations of Phillimore at [2001] EWCA Civ 713 para 31; [2003] UKHL 37 paras 61 and 156.

[23] For a full discussion of this point see A Pearce, 'Aston Cantlow: Chancel Repairs and the Status of Church of England Institutions' (2003) 151 *Law and Justice* 163 and C Smith, 'A Very English Affair: Establishment and Human Rights in an Organic Constitution' in C Evans and P Cane (ed), *Law and Religion in Theoretical and Historical Context* (Cambridge, Cambridge University Press, 2009).

[24] Ahdar and Leigh, *Religious Freedom in the Liberal State* 133.

[25] On this point see J Martinez-Torron, 'The European Court of Human Rights and Religion' in R O'Dair and A Lewis (eds), *Law and Religion* (Oxford, Oxford University Press, 2001) 185 at 190.

affirmed the right of signatory States to determine Church-State relations as a matter of national law. In *Darby* v *Sweden*[26] it was confirmed that, providing adequate provision was made for safeguarding the religious liberty of all citizens, Establishment *per se* would not breach the Convention. The Convention required provision for adequate religious freedom, and not necessarily equality of privilege[27]. As such it seems that legal arrangements which privilege one religious group over another will not breach Article 14 unless they impinge upon the religious freedom of those who are not members of the privileged group[28].

In certain respects the European jurisprudence also appears to uphold that aspect of Establishment which assumes that the State can properly take an interest in the moral and spiritual welfare of its citizens, or at least that it should do all necessary to guarantee to them adequate religious liberty. Thus the European Court has upheld restrictions to freedom of speech under Article 10(2) where the speech concerned was calculated to outrage or offend religious believers or members of the majority faith[29].

Though the European jurisprudence appears consistently to have upheld the legality of weak models of Establishment two aspects of it seem to pose particular problems for such constitutional arrangements. Probably the least important of these is the rule that the State must not intervene in the internal affairs of churches or make judgments as to the merit or validity of beliefs[30]. This might strike at the roles of Parliament and the Prime Minister in the government of the Church of England. It seems likely, however, that adequate constitutional safeguards have been put in place to avoid a breach. Further, though some writers have characterised Establishment as entailing some level of State endorsement of the theological position of the Established church, and thus presumably some judgment of its merits, many Anglican theorists long ago abandoned this as a justification of the Church of England's constitutional position. From the mid-nineteenth century onwards the Establishment of the Church of England has been justified by many not (at least solely) on the basis of its doctrinal purity, but rather on the ground that that church

---

[26] (1991) 13 EHRR 774.

[27] See also *Kokkinakis* v *Greece* (1993) 17 EHHR 397.

[28] See e.g. *Choudhury* v *UK* Appl. No. 17439/90 (1991) 12 HRLJ 172 and *Cha'are Shalom Ve Tsedek* v *France* [2000] ECHR 27417/95.

[29] See e.g. *Wingrove* v *The UK* (1997) 24 EHRR 1 at 48 and *Otto-Preminger Institute* v *Austria* (1994) 17 EHRR 293.

[30] *Metropolitan Church of Bessarabia* v *Moldova* [2001] ECHR 45701/99.

is organisationally and practically the religious body best able to fulfil a national mission[31].

The more seriously problematic aspect of European jurisprudence is the consistent treatment of churches, whether Established or not, as private voluntary bodies. In the context of Article 34 Establishment will never serve to deny a church the enjoyment of Convention rights and the status of a potential victim of State interference. Nor will it ever render the actions of an Established church acting as a religious body matters for which the State will be held responsible at international law[32].

The emphasis engendered by Article 34 upon the distinction between governmental and non-governmental bodies serves both to exclude the liability of the State for the religious actions of religious bodies, and to protect the religious liberty of Established churches by allowing them to vindicate their Convention rights. It also, however, as will be argued below, strikes at the ideological foundations of Establishment. It does so by confining religion to the private sphere and denying that public provision for religion, rather than the guarantee of liberty of private provision, can ever be part of the mandate or responsibility of the State. The result is a focus on the private or voluntary aspects of Established churches to the exclusion of their history and identity as public or national entities[33].

The effects of this jurisprudence can be seen in the decisions and reasoning of the majority in the House of Lords in the case of *Aston Cantlow and Wilmcote with Billesley Parochial Church Council* v *Wallbank and Another*[34]. In answering the question whether a parochial church council was acting as a public authority (and thus bound to

---

[31] See e.g. Coleridge, *On the Constitution of Church and State*, 46 and S L.Holland, *The National Church of a Democratic State* (London, Rivingtons, 1886) 8-10. Many were plainly uncomfortable with the idea of a national church as a repository of incontrovertible truth, or with the idea that it should be a narrowly defined body. See e.g. T Arnold, *Fragments on Church and State* (London, B. Fellowes, 1845) 55ff and F D Maurice, *The Kingdom of Christ or Hints to a Quaker Respecting the Principles, Constitution, and Ordinances of the Catholic Church* (3rd Edition, London, Macmillan and Co, 1883) introduction. A variation on this appears to have been one of the justifications of retaining the *ex officio* seats for Anglican bishops in the reformed second chamber. See *A House for the Future* (Cm 4534, 2000) Para 15.8.

[32] See *Holy Monasteries* v *Greece* (1995) 20 EHRR 1; *Hautanemi* v *Sweden* (1996) 22 EHRR CD 155.

[33] For a detailed analysis of the jurisprudence see J Martinez-Torron, 'The European Court of Human Rights and Religion' in O'Dair and Lewis (eds), *Law and Religion*, 185 – 204; J Martinez-Torron, 'Religious Liberty in European Jurisprudence' in M Hill (ed), *Religious Liberty and Human Rights* 99-127; Ahdar and Leigh, *Religious Freedom in the Liberal State* chapter five.

[34] [2003] UKHL 37.

respect Convention rights) when it enforced a chancel repair obligation the majority denied the public nature of that act. Focussing on the private law form which that obligation currently takes, and upon those aspects of the council's role which concern the private voluntary activity of active conformists, they contrived to obscure the public face of the Church of England. They ignored the origins of the chancel repair obligation as a means of making public provision for religious services. They ignored, too, the continuing legal obligations owed by the Church of England to all parishioners, whether active conformists or not. In doing so the majority were apparently unable to accept that provision for the spiritual and moral welfare of its citizens was something with which the State could concern itself[35].

The Ideological Foundations of Establishment and Human Rights

An analysis of the jurisprudence leads to the conclusion that, as a matter of law at least, there is nothing irreconcilable in the relationship between Establishment and human rights. That analysis has, though, highlighted several possible ideological conflicts which must now be considered in greater detail.

Ahdar and Leigh identify several continuing ideological justifications for Establishment in the modern pluralist and liberal democratic State. The first of these is that the presence of an Established church serves as a reminder that government will be accountable to God, as well as the electorate, for its actions. It serves also as a reminder that the State has not been formally or legally secularised, and that religion is in some sense or capacity relevant beyond the sphere of the private individual[36]. Such arguments are a pale shadow of centuries of Anglican writing on the relationship between church and State[37].

---

[35] [2003] UKHL 37 at paras 14-15, 64, 83, 86,138 and 149-52. For a detailed examination of this case see A Pearce, 'Aston Cantlow: Chancel Repairs and the Status of Church of England Institutions' (2003) 151 Law and Justice 163 and C Smith, 'A Very English Affair: Establishment and Human Rights in an Organic Constitution' in C Evans and P Cane (eds), Law and Religion in Theoretical and Historical Context (Cambridge, Cambridge University Press, 2009).

[36] See Ahdar and Leigh, Religious Freedom in the Liberal State chapter five.

[37] For a general overview see P Avis, Church, State and Establishment (London, SPCK, 2001) and A R Vidler, The Orb and the Cross: A Normative Study of the Relations of Church and State with Reference to Gladstone's Early Writings (London, SPCK, 1945).

In English history Establishment has rested upon several key assumptions, the most basic of which was the assumption that it was fundamentally good for people to live in societies and communities[38]. Beyond this, much Anglican theory asserted a dualist and corrective relationship between Church and State in which each had a distinct set of qualities and powers, and exercised rightful jurisdiction over certain things. Most commonly the role of the Established Church was seen as being to provide the State with moral knowledge, while that of the State was to provide the Church with the means of external action which enabled it to further its religious purpose and mission[39].

From the point of view of the State one of the most important historical rationales for Establishment, particularly in a liberal democratic State, was that it provided a means by which the State could secure the moral and spiritual education of its citizens so that they were fitted to be worthy citizens of a State which was governed by law rather than by force[40]. On this basis the State had a legitimate interest and role in ensuring the provision of public services of religion for all of its citizens.

From the perspective of both Church and State, Establishment was also valuable as a means of ensuring that the lives of believing citizens were not pulled apart and fragmented by divisions and disagreements between the spiritual and the secular. This served to ensure an environment in which the Church could flourish, and to safeguard against instances where citizens were forced to choose between competing religious and secular obligations, with Church and State set up in opposite to each other[41].

Historically, then, Anglican Establishment theory has hallowed a close relationship between Church and State, and between the sacred and secular aspects of life. It assumes that the State has a legitimate interest in

[38] See e.g. T Arnold, *Fragment on the Church* (Second edition, London, B. Fellowes, 1845) 6ff and W. E Gladstone, *The State in its Relations with the Church* (2 Volumes) (Fourth edition, London, John Murray, 1841) 50ff. It is also a key theme in F D Maurice, *The Kingdom of Christ*.

[39] See e.g. Arnold, *Fragment on the Church* 9-13.

[40] This justification depends on the assumption of a necessary link between religion and morality, and between the moral sense of individuals and their capacity to obey law. See e.g. W E Gladstone, *The State in its Relations to the* Church 60-3; R Palmer, *A Defence of the Church of England against Disestablishment* (Fifth edition, London, Macmillan and Co, 1911) 73; S T Coleridge, *On the Constitution of Church and State According to the Idea of Each* 58 and 76; S L Holland, *The National Church of a Democratic State* (London, Rivingtons, 1886) 5-8.

[41] See e.g. See T Arnold, *Fragment on the Church* 11 and F D Maurice, *The Kingdom of Christ* at 238-9. For a modern discussion of this question see M W McConnell, 'Religious Souls and the Body Politic' (Spring 2004) *The Public Interest* 126- 42.

religion, and that the Church has a role to play in the public sphere. This contrasts strongly with many of the assumptions upon which the human rights framework rests.

Though, in part, human rights owe their ideological heritage to Judeo-Christian traditions, they are also substantially the offspring of traditions which are, to some extent at least, antithetical to these[42]. Human rights are as much the birth child of liberalism and Enlightenment rationalism as they are that of Christianity. It is in the link between human rights and the central assertions of liberalism and the Enlightenment that a potential difficulty can be found in the relationship between human rights and Establishment[43].

At the heart of liberalism is a dichotomy between fact and value, or between the objective and subjective, and the corresponding dichotomy between what is public and what is private. Religion, which is assumed always to be subjective and irrational, is thus defined as belonging to the private sphere. As such liberalism requires the State to be neutral as between religions and, in some manifestations, to withdraw from any dealings with religion as being an essentially private matter in which it has no proper role[44]. While neutrality may be as well served by allowing all religions a voice and role in the public square as it is by the exclusion of all, and while many would dispute the existence of State neutrality as anything more substantial than a myth[45], the general thrust of liberal doctrine is contrary to the ideological basis of Establishment.

Establishment assumes that the State will take an interest in religion, that religion has a role to play in the public sphere, and that life should not and cannot be fragmented between the spiritual and the secular. In contrast Enlightenment liberalism tends rigidly to distinguish the public from the private. It excludes the State from any concern with religion except insofar as it polices the boundary between the public and private, or acts to guarantee the religious freedom of its citizens within the private sphere to which religion and religious belief are to be confined.

---

[42] For a discussion of this, see Frank Cranmer's contribution to this volume.

[43] There is not sufficient space here to engage in a full analysis of the ideological and conceptual foundations of human rights. For a more complete discussion of this see M De Blois, 'The Foundation of Human Rights: A Christian Perspective' in P R Beaumont (ed), *Christian Perspectives on Human Rights and Legal Philosophy* (Cumbria, Paternoster Press, 1998) 7-30; N Doe, 'Canonical Approaches to Human Rights in Anglican Churches' in Hill, *Religious Liberty and Human Rights*, 185-206

[44] See T Rowland, 'The Liberal Doctrine of State Neutrality: a Taxonomy' (2000) 2 *U. Notre Dame Austrl L Rev* 53 – 66.

[45] Ahdar and Leigh make this point throughout their book.

Religious belief is something which is left at home when the believer steps across the threshold into the outside world[46].

Establishment and Human Rights as Competing Sources of Authority and Identity

The tension between the ideological foundations and intellectual heritage of Establishment and human rights may create difficulties precisely because it creates competing sources of authority and identity for and in the State.

Historically one of the roles served by Establishment, particularly in the English experience, has been to provide a source of moral authority for the State and to reinforce the idea that government is subject to a higher authority[47]. Another related role for Establishment and the Established Church has been to reinforce national identity and citizenship by the provision of a common national religion, the exclusion of foreign power, and by guaranteeing the role of the Established church in training people to be good citizens[48]. The liberal conception of human rights is problematic for this on a number of levels.

At the most basic level, as noted above, Establishment theory has tended to assume the moral good of men living in communities, States and nations. States are generally seen as being morally good, at least when subjected to the corrective influence of the church. In contrast, human rights, with their emphasis upon the individual and their rigid distinction between States and victims[49], tend to cast the State in the role of a dangerous villain and a potential enemy of liberty. Viewed in such a light the State can rarely be seen as a suitable ally for a church.

Further problems might be caused because appeals to the idea of respect for human rights appear to provide the State with an alternative source of authority and cohesion, and one which is broader in scope than any religious body can ever be. Human rights might, then, usurp the role traditionally played by the Established church. This, though it does not answer how citizens should reconcile competing religious and secular

---

[46] See McConnell, 'Religious Souls and the Body Politic'.

[47] The remnants of this are seen in the formula of 'the Queen in Parliament under God' and a somewhat muted reference to it in The Report of the Royal Commission on House of Lords Reform *A House for the Future* (Cm 4534, 2000) Para. 15.9.

[48] See generally A Hastings, *Church and State: The English Experience* (Exeter, University of Exeter Press, 1991).

[49] E.g. under ECHR Article 34.

obligations, might appeal to a State which is seeking ways to promote national cohesion within a citizenry which is culturally and religiously diverse. It provides a non-doctrinal source of unity and, potentially at least, avoids the danger of excluding or marginalising those who do not adhere to the Established church[50].

Such changes in the appearance and political concerns of the State, taken together with the reality of a religiously plural nation, may further undermine Establishment through the reactions they provoke on the part of the Established church. The almost inevitable reaction of at least some sections of that church will be a loss of confidence in that church's national identity and mission, and a reassertion of a narrower spiritual and doctrinal identity for that church which does not depend upon its Established status[51]. This in turn undermines the ability of the church to engage in a national mission by rendering it less comprehensive and reducing its catholicity and breadth[52].

Conclusion

At the outset the question posed was whether Establishment and human rights were happy bedfellows or uneasy allies in the English constitution. The answer which law provides to this question appears to be, in large part at least, that they can co-exist quite happily. The jurisprudence of the European Convention has accepted and accommodated Establishment and upheld its consistence with the requirements of human rights. Further, the provisions of the Human Rights Act 1998 seem to have successfully safeguarded the religious liberty of the Church of England without altering the legal fact of its Establishment.

Looking beyond matters of strict legal compliance, however, the answer to the initial question seems more problematic, and is arguably that human rights and Establishment are at best uneasy allies. This answer is given not on the basis that the Church of England is in ethos or action opposed to human rights, but rather on the grounds that the assumptions upon which Establishment and human rights rest pull in opposing constitutional

---

[50] Edge, 'Reorienting the Establishment Debate: From the Illusory Norm to Equality of Respect'.

[51] For an account of Anglican High Church reactions to such challenges in the nineteenth century see e.g. O Chadwick, *The Spirit of the Oxford Movement* (Cambridge, Cambridge University Press, 1990) and J S Reed, *Glorious Battle: The Cultural Politics of Victorian Anglo-Catholicism* (Nashville, Vanderbilt University Press, 1996).

[52] See Medhurst, 'The Church of England: a Progress Report' at 16.

directions. Establishment in its essence demands a public role for religion while the general effect of human rights is to make religion an innately private matter. An emphasis upon human rights norms and thinking obscures the public face of the Established church, denies the public aspects of what it does and may deny it key aspects of its historical constitutional role.

The final question is whether this ideological tension matters in the absence of legal conflict. If your only concern is State compliance with international legal obligations, or with the rights guaranteed to religious bodies, then the answer is that it probably does not. If, though, your concern is to find a logical basis for the continuance of Establishment as a constitutional arrangement with any significance or future, then it does matter. Even if you have no particular attachment to the idea of Establishment, then unquestioning acceptance of the desirability and rationality of a jurisprudence based on silence and a refusal to examine Church-State relations must be questioned.

CHURCH, STATE AND CIVIL PARTNERS:
ESTABLISHMENT AND SOCIAL MORES IN TENSION

Mark Hill

Introduction

The Civil Partnership Act 2004 came into force on 5 December 2005 amidst a furore of media attention, much of it prurient, and under protest from evangelical Christian groups and others. It generated a spirited exchange in periodicals such as the *Ecclesiastical Law Journal*[1], but the practical implications are yet to be fully evaluated. This chapter will provide an analysis of three particular ways in which the Act necessitates a re-visiting of the constitutional relationship of Church and State: first, the sacramental and secular concepts of marriage and the degree to which they have been altered by the creation of the legal construct of the civil partnership[2]. Secondly, the implications for clergy of the Church of England, who are commonly understood to be under a legal duty to solemnise the marriage of parishioners irrespective of the couple's religious beliefs or lack of them, and yet are canonically restrained from blessing a same-sex union. Thirdly, two specific provisions of the Act which empower Ministers of the Crown by order to amend or repeal Church legislation, thereby jeopardising a century of progress towards self-governance and autonomy on the part of the Established Church in England.

Gay Marriage?

The Civil Partnership Act 2004 was welcomed by civil rights jurists, and produced – perhaps inevitably – a flurry of camp innuendo from the popular press. Few could have missed the coverage of Sir Elton John and David Furnish at the same Windsor register office as had been used a

---

[1] J Humphreys, 'The Civil Partnership Act 2004, Same-Sex Marriage and the Church of England' (2006) 8 *Ecc LJ* 289, M Scott Joynt, 'The Civil Partnership 2004: Dishonest Law?' (2007) 9 *Ecc LJ* 92.

[2] In a pastoral letter to the parishes of his diocese in March 2008, the Rt Revd Jonathan Gledhill, Bishop of Lichfield, criticized 'the Great British experiment to downplay marriage and the family'. He said the experiment had failed: <http://www.lichfield.anglican.org/news&newsID=492>.

few months earlier for the marriage of HRH Prince Charles (the future Supreme Governor of the Church of England) and Camilla Parker-Bowles[3]. But what was the status and legal effect of the respective ceremonies and why was the latter but not the former followed by an Anglican service of blessing in St George's Chapel, Windsor conducted by the Archbishop of Canterbury?

The answer, as is so often the case, lies in matters of definition: terminological precision articulates a conceptual distinction whereas linguistic laxity obfuscates and confuses. Prior to the introduction of the legislation, the Government asserted that it had no plans to allow same-sex couples to marry; its proposals were for an entirely separate concept: 'civil partnership is a completely new legal relationship, exclusively for same-sex couples, distinct from marriage'[4]. Quite how distinct, however, is far from clear. In *Wilkinson v Kitzinger*, it was said that 'Parliament has taken steps by enacting the Civil Partnership Act to accord to same-sex relationships effectively all the rights, responsibilities, benefits and advantages of civil marriage save the name'; and the concept of civil partnership was described as a 'parallel and equalizing institution designed to redress a perceived inequality of treatment of long-term monogamous same-sex relationships, while at the same time, demonstrating support for the long established institution of marriage'[5]. In *Secretary of State for Work and Pensions v M*, it was noted that civil partnerships have 'virtually identical legal consequences to marriage'[6]. Herring criticises the judgment on the basis that although the President of the Family Division recognised that civil partnerships were as a matter of nature and common understandings different from marriage, it is not clear how he thought they were different[7]. Attempts at jurisprudential precision have not prevented the expression 'gay marriage' achieving popular currency and widespread parlance[8].

---

[3] I have elsewhere addressed the dubious legality of a Royal Marriage being contracted in a civil ceremony: (2005) 8 *Ecc LJ* 244, its status hinging in nothing more than a written statement of Lord Falconer of Thornton (then Lord Chancellor) in the House of Lords. Civil marriage is a creature of statute, and its application to members of the Royal Family was expressly excluded from the scheme: Marriage Act 1836, s 45.

[4] This statement was for a long time to be found in response to 'Frequently Asked Questions' on the website of the Women and Equality Unit of the Department for Trade and Industry.

[5] *Wilkinson v Kitzinger* [2006] EWHC (Fam) 2022 at para 121.

[6] *Secretary of State for Work and Pensions v M* [2006] 1 FCR 497 at para 99, per Sir Mark Potter P. He disavowed the concept of 'gay marriage' as a contradiction in terms.

[7] J Herring, *Family Law* (Third edition, Essex, Pearson, 2007) 70.

[8] Note that gay marriage in its full sense has been adopted in both Belgium and Spain. The Constitutional Court of South Africa in *Minister of Home Affairs v Fourie, Lesbian*

The great repository of English law, *Halsbury's Statutes*, now has a generic section entitled 'Matrimonial Law and Civil Partnerships' following directly after 'Markets and Fairs'[9].

In England, the solemnization of matrimony traditionally lay with the churches. Sacramental marriages in religious ceremonies had – and continue to have – direct legal effect in English secular law. To this day, ministers of the Church of England are under a duty to conduct a marriage service according to the rites of the Church for any resident of their parish regardless of religious affiliation[10]. Civil marriage, by contrast, is a creature of statute, introduced by the Marriage Act 1836. The legislation empowers registrars (who are civil servants and officers of the state) to solemnize marriages. But, as was made clear in the case of *R v Dibdin*[11]:

> Marriage … is one and the same thing whether the contract is made in church with religious vows superadded, or whether it is made in a Nonconformist chapel with religious ceremonies, or whether it is made before a consul abroad, or before a registrar, without any religious ceremonies.

Marriage is the lifelong union of one man and one woman. This is not merely a Christian definition, but one recognised and articulated by the secular courts. Lord Penzance in *Hyde v Hyde* defined marriage as 'a voluntary union for life of one man and one woman to the exclusion of all others'[12].

In contrast, a civil partnership is a legally formed 'relationship between two people of the same sex'[13], contracted in accordance with the detailed procedures of the Civil Partnership Act 2004[14]: notice must be given of an intention to form a civil partnership, the notice must be publicised,

---

and Gay Equality Project v Minister of Home Affairs (CCT 60/04, 10/05, 1 December 2005) declared the common law definition of marriage (between a 'man' and a 'woman') to be inconsistent with the South African Constitution. However the Court suspended the declaration of invalidity for twelve months to allow Parliament to correct the defect by introducing, should it so wish, legislation permitting civil unions. The dissenting judgment of O'Regan J would not have allowed the suspension but would have corrected the law with immediate effect.

[9] *Halsbury's Statutes of England and Wales* (Fourth edition, London, Butterworths LexisNexis, 2006 Reissue), Volume 27.

[10] See M Hill, *Ecclesiastical Law* (Third edition, Oxford, Oxford University Press, 2007) paras 5.31-5.50.

[11] [1910] P 57, CA.

[12] *Hyde v Hyde* (1868) LR 1 P&D 130 at 133.

[13] Civil Partnership Act 2004, s1(1), 3(1)(a).

[14] See, generally, N Gray and D Brazil, *Blackstone's Guide to the Civil Partnership Act 2004* (Oxford, Oxford University Press, 2005).

and the partnership cannot be entered into until 15 days after the notice
has been given. These preliminaries broadly replicate those for civil marriage under a registrar's certificate. The partnership itself is entered into
by signing a document in the presence of each partner, the registrar
and two witnesses. The Act provides that civil partners are to be treated
by law in the same way as married couples in respect to, amongst other
things, property disputes between them, the law relating to wills, administration of estates and family provision.

Like marriage, a civil partnership 'ends only on death, dissolution
or annulment'[15]; and the provisions of the Civil Partnership Act 2004
as regards termination 'mirrors, to a large extent, the provisions contained in the Matrimonial Causes Act 1973'[16] with the order of dissolution being equivalent to a divorce[17]. There are two main differences
between the termination of a marriage and termination of a civil partnership[18]. First, whilst adultery is a ground for a divorce[19], there is no like
provision for the dissolution of a civil partnership[20]. Second, in relation
to annulment, whilst section 12 of the Matrimonial Causes Act 1973
provides that a marriage may be voidable if one party petitions that the
marriage has not been consummated[21], there is no equivalent provision
to that in the Civil Partnership Act 2004[22].

[15] Civil Partnership Act 2004, s 1(3).

[16] Gray and Brazil, *Blackstone's Guide to the Civil Partnership Act 2004* 25.

[17] Herring, *Family Law* 63.

[18] Another difference is that under the Civil Partnership Act 2004, s49(b), in the case
of a minor, if a person whose consent is required has forbidden the issue of the civil
partnership document then a later civil partnership is void. In contrast, in relation to
marriage, unless a person has objected to the calling of banns, a marriage contracted in
the absence of the necessary consent is not void: N Lowe and G Douglas, *Bromley's
Family Law* (Tenth Edition, Oxford, Oxford University Press, 2007) 98.

[19] Matrimonial Causes Act 1973, s1(2) (a).

[20] Although a relationship with a third party may constitute the ground of 'behaviour'
under section 44(1) of the Civil Partnership Act 2004: see Lowe and Douglas, *Bromley's
Family Law* 301 and Gray and Brazil, *Blackstone's Guide to the Civil Partnership Act
2004* 27.

[21] Owing to the incapacity of either party to consummate or that it has not been consummated due to the respondent's wilful refusal to do so: Matrimonial Causes Act 1973,
s 12. Section 12 also provides that a marriage may be voidable if one of the parties was
suffering from a communicable venereal disease at the date of the marriage. See Lowe
and Douglas, *Bromley's Family Law* 79.

[22] See Civil Partnership Act 2004, s 50. It is 'unclear' why the provision of section 12
of the Matrimonial Causes Act 1973 that a marriage may be voidable if one of the parties
was suffering from a communicable venereal disease at the date of the marriage has been
omitted from the grounds on which a civil partnership is voidable: Lowe and Douglas,
Bromley's Family Law 98.

The Act contains specific provision relating to faith communities. A civil partnership may not be entered into on religious premises and no religious service may be used while the registrar is officiating at the signing of a civil partnership document[23]. Similarly, marriages that take place in register offices or non-religious 'approved premises' are also prohibited from including any religious service[24]. A Pastoral Statement issued by the House of Bishops of the Church of England on 25 July 2005 states,

> The legislation does, however, leave entirely open the nature of the commitment that members of a couple chose to make to each other when forming a civil partnership. In particular, it is not predicated on the intention to engage in a sexual relationship. Thus there is no equivalent of the marriage law provision either for annulment on the grounds of non-consummation or for its dissolution as a result of sexual infidelity[25].

Whilst it is self-evident that, in contradistinction to married couples, biological procreation cannot be achieved by civil partners, the issue of the extent to which civil partnerships carry with them the concept of a sexual union is debatable. An argument that it does has been made by Jacqueline Humphries[26]. She maintains that the Act has an understanding of civil partnerships that are voluntary, permanent, sexual, monogamous, mutually supportive and nurturing of children in the same ways that a marriage is understood to be within English law. I disagree. There is nothing in the provisions of the Act to suggest that it is concerned with anything more that the financial affairs of participating partners and inheritance upon death. Physical intimacy, still less sexual fidelity, fail to feature in the provisions of the Act, whether conceptually or substantively.

In relation to marriage, non-consummation has already been mentioned[27]. It is the act of heterosexual penetration[28] which is required to

---

[23] Civil Partnership Act 2004, s2(5), 6(1)(b).

[24] Ibid; Marriage Act 1949, s45A(4); Marriages and Civil Partnerships (Approved Premises) Regulations 2005/3168, Schedule 1.

[25] *Civil Partnerships: A Pastoral Statement from the House of Bishops of the Church of England*, July 2005.

[26] J Humphreys, 'The Civil Partnership Act 2004, Same-Sex Marriage and the Church of England' (2006) 8 *Ecc LJ* 289.

[27] See Lowe and Douglas, *Bromley's Family* Law. They contend that the reason for this omission is 'because the concept of consummation, which is inherently heterosexual (if not heterosexist) does not apply to a same-sex relationship': page 79.

[28] It has been judicially defined as the penetration of the vagina by the penis: *D-E v Attorney General* (1845) 1 Rob Eccl 279. See G Douglas, *An Introduction to Family Law* (Second Edition, Oxford, Oxford University Press, 2004) 34.

consummate a marriage, as opposed to the prospect of that act resulting in the birth of a child[29]. Does the omission of non-consummation as a ground for dissolving a civil partnership simply recognise that heterosexual sex is not an element of a civil partnership or is it an acknowledgment that sexual intimacy of any type is not a component part?[30] The second interpretation seems preferable. Since section 12 of the Matrimonial Causes Act 1973 underlines that 'heterosexual sex is an important element, if not the purpose of marriage'[31], the absence of any equivalent provision in section 50 of the Civil Partnership Act 2004 may be taken to reveal that sexual intimacy is not an element of a civil partnership[32]. This interpretation is supported by Baroness Scotland's explanation of the omission: 'There is no provision for consummation in the Civil Partnership Bill. We do not look at the nature of the sexual relationship, it is totally different in nature'[33].

Moreover, the fact that siblings, parents cared for by children, and others living together cannot enter a civil partnership further suggests that sexual intimacy is not a definitional element of a civil partnership[34]. If it were solely the sexual element that was distinctive then heterosexual cohabitees, who are not related, would be included. The Grand Chamber of the European Court of Human Rights has recently stated that: 'Rather than the length or the supportive nature of the relationship, what is determinative is the existence of a public undertaking, carrying with it a body of rights and obligations of a contractual nature'[35]. A civil partnership, as the Act makes clear, is no more and no less than a 'relationship between two people of the same sex'[36]. There is no requirement – either prescriptive or normative – that a civil partnership relationship must or should be sexual.

[29] Lowe and Douglas, *Bromley's Family Law* 79.

[30] It has been suggested the absence of a non-consummation provision in the Civil Partnership Act 2004 'demonstrates the law's failure to recognise that gay sex is real sex': Herring, *Family Law* 64.

[31] See Douglas, *An Introduction to Family Law* 34.

[32] Certain other grounds that are inherently heterosexual have not been omitted: for instance, being pregnant by someone else is a ground upon which the civil partnership can be voidable. See Lowe and Douglas, *Bromley's Family Law* 98.

[33] Baroness Scotland of Asthal, House of Lords, Hansard 17 November 2004, col 1479.

[34] Herring, by contrast, contends that the arguments used against the unsuccessful 'wrecking amendment' introduced in the House of Lords to extend the application of the Bill to siblings and similar 'showed that it is the sexual element of the relationship, with what that represents, which leads us to regard a relationship as being different from a relationship between friends'. Herring, *Family Law* 68.

[35] *Burden v United Kingdom* (Application no. 13378/05) para 65.

[36] Civil Partnership Act 2004, s1(1), 3(1)(a).

It therefore follows that the clergy of the Church of England are free under both civil law and canon law to enter into a civil partnership since the act of registration does not of itself constitute a declaration of homosexual orientation or practice. Were a cleric to be disciplined on the basis that he or she were in a doctrinally offensive non-celibate same-sex relationship, the mere fact that a civil partnership had been entered would be evidentially neutral, and would not of itself demonstrate an infringement of the doctrinal Statement 'Issues in Human Sexuality'[37]. The document is lengthy and closely reasoned but its ultimate conclusion is that whilst homosexual orientation is acknowledged and accepted, the active practice of such orientation in a same-sex relationship incorporating physical intimacy is regarded as incompatible with the clerical state:

> We have, therefore, to say that in our considered judgement the clergy cannot claim the liberty to enter into *sexually active* homophile relationships. Because of the distinctive nature of their calling, status and consecration, to allow such a claim on their part would be seen as placing that way of life in all respects on a par with heterosexual marriage as a reflection of God's purpose in creation. The Church cannot accept such a parity and remain faithful to the insights which God has given it through Scripture, tradition and reasoned reflection on experience[38].

The House of Bishops' statement also 'affirms' that clergy of the Church of England should not provide services of blessing for those who have registered a civil partnership. However, 'where clergy are approached by people asking for prayer in relation to entering into a civil partnership they should respond pastorally and sensitively in the light of the circumstances of each case'[39].

---

[37] 'Issues in Human Sexuality': A Statement by the House of Bishops of the General Synod of the Church of England, December 1991 (Church House Publishing, 1991). For additional prescriptive description of clerical lifestyle and sexual conduct, see a resolution of the General Synod of the Church of England dated 11 November 1987, a resolution of the General Synod dated 14 July 1997, and resolution 1.10 of the Lambeth Conference 1998.

[38] 'Issues in Human Sexuality' at paragraph 5.17 (emphasis added). The rigour of this House of Bishops' Statement must be contrasted with the known fact of practising homosexual clergy ministering openly and effectively in the Church of England. Media attention surrounding the proposed appointment of Canon Jeffrey John as Bishop of Reading, and the consecration of the Reverend Gene Robinson to be a bishop in the Episcopal Church of the USA have exposed the divide which some perceive to exist between the official doctrinal teaching of Anglicanism and its routine practice. These matters, though highly significant, are beyond the scope of this paper.

[39] A survey of same-sex couples which found that a significant minority wanted a religious element in a civil partnership celebration: P Readhead, *Same-Sex Couples Tie the Knot* (ESRC, 2006).

Only time will tell how the tension between the legislature and faith communities will be played out. The statutory provisions of the Act currently ensure that the doctrinal purity of sacramental marriage as a life-long union between one man and one woman is preserved. However this jurisprudential precision has not prevented the expression 'gay marriage' achieving popular and widespread parlance. As to the controversial question on whether the passing of the Civil Partnership Act 2004 undermines the institution of marriage, General Synod passed several resolutions in its February 2007 group of sessions including one which acknowledged:

> the diversity of views within the Church of England on whether Parliament might better have addressed the injustices affecting persons of the same sex wishing to share a common life had it done so in a way that avoided creating a legal framework with many similarities to marriage.

Conscientious Objection

The duty on the part of a priest of the Church of England to solemnise the marriage of parishioners who present themselves is subject to a number of statutory exceptions[40]. The first of these, often styled a 'conscience clause' is to be found in the Matrimonial Causes Act 1965 and provides that clergy [41] cannot be compelled to solemnise the marriage of any person whose former marriage has been dissolved and whose former spouse is still living[42]. This permits them not only to refuse to solemnise the marriage but also to prohibit the use of the church or chapel of which they are minister for such a purpose[43]. The same model was adopted by the Marriage (Prohibited Degrees of Relationship) Act 1986, which permits the clergy to refuse to marry those related by affinity whose marriage would have been void but for that Act, and to prohibit the use of his church accordingly[44]. However, the more recent exception created by

---

[40] Assuming that the legal requirements are satisfied, it is generally understood that there is a legal right to be married in the parish church: *Argar v Holdsworth* (1758) 2 Lee 515; M Hill, *Ecclesiastical Law* para 5.34. However, the existence of this right has been questioned in recent years by N Doe, *The Legal Framework of the Church of England* (Oxford, Clarendon Press, 1996) 358-362 and M Smith, 'An Interpretation of *Argar v Holdsworth*' (1998) 5 *Ecc LJ* 34. For a defence of the orthodox view, see J Humphreys, 'The Right to Marry in the Parish Church: A Rehabilitation of *Argar v Holdsworth*' (2004) 7 *Ecc LJ* 405.

[41] It also applies to clergy of the Church in Wales.

[42] Matrimonial Causes Act 1965, s 8(2).

[43] Ibid, s 8(2)(b).

[44] Marriage Act 1949, s 5A (amended by the Marriage (Prohibited Degrees of Relationship) Act 1986, s 3). Note also the Marriage Act 1949 (Remedial) Order 2006, which

the Gender Recognition Act 2004 is more narrowly drawn[45]. A Church of England minister is not obliged to solemnise the marriage of a person if he reasonably believes the person's gender to be an acquired gender under the 2004 Act[46]. It should be noted that section 22 of the Gender Recognition Act 2004 creates a general offence of unauthorised disclosure of information relating to a person's 'gender history'[47]. Although this applies only to those who have gained the information in an official capacity, that concept is broad enough to include receipt of information in connection with a voluntary organisation. The Gender Recognition (Disclosure of Information) (England, Wales and Northern Ireland) (No 2) Order 2005[48] makes provision for exceptions for certain legal, medical, financial and religious purposes. In respect of the religious purposes, disclosure is permitted to enable any person to make a decision whether to officiate or permit the marriage of the person[49].

The teaching and the practice of the Church of England with respect to a further marriage by a divorced person whose spouse is still alive has been subject to review and re-articulation[50]. The Canons still provide that 'marriage is in its nature a union permanent and lifelong' terminable by

---

preserved the clerical conscience clause in relation to the marriage of former parents-in-law to children-in-law. This underlying legislative change came about in consequence of the decision in the European Court of Human Rights in *B and L v United Kingdom* (2006) 42 EHRR 11.

[45] And they differ as between the Church of England and the Church in Wales.

[46] Marriage Act 1949, s 5B (1) (amended by the Gender Recognition Act 2004, s 11, Sch 4). A clerk in holy orders of the Church in Wales is not obliged to permit the marriage to be solemnised in his church or chapel: ibid s 5B (2) (as so amended).

[47] This is punishable by a fine of up to £5,000.

[48] Gender Recognition (Disclosure of Information) (England, Wales and Northern Ireland) (No 2) Order 2005, SI 2005/916.

[49] It also includes whether to appoint the person as a minister, office-holder or to any employment for the purposes of the religion, whether to admit them to any religious order or to membership, or to determine 'whether the subject is eligible to receive or take part in any religious sacrament, ordinance or rite, or take part in any act of worship or prayer, according to the practices of an organised religion': ibid art 4. If a decision other than one relating to marriage is being made, the person making the disclosure must reasonably consider that that person may need the information in order to make a decision which complies with the doctrines of the religion in question or avoids conflicting with the strongly held religious convictions of a significant number of the religion's followers.

[50] See *An Honourable Estate* (Church House Publishing, London, 1988), *Marriage: A Teaching Document from the House of Bishops* (Church House Publishing, London, 1999), *Marriage in Church After Divorce*, the Winchester Report (GS 1361, 2000), *Marriage in Church After Divorce*, A Report from the House of Bishops (GS 1449, May 2002). The latter states, 'The Church of England has sought both to uphold the principle of life-long marriage and to provide a pastoral ministry to divorced persons who seek a further marriage in church': para 1.

the death of one partner[51]. With the rescission of paragraph 1 of the 1957 Act of Convocation[52], the term 'indissoluble save by death' was lost, as was the exhortation not to use the marriage service in the case of anyone who had a former partner still living[53], but marriage should always be undertaken as 'a solemn, public and life-long covenant between a man and a woman'[54].

As noted above, a priest is relieved of his duty to marry those who are entitled by law to be married in his church if one or both of the intended parties has been divorced and his or her partner is still living[55]. He may also refuse to allow his church to be used for such a purpose[56]. The Act does not preclude the priest from conducting such a marriage; it merely creates a permissive right entitling him lawfully to decline if his conscience so dictates. A capricious refusal, not based upon a conscientious objection, might be actionable under the Human Rights Act 1998[57]. Equally, the right being personal to the priest exercisable according to his conscience, it is not open to the bishop or archbishop to seek to fetter its exercise by mandatory direction[58].

Thus we find ourselves in the curious position whereby Church of England clergy (i) are under a legally enforceable duty to solemnise the matrimony of atheists and adherents; (ii) have a statutory discretion to

---

[51] See Canon B 30 para 1. The unanimous advice of the legal officers of General Synod (appearing as annex 2 to *Marriage in Church After Divorce*, A Report from the House of Bishops (GS 1449, May 2002)) was that the further marriage of a divorced person was not necessarily incompatible with the Church's doctrine of marriage since the characteristic and normative nature of marriage as a lifelong union was unchanged.

[52] *Regulations Concerning Marriage and Divorce*, Canterbury Convocation passed in May 1957, and declared an Act of Convocation on 1 October 1957, affirming resolutions of 1938 common to both the Canterbury and York Convocations.

[53] Paragraph 1 of the Act of Convocation of 1 October 1957, and the resolutions of 1938, were rescinded by General Synod with effect from 14 November 2003.

[54] See the *Pastoral Introduction* to the Common Worship Marriage Service.

[55] Matrimonial Causes Act 1965, s 8(2)(a).

[56] Ibid, s 8(2)(b).

[57] The right to marry is set out in Article 12 of the European Convention on Human Rights, and it is suggested that a minister of the Church of England, in performing functions relating to the solemnisation of marriage is a public authority for the purposes of s 6(1) of the Human Rights Act 1998: see *Aston Cantlow Parochial Church Council v Wallbank* [2004] 1 AC 546, particularly (albeit *obiter*) per Lord Hobhouse of Woodborough at para 86, and Lord Rodger of Earlsferry at para 170.

[58] There is nothing objectionable to the issuing of guidelines, and these may be useful to ensure procedural consistency, but the priest's statutory discretion must not be eroded. *Advice to Clergy Concerning Marriage and the Divorced* was issued by the House of Bishops in November 2002, and is included in the supplementary material to the Canons of the Church of England.

refuse to marry divorcées, transgendered and certain others exercisable in accordance with their conscience irrespective of the religious beliefs and affiliations of the couple; and (iii) are canonically prohibited[59] from conducting a service of blessing following the registration of a civil partnership. Ironically, devout Christians in the latter category are denied the ministrations of the Church by way of a blessing whereas Muslims, Budhists, Sikhs, Jews and non-believer couples[60] can compel the use Church of England rites and liturgy and the ministrations of its clergy. The pastoral damage which might result from this mixed message cannot be adequately explained away as an anomaly of the historic accident of establishment in a plural society[61].

The Legislative Autonomy of the Church of England

Turning to constitutional matters, certain obscure sections of the Civil Partnership Act 2004 strike a somewhat discordant note when seen against a century of progress towards self-governance and autonomy on the part of the established church in England[62]. The year 1919 saw the passage of what is usually referred to as the Enabling Act[63]. This gave to the National Assembly of the Church of England (or 'Church Assembly' as it was more commonly known)[64] the power to legislate by Measure[65]. As a result of the Synodical Government Measure 1969, the Church Assembly was reconstituted and renamed the General Synod of the Church of England[66] and Synod was additionally empowered to legislate by Canon, a power which had hitherto vested in the Convocations of

[59] See *Civil Partnerships: A Pastoral Statement from the House of Bishops of the Church of England*, July 2005 (discussed above) and note Canon C14 of the Canons of the Church of England which requires clergy to take the Oath of Canonical obedience to the diocesan bishop and his successors 'in all things lawful and honest'.

[60] Provided that one or both are resident within the particular parish.

[61] For a more forthright discussion of the subject see M Hill, 'Rent Asunder: Westminster's War on Marriage', a paper presented at the Tenth Anniversary Conference of the Centre for Law and Religion, Cardiff University, 11-12 March 2008 (publication forthcoming).

[62] See M Hill, 'Uncivil partnership with the state?' *Church Times* 2 February 2007.

[63] Namely the Church of England Assembly (Powers) Act 1919, a statute allowing the laity (other than members of Parliament) to participate in Church government for the first time.

[64] It was created by the conflation of the Convocations of Canterbury and of York.

[65] See W McKay, *Erskine May's Treatise on the Laws, Privileges, Proceedings and Usage of Parliament* (Twenty-third edition, London, 2004) 701–705. The legal status of a Measure is considered in Hill, *Ecclesiastical Law* paras 1.25 and 1.30.

[66] Hereafter 'Synod'.

Canterbury and York[67]. The formation of the Church Assembly marked a significant reduction in the legislative role of Parliament over the affairs of the Church of England. However, as the passage of the draft Churchwardens Measure in 1999 served to illustrate, the residuary powers retained by Parliament are from being a dead letter, the Ecclesiastical Committee declining to approve provisions which would have enabled bishops to suspend churchwardens from office[68].

Measures have the full force and effect of Acts of Parliament and can amend or repeal Acts of Parliament[69]. Once a Measure has received the Royal Assent, its *vires* may not be challenged in the courts[70]. A Measure may relate to 'any matter concerning the Church of England'[71]. This expression carries its ordinary meaning and is not to be narrowly construed so as to prevent Synod passing a Measure concerning a fundamental change in doctrine[72]. However, a Measure may not make any alteration in the composition or powers or duties of the Ecclesiastical Committee of Parliament or in the parliamentary procedures prescribed under section 4 of the 1919 Act[73]. The Human Rights Act 1998, which came into effect in England on 2 October 2000, requires all Measures, whenever passed, to be read and given effect in a way which is compatible with the rights contained in the European Convention on Human Rights[74].

---

[67] Synodical Government Measure 1969, s 1; Canon H 1. Note also the Church of England (Worship and Doctrine) Measure 1974, s 1, which makes particular provision for Canons concerning worship.

[68] See B Hanson, 'Report on the General Synod of the Church of England, July and November Sessions, 1999', (2000) 5 *Ecc LJ* 382. Note also amendments to the proposed Church of England (Pensions) Measure 2003 made at the behest of the Ecclesiastical Committee of Parliament, noted in S Slack, 'Report on the General Synod of the Church of England, July Session, 2002', (2003) 7 *Ecc LJ* 78.

[69] Church of England Assembly (Powers) Act 1919, s 4. See, for example, the Priests (Ordination of Women) Measure 1993, s 6, which ousted the provisions of the Sex Discrimination Act 1975. Note that this is no longer the case.

[70] *R v Archbishops of Canterbury and York, ex parte Williamson, The Times*, 9 March 1994, CA, reproduced in the Materials in Hill, *Ecclesiastical Law*.

[71] Church of England Assembly (Powers) Act 1919, s 3(6).

[72] *R v Ecclesiastical Committee of Both Houses of Parliament, ex parte The Church Society* (1994) 6 Admin LR 670; *R v Archbishops of Canterbury and York, ex parte Williamson* (1994) *The Times*, 9 March; *Williamson v Archbishops of Canterbury and York*, 5 September 1996, (unreported). The judgments in the two former cases are reproduced in the Materials section of M Hill, *Ecclesiastical Law* (Second edition, Oxford University Press, 2001).

[73] Church of England Assembly (Powers) Act 1919, s 3(6) proviso.

[74] See M Hill, *Ecclesiastical Law* paras 1.26–1.27.

Two sections of the Civil Partnership Act 2004 now sit somewhat uncomfortably with this process of autonomy[75]. They provide that a Minister of the Crown may by order amend, repeal or revoke Church legislation, a term defined so as to include Measures of the Church Assembly or General Synod and any orders, regulations or other instruments made by virtue of such Measures. Section 255 of the Civil Partnership Act is anodyne enough, limiting this new form of ministerial intervention to amendments, repeals or revocations in any Church legislation relating to pensions, allowances or gratuities with respect to surviving civil partners or their dependants. However, section 259 goes further and is much more widely drafted. It empowers a Minister by order to make 'such further provision as he considers appropriate for the general purposes, or any particular purpose, of the Civil Partnership Act, or for giving full effect to the Act or any provision of it'.

This amounts to a curtailment of autonomy on the part of the Church of England, albeit partial, with a specificity of purpose, and reliant upon benign and consensual exercise by the Government. In the course of parliamentary debate on an amending statutory instrument, the Under-Secretary of State in Department for Trade and Industry stated,

> by convention the Government do not legislate for the Church of England without its consent. I stress that the provisions in the order amending Church legislation have been drafted by Church lawyers, consulted on internally within the Church, and finally have been approved by the Archbishops' Council and the House of Bishops. The Church has asked that we include the amendments in the order, which we are content to do[76].

However the terms of sections 255 and 259 of the Civil Partnership Act are clear and unambiguous. The absence of any express provision for seeking (still less procuring) concurrence gives considerable power to the Executive (as opposed to Parliament) to legislate for the Church of England[77]. The fact that concurrence was in fact sought would give

[75] See M Hill, 'Uncivil partnership with the state?' *Church Times* 2 February 2007, and 'Editorial' (2007) 9 *Ecc LJ* 1, and, for a contrary view by way of response, see S Slack, 'Church Autonomy and the Civil Partnership Act: A Rejoinder' (2007) 9 *Ecc LJ* 206.

[76] Lord Sainsbury of Turville speaking on the proposed Civil Partnership Act 2004 (Overseas Relationships and Consequential, etc Amendments) Order (Grand Chamber, 19 July 2005, GC192-193). This was confirmed in debate by the Bishop of Worcester and there was a similar exchange on the Civil Partnership (Judicial Pensions and Church Pensions, etc) Order in which Lord Evans of Temple Guiting spoke for the Government and the Bishop of St Albans for the Church of England (30 November 2005, Column 293-295).

[77] The Parliamentary debates in the above instances curiously referred to consent being forthcoming from the Archbishops' Council and the House of Bishops. No reference is

modest comfort for the future exercise of this express power were it not
for the fact that the so-called approval came from the Archbishops'
Council and the House of Bishops as opposed to the General Synod to
whom Parliament delegated the power to legislate in relation to matters
concerning the Church of England.

Conclusion

The Civil Partnership Act 2004 is one of a number of pieces of legislation that have had an impact upon religious communities and individuals[78]. Indeed, the Act has particularly profound implications for the
constitutional relationship of Church and State. These are yet to be fully
appreciated. The Act creates a newly recognised legal relationship which
cannot be entered into on religious premises, at which no religious service
can be used, and the blessing of which is expressly forbidden by the
Church of England. Moreover despite political and judicial rhetoric that
civil partnerships are different and distinct from marriage, the exact differences have yet to be fully explored and clearly articulated. Although
the Act defines the relationship as being for two individuals of the same
gender, physical intimacy, still less sexual fidelity, do not feature in the
provisions of the Act. This means that the House of Bishops' Pastoral
Statement is wholly consistent with the letter of the legislation; whether
it accords with popular perceptions of the legislation is another matter.
Future judicial interpretation of the Act may pose challenges for the
clergy of the Established Church. The implications for Church of England clergy who are commonly understood to be under a legal duty to
solemnise the marriage of parishioners creates what can at best be styled
a pastoral anomaly. The specific provisions of the Act empowering Ministers of the Crown by order to amend or repeal Church legislation is a
dangerous precedent for the continuing autonomy of the Established
Church. Whether promoted by accident or design, the effects of the Civil
Partnership Act on the nature of Establishment in times of changing
social mores are far from insignificant and not yet fully understood.

made to the General Synod, which is the legislative body of the Church of England. The
consequence for the Church of England of this arrogation of legislative authority remains
to be seen.

[78] See other chapters in this volume for discussion of the impact of other statutes such
as the Charities Act 2006, the Racial and Religious Hatred Act 2006 and the new law on
religious discrimination.

RELIGION AND DISCRIMINATION: BALANCING INTERESTS WITHIN THE ANTI-DISCRIMINATION FRAMEWORK

Pauline Roberts

Introduction

Until 2003, discrimination on grounds of religion or belief in any context was not prohibited in Great Britain[1]. Certain groups with strong religious identities had been identified as racial groups by reference to their ethnic origins, and hence were protected under the Race Relations Act 1976 from discrimination on racial grounds, but not specifically against discrimination on grounds of religion[2]. Since 2003, significant legislative developments have occurred, which have seen the introduction of a prohibition on religious discrimination throughout Britain, first in the employment context as part of the implementation of the EC General Framework Directive and, more recently, in relation to the provision of goods and services and the exercise of public functions[3]. At the same time, non-discrimination regulations relating to sexual orientation have been introduced[4], as well as those relating to age[5].

The extension of equality rights increases the potential for conflict between different rights, in particular between those related to sexual orientation and religion or belief, as some religious practices and belief may discriminate on grounds of gender or sexual orientation[6]. Any attempt

[1] Though discrimination on grounds of religion was first prohibited in Northern Ireland by the Fair Employment Act 1976; see now the Fair Employment and Treatment (Northern Ireland) Order 1998.

[2] Namely, Jews (*Seide v Gillette* [1980] IRLR 427) and Sikhs (*Mandla v Dowell Lee* [1983] 2 AC 548).

[3] The Employment Equality (Religion or Belief) Regulations 2003 SI 2003/1660, which implement part of the EC Directive 2000/78 establishing a general framework for equal treatment in employment and occupation, [2000] OJ L303/16; Part 2 of the Equality Act 2006 covers the provision of goods and services.

[4] The Employment Equality (Sexual Orientation) Regulations 2003 SI 2003/1661 and the Equality Act (Sexual Orientation) Regulations 2007 SI 2007/1263.

[5] The Employment Equality (Age) Regulations 2006 SI 2006/1031.

[6] See, for example, M Bell, *Anti-Discrimination Law and the European Union* (Oxford, Oxford University Press, 2002) 112-118; L Vickers, 'Freedom of Religion and the Workplace: The *Draft* Employment Equality (Religion or Belief) Regulations 2003' (2003) 32 *Industrial Law Journal* 23-36; N Bamforth, M Malik and C O'Cinneide, *Discrimination Law: Theory and Context* (London, Sweet & Maxwell, 2008) chapter 13.

to maintain such a distinction will be contrary to the principle of non-discrimination and must therefore either be justifiable or fall within one of the exceptions permitted by the legislation if it is not to be found unlawful. A balance needs to be struck not just between the various equality rights, but also between these statutory rights and human rights, in particular the right to freedom of thought, conscience and religion contained in Article 9 of the European Convention on Human Rights[7]. This chapter focuses on three areas of conflict, each of which has resulted in a lot of media interest in the issues raised. In addition, two of the areas have seen the involvement of different interest groups in the debate surrounding the scope of the legislative provisions, particularly in respect of whether an appropriate balance has been struck by the legislation.

This chapter begins by introducing the main statutory provisions which prohibit discrimination on grounds of religion or belief in Great Britain, focusing on the concept of indirect discrimination in the workplace. The cases which are discussed in this part have been chosen to highlight how the application of the concept of indirect discrimination seeks to balance the religious rights of the employees against either the commercial interests of the employer or the duty of the employer to fulfil obligations to third parties, such as school pupils or those in residential care. It will then examine in detail two other issues which illustrate the potential for conflict between religious rights and other equality or human rights and will assess how the various interests have been balanced in these areas. First, the paper will discuss the religion-based exceptions from the statutory prohibition on sexual orientation discrimination, which have proved controversial[8]. The final issue is that of religious harassment, which poses particular problems as the legislation impacts on the right to freedom of expression alongside the right to religious freedom[9]. There are also general concerns about the possible extension of the prohibition on harassment on all grounds within the anti-discrimination legislation to beyond the workplace[10].

---

[7] See, for example, R Allen and G Moon, 'Substantive Rights and Equal Treatment in Respect of Religion and Belief: Towards a Better Understanding of the Rights, and their Implications' [2000] *European Human Rights Law Review* 580-602.

[8] R Sandberg and N Doe, 'Religious Exemptions in Discrimination Law' (2007) 66 *CLJ* 302-312.

[9] L Vickers, 'Is All Harassment Equal? The Case of Religious Harassment' (2006) 65 *CLJ* 579-605.

[10] *Discrimination Law Review. A Framework for Fairness: Proposals for a Single Equality Bill for Great Britain*, (London, Department for Communities and Local Government, June 2007) chapter 14. The Race Relations Act 1976 already prohibits harassment

Discrimination on Grounds of Religion or Belief

The Employment Equality (Religion or Belief) Regulations 2003 prohibit direct and indirect discrimination, victimisation, harassment and instructions to discriminate on the grounds of religion or belief in employment and occupation[11]. These are familiar concepts of discrimination which can be found also in the Sex Discrimination Act 1975 and Race Relations Act 1976, in relation to unlawful discrimination on grounds of sex and race. An employer discriminates directly against someone if he treats that person less favourably 'on grounds of religion or belief'. This is as broad an approach as is taken elsewhere in the anti-discrimination framework, in that a claimant may argue that she has been discriminated against on the basis of perceived religion, or because of the religion of someone with whom she associates, even if it is not her own religion[12]. A general exception is provided where being of a particular religion is a genuine and determining occupational requirement, having regard to the nature of employment, and that it is proportionate to apply the requirement[13]. A specific exception for 'organisations with a religious ethos' may be relied upon where certain criteria are met[14].

While the 2003 Religion or Belief Regulations were introduced in response to obligations under EC law, the Equality Act 2006 outlawed discrimination (though not harassment) on grounds of religion or belief in the provision of goods or services as part of the Government's policy of ensuring equal treatment and opportunities irrespective of factors such as religion[15]. Discussion of what is meant by 'equality' and the principles underlying the anti-discrimination legislation is beyond the scope of this chapter, which simply focuses on the current approach to balancing competing interests within the equality legislation[16]. In respect of goods and

on grounds of race or ethnic or national origins in the provision of goods and services and similar provisions are to be included in the Sex Discrimination Act 1975, to comply with the Directive 2004/113/EC implementing the principle of equal treatment between men and women in the access to goods and services.

[11] See L Vickers, *Religious Discrimination at Work* (Liverpool, Institute of Employment Rights, 2008) and L Vickers, *Religious Freedom, Religious Discrimination and the Workplace* (Oxford, Hart, 2008).

[12] For commentary on case law, see R Sandberg, 'Flags, Beards and Pilgrimages: A Review of the Early Cases on Religious Discrimination' (2007) 9 *Ecc LJ* 87-91.

[13] Regulation 7(2).

[14] Regulation 7(3). See Vickers, *Religious Discrimination at Work* at 13-15.

[15] Equality Act 2006, s 46.

[16] See for example S Fredman, *Discrimination Law* (Oxford, Clarendon Press, 2002); H Collins, 'Discrimination, Equality and Social Exclusion' (2003) 66 *MLR* 16-43.

services, there is an exemption for an 'organisation relating to religion or belief' which permits restriction of the provision of goods and services and membership of or participation in that organisation, either in order not to cause offence to persons of that religion or because of the purpose of the organisation[17]. Section 57 provides a definition of 'organisation relating to religion or belief' which focuses on the purpose of the entity involved. To be covered, the main purpose of the organisation must not be commercial and must fall within the list contained in section 57, namely to practise or advance a religion or belief, to teach the practices or principles of a religion or belief, to enable individuals to receive a benefit within the framework of that religion or belief, or to improve relations between persons of different religions or belief.

Indirect Discrimination

Indirect discrimination occurs where an employer introduces a provision, criterion or policy which is applied to everyone, regardless of religion, but which puts persons of a particular religion, including the individual claimant, at a particular disadvantage when compared with other persons[18]. If a *prima facie* case of discrimination can be established, the employer may still avoid liability if he is able to show that the policy is 'a proportionate means of achieving a legitimate aim'[19]. It has been traditional to balance the interests of employers and employees in this context through the concept of justification of indirect discrimination[20]. Thus, in the context of goods and services, section 45 of the Equality Act 2006 requires the service provider to 'reasonably justify' the otherwise discriminatory 'requirement, condition or practice'. The factors taken into account by tribunals and courts when determining the issue of justification in indirect discrimination cases will vary according to the facts of each case, but may include the right to freedom of religion and the public/private distinction[21].

Cases involving dress codes and religious symbols provide an illustration of the various interests which may be engaged in an indirect discrimination case. For example, the employer may well have a corporate identity which is reflected in its dress policy, while individual human

---

[17] Equality Act 2006, s 57.
[18] Regulation 3(1)(b).
[19] Regulation 3(1)(b)(iii).
[20] See Vickers, *Religious Discrimination at Work* at 21-23.
[21] Ibid at 46-51.

rights involved include the right to freedom of expression and the right to freedom of thought, conscience and religion[22]. Furthermore, in relation to the debate concerning the legitimacy of restrictions on headscarves in the workplace, one academic has commented that there is a 'conflict between positive and negative aspects of freedom of religion', as employees may wish to work in a 'non-religious environment', just as much as others wish to exercise their religious freedom to wear religious dress[23]. Two cases have illustrated the public interest in how employers approach competing interests when determining workplace rules for dress and it is to these we now turn.

The high profile case of *Azmi v Kirklees Metropolitan Council*[24] involved a claim brought by a teaching assistant who was suspended when she refused to remove her face veil when requested to do so while working with the children[25]. The Employment Appeal Tribunal (EAT) confirmed the employment tribunal's decision that Ms Azmi had been neither harassed nor discriminated against on the ground of religion, either directly or indirectly, by the school's conduct in requiring her to remove her veil in these circumstances[26]. The EAT found that the tribunal had adopted the correct approach to finding a comparator for direct discrimination purposes, namely a person who, whether Muslim or not, covered her face for a non-religious reason. As the evidence supported the view that such a comparator would have been suspended had she refused to comply with an instruction to remove the face covering, the tribunal concluded that there was no less favourable treatment on grounds of religion or belief.

With regard to indirect discrimination, the tribunal identified the discriminatory practice as the requirement not to cover one's face nor to wear clothing which interfered too much with the claimant's ability to communicate appropriately with the children. The EAT found that the tribunal was entitled to conclude that this was an 'apparently neutral' practice, noting that the employer's policy stressed that each case should be considered on its merits. The practice was discriminatory as there was

[22] See M Hill and R Sandberg, 'Is Nothing Sacred? Clashing Symbols in a Secular World' [2007] *P L* 488-506.

[23] Vickers, *Religious Discrimination at Work* at 24.

[24] [2007] ICR 1154.

[25] For discussion see Hill and Sandberg, 'Is Nothing Sacred?' at 502-504.

[26] The employment tribunal had upheld her claim of victimisation on the ground of religion, in that the council had failed to deal with her grievance properly and had treated her less favourably than they would have treated her had she not made an allegation of religious discrimination. This was not the subject of appeal.

no dispute that the practice put Muslim women at a particular disadvantage when compared with others, given the claimant's belief that her religion obliged her to wear the veil, unlike persons of another religion or no religion. However, the EAT confirmed that the indirect discrimination was justified objectively, notwithstanding its discriminatory effect. The council's legitimate aim was to ensure the best possible education for the pupils and the means adopted were proportionate. The principle of proportionality requires a tribunal to consider the reasonable needs of the employer but to make its own judgment as to the appropriateness of the practice in question[27]. In *Azmi* the employer had observed the claimant in the classroom and concluded that her communication was not as effective when she wore the face veil. In addition, the employer required her to remove the veil only when teaching, not at other times, such as when moving about within the school.

The second case suggests a further point, namely the potential for religious (or any other interest) groups to exert influence, whether political or commercial. The uniform policy of British Airways prohibited the wearing of visible items of jewellery. Employees whose religion required them to wear certain items of clothing or any other accessory could do so only if the company had first approved their design, if the items could not be covered up by the uniform. When a female employee was sent home for refusing to conceal her silver cross, the ensuing publicity included the announcement by the Church of England that it was reviewing its investment policy, in particular its shareholding in British Airways[28]. Shortly afterwards, the airline announced a review of its uniform policy[29].

In the subsequent claim of discrimination under the 2003 Religion or Belief Regulations, the female employee, Miss Eweida, was unsuccessful[30]. There was no direct discrimination as British Airways would have

---

[27] *Hardy & Hansons plc v Lax* [2005] ICR 1565.

[28] Church of England Press Release, 'Archbishop of Canterbury comments on British Airways', 24 November 2006, available at <http://www/cofe.anglican.org/news/pr118a06.html>.

[29] See for example, 'How the archbishop took on the world's favourite airline – and won', *The Guardian*, November 25 2006. British Airways subsequently changed its uniform policy to allow the display of faith and charity symbols, subject to an application process. The cross and Star of David were given general approval as authorised symbols, subject to certain rules.

[30] *Eweida v British Airways plc*, ET, Case Number 2702689/2006 (7 January 2008). In addition to dismissing the claims of discrimination and harassment in respect of the dress policy, the tribunal found no evidence of discrimination in relation to its rostering system, its management of break-times or a perceived anti-Christian bias in the company's policy and training materials. Confirmed by the EAT, *Eweida v British Airways plc* [2009] ICR 303.

treated any person displaying a cross, a symbol of any faith or a visible plain silver necklace in the same way, irrespective of religion[31]. There was no indirect discrimination as the employment tribunal found that Christians were not put at a particular disadvantage by the rule that personal jewellery should be concealed[32]. It was a matter of personal choice to wear a cross, not a requirement of the Christian faith[33]. This may be contrasted with *Azmi*, where the tribunal had found the policy to be discriminatory (albeit justified) as Ms Azmi *did* believe that her religion required her to wear the veil. Though the issue of justification did not arise in *Eweida*, as the policy was not indirectly discriminatory, the tribunal commented that it did not consider the policy to be a proportionate means of achieving what was undoubtedly a legitimate aim (a uniform corporate identity). One factor which influenced the tribunal was the company's acknowledgment that it had not considered formally the discriminatory impact of this policy prior to November 2006, after attracting the interest of both the Church of England and the media[34]. The employment tribunal criticised the requirement's failure to distinguish items such as religious symbols from other purely decorative pieces of jewellery, noting that they did not consider this 'struck the correct balance between corporate consistency, individual need and accommodation of diversity'[35].

It has been noted that the religious beliefs of the claimant in *Azmi* required her to treat men less favourably than women, in that men were not permitted to see her face[36]. Thus, there is a clash between gender rights and religious rights, as well as the duty of the employer to ensure the best possible education for the children in its school. Criticism has been made of the tribunal's approach to direct discrimination, as the claimant's wish to wear the veil was so closely linked to her religious convictions[37]. However, there is no justification for direct discrimination and by viewing the facts as providing the basis for an indirect discrimination claim, the tribunal ensured that the interests could be balanced through the justification defence. The EAT stressed that each case should

---

[31] At para 31.7.
[32] At para 33.6.
[33] At para 33.4.
[34] At para 33.10.
[35] At para 33.11.
[36] S Ashtiany, 'Gay Couples and Catholic babies are simply the start', *The Times* February 6, 2007.
[37] See B Fitzpatrick, *Sexual Orientation and religion or belief cases* (TUC, June 2007) at 46-47, available at <http://www.tuc.org.uk/extras/SORBreport.pdf>.

be decided on its facts and that not all cases of manifestation of religious beliefs would be classified as potentially indirect discrimination, but could well involve direct discrimination[38].

Sexual Orientation Discrimination: Religious-Based Exceptions

This part focuses on the exceptions within the sexual orientation regulations, rather than the exceptions within the religious discrimination legislation, as these are the areas which have caused particular controversy and which illustrate the tension between religion and sexual orientation in the anti-discrimination framework. There are two examples in which the legislature attempted to balance competing equality and human rights interests: first, the genuine occupational requirement exception, where employment is for the purpose of organised religion, in the 2003 Employment Equality (Sexual Orientation) Regulations and, secondly, the refusal to grant a specific exemption to Roman Catholic Adoption Agencies from the prohibition on discrimination on grounds of sexual orientation in the provision of goods and services[39].

Exception for Purpose of Organised Religion

Article 4(1) of the General Framework Directive provides the basis for the genuine and determining occupational requirement concept which is found in the employment equality regulations. Article 4(1) provides that:

> a difference of treatment which is based on a characteristic related to any of the [protected] grounds....shall not constitute discrimination where, by reason of the nature of the particular occupational activities concerned or of the context in which they are carried out, such a characteristic constitutes a *genuine* and *determining* occupational requirement, provided that the objective is *legitimate* and the requirement is *proportionate*[40].

Recital 23 to the preamble to the Directive envisages that such exceptions will be relevant in very limited circumstances. Regulation 7 of the 2003 Sexual Orientation Regulations contains two exceptions to the general prohibition on discrimination on grounds of sexual orientation. The first, regulation 7(2), is a 'general exception' where, 'having regard

---

[38] *Azmi* at para 76.
[39] The Equality Act (Sexual Orientation) Regulations 2007 SI 1263.
[40] (italics added).

to the nature of the employment or the context in which it is carried out' the employer can demonstrate that there is a '*genuine* and *determining* occupational requirement' that the position-holder must be of a 'particular sexual orientation' and that it is proportionate to apply that requirement in the particular case. Finally, either the person concerned does not meet the requirement or it must be reasonable for the employer to so conclude.

In comparison, regulation 7(3) applies only where the employment is 'for the purposes of organised religion'. To fall within regulation 7(3), an employer must satisfy certain criteria: in all cases, the employment must be 'for purposes of an organised religion'. But the employer must also then demonstrate that the requirement related to sexual orientation is applied either (i) so as to comply with the doctrines of the religion, or (ii) 'so as to avoid conflicting with the strongly held religious convictions of a significant number of the religion's followers' in the light of the nature of the employment and the context in which it is carried out[41]. The final condition is that either the person to whom the requirement is applied does not meet it or the employer reasonably is not satisfied that he or she does so. Section 19 of the Sex Discrimination Act 1975 provides a similar exception from the 1975 Act where the employment is restricted to one sex[42]. However, there is no case law on the meaning of 'purposes of an organised religion' in section 19 and thus this provides little assistance in resolving the uncertainty as to its scope[43].

In Parliamentary debate, the Government justified the introduction of regulation 7(3) by arguing that it 'will enable a tribunal to consider whether it is a matter of religious doctrine that a requirement relating to sexual orientation applies to a particular job', rather than be obliged to decide whether it was right that religious doctrine required someone to be heterosexual[44]. It was thus regarded as easier and less controversial for the tribunal to identify religious doctrine than to determine its reasonableness

---

[41] Regulation 7(3)(b).

[42] Regulation 20 of the Employment Equality (Sex Discrimination) Regulations (SI 2005/2467) amended section 19 of the Sex Discrimination Act 1975 with effect from 1 October 2005, in order to comply with the amended Equal Treatment Directive 2002/73/EC. Section 19 now mirrors regulation 7(3), whereas it previously referred to the need to 'avoid offending the religious susceptibilities of a significant number' of a religion's followers.

[43] R Sandberg and N Doe, 'Religious Exemptions in Discrimination Law' at 310-311.

[44] G Sutcliffe, Minister for Employment Relations, Competition and Consumers, Fourth Standing Committee on Delegated Legislation, 17 June 2003, Col 048.

or the proportionality of its application to a job requirement. Regulation 7(3)(b)(ii) seems to go further, in that it applies where a 'significant number' of a religion's followers hold particular views which do not form part of an accepted doctrine, otherwise it would fall within the first exception. However, an employer must show that the nature of employment and the context in which it is performed makes strongly held religious convictions a relevant matter to take into account. Thus, tribunals may limit the scope of this exception through a narrow interpretation of the types of employment for which it is reasonable to take account of the employee's sexual orientation.

Judicial review proceedings were brought in relation to both regulations 7(2) and 7(3) of the 2003 Sexual Orientation Regulations[45]. In *Amicus* the main argument in respect of Regulation 7(3) focused on its compatibility with the General Framework Directive[46]. Richards J referred to the obligation to apply a purposive construction when interpreting legislation which implements EC law, which enables the courts to consider extraneous materials[47]. Key to his approach to the question of compatibility was his view that regulation 7(3) could be construed as having very limited application. With regard to the first criterion, that employment must be for the purposes of an organised religion, Richards J accepted the Government's argument that this is a much narrower expression than 'religious organisations' or 'where an employer has an ethos based on religion or belief'. He was persuaded by the argument that a teacher in a faith school is *likely* to be employed 'for purposes of a religious organisation', rather than 'for purposes of organised religion'[48]. There was certainly a fair amount of support for this conclusion within Parliamentary

---

[45] *R (on the application of Amicus – MSF Section and others) v Secretary of State for Trade and Industry and others (Amicus)* [2004] EWHC 860 (Admin).

[46] Regulation 7(3) was challenged also on the basis of breach of legal certainty and breach of the European Convention on Human Rights. This was rejected, as was the challenge to other regulations, namely the exception for benefits dependent on marital status (regulation 25) and an exception to the prohibition of discrimination by further and higher education institutions in limited circumstances (regulation 20(3)).

[47] *Amicus* at para 46-66. In *Pickstone and others v Freemans plc* [1989] AC 66, the House of Lords held that the Equal Pay (Amendment) Regulations 1983 were reasonably capable of being construed so as to conform with EC law, having regard to the purpose of the equal pay legislation and its history. Richards J also referred to further recent support for the admissibility of background material in *Wilson v First County Trust Ltd. (No 2)* [2003] UKHL 40, in which the House of Lords had held that such material is admissible for the purpose of evaluating compatibility of legislation with rights under the European Convention of Human Rights, 'including the value judgment inherent in the test of proportionality'.

[48] At para 117.

statements, in which it seemed clear that the Government intended primarily that ministers of religion be covered by the exception, as well as a
'small number of posts outside the clergy' which 'exist entirely to promote religion', such as senior employees of the archbishops' conference
and of the General Synod of the Church of England[49]. Statements support
the view that the Government did not intend the exemption to apply to
employment such as a nurse in a care home or a teacher at a faith school,
which the Government preferred to describe as jobs existing for the
purpose of health care and education, rather than for the purposes of
an organised religion[50]. There remains a degree of uncertainty as to the
limiting effect of these comments, as whether employment is for the
purposes of an organised religion remains a question of fact for the
tribunal to determine. However, in light of the obligation to interpret the
regulations purposively and various Parliamentary statements, a narrow
construction of 7(3) would mean that very few employees would be
affected by the exception.

Turning to the second criteria, *Amicus* suggests that these conditions
impose 'very real additional limitations', both of which Richards J viewed
as setting objective tests which would be very hard to satisfy in practice[51].
He concurred with the views expressed in Parliamentary materials that
the first alternative would be satisfied in very few cases, as it would have
to be shown that employment of a person not meeting that requirement
would be incompatible with the doctrines of the religion. With regard
to the second alternative, Richards J noted that reference to a 'significant number', rather than to a majority, reflected both the need to avoid
detailed statistical analysis and to take due account of the presence of
differing views even within an organised religion[52]. He noted that sexual
orientation is a subject on which some followers of a religion may hold
stronger religious convictions than others and, in his view, it was acceptable to consider a possible exception even if the convictions were held
'only by a significant minority of followers'[53].

In one sense, it was acknowledged that regulation 7(3)(b) may be wider
than 7(2), in so far as it refers to an employer applying a 'requirement
related to sexual orientation', whereas in 7(2) the relevant occupational

[49] G Sutcliffe, Minister for Employment Relations, Competition and Consumers,
Fourth Standing Committee on Delegated Legislation, 17 June 2003, Col 030.
[50] Ibid.
[51] *Amicus* at para 117.
[52] At para 118.
[53] At para 118.

requirement is described as 'being of a particular sexual orientation'. Richards J noted that the derogation permitted by Article 4(1) refers to a difference of treatment 'which is based on a characteristic *related* to' sexual orientation; such wording is arguably wide enough to include discrimination based on sexual behaviour *related* to sexual orientation[54]. However, it is also arguably wide enough to cover the situation where, say, a priest is removed from office due to his known tolerance of homosexuality, rather than for his own sexual orientation or behaviour. Thus, a requirement that an employee accept others' views on sexual orientation could also fall within 7(3), subject to the employer meeting the other conditions.

The exception may apply where the employer *reasonably believes* that the person fails to meet the requirement as to sexual orientation[55]. Objections had been made that this condition provided scope for both intrusive questions concerning an employee's personal life and for decisions made upon assumptions about the individual's sexual orientation[56]. Richards J concluded that this was a lawful provision, by adopting a narrow construction which would mean that any decision based upon mere stereotyping could not satisfy the 'reasonableness' requirement[57]. He expressed doubt over the Secretary of State's argument permitting differential treatment on grounds of *perceived* sexual orientation. It may well also be the case that the risk of liability for harassment will deter too intrusive a line of enquiry. After an initial query as to whether the individual meets the requirement, further questions may be discouraged, though Richards J accepts that employers need not always be bound 'to accept at face value' the answer given to the initial question and may, if no answer is given, form their own opinion[58]. The onus is clearly on tribunals to apply the reasonableness test narrowly and to expect the employer to demonstrate the objective grounds for his belief[59].

---

[54] At para 119.

[55] For further discussion in relation to regulation 7(2) see H Oliver, 'Sexual Orientation Discrimination: Perceptions, Definitions and Genuine Occupational Requirements', (2004) 33 *Industrial Law Journal* 1-21.

[56] See H Oliver, 'Sexual Orientation Discrimination: Perceptions, Definitions and Genuine Occupational Requirements' at 15-18, and R Allen QC and R Crasnow, *The Times*, June 24, 2003.

[57] *Amicus* at para 81.

[58] *Amicus* at para 80 (in respect of regulation 7(2)(c)(ii), to which he applied the same reasoning as 7(3)(c)(ii)).

[59] Robert Wintemute believes that if the courts apply the test with 'sufficient strictness' it should comply with Article 4(1). See R Wintemute, 'United Kingdom' in K Waaldijk, M Bonini-Baraldi and A Littler (ed) *Combating Sexual Orientation Discrimination in*

As discussed in the *Amicus* case, the Government acknowledges that regulation 7(3) provides a 'broader exception' than the one contained in regulation 7(2)[60]. This might indicate that special treatment is being afforded to organised religions, rather than relying on the tribunals to interpret and apply 7(2) to such circumstances, as they will have to for any other employment. In recognising the concern expressed by representatives of certain organised religions, the Government has, at the very least, *appeared* to confer an exception which has not been granted to other employers[61]. In response to those who think the balance of rights in the exception is not appropriate, and would argue for a wider exception, it should be noted that if the doctrine of an organised religion included a belief, say, that persons with a disability should not serve as religious ministers, there is no specific exception upon which the organised religion could rely, comparable to either section 19 of the Sex Discrimination Act 1975 or regulation 7(3) of the 2003 Sexual Orientation Regulations. While discrimination for a reason which relates to the disabled person's disability may be justified, *direct* discrimination cannot be justified[62]. Similarly, an organised religion whose doctrine differentiated between racial groups would have to argue under the general exception in section 4A of the Race Relations Act 1976, which is similar to regulation 7(2), namely where being of a particular race or of particular ethnic or national origins is a genuine and determining occupational requirement, it is proportionate to apply that requirement and either the person does not meet it or the employer is reasonably not satisfied that that person meets it.

In the case of *Reaney v Hereford Diocesan Board of Finance*[63] the respondent was found to have discriminated against the claimant on the grounds of sexual orientation after not being appointed as Diocesan Youth Officer. In considering whether the respondent could rely on the

---

Employment: Legislation in Fifteen EU Members States, Report of the European Group of Experts on Combating Sexual Orientation Discrimination about the implementation up to April 2004 of Directive 2000/78/EC establishing a general framework for equal treatment in employment and occupation (Leiden, Universiteit Leiden, 2004) at para 17.4.4, available on the website of the European Commission: <http://ec.europa.eu/employment_social/fundamental_rights/pdf/aneval/sexorfull_uk.pdf>.

[60] Joint Committee on Statutory Instruments Twenty-First Report, Appendix 2, para 14 (Memorandum from the DTI to the Joint Committee on Statutory Instruments, Draft Employment Equality (Sexual Orientation) Regulations 2003).

[61] It has been suggested that 7(3) does not properly take account of religious freedom: see J Rivers, 'Law, Religion and Gender Equality', (2007) 9 *Ecc LJ* 24 at 44.

[62] Disability Discrimination Act 1996, s 3 A(4).

[63] ET Case No 1602844/2006.

Regulation 7(3) exception, the tribunal found that the employment was for the purposes of an organised religion. In reaching this conclusion, the tribunal was guided by the decision in *Amicus* and relevant Parliamentary statements[64]. The role of the Diocesan Youth Officer was different from that of a Parish Youth Worker, who takes part in youth work. The Diocesan Youth Officer had a representative role, closely connected to the promotion of the Church and its religion. Thus, the tribunal felt that this post was one of the few beyond the clergy which was employment for the purposes of an organised religion. Furthermore, the Bishop's requirement concerning the claimant's future sexual behaviour was in accordance with the doctrines of the Church of England. Alternatively, the evidence supported the finding that a significant number of people within the Church of England have strong views against homosexuality. Interestingly, the tribunal felt that this should be interpreted by reference to the general position within the whole of the Church of England, rather than be restricted geographically to the Diocese of Hereford[65].

However, the respondent failed to satisfy the third part of the exception, namely that the claimant did not meet the requirement or that the employer is not satisfied in all the circumstances and it is reasonable for him to conclude that the person does not meet the requirement. The tribunal found that the claimant did meet the requirement, as he was committed to remaining celibate while working as Diocesan Youth Officer. The tribunal considered that it was not reasonable for the Bishop to doubt the claimant's commitment, given the strength of the references in support of the claimant's good character. It was not reasonable 'to rely on some vague idea' that the claimant could not be relied upon, having recently ended a relationship[66]. This reflects the view in *Amicus* that the reasonableness test should be applied strictly, with the employer required to provide evidence to support his view.

Exception for Organisation Relating to Religion or Belief

Regulation 14 of the 2007 Sexual Orientation Regulations provides an exception for 'organisations relating to religion or belief' from the general prohibition of discrimination on ground of sexual orientation in

[64] At para 102.
[65] At para 104.
[66] At para 105-107.

relation to goods and services[67]. If the organisation satisfies certain conditions then it may apply restrictions on the ground of sexual orientation in relation to membership, participation in activities or the provision of goods and services during activities 'undertaken by the organisation', and the use or disposal of premises 'owned or controlled by the organisation'[68]. Participation in activities and the benefit of goods and services related thereto may also be restricted where undertaken on behalf of the organisation 'or under its auspices'[69]. For example, this might cover residential care services for the elderly provided by an individual or group acting under the auspices of an organisation relating to religion.

This exemption does not apply to an organisation whose 'sole or main purpose is commercial' or when an organisation is providing services or exercising a public function on behalf of a public authority pursuant to a contractual arrangement[70]. Otherwise, an organisation will qualify for the exemption if it meets the following conditions, which are very similar to those contained in section 57 of the Equality Act 2006. The first criterion is that the purpose of the organisation must fall within the list contained in regulation 14, namely to practise or advance a religion or belief, to teach the practice of a religion or belief or to enable individuals of a religion or belief to receive benefits or pursue activities within the framework of that religion or belief[71]. Secondly, any restriction in the provision of goods and services by that organisation or restriction of membership or participation in activities of the organisation must either be 'necessary to comply with the doctrine of the organisation' or be imposed 'so as to avoid conflicting with the strongly held religious convictions of a significant number of the religion's followers'[72]. Under this exception ministers may restrict participation in activities or the provisions of goods and services when completing functions connected to an organisation which falls within the scope of regulation 14[73].

There was a wide-ranging debate concerning the scope of this exemption during the drafting of the 2007 Regulations and many people

---

[67] The Equality Act (Sexual Orientation) Regulations 2007 SI 1263, regulation 4. It is also unlawful to discriminate in relation to disposal of premises (regulation 5), education (regulation 7) and the exercise of functions by public authorities (regulation 8).

[68] Regulation 14(3).

[69] Regulation 14(3).

[70] Regulation 14(2) and (8).

[71] Regulation 14(1).

[72] Regulation 14(5).

[73] Regulation 14(4).

responded to the consultation paper[74]. In particular, there were strongly held views from different interest groups on the attempt by the Roman Catholic Church, supported by other religions, to persuade the Government to include a specific exemption to permit the Catholic Adoption Agencies to refuse to place children with homosexual couples[75]. As these agencies are providing services on behalf of public authorities, they do not fall within the exception provided by Regulation 14, hence the argument that a specific exemption be provided. These arguments did not succeed, instead the interests of the Catholic Church were balanced through a transitional provision, which provides a period until 31st December 2008 in which adoption and fostering agencies may adapt their practices in order to comply with the Regulations[76]. During this transition period, a faith-based adoption or fostering agency which wishes to restrict provision on grounds of sexual orientation is obliged to refer same-sex couples to other agencies which it believes provides similar services regardless of sexual orientation[77].

It was clear from the outset, when the proposals to prohibit sexual orientation discrimination in this area were first published, that the Government intended the exception for religious organisations to be as narrow as possible and to be 'limited to activities closely linked to religious observance' or practices based on the doctrines of a faith, such as marriage or baptism ceremonies or public worship[78]. The consultation paper suggested that the exception would not be extended to the provision of services such as social groups for the elderly or for parents and younger children[79]. However, as indicated above, if such services were provided neither on a commercial basis nor under a contract with a public authority, then a qualifying organisation providing these services would fall within the exception in Regulation 14 if it could demonstrate that the restriction was imposed to avoid a clash with the 'strongly held religious convictions of a significant number' of those who followed the religion.

[74] Department of Communities & Local Government, *Getting Equal Getting Equal: Proposals to Outlaw Sexual Orientation Discrimination in the Provision of Goods and Services -Government Response to Consultation* (March 2006), at 9-10.

[75] Letter from Cardinal Cormac Murphy-O'Connor to the Prime Minister, 22 January 2007, available at the Diocese of Westminster website <http://www.rcdow.org.uk/includes/dow_content_print.asp?content_ref=1179>.

[76] Regulation 15.

[77] Regulation 15(3).

[78] Women and Equality Unity, *Getting Equal: Proposals to Outlaw Sexual Orientation Discrimination in the Provision of Goods and Services* (March 2006), at para 3.32-3.36.

[79] Ibid, para 3.34.

In contrast with the success of the Church of England and representatives of other religions who requested the inclusion of the specific exception provided by Regulation 7(3) of the 2003 Sexual Orientation Regulations, the Roman Catholic Church did not achieve the indefinite exemption it sought. However, in terms of the balance of interests achieved, arguably there is little difference in the outcome. This is because *Amicus* and *Reaney* indicate that Regulation 7(3) should be interpreted as narrowly as possible, to ensure compliance with EC legislation.

Although there has been no legal challenge to the 2007 Sexual Orientation Regulations, there has been judicial review of the corresponding measures introduced in Northern Ireland[80]. In *Re Christian Institute*[81] it was argued that the Northern Ireland Regulations breached the applicants' rights under the European Convention on Human Rights. A detailed analysis of all the arguments raised is beyond the scope of this chapter and, indeed, the judge rejected this part of the application, on the basis that such a challenge had to be made within civil proceedings under the Regulations[82]. This would enable the court to examine the issues of 'interference' with rights and 'justification' for such interference through a detailed consideration of the evidence in any particular case[83]. Weatherup J stressed that the balance of interests 'requires close consideration' of various issues, including how the parties have acted, 'the measures in question, the value of the policy being promoted and the right being diminished and the effects of the introduction or the failure to introduce the measures'[84].

In addition, Weatherup J provided valuable comments on the argument that, in the provision of goods and services, people who 'subscribe to the orthodox religious belief on homosexuality' will be obliged to promote views to which they object on religious grounds[85]. Regulation 5 of the Northern Ireland Regulations prohibits discrimination on grounds of sexual orientation in the provision of goods and services to the public. An exception is provided in regulation 16 for organisations relating to religion or belief, similar to that in the 2007 Sexual Orientation Regulations.

---

[80] The Equality Act (Sexual Orientation) Regulations (Northern Ireland) 2006 SR 439 ('the Northern Ireland Regulations').

[81] [2007] NIQB 66.

[82] See R Sandberg, 'Gods and Services: Religious Groups and Sexual Orientation Discrimination' (2008) 10 *Ecc LJ* 205-209.

[83] At para 64-65.

[84] At para 65.

[85] At para 85.

The applicants in *Re Christian Institute* relied on the example of a Christian printer who would be happy to print material for a person who is homosexual but would object, due to his orthodox religious belief, to printing material that promoted homosexuality. The printer would not fall within the scope of the exception under regulation 16 if acting for a commercial purpose.

Weatherup J referred to a Canadian decision based on similar facts, *Ontario Human Rights Commission v Brockie*[86], in which the Ontario Superior Court of Justice discussed rights to religious freedom in the commercial context and considered that service of the public in a commercial service should be regarded as on 'the periphery of activities protected by freedom of religion'[87]. However, he noted that in *Brockie* the Court ruled that the printer should not be required to print material which could 'reasonably be held to be in direct conflict with the core elements of his religious beliefs'[88]. This approach was 'clearly not consistent' with the approach taken in regulation 16, in which a religious organisation whose sole or main purpose is commercial is excluded from the scope of the exception[89]. As outlined above, the same qualification is found in regulation 14 of the 2007 Sexual Orientation Regulations. The exclusion for commercial organisations suggests that a public/private distinction is being drawn, in which those who may rely on the exception must not be benefiting from public funds nor acting in the public market. However, with no definition of 'commercial' in the Equality Act 2006 or the relevant regulations, there seems little scope for recognising the point made in *Brockie* that, while on the boundary of areas protected by freedom of religion, engagement in commercial activity does not rule out such protection.

On a separate point, the judge rejected the argument that the exemption would be lost in respect of all activities of the organisation when it contracts with a public authority in respect of certain matters. He said the correct interpretation of regulation 16(8) is that the exemption would not apply in respect of the activities the organisation has contracted to provide on behalf of the public authority, but that any other activities of the religious organisation would remain covered if otherwise entitled to the exemption[90]. Again, this reflects the distinction being drawn between

---

[86] [2002] 22 DLR (4th) 174, cited in paras 86-88.
[87] *Re Christian Institute* at para 87.
[88] At para 87.
[89] At para 88.
[90] At para 57.

'public' activities, which cannot fall within the exception, and 'private' non-commercial activities, which can be exempt.

Harassment

This section begins with an introduction to the definition of religious harassment in employment and the similarities to the definition of harassment elsewhere in the anti-discrimination legislation. It identifies a likely challenge to the provision on religious harassment on the basis that it fails to implement properly the EC Framework Directive, following a similar ruling in relation to the definition of harassment on grounds of sex. It then considers the various interests which need to be balanced when prohibiting religious harassment. This leads on to the final part which looks at the debate concerning the extension of harassment to goods and services, both in relation to religion and sexual orientation.

Religious Harassment

It is unlawful for an employer to subject an employee to harassment on grounds of religion or belief[91]. Harassment is defined as unwanted conduct, which has the 'purpose or effect' of violating an individual's dignity or 'creating an intimidating, hostile, degrading, humiliating or offensive environment' for the individual, where the harasser acts 'on grounds of religion or belief'[92]. Whether the conduct has such an effect is to be determined by whether it should reasonably be considered as having the effect, taking account of all the circumstances, with particular regard the perception of the individual who suffers the unwanted conduct[93].

A similar definition of harassment is found in the other anti-discrimination legislation, where the harasser acts on other protected grounds[94]. This is significant for religious harassment following judicial review of the harassment provisions in section 4A of the Sex Discrimination Act 1975, which found that these measures did not implement correctly the provisions of the EC Equal Treatment Amendment Directive[95]. This

---

[91] Employment Equality (Religion or Belief) Regulations 2003, regulation 6(3).
[92] Regulation 5(1).
[93] Regulation 5(2).
[94] Race Relations Act 1976, s 3A; Disability Discrimination Act 1995, s 3B; the Employment Equality (Sexual Orientation) Regulations 2003, regulation 5.
[95] *Equal Opportunities Commission v Secretary of State for Trade and Industry* [2007] EWHC 483 (Admin).

was because unwanted conduct 'on the *ground* of her sex' suggested
the need for causation, whereas the Directive uses the phrase 'related to',
which can cover a wider range of conduct[96]. As the Framework Directive
contains an identical reference to 'unwanted conduct *related to* any of
the grounds' covered by the Directive, it is likely that the definitions of
harassment on grounds of religion or belief and sexual orientation in the
2003 Employment Equality Regulations also fail to implement properly
European Law, as noted in a recent case involving sexual orientation
harassment[97]. In the latter case the EAT confirmed the tribunal's finding
that there was no evidence that the harassers had engaged in homophobic
banter on the ground of sexual orientation, as it was accepted by the
claimant that the harassers knew that he was not gay and did not perceive
him to be gay[98]. So, although the unwanted conduct was *related* to sexual
orientation, in that the conduct involved homophobic comments, it was not
said to be *on the ground* of sexual orientation. A similar argument would
defeat a claim, for example, brought by someone who felt an offensive
environment was created by constant comments about the Muslim faith,
when it was accepted that the individual was not himself a Muslim, nor
perceived to be by his colleagues.

It has been argued that it is not appropriate to treat religious harassment in the same way as racial or sexual harassment, not because one
form is worse than the other, but because different considerations arise
in relation to religious harassment[99]. For example, if an employee is keen
to express her particular religious views but is prevented from doing
so because a colleague finds them offensive, then the law must find a
balance between the freedom to manifest religion and belief and the
right not to be harassed on grounds of religion[100]. In the European Convention on Human Rights, the right to freedom to manifest religion and
belief can be restricted where it is proportionate to do so for the protection of others, unlike the absolute right to believe[101]. An employer has
a legitimate interest in maintaining a workplace environment in which
all workers are free to discuss matters in an inoffensive manner, whether
the views expressed are religious or secular.

---

[96] The Sex Discrimination Act 1975 (Amendment) Regulations 2008, SI No 656
amends section 4A of the Sex Discrimination Act 1975, to cover 'unwanted conduct that
is related to her sex or that of another person'.
[97] *English v Thomas Sanderson Blinds Ltd* [2008] IRLR 342.
[98] Ibid.
[99] L Vickers, 'Is All Harassment Equal? The Case of Religious Harassment' (2006)
65 *CLJ* 579-605.
[100] Vickers, 'Is All Harassment Equal?' at 584-586.
[101] Article 9. See discussion in Vickers, 'Is All Harassment Equal?' at 585-586.

Extension of Harassment to Goods and Services

When the Equality Act 2006 was introduced, there was an extensive Parliamentary debate on whether to include religious harassment in the prohibition of discrimination in the provision of goods and services to the public, housing and education[102]. The first draft of the legislation contained a prohibition of harassment, as well as discrimination, in this context, but only where the religion or belief was different from that of the harasser[103]. A number of exceptions were included, namely faith schools, any educational establishment in relation to content of curriculum or religious worship and certain landlords. However, following concern expressed in the House of Lords and by the Joint Committee on Human Rights, harassment was removed from the bill[104].

Thus, the current position in Britain is that harassment on grounds of religion or sexual harassment is prohibited only in the employment and vocational training context. However, harassment on grounds of sexual orientation beyond the workplace *was* included in the Northern Ireland Regulations which correspond to the 2007 Sexual Orientation Regulations[105]. As noted above, judicial review proceedings were brought in relation to the Northern Ireland Regulations[106]. In addition to the claim that the Regulations breached the applicants' rights under the European Convention on Human Rights, it was also argued that the consultation process was procedurally unfair, with particular reference to the harassment provisions. It was found that there *was* an absence of proper consultation with regard to the harassment provisions, as the consultation paper had clearly indicated that it would be more appropriate to deal with the issue of harassment in relation to goods and services through the Government's intended Single Equality Bill[107]. Thus, the process was unfair to those consultees who had been induced not to set out their objections by the way in which the consultation referred to harassment being postponed, in order to be part of the major review of all anti-discrimination legislation in the United Kingdom.

[102] See for example Lord Lester, Col 648-652, Hansard HL 9 November 2005.

[103] Joint Committee on Human Rights, *Equality Bill* Sixteenth Report of Session 2004-2005, HL Paper 98, HC 497 (March 2005, London: The Stationery Office Limited) para 41.

[104] Joint Committee on Human Rights, *Equality Bill* Sixteenth Report of Session 2004-2005, HL Paper 98, HC 497 (London: The Stationery Office Limited, March 2005) at para 41-52.

[105] Regulation 5(2), the Equality Act (Sexual Orientation) Regulations (Northern Ireland) 2006 SR 439.

[106] *Re Christian Institute* [2007] NIQB 66.

[107] At para 34.

With regard to the specific provisions on harassment, Weatherup J noted the concerns of the House of Lords and House of Commons Joint Committee on Human Rights that the provisions were too wide and vague, with a risk of incompatibility with both freedom of speech in Article 10 and freedom of thought, conscience and religion in Article 9 of the European Convention on Human Rights[108]. He discussed the balance of rights which is sought in the prohibiting of harassment with regard to race, religion and gender, which involves justifying the interference with freedom of speech on the basis that others have the right not to be subject to harassment on these various grounds. He concluded that it was unclear as to whether any consideration had been given to the additional factor which may be present in cases of harassment on the ground of sexual orientation, namely the right to manifest a religious belief[109].

Recognising the 'importance of balancing' the rights to freedom of speech and 'doctrinal activities of religious bodies' with the need to safeguard individual dignity, the Discrimination Law Review has expressed the need to proceed cautiously in extending protection against harassment, while seeking to ensure 'consistency, fairness and legal certainty' in any future Single Equality Bill[110]. Nevertheless, the Equality and Human Rights Commission is of the view that such legislation should include 'consistent' protection against harassment on all grounds and in respect of all activities which are covered by the new legislation[111]. The Equality and Human Rights Commission indicates that the rights to freedom of expression and religious freedom would be taken into account by the courts and tribunals in any claim of unlawful harassment, for example if they need to determine the reasonableness of regarding the unwanted conduct 'as having the effect of violating the person's dignity or creating an intimidating, hostile, degrading, humiliating or offensive environment[112].

---

[108] At para 40.

[109] At para 42.

[110] *Discrimination Law Review. A Framework for Fairness: Proposals for a Single Equality Bill for Great Britain*, (London, Department for Communities and Local Government, June 2007) at para 14.14-14.17.

[111] Equality and Human Rights Commission, *Response to the Discrimination Law Review a Framework for Fairness: Proposals for a New Equality Bill for Great Britain* at 30.

[112] Equality and Human Rights Commission, *Response to the Discrimination Law Review a Framework for Fairness* at 31.

Conclusion

The potential for conflict between various rights in the recent extensions to the anti-discrimination legislation has been visible in the areas discussed above. Courts and tribunals have an important role in ensuring that any interference with human rights, where permitted, is proportionate. This is illustrated in the application of the law on indirect religious discrimination, such as *Azmi* and *Eweida*. In the *Amicus* case it was argued that the Government was attempting to find a 'delicate balance' between the employment rights of gay and lesbian workers, and the rights of religious groups to freedom of religion[113]. It seems that the balance sought was to avoid the 'practical' problems which may arise from an employment tribunal deciding issues of religious doctrine. Yet, the wording of regulation 7(3) in itself contains uncertainty, such as what is meant by 'organised religion' and what constitutes a 'significant number of the religion's followers'[114].

Harassment is an area which poses a particular challenge with regard to competing rights, as highlighted by the controversy in relation to recent attempts to prohibit harassment on grounds of religion and sexual orientation in the provision of goods and services. While the Discrimination Law Review, as far as possible, seeks to ensure consistency of grounds in any future single equality Bill, there is much concern as to the appropriateness of using the existing definition of religious harassment, both in relation to the workplace and if it were to be extended to the provision of goods and services to the public[115].

Finally, while the primary focus of the chapter has been on the legislative and judicial approach to balancing competing interests, this is an area of law in which interested organisations, be they religious or secular, have responded in depth to consultations on proposed legislation[116]. As seen above, they have applied also for the judicial review of certain regulations. Thus, there is considerable public engagement in the legal

---

[113] *Amicus* at para 90.

[114] See Sandberg and Doe 'Religious Exemptions in Discrimination Law' at 310-312.

[115] See *Re Christian Institute* [2007] NIQB 66 and Vickers 'Is All Harassment Equal?' at 605.

[116] Col WA96, Hansard HL 1 July 2003, Written Answers: Lord Sainsbury noted that a range of groups and individuals had responded with regard to the draft Sexual Orientation Regulations 2003. 'These included representations from the archbishops' Council of the Church of England, the Catholic Bishops' Conference of England and Wales, the Muslim Council of Great Britain and the Baha'I Community of the UK'.

process concerning the balance of rights and interests. In the future, there may be scope for participation at a different level, at least in relation to public authorities, as the Discrimination Law Review sought views on whether the duties of public bodies to promote equality should be extended, in addition to the proposed replacement of the current duties with a single equality duty[117]. Currently, there are duties to promote equality of opportunity which require public bodies to take proactive steps to eliminate unlawful discrimination on grounds of race, gender and disability[118]. It is not envisaged that a single equality duty which extended to religion or belief would require public authorities to place the needs of one religious group 'above the needs of the wider community' but it would enable authorities 'to consider the needs of their employees and service users and take action proportionate to the need identified, within what is permitted by discrimination law.'[119] Thus, in addition to encouraging participation by religious and other interest groups in the policy making of public bodies, compliance with the duty could be evidence also of a proportionate policy which seeks to achieve a fair balance between competing interests.

---

[117] *Discrimination Law Review. A Framework for Fairness: Proposals for a Single Equality Bill for Great Britain*, (London, Department for Communities and Local Government, June 2007).

[118] Race Relations Act s 71; Disability Discrimination Act s 49A; Sex Discrimination Act 1975 s7.

[119] *Discrimination Law Review. A Framework for Fairness: Proposals for a Single Equality Bill for Great Britain*, (London, Department for Communities and Local Government, June 2007) at para 5.72.

FREEDOM OF SPEECH, RELIGIOUS SENSIBILITIES AND INCITING HATRED IN ENGLISH LAW

Richard Clarke

Introduction

During the opening decade of the twenty-first century, the law of England and Wales relating to freedom of speech and religion has been subject to the most radical programme of reform in over three hundred years. First, the Racial and Religious Hatred Act 2006 introduced a new offence of inciting religious hatred. Second, section 79 of the Criminal Justice and Immigration Act 2008 abolished the common law offences of blasphemy and blasphemous libel. As a result the legal framework for judging whether an utterance relating to religion is illegal has been altered. This chapter reviews this legislation, critically assessing the effects that the changes will have on freedom of speech. It concludes that the abolition of blasphemy is a welcome development, and that although the new offence of inciting religious hatred fixes a tiny gap in the law relating to race and religious identity, its actual effect is so limited it does not present a threat to freedom of speech.

The Tradition of English liberty

Historically, freedom of speech has always been a highly valued aspect of British society. Intellectually its antecedents can be traced through such illustrious figures as John Locke, John Milton, Thomas Paine, John Stewart Mill and George Orwell, all of whom, in their various times, expressed a commitment to free speech that continues to resound today. But this is not to say that free speech has always been expressly protected. Until the advent of the modern culture of guaranteed rights, it depended simply on the fact that, under the common law, individuals can do anything that is not legally forbidden. However, English law has for a long time forbidden and punished speech in a wide range of areas to varying degrees. Obscenity, sedition, defamation, fraudulent advertising, disclosure of trade or official secrets, treason-felony, incitement to commit crime and conduct liable to excite a breach of the peace, to name but a few, are the subject of longstanding restrictions. Furthermore, on the subject of religion, utterances of various sorts were for a long time prohibited, by the specific offences of blasphemy, heresy, and unlicensed preaching. Fortunately, the second and third ceased many years ago to concern the general law[1], and following the Criminal Justice and Immigration Act 2008, the offences of blasphemy and blasphemous libel have finally been abolished[2]. However, it has often been said that the new offence of inciting religious hatred is a modern replacement for the defunct crime of blasphemy[3]. This would suggest that they are both attempts at dealing with the same public nuisance. However, it is actually necessary to distinguish between two very separate issues from the outset. The first is where religious groups seek protection of their beliefs from insult and criticism, which causes certain adherents of the faith to be offended; and the second is where religion is used by extremist preachers and far-right politicians to justify or mask, what is essentially racial hatred against people.

It is certainly true that in recent years conflicts between individuals professing a religious belief and those who criticise, insult or ridicule that belief, have resulted in widespread protests, legal challenges and occasionally violence. It is not difficult to pick out such occurrences across almost all faiths within the domestic sphere. Christians tried to ban *Jerry Springer: The Opera*, and prosecute its creators for the production and its subsequent airing on television. A far more violent protest ensued on the first night of the play *Behzti* (Dishonour) in Birmingham in 2005 when 400 Sikhs stormed the theatre throwing stones and injuring police officers in the process[4]. And following the knighthood of Sir Salman Rushdie for his 'lifelong body of literary work'[5], fresh protests erupted against the treatment of Islam in his novels. In all of these examples it is predominantly the tenets of the religion that are being insulted, offended

---

[1] By the late Stuart times heresy had been narrowed in scope (Act of Supremacy 1558, s 20) and left to spiritual sanctions alone (Act of 1677 abolishing the writ *De Heretico Comburendo*), and by the mid-nineteenth century universal religious toleration had ended any need for preaching to be authorised by public authority, except in official public worship.

[2] Section 74 of the Act also makes it an offence to incite hatred against a group of people on grounds of sexual orientation, though this is beyond the remit of this chapter.

[3] Hansard HL vol 669 col 1118 (Debate) (5 March 2008), Baroness Andrews of Southover,

[4] T Kirby, 'Violence and vandalism close production' *The Independent* (21 December 2004) <http://enjoyment.independent.co.uk/theatre/news/article25779.ece>

[5] Nico Hines, 'British Minister: We Stand By Rushdie knighthood' *The Times* (20 June 2007) <http://www.timesonline.co.uk/tol/news/uk/article1963407.ece>

or ridiculed[6]. In terms of the Church of England, this is traditionally where the offence of blasphemy provided recourse in law. However, there are compelling reasons for saying that this kind of law protecting religious sensibilities is inappropriate and unreasonable, and that there is no right not to be offended in a liberal, plural society.

On the other hand, the second issue is a very different type of public nuisance. Namely, the increasing use of religion as an incendiary issue to further the ultimately racist agendas of far-right political groups, and extremist religious preachers. The leader of the British National Party, Nick Griffin, illustrated the point well after his acquittal at trial for inciting racial hatred, stating that he was a 'religionist'. In addition, certain extremist religious leaders use their particular faith as an excuse for, and source of, what is essentially racial hatred. As a result the new legal framework is intertwined with difficult questions relating to the politics of identity. But ultimately the question is how should the law respond to these two very different and delicate problems, which both have repercussions for free speech?

Regrettably, throughout the parliamentary and public debate the philosophical arguments submitted as the basis for the protection of free speech were, at times, woefully inadequate. Many made torpid use of Voltaire's spectacular declaration in support of free speech, 'I disapprove of what you say but I will defend to the death your right to say it'[7], without ever asking why it should be defended at such cost, or indeed ever expecting to pay such a price. On the other side of the argument those arguing for greater protection of religious believers and beliefs referred to rather vague concepts of 'communities', 'hurt' and 'offence', often without exploring with precision what these mean, let alone why they should trump rights of free expression. This confusion is certainly not helped by the fact that the English judiciary, has not taken a lead on these issues, and 'is still far from having a philosophically coherent method for dealing with free speech disputes.'[8] As a result it is useful to very briefly recap the compelling reasons for protecting freedom of expression in Britain today.

---

[6] I use the qualification 'predominantly' because, as I will argue later, the distinction between criticism of a belief and someone who adheres to such a belief, is not always a clear one.

[7] S Lee, *The Cost of Free Speech* (London, Faber and Faber, 1990) 3, Lee also explains how the phrase was attributed to Voltaire by the biographer Evelyn Beatrice Hall as a summary of his view.

[8] I Hare, 'Crosses, Crescents and Sacred Cows: Criminalising Incitement to Religious Hatred' (2006) *PL* 521 at 526.

'The instrumental importance of free speech is generally thought to derive from the contributions it makes to the functioning of democratic self-governance, to the pursuit of truth in the market-place of ideas and to individual self-fulfilment.'[9] The first argument is based on the need for free speech in order to have effective political debate and decision making. Mill warns us of the tyranny of a government that retreats into the comfort of consensus and majority public opinion and bans dissident speech, by saying 'if all mankind minus one, were of one opinion, mankind would be no more justified in silencing that one person, than he, if he had the power, would be justified in silencing mankind.'[10] Furthermore, as religion plays such an important role for some in the formulation of political positions, it follows that expression about religion must not be censored. This is especially true as religion often makes very large claims for itself. Secondly, 'historically the most durable argument for a free speech principle has been based on the importance of open discussion to the discovery of truth.'[11] The argument is based on the assumptions that truth is a universal good, and that it can be obtained through open discussion. Phrased beautifully in Milton's *Areopagitica*, he champions truth, by saying 'let her and falsehood grapple; who ever knew truth put to the worse in a free and open encounter?'[12] Thus, if the State intervenes in the marketplace by silencing certain speech, it may jeopardise the process of discovering the truth. The final argument for free speech sees it as an essential part of individual self-development. The basis of the argument is that individuals need to be able to read and hear a variety of differing views and ideas to develop intellectually and emotionally. Restrictions imposed on the speech of others will invariably diminish the flourishing of individual personality, creativity and the arts. Indeed from a spiritual perspective it is easy to see why this is a very attractive argument. It follows that the individual needs to be able to express their religion or lack of religion, because it is integral to their personal growth and fulfilment. To silence or punish this would clearly be detrimental, especially as many people define themselves in reference to their religious beliefs.

[9] Ibid.

[10] J S Mill, *On Liberty and Other Essays* (Oxford, Oxford University Press, 1998) 21.

[11] E Barendt, *Freedom of Speech* (Oxford, Oxford University Press, 2005) 7.

[12] J Milton, *Areopagitica taken from The Major Works* (Oxford, Oxford University Press, 2003) 269.

In light of these philosophical considerations, it is necessary to address the first identified issue, namely the protection of religious beliefs from insult, criticism and ridicule. In the English legal framework this has been historically addressed by the law of blasphemy, with regard to the Church of England, but it has also at times been subject to potential extension to other faiths.

The Offences of Blasphemy and Blasphemous Libel

The Evolution of Blasphemy

Criminal sanctions against blasphemy have an extensive history in English law, dating back to the seventeenth century to a time when the religion of the realm was an intensely political issue. Most of the previous law developed alongside an even older law of heresy, restricting all forms of dissidence against the mainstream Christian Church[13]. However, by this time any such dissidence against the Church was implicitly an attack on the monarch and the State as the two were, and arguably still are, inextricably linked. Common law blasphemy was thus, at its inception, an offence to ensure good public order as much as protect religious faith. The point is made well by reference to the case of Nicholas Atwood in 1617[14] who 'was fined for sneering at Anglican preachers, thereby attacking both the king and the law – the King in his capacity as head of the Church and the law which had by this time established Anglicanism as the only official religion.'[15] However, the first case to be tried by the criminal courts, as opposed to the ecclesiastical courts, came in 1677 in the case of John Taylor[16]. Mr Taylor, who claimed amongst other things that Jesus was a bastard, a whoremaster and that religion was a cheat, had clear mental deficiencies but was nonetheless convicted and sent to the pillory. In judgment, Lord Chief Justice Hale stated, 'to say, Religion is a Cheat is to dissolve all those Obligations where the civil societies are preserved, ...Christianity is a parcel of the laws of England and therefore to reproach the Christian religion is to speak in subversion of the law.'[17]

---

[13] R Webster, *A Brief History Of Blasphemy: Liberalism, Censorship and 'The Satanic Verses'* (Southold, Orwell Press, 1990) 22.

[14] *R v Atwood* (1617) Cro Jac 421.

[15] G Robertson, *Obscenity* (London, Wiedenfeld and Nicolson, 1979) 236.

[16] 1 Ventris 293.

[17] Ibid.

Following on from this case there were countless other convictions against people from all walks of life. Even the Cambridge academic Thomas Woolston was charged and detained until his death in 1733 for suggesting that the New Testament miracles were allegorical[18]. This continued until well into the nineteenth century where the zealous nature of prosecutors came at an embarrassment to the government. In 1851 the Home Office was advised that John Stuart Mill was liable to prosecution for expressing agnostic views in public, although the brief went on to say, 'we should in this case consider it highly inexpedient for the Government to institute such proceedings.'[19] Another integral part of blasphemy was decided around this time, in the case of *R v Gathercole*[20] where it was affirmed that the offence protected only the tenets of the Church of England. In judgement Baron Alderson ruled, 'If this is only libel on the whole Roman Catholic Church generally, the defendant is entitled to be acquitted. A person may, without being liable to prosecution for it, attack Judaism or Mahometanism; or even any sect of the Christian religion, save the established religion of the country.'[21] This did of course mean that where other religions beliefs overlapped with the established church, they would too be protected.

Yet it is not the case that the courts were unable to change the offence of blasphemy at all, indeed Robertson notes 'judges had made the law, and in the nineteenth century it was the judges who changed the law to serve different social conditions.'[22] In 1883 a significant change in the law of blasphemy came about in *R v Ramsey & Foot*[23]. Lord Chief Justice Coleridge directed the jury that 'if the decencies of controversy are observed, even the fundamentals of religion may be attacked without the attackers being guilty of blasphemous libel.' This clearly restated the ambit of blasphemy but was nonetheless adopted by the House of Lords in *Bowman v Secular Society*[24]. All five Law Lords agreed and said that the rationale for the offence was now public order. Lord Parker's judgement is of particular interest; he suggested that 'to constitute blasphemy at common law there must be such an element of vilification, ridicule or

---

[18] Webster, *A Brief History Of Blasphemy* 23.

[19] Submission quoted in Robertson, *Obscenity* 237.

[20] (1838) 168 ER 1140.

[21] Ibid. The 'established religion' was not then, of course, considered a sect. What it believed about Christianity was not regarded as a denominational viewpoint but as Christianity 'pure'.

[22] Robertson, *Obscenity* 238.

[23] (1883) 48 LT 733.

[24] [1917] AC 406.

irreverence as would be likely to exasperate the feelings of others and so lead to a breach of the peace.'[25] Following on from this case the only person to be publically prosecuted came in 1922, in the case of *R v Gott*[26]. The case involved a free thinking pamphlet describing Jesus entering Jerusalem 'like a circus clown on the back of two donkeys'[27]. The Court of Appeal upheld the offence on the grounds that the material was 'offensive to anyone in sympathy with the Christian religion, whether he be a strong Christian, or a lukewarm Christian, or merely a person sympathizing with their ideals.'[28]

The following 27 years passed without a single prosecution, leading to Lord Denning, notably a devout Christian, declaring in 1949 that Hale's *ratio* in defence of blasphemy was outdated, and the entire offence was obsolete:

> The reason for this law was because it was thought that a denial of Christianity was liable to shake the fabric of our society, which was itself founded on the Christian religion. There is no such danger to society now and the offence of blasphemy is a dead letter[29].

Following this sounding of the death knell on blasphemy there were no prosecutions for another thirty years. However, in 1977 in *R v Lemon*[30] the crime of blasphemous libel was dragged back into the courtroom in a now infamous case. Mr Lemon, the proprietor of Gay News Ltd., published a poem by Professor James Kirkup entitled 'The Love That Dare Speak Its Name'. The poem describes 'as a sort of allegory of religious experience, acts of sodomy and fellatio with the body of Christ immediately after the moment of His death'[31] and was printed with a cartoon illustration of the subject matter. Mary Whitehouse brought a private prosecution for blasphemous libel against both Lemon as the editor, and Gay News Ltd. as a corporate body. At the trial, before Judge King-Hamilton and a jury at the Central Criminal Court in July 1977, the defendants were convicted, Lemon being sentenced to nine months' imprisonment, suspended for 18 months, and fined £500 and the Gay

---

[25] At 446.

[26] (1922) 16 Cr App R 87.

[27] See further, A Bradney, *Religion, Rights and Laws* (Leicester, Leicester University Press, 1993) 83.

[28] (1922) 16 Cr App R 87 at 89-90.

[29] A Denning, *Freedom Under Law – Hamlyn Lecture* (London, Stevens & Co, 1949) 46.

[30] [1979] AC 617.

[31] J R Spencer, 'Blasphemous Libel Resurrected – Gay News and Grim Tidings' [1979] *CLJ* 245 at 246.

News Ltd being fined £1000[32]. Lemon then appealed to the Court of
Appeal who affirmed the decision on 17 March 1978, and finally to the
House of Lords in a consolidated appeal. The question for the Lords was
whether it was 'necessary for the Crown to establish any further intention
on the part of the appellants beyond an intention to publish that which in
the jury's view was a blasphemous libel?'[33] Their lordships produced a
split 3:2 majority[34], in favour of the trial judge's view that all that is
required to commit blasphemous libel is an intention to publish the material that a jury would deem blasphemous. The dissenting Law Lords suggested that 'the effect of the decision of the majority is that the offence
becomes one of strict liability.'[35] Lord Scarman in his judgment, added a
further issue into the mix by suggesting *obiter* that the offence should be
applied to all religions as a policy decision, because 'in an increasingly
plural society such as that of modern Britain it is necessary not only to
respect the differing religious beliefs, feelings and practices of all but also
to protect them from scurrility, vilification, ridicule and contempt.'[36]

The Possible Extension of Blasphemy

As a result of *Lemon*, the idea of extending blasphemy to cover
all religions had begun to be considered as a possible option. In 1988
Salman Rushdie published a novel entitled *The Satanic Verses*. In the
UK the novel was a Booker prize finalist, Whitbread prize winner and
received widespread critical acclaim. However, international and notably
Islamic reactions to the book were very different as it was immediately
banned in a number of countries including India, Pakistan, and Iran.
Iranian Ayatollah Khomeini issued a now notorious *fatwa* stating:

> I inform the proud Muslim people of the world that the author of the Satanic
> Verses book, which is against Islam, the Prophet and the Koran, and all
> those involved in its publication who were aware of its content, are sen-
> tenced to death. I ask all the Muslims to execute them wherever they find
> them[37].

---

[32] *R v Lemon* [1979] AC 617 at 620.
[33] Ibid.
[34] Lord Scarman, Viscount Dilhorne and Lord Russell (Lord Diplock and Lord
Edmund Davies dissenting).
[35] JC Smith, 'Blasphemy: R v Lemon and Another' [1979] *Crim LR* 311 at 312.
[36] *R v Lemon* [1979] AC 617 at 658,
[37] See S Akhtar, *Be Careful With Muhammad! The Salman Rushdie Affair* (London,
Bellew Publishing, 1989) 64.

As a result, bookshops were targeted, translators of the text were attacked, riots and book burnings took place, diplomatic relations between Iran and Britain were severed, and Rushdie was forced into hiding under the protection of the British Government[38]. Such a violent and direct challenge to free expression was unprecedented in Britain, and consequently numerous movements mobilized in as a result caused a movement of support for Rushdie.

However, a legal challenge was brought against him and his publishers, alleging that they had committed blasphemous libel (thus implicitly extending the crime of blasphemy to cover Islam). At first instance, the magistrate refused to issue the summonses on the grounds that the common law offence of blasphemy was restricted to the Christian religion and the applicant had failed to show that the alleged seditious libel was an attack on the State[39]. The appellants sought judicial review of the decision and in *R v Chief Stipendiary Magistrate ex parte Choudhury*[40], the High Court dismissed the application, and with regard to blasphemous libel upheld the magistrates' decision that blasphemy is confined to the established Christian religion and noted that it was not the place of the court to change this. It also stated that, even if it was extended to cover Islam, on the facts of the case, *The Satanic Verses* would not be blasphemous because it 'is not designed to vilify or insult Islam, or to encourage disaffection or discontent.'[41] Ultimately the extension of blasphemy on policy grounds, in light of the fact that the Law Commission had some six years earlier expressly asked for its complete repeal, was a rather hopeless argument[42]. As Geoffrey Robinson QC stated, 'where parliament fears to tread, it is not for the court to rush in.'[43]

The case did, however, go on to the European Court of Human Rights in *Choudhury v UK*[44], where the question of whether blasphemy was discriminatory in only protecting the tenets of the Church of England was answered in the negative. Counsel for the appellants contended, *inter alia,* that the English blasphemy law was prejudicial against Islam under Articles 9 and 14 ECHR. The case was 'declared inadmissible

---

[38] C Bedford, *Fiction, Fact and the Fatwa: 2,000 days of Censorship* (Fifth edition, London, Article 19, 1994).

[39] [1991] 1 QB 429.

[40] Ibid.

[41] Ibid at 432.

[42] Law Commission, 'Offences Against Religion and Public Worship' (Law Com No 145, 1985) para 2.57.

[43] [1991] 1 QB 429 at 433.

[44] (1991) 12 HRLJ 172.

by the Commission as manifestly ill-founded because Article 9 could not be interpreted as including a positive obligation on states to protect all religious sensibilities.'[45] Following this decision Strasbourg had another chance to review UK blasphemy law in Wingrove v UK[46]. The facts again concerned a film, this time a silent one, on the subject of St Teresa of Avila, a nun who purportedly experienced ecstatic visions of Jesus. The film was denied a licence by the British Board of Film Classification as its screening would constitute a blasphemy[47]. Leaving Article 9 aside, the action focused on the infringement of Nigel Wingrove's freedom of expression under Article 10. The Court, in disagreement with the Commission, held that under Article 10(2) the violation of the victim's right of free expression, was justified. The reasoning followed Otto-Preminger[48] to hold that the national courts were in a better position to decide whether the law was necessary than a panel of international judges[49]. Furthermore, it suggested that there was a duty to avoid so far as possible an expression that is, in regard to objects of veneration, gratuitously offensive to others[50]. This apparent favouring of local and domestic concepts of proportionality has meant that those individuals who find their speech restricted have little hope of achieving a remedy from the ECHR. This has been rightly criticised by Kearns, who notes that the

> preference for upholding blasphemy law over [free expression] not only permits the silencing of artistic enterprise in favour of galvanising religious belief, but disfavours art, which is more universally participated in, in favour of what is in practice a small censoring lobby which happens to be religious in its justification[51].

The Abolition of Blasphemy

The Criminal Justice and Immigration Act 2008 was not the first challenge to the blasphemy laws. Baroness Andrews noted during the debates that it was 'the fifth time that [the House of Lords had] considered this

[45] P Kearns, 'The Uncultured God: Blasphemy Law's Reprieve and the Art Matrix' (2000) EHRLR 512.

[46] (1997) 24 EHRR 1.

[47] For a detailed review see S Stokes, 'Blasphemy and Freedom of Expression under the European Convention on Human Rights: The Decision of the European Court in Wingrove v United Kingdom' (1997) 8(2) Ent LR 71.

[48] (1994) 19 EHRR 34.

[49] (1997) 24 EHRR 1 at para 48.

[50] See P M Taylor, Freedom of Religion: UN and European Human Rights Law and Practice (Cambridge, Cambridge University Press, 2005) 88.

[51] Kearns, 'The Uncultured God' 520.

issue. It had previously been previously considered in 2005 during the passage of the Racial and Religious Hatred Bill, in 2002 during the Religious Offences Bill, in 2001 during the Anti-terrorism, Crime and Security Bill, and in 1995 during the Blasphemy (Abolition) Bill.'[52] However, the antecedence before this final successful attempt had an important bearing on the outcome. The most recently attempted prosecution of blasphemy came in response to *Jerry Springer: The Opera*. After being broadcast on the BBC in 2005, the corporation received 45,000 complaints about the performance[53] and a number of demonstrations took place across the country. The plot involves a *Jerry Springer Show* in hell following the shooting of Jerry in the first Act, where the Devil seeks to solve his problems, with the guests of the show all appearing as religious characters, such as Jesus, Mary, Adam and Eve. Following the broadcast, Christian Voice, a pressure group, brought a private prosecution for blasphemous libel. At first instance, the District Judge refused to issue a summons because section 2(4) Theatres Act 1968 prevented prosecution[54], and furthermore there was no *prima facie* case.

In response, Mr Green applied for judicial review of the decision, requiring a mandatory order of the summons. In judgment, Lord Justice Hughes and Mr Justice Collins upheld the decision of the District Judge, agreeing that the Theatres Act prevented prosecution.[55]

Furthermore, although the Theatres Act did not apply to the broadcast by the BBC, the Broadcasting Act 1990, Schedule 15 paragraph 6 contained identical provisions applicable to broadcasts[56]. In relation to the District Judge's decision that there was no *prima facie* case, the High Court noted that 'the gist of the crime of blasphemous libel is material relating to the Christian religion, or its figures or formularies, so scurrilous and offensive in manner that it undermines society generally, by endangering the peace, depraving public morality, shaking the fabric of

---

[52] Hansard HL vol 699 col 1119 (Lords Committee) (5 March 2008), Baroness Andrews.

[53] BBC News, 'Protests as BBC screens Springer' (10 January 2005) <http://news.bbc.co.uk/go/pr/fr/-/1/hi/entertainment/tv_and_radio/4154071.stm>.

[54] 'No person shall be proceeded against in respect of a performance of play or anything said or done in the course of such a performance ... for an offence at common law where it is of the essence of the offence that the performance or, as the case may be what was sad or done was obscene, indecent, offensive, disgusting or injurious to morality'.

[55] *Green, R (on the application of) v The City of Westminster Magistrates' Court* [2007] EWHC (Admin) 2785.

[56] At para 21.

society or tending to be a cause of civil strife.'[57] As a result, on the facts, they held that the opera 'could not in context be regarded as [blasphemous] because the play as a whole was not and could not reasonably be regarded as aimed at, or an attack on Christianity or what Christians held sacred.'[58] This was a clear victory for free expression not least because it prevented any theatre, the BBC and any other broadcaster being charged with blasphemous libel.

In the subsequent week, blasphemy was again in the headlines following the arrest of a British schoolteacher in Sudan for allowing her pupils to name a teddy bear Muhammad[59]. Whilst there was widespread anger at her treatment and draconian punishment (only avoided by diplomatic intervention), critics at home were quick to point out that England itself had blasphemy laws, and should be wary of criticising the Sudanese law. In a letter to the *Daily Telegraph* a number of prominent public figures – including Philip Pullman, Lord Carey, Lord Lester, Lord Harries, Richard Dawkins, and Shami Chakrabarti – asked 'is it not time to repeal our own blasphemy law?', and called on the government to support the amendment to the Criminal Justice and Immigration Bill to abolish the offence, tabled by Evan Davies, Frank Dobson and David Wilshire[60]. When introduced, the government minister in response declared 'every sympathy for the case for formal abolition'[61], and announced that after a short consultation with the Church of England, it would introduce an amendment into the House of Lords to that end. The consultation period somewhat divided the Church, although in a letter to the Minister for Communities and Local Government Hazel Blears, the Archbishops of Canterbury and York agreed with the abolition, stating:

> having signalled for more than 20 years that the blasphemy laws could, in the right context, be abolished, the Church is not going to oppose abolition now provided we can be assured that provisions are in place to afford the necessary protection to individuals and to society[62].

---

[57] At para 16.

[58] Ibid para 32.

[59] BBC News, "'Muhammad' Teddy Teacher Arrested" (26 November 2007) <http://news.bbc.co.uk/1/hi/world/africa/7112929.stm>.

[60] Letter to the *Daily Telegraph*, 'Repeal of blasphemy law' (8 January 2008) <http://www.telegraph.co.uk/opinion/main.jhtml?xml=/opinion/2008/01/08/nosplit/dt0801.xml>.

[61] Hansard HC vol 470 col 454 (Debate) (9 January 2008), Maria Eagle.

[62] Hansard HL vol 699 col 1118 (Lords Committee) (5 March 2008), Baroness Andrews.

As a result, on 5 March 2008, Baroness Andrews moved amendment number 144B in the House of Lords, presenting two main arguments. 'First, the law has fallen into disuse and therefore runs the risk of bringing the law as a whole into disrepute. Secondly, we now have new legislation to protect individuals on the grounds of religion and belief.'[63] It was almost universally accepted that the laws served no useful legal purpose, especially following the decision in *Green* and also the sporadic use of the law over history, described above. The real debate as such rested on what the repeal meant symbolically. The minister went to great lengths to placate the Christian community, by insisting that the measure did not 'represent further evidence of a drift towards secularisation.'[64] However, those who welcome secularisation as a positive and progressive measure, can certainly rejoice in the dismantling of one of the most oppressive remnants of established authoritarian religion in England and Wales. However, whether the abolition is a step towards the disestablishment of the Church of England is yet to be seen. The amendment finally passed by 148 votes to 87, and following a short debate rehearsing the same arguments in the House of Commons on 6 May 2008, the amendment was passed 378 votes to 57, consigning blasphemy to history.

The New Offence of Inciting Religious Hatred

The Racial and Religious Act 2006 creates a new offence of stirring up hatred against a group of people based on religious grounds. It amends the Public Order Act 1986, inserting Part 3A following the pre-existing and separate offence of stirring up racial hatred. The difference between these two offences will be discussed below. The *actus reus* of the offence is committed when religious hatred is stirred up in one of the ways individually listed from s 29B to s 29F. In order they are: by using words or behaviour or displaying written material; publishing or distributing written material; performing a play in public; distributing, showing or playing a recording and broadcasting in a programme service. In summary, this list encapsulates every conceivable form of communication that hatred could be incited by. Additionally there is an inchoate form of the offence, by way of possession of inflammatory material, which allows law enforcement agencies to tackle those who harbour material with a view to commit one of the above communications. This is in itself 'highly

---

[63] Ibid.
[64] Ibid col 1122.

unusual in creating a form of inchoate criminal liability with no equivalent substantive offence.'[65] The requisite *mens rea* of the offence is an intention to stir up religious hatred. Consequently, in order to seek a conviction, prosecutors will need to prove first that a person has used 'threatening' words or behaviour or written material, and has communicated it in one of the above ways. And second, that they have made such a communication with the specific intention of stirring up hatred against a group of people on religious grounds. Once they have evidence of this they will need to consider whether the speech is protected by s 29J and seek the permission to bring a prosecution from the Attorney General.

However, if the Government had originally succeeded in Parliament, provisions outlawing stirring up religious hatred would have been on the statute book by the end of 2001. As it happened, it would take five years and four separate attempts, for the legislation to receive royal assent, and only after a radical overhaul of the provisions contained within. The first attempt came in 2001 as part of statutory response to the events of 9/11, culminating in the Anti-Terrorism, Crime and Security Bill 2001. The second attempt came when Lord Avebury revived the provisions as the private member's Religious Offences Bill 2002. For the third attempt, the Home Office included the provisions in the Serious Organised Crime and Police Bill in November 2004 but these provisions were removed from the Bill at a late stage in order to secure its passage into law before the election in May 2005[66]. The fourth and final attempt began after the 2005 general election, since in their manifesto the Labour Party had restated their intention to outlaw inciting religious hatred[67].

In the subsequent Parliamentary session, the Racial and Religious Hatred Bill was introduced to the floor of the Commons on 9 June 2005. Government ministers showed determination to succeed on this occasion, outraging Lord Lester who stated: '...the government have even threatened this House with the use of the Parliament Act to ram the bill through if we do not do their bidding.'[68] However the House of Lords refused to accept the original Bill and proposed four substantial amendments after a number of long and detailed debates. Firstly, they separated the offence from incitement to racial hatred creating separate offences under Part 3A. Secondly, they changed the *actus reus* of the offence to include only

---

[65] Hare, 'Crosses, Crescents and Sacred Cows' 533.

[66] R Ahdar and I Leigh, *Religious Freedom in the Liberal State* (Oxford, Oxford University Press, 2005) 379.

[67] Labour Party General Election Manifesto (2005) 111-112.

[68] Hansard HL vol 674 col 1074 (Lords Committee) (25 October 2005), Lord Lester of Herne Hill.

'threatening' words and behaviour, and not as original wider 'threatening, abusive or insulting' test. Thirdly, it narrowed the *mens rea* of the office to require intention to stir up hatred, as opposed to the government proposed test that the speech was 'likely' to stir up hatred. And finally, by the insertion of section 29J, the Lords expressly protected freedom of speech. In response, the Government opposed these amendments and sought to return to the original form of the Bill. However, on 31 January 2006, the government proposals lost by a single vote in the House of Commons, after the then Prime Minister Tony Blair had left early, inflicting only the second government defeat of his term. Thus the narrower Bill received Royal Assent on 16 February 2006, and came into force on 1 October 2007[69].

Justifications for the Offence

It would seem from the repetitive reintroduction of the Bill that the Government was committed to enacting the above legislative framework, and therefore must have had strong reasons for doing so. From the parliamentary debates, it is clear that two prevailing arguments were used. The first is that the harm caused by those who incite religious hatred is a terrible menace to society, which leads to further problems and crimes as a result. The second argument put forward by the government is that the existing law of inciting racial hatred was discriminatory in that it protected some religious groups and not others. The reason behind this is that certain faiths including Judaism and Sikhism were deemed monoethnic and adherents thus received protection from the existing racial hatred law while other faiths were not so protected[70]. There has been plenty of confusion surrounding these points.

First, in addressing the argument that inciting religious hatred leads to a breakdown of communities, much worse criminal offences, and leaves certain groups vulnerable and unprotected, it is important to remember the universal and wide protection afforded to individuals under the existing criminal law. Most of the extreme types of incidents that the government suggested in Parliament were clearly already criminal offences[71].

---

[69] The Racial and Religious Hatred Act 2006 (Commencement No.1) Order 2007 SI 2007/2490.

[70] *Mandla v Dowell Lee* [1983] 2 AC 548.

[71] Examples given included Muslim women being spat at, verbally abused, assaulted and incitement to firebomb Muslim homes – all of which would be amply dealt with by existing law. See Hansard HC Deb (21 June 2005) vol 435 col 668-762.

Where an individual incites another to violence there are plenty of laws to catch such behaviour. As Hare notes, 'In these situations, the legal response is based on whether the speaker actually advocates acts of intimidation or violence against the impugned group and not merely that he seeks to affect the emotional response of the audience to them provoking feelings of hatred.'[72] Furthermore, if a person does commit certain existing crimes, notably public order offences, and they can be proved to have acted with racial or religious aggravation, the sentence and crime is more severe as a result[73]. So the idea that the existing criminal law enabled individuals to threaten and assault members of religious minorities with impunity was clearly mistaken.

Second, the argument that there was a gap in law, discriminating against non-mono-ethnic religious groups was the point upon which most of the debate was constructed. We have already seen that the right to free speech is not absolute, in that the government does curtail it in certain circumstances. One such example is in relation to inciting racial hatred, where the law punishes speech that is likely to incite hatred against other people in regard of their race[74]. The reason being that 'racial harmony and the protection of the sensitivities of ethnic groups is considered a more important goal than absolute tolerance in this context of free speech.'[75] As Goodhall states, 'it is not unlawful to feel hatred, so incitement to hatred is not in itself an offence. Incitement to racial hatred is unlawful because it has been made so within the Public Order Act 1986 ... This is the crux.'[76] However it is vital to note at the outset that this discrepancy 'does not necessarily lead to the conclusion that a broader definition of religious hatred is the appropriate response.'[77] There are reasons why the gap should not be so filled.

First, much of what the new Act aims to address, could be covered by the existing offence of racial hatred, where 'there is a strong argument that incitement to religious hatred against Muslims could be held as incitement to racial hatred against, say, Pakistanis or Bangladeshis or those of Arab origin.'[78] Also, the existing racial hatred law only

[72] Hare, 'Crosses, Crescents and Sacred Cows' 532.
[73] ss 28 – 32 Crime and Disorder Act 1998, as amended by s 39 Anti-terrorism, Crime and Security Act 2001, and s 145 Criminal Justice Act 2003.
[74] Public Order Act 1986 Part III.
[75] E Barendt, *Freedom of Speech* (Oxford, Oxford University Press, 2005) 8.
[76] K Goodall, 'Incitement to Religious Hatred: All Talk and No Substance?' (2007) 70 *MLR* 89 at 92.
[77] Hare, 'Crosses, Crescents and Sacred Cows' 532.
[78] Ibid at 533.

protects mono-ethnic religious groups on their ethnic or racial basis, and so it is not true that Judaism and Sikhism are protected as religions *per se*.

Second, it is highly problematic to draw a comparison between race and religion as identities. Race, though a contested social construct, is primarily concerned with the immutable characteristic of the colour of ones skin, and this is vastly different to the issue of one's religious or non-religious views. As Hare notes, 'it remains the case that for the vast majority who live in liberal democracies, religious adherence is a matter of choice rather than birth and the law does not usually provide the protection of the criminal law for vilification based upon the life choices of its citizens.'[79] Furthermore, religious groups are not usually just concerned with the life choices of their own followers. There is often an effort to attract new believers, and also a willingness to contribute to public debate on science, morality and the state of society[80]:

> These sorts of claims are not mirrored in racial discourse. In addition, unlike most minority groups who are the victims of racial incitement, many religious entities are highly organised and well-funded and therefore have the resources to counter extreme speech against them[81].

Therefore, the justifications for the offence are not particularly convincing, and should be treated with perhaps even more suspicion than other pieces of the criminal law since it has been argued that the new offence is an anomaly 'to the general rule that the law permits people blatantly to mislead each other.'[82] Thus proponents of the offences effectively want the state to criminalise a viewpoint the majority regards as certainly false. This necessarily implies the infallibility of the state to decide what is true, and is not responsible law making. Mill reminds legislators that they 'ought to be moved by the consideration that however true [an opinion] may be, if it is not fully, frequently, and fearlessly discussed, it will be held as a dead dogma, not a living truth.'[83]

---

[79] Ibid at 533.

[80] As seen in the public and Parliamentary debate surrounding the Human Fertilisation and Embryology Bill 2007.

[81] Hare, 'Crosses, Crescents and Sacred Cows' 534.

[82] Goodall, 'Incitement to Religious Hatred' 109.

[83] J S Mill, *On Liberty and Other Essays* (Oxford, Oxford University Press, 1998) 40.

How Will the Offence Work in Practice?

The meaning of 'religious hatred' is crucial to the operation of the Act, and is defined in section 29A as 'hatred against a group of persons defined by reference to religious belief or lack of a religious belief.'[84] The effect of including lack of a religious belief in the definition, is that it has an internal and external application. Externally, a non-believer covers any person other than the adherents of a particular religion, which would include all agnostics and atheists, who evidently cannot be described as part of a religion. However, this provision also acts internally on members of the specified religion who not perhaps agree with certain interpretations of that faith. Thus, it is possible for someone to incite religious hatred against another group within the same religion. In this way the Act is just as useful for policing internal religious disputes as it is when applied to different religions. As Addison notes, 'this makes the offence of religious hatred distinctly different from the offence of racial hatred. It would be very difficult for a person to incite racial hatred against their own race because they would of course be inciting hatred against themselves.'[85] The meaning of 'religious belief' is not specifically defined in the Act, however its likely effect is 'that groups defined by non-religious beliefs or philosophies are not protected'; it is therefore a much narrower definition that the definition 'religion or belief' used in the Equality Act 2006 and Article 9 of the European Convention on Human Rights[86]. However, it will be necessary for a court to determine whether a certain group's beliefs are of religious nature.

The significance of the phrase 'group of persons'[87] is to exclude incitement of hatred towards individuals from the scope of the Act. The strange effect of this exclusion is to afford greater protection to religious groups than religious individuals. However, as Addison notes, with reference to Salman Rushdie affair:

> if the legislation had been in force…it would not have applied to those who were inciting hatred of Salman Rushdie because, even though they were inciting hatred on a monumental scale, the hatred they were inciting was against an individual and not against a group. Paradoxically, however, those who defended Salman Rushdie and criticised those aspects of Islamic

---

[84] Racial and Religious Hatred Act 2006 s 29A.
[85] N Addison, *Religious Discrimination and Hatred Law* (London, Routledge, 2007) 142.
[86] Ibid.
[87] Racial and Religious Hatred Act 2006 s 29A.

belief which were being used to justify the campaign against him could have found themselves threatened with prosecution for stirring up religious hatred against Muslims[88].

As we have seen, in all of the methods capable of inciting religious hatred, listed from 29B to 29F, there is a common test. In each case the speech, behaviour, written material, recording, play or programme must be 'threatening'. There is no definition of threatening to be found in the Act and thus it must be given its ordinary and natural meaning. The *Oxford English Dictionary* defines it as 'having a hostile or deliberately frightening quality or manner'. However, deciding whether a person's actions were hostile or deliberately frightening is a question of fact to be decided by juries[89].

In a recent unreported case at the Old Bailey, a man from Birmingham was convicted of stirring up racial hatred and soliciting murder at a protest against the publication of the *Jyllands-Posten* cartoons. It was accepted at trial that he had said 'Bomb, bomb Denmark, bomb, bomb USA', and that 'disbelievers would pay a heavy price and Denmark would pay with blood'[90]. These kinds of statements are clearly threatening and could almost certainly result in an additional conviction for inciting religious hatred, as the direction of the threat is to disbelievers. An interesting question is whether a threat of divine punishment or judgment could be perceived as threatening. For example, if a religious person held a placard stating 'God will send all unbelievers to hell' this would probably not be perceived as threatening. The reason is that 'it is not a threat or an exhortation to anyone to do anything but, in essence, merely expressing a personal religious belief as to what God will do.'[91] It does highlight however that context is very important when determining what is threatening.

As already noted, the Act specifies a number of different ways that effectively religious hatred can be stirred up. The most widely drafted, and probably be the most common method to be prosecuted is the use of words or behaviour or display of written material, outlined in section 29B. Its effect is straightforward, although there is a statutory

---

[88] Addison, *Religious Discrimination and Hatred Law* 143. Although this is perhaps an overstatement, as such criticisms would probably not be threatening and certainly would be covered by the express protection of free expression found in s 29J.

[89] *R v Cakmak* [2002] EWCA Crim 500.

[90] BBC News, 'Cartoons protester found guilty' (5 January 2007) <http://news.bbc. co.uk/go/pr/fr/-/1/hi/uk/6235279.stm>.

[91] Addison, *Religious Discrimination and Hatred Law* 142.

defence in section 29B(4) that protects a person committing the offence inside a dwelling house if he had no reason to believe his words would be heard outside. The reason for this is simply to stop the Act criminalising the private discussions that go on inside a person's home. However, this defence does not apply to all private places and so there would be no problem prosecuting on the basis of an incriminating speech made in a place of worship.

Under section 29C, a person is guilty of the offence if they publish or distribute threatening written material with the intention of stirring up religious hatred. In section 29C (2) the distribution or publishing must be 'to the public or a section of the public' and thus is very wide. The offence is likely to engage publishers and bookstores primarily, although publishing could also be applied to other more recent disciplines such as the recent internet phenomenon of blogging. Additionally, handing out leaflets or posting material to people will be covered by the offence. Section 29E makes it an offence to distribute or show a recording containing threatening content with the intention of stirring up religious hatred. This will operate in the same way as section 29C, other than it will catch recordings of speeches and so forth. Furthermore, the Act specifically addresses the arts and media by including specific provisions for public broadcasts and plays, in sections 29D and 29F respectively. As already noted, in recent years plays and broadcasts have become the focus of huge media storms regarding their religiously offensive content. But one can be certain that both *Behzti* and *Jerry Springer: The Opera* would fall short of the offence because whilst they may ridicule and criticise in strongest terms, they could not be perceived as threatening.

In terms of sentencing and police powers there are a number of interesting points to consider. Firstly, under section 29L(3) the penalty for anyone found guilty of an offence under the Act is seven years imprisonment if convicted on indictment, or if convicted on summary the sentence is limited to six months imprisonment or a fine or both. This is the same penalty as was prescribed for racial hatred and offers judges and magistrates a large amount of sentencing discretion. A major procedural limitation on the workings of the Act is that the permission of the Attorney General is required for a prosecution to begin. Spelled out in section 29L(1), it effectively prevents private prosecutions from taking place. 'This is an important provision and not a mere technicality because where a prosecution which requires the consent of the Attorney General is brought without his consent first being obtained, any conviction is a nullity.'[92] It further highlights the much politicised nature of the offences.

Finally section 29J is the clause added into the legislation by the House of Lords designed to explicitly protect freedom of expression being unnecessarily curbed by the Act. It provides that:

> Nothing in this Part shall be read or given effect in a way which prohibits or restricts discussion, criticism or expressions of antipathy, dislike, ridicule, insult or abuse of particular religions or the beliefs and practices of its adherents, or proselytising or urging adherents of a different religion or belief system to cease practising their religion or belief system.

This is laudable even if it only codifies the existing rights of individuals in Britain today. As we have seen, the offence has been narrowed to such an extent, that even without section 29J, it is difficult to envisage a conviction of someone who does not plead guilty to having the intention of stirring up hatred.

Conclusion

The abolition of blasphemy and blasphemous libel is a welcome development and a long overdue victory for freedom of speech. Whilst the antiquated offences had been rendered practically redundant by a recent judicial decision[93], over the past few decades repeated attempts to revive and even expand them have been a constant threat. Removing the privilege of the Church of England to have legal protection from criticism and insult of the most scurrilous and offensive nature, has the obvious effect of rendering all religious beliefs equally exposed. But perhaps more importantly it is a symbolic statement that there is no right not to be offended in English law. Individuals may well find their religious beliefs the subject of strong insult and ridicule, but this is a necessary part of a plural and free society.

The new offence of incitement to religious hatred is a very different type of offence in that it protects people rather than intangible beliefs and ideas. Whilst religious communities may welcome the fact that it results in the equal protection all religions, the level of protection afforded is so specific, and subject to such strict caveats, it is only applicable to a small amount of incidents. Thus the right for people to criticise, vilify, and

---

[92] *Ibid* 148. See *R v Pearce* (1981) 72 Cr App R 295.
[93] Green, R (on the application of) v The City of Westminster Magistrates' Court [2007] EWHC (Admin) 2785.

insult religious beliefs and believers remains a legitimate use of an individuals right to free speech. The persistence of certain people to go and seek out that which offends them, and then protest in the strongest terms is a worrying trend, most notably within the arts. That a play can be forcibly and violently closed by the direct action of a religious group, simply because they disapprove of the plot, in twenty-first century Britain is a disturbing reality.

As a result, the antecedence of this legislation is deeply concerning. If it were not for the narrow success of the Lord Lester amendments, the result would have been a far greater incursion into the right to freedom of speech. In trying to criminalise bigoted and odious far-Right politicians and extremist preachers, who no doubt exploit tensions and are a menace to society, the government displayed a willingness to cut away fundamental rights. This is a dangerous precedent, and one which indicates the very individualistic nature of the offences. Indeed, Gordon Brown responded to the second acquittal of Nick Griffin of the BNP by saying:

> I think any preaching of religious or racial hatred will offend mainstream opinion in this country and I think we've got to do whatever we can to root it out from whatever quarter it comes ... if that means we've got to look at the laws again I think we will have to do so[94].

In light of this it is worth remembering the advice of Sir Thomas More in Robert Bolt's play *A Man for All Seasons*. In response to William Roper's claim that he would 'cut down every law in England to [get after the Devil]', More declares:

> Oh? And when the last law was down, and the Devil turned on you – where would you hide, Roper, the laws all being flat? This country's planted thick with laws from coast to coast – Man's laws, not God's – and if you cut them down ... d'you really think you could stand upright in the winds that would blow then?[95]

We must remain wary of any law that purports to do good by stifling freedom of speech, even if this means permitting views that are almost universally perceived as repugnant and wrong. To do so, is the true test of whether we believe in free speech at all.

---

[94] BBC News, 'BNP Leader Cleared of Race Hate' (10 November 2006) <http://news.bbc.co.uk/1/hi/england/bradford/6135060.stm>.
[95] R Bolt, *A Man For All Seasons* (London, Heinemann Books, 1960) 39.

PUBLIC BENEFIT IN THE ADVANCEMENT OF RELIGION AFTER THE CHARITIES ACT 2006: ANOTHER CHARITY MUDDLE?

Peter Luxton

Introduction

One of the most difficult issues arising from the Charities Act 2006 concerns the impact of the new statutory provisions on the advancement of religion, which came into force on 1 April 2008[1]. The impact of these provisions is two-fold.

First, the Act has introduced a statutory list of purposes, and advancement of religion appears as paragraph (c) on this list[2]. It is stated that 'religion' in paragraph (c) includes 'a religion which involves belief in more than one god'[3] and 'a religion which does not involve belief in a god[4]. The scope of these provisions is by no means clear. The former may simply be a statutory recognition of what had already probably been accepted as the law, albeit without the benefit of a clear judicial statement, namely that the advancement of religion includes the advancement of polytheistic religions[5]. On one interpretation, the latter provision merely clarifies the previous law that recognised that religion for this purpose embraces Buddhism[6] and perhaps other faiths that, whilst not believing in a god, nevertheless believe (to use the words of the Charity Commission)[7] in 'a divine or transcendental being, entity or principle'. It seems unlikely that it was intended that purely secular belief systems, such as humanism or ethics[8], were intended to be brought within the

---

[1] Charities Act 2006 (Commencement No. 4, Transitional Provisions and Savings) Order 2008 (2008/945).

[2] Charities Act 2006, s 2(2)(c).

[3] S 2(3)(a)(i).

[4] S 2(3)(a)(ii).

[5] cf *Varsani v Jesani* [1999] Ch 219.

[6] See comments of Lord Denning MR in *R v Registrar General, ex p Segerdal* [1970] 2 QB 697, 707.

[7] Charity Commission, *Public Benefit and the Advancement of Religion: draft supplementary guidance for consultation*, February 2008, at 13; and see Charity Commission, *Analysis of the law underpinning* Public Benefit and the Advancement of Religion, February 2008, para 2.21-2.24 (pages 11-12).

[8] *Re South Place Ethical Society* [1980] 1 WLR 1565.

fold. The Commission's draft guidance indicates that it is intending to take a narrow view of this provision, and will continue to regard worship or something akin to worship (such as what it describes as having 'reverence or respect for' or having 'a connection with' the supreme being or entity) as an essential ingredient for a religion[9].

Second, the Act puts the requirement for public benefit into statutory form[10], and provides that it is not to be presumed that any particular description of charitable purposes is for the public benefit[11]. This chapter concentrates on an analysis of the public-benefit provisions, these being of fundamental importance, their impact being unclear, and (as will be seen) the Charity Commission's interpretation of them being particularly controversial[12]. The ensuing pages look at public benefit in the advancement of religion as it existed before 1 April 2008, and, in the light of this investigation, examine what the likely impact of the Act will be on public benefit under this head of charity. To do this, it is necessary to begin by examining the background to the advancement of religion as a charitable purpose in English law.

Background

The advancement of religion has for centuries been recognised as a charitable purpose. Although the Preamble to the Statute of Elizabeth 1601[13] makes only an indirect passing reference to religion, namely to the repair of churches, it would appear that this was because religion was a sensitive issue in Tudor times, with the break from Rome under Henry VIII, the restoration of the Catholic faith under Mary, and renewed Protestantism under Elizabeth. It being dangerous in the sixteenth century to profess anything but the established faith for the time being, it was thought safer to exclude religious purposes from the jurisdiction of the commissioners established by the Act[14]. Perhaps the repair of churches was included because it relieved the parishioners upon whom the cost

---

[9] Charity Commission, *Public Benefit and the Advancement of Religion: draft supplementary guidance for consultation*, February 2008, 15; and see Charity Commission, *Analysis of the law underpinning* Public Benefit and the Advancement of Religion, February 2008, para 2.25 (page 12).

[10] Charities Act 2006, s 2(1), s 3.

[11] S 3(2).

[12] Ss 2(1) and 3.

[13] 43 Eliz I c 4.

[14] See F Moore, *Readings upon the Statute 43 Elizabeth*, reproduced in Duke, *Law of Charitable Uses* (1676; reprinted London, W Clarke, 1805).

would otherwise fall. The only lawful religious purpose under the reign of the first Elizabeth was that of the established church; other religions were accounted superstitious, and land given for such purposes could be confiscated by the Crown[15]. That the advancement of religion was nevertheless recognised as a charitable purpose became clear within a few decades after the Act was passed, when it was held that a gift to maintain a preaching minister was within the equity of the statute[16]. The Court of Chancery, however, recognised that gifts on trust for the purpose of other religions, whilst unlawful, could be charitable, and so applicable cy-près under the sign manual[17]. Over several centuries, the impediments on other religions were gradually lifted[18]. Equity's stance remained unchanged, and in the 1860s, Sir John Romilly MR held that 'the Court of Chancery makes no distinction between one sort of religion and another'[19], a statement that has been approved and followed ever since[20].

In a well-known passage in his speech in the House of Lords in what is conveniently generally known simply as *Pemsel's* case[21], Lord Macnaghten indicated four principal divisions of charitable purposes: the relief of poverty, the advancement of education, the advancement of religion, and other purposes beneficial to the community not falling under the preceding three heads. The advancement of religion thereby acquired the distinction of becoming the third of only three purposes that his Lordship specified as charitable, all other charitable purposes merely falling under the broad description of the fourth head[22].

---

[15] Moore, *Readings upon the Statute 43 Elizabeth*; and see G Jones, *History of the Law of Charity 1532-1827* (Cambridge, Cambridge University Press, 1969).

[16] *Pember v Inhabitants of Kington* (1639) Tot 34 (gift to maintain a preaching minister).

[17] *Da Costa v De Paz* (1754) 2 Swan 487n.

[18] Toleration Act 1688 (relieved Protestant Dissenters), Unitarian Relief Act 1813, Roman Catholic Charities Act 1832, Religious Disabilities Act 1846 relieved Jews; but a bequest to enable persons professing the Jewish religion to observe its rights had been held charitable and not illegal seven years earlier in *Strauss v Goldsmid* (1837) 8 Sim 614.

[19] *Thornton v Howe* (1862) 31 Beav 14; *Gilmour v Coats* [1949] AC 426, 457 (Lord Reid); see also Cross J in *Neville Estates Ltd v Madden* [1962] Ch 832, 853: 'As between different religions the law stands neutral, but it assumes that any religion is at least likely to be better than none.'

[20] *Re Watson* [1973] 1 WLR 1472, *Holmes v A-G* (1981) The Times 12 February 1981.

[21] *Commissioners for Special Purposes of the Income Tax v Pemsel* [1891] AC 531, 583.

[22] In his argument as counsel in *Morice v Bishop of Durham* (1805) 10 Ves Jun 522, 532, Samuel Romilly had suggested a similar (but not identical) four-fold classification, his third head being also 'the advancement of religion'.

The case law before the Charities Act 2006 had laid down what was meant by the advancement of religion. First, it had established the need for belief in a supreme being[23]; secondly, the need for worship of that being[24]; thirdly, it had been held that the purpose must not be immoral or adverse to the foundations of religion[25]; and, fourthly, it was emphasized that the purpose must advance religion[26]. Although the courts had for centuries accepted the advancement of religion as a charitable purpose, it was not until towards the end of the nineteenth century that it was judicially classified as a separate head of charity[27], and it was not until the following century that the courts started making reference to public benefit as an additional and separate requirement for charitable status[28].

At the time of *Pemsel's* case, the courts did not expressly refer to the need for a purpose to have a public benefit in order to be charitable. However in the decades after that decision of their Lordships' House, the courts began to specify a further requirement for a charitable trust[29]; namely, that in addition to being for a charitable purpose it had to be for the public benefit[30]. It would be wrong, however, to infer from this that the law of charities had not previously required a charitable purpose to be for the public benefit; rather it would appear that the notion that a charitable purpose is for the public benefit is intrinsic to a purpose being held to be charitable[31]. This would seem to be what Lord Macnaghten

---

[23] See *Bowman v Secular Society* [1917] AC 406, 449 (Lord Parker); *Re South Place Ethical Society* [1980] 1 WLR 1565.

[24] *R v Registrar General,ex p Segerdal* [1970] 2 QB 697, 709 (Buckley LJ); *Re South Place Ethical Society* [1980] 1 WLR 1565.

[25] *Thornton v Howe* (1862) 31 Beav 14, 20 (Romilly MR).

[26] See *United Grand Lodge of Masons v Holborn BC* [1957] 1 WLR 1080, 1090 (Donovan J): 'To advance religion means to promote it, to spread its message ever wider among mankind; to take some positive steps to sustain and increase religious belief; and these things are done in a variety of ways which may be comprehensively described as pastoral and missionary.' Thus private prayer, whilst a religious activity, does not advance religion: *National Deposit Friendly Society Trustees v Skegness UDC* [1959] AC 293, 322 (Lord Denning).

[27] *Commissioners for Special Purposes of the Income Tax v Pemsel* [1891] AC 531, 583 (Lord Macnaghten).

[28] *Re Hummeltenberg* [1923] 1 Ch 237, 242 (Russell J); *National Anti-Vivisection Society Ltd v IRC* [1948] AC 31, 42 (Lord Wright).

[29] There is also a third requirement, that the purpose be wholly and exclusively charitable, which was well established before *Pemsel's* case, but this requirement is not material to the argument in this chapter.

[30] *Re Hummeltenberg* [1923] 1 Ch 237, 240-241 (Russell J); *National Anti-Vivisection Society Ltd v IRC* 1948] AC 31, 42 (Lord Wright).

[31] See Jones, *History of the Law of Charity* at 27, who states that public benefit 'was the key to the statute [of 1601]'.

meant when he explained his fourth head of charity as being 'other purposes beneficial to the community'[32], its being understood that the first three purposes he had specified already possessed this quality. It may be that it was the manner in which Lord Macnaghten described his fourth head – 'other purposes beneficial to the community' – that led later courts to treat this as a necessary ingredient for the other three heads. In any event, in *National Anti-Vivisection Society Ltd v IRC*[33], Lord Wright explained that, whereas in the fourth head of *Pemsel* the existence of public benefit must be proved, in Lord Macnaghten's first three heads (including therefore the advancement of religion) public benefit is *prima facie* presumed.

The Two Meanings of 'Public Benefit'

Any analysis of the presumption of public benefit in the advancement of religion has to explain the difficult decision of the House of Lords in *Gilmour v Coats*[34], where a gift for the purposes of a Carmelite convent was held not to be charitable for the advancement of religion because it lacked the ingredient of public benefit, which their Lordships held to be necessary under this head of charity. Their Lordships rejected the arguments of the Catholic Church that public benefit was satisfied either because the nuns engaged in intercessory prayer or because there was spiritual edification in the public's awareness that women in the convent were devoting their lives exclusively to the service of God: these were matters of belief and were not susceptible to judicial proof. It is evident from Lord Simonds' speech that that he treated the gift as being for a charitable purpose (the advancement of religion), but denied it charitable status on the separate ground that it was not for the public benefit in the sense that it did not benefit a sufficient section of the community.

It is manifest from this and other decisions that the expression 'public benefit' as it appears in the case law is ambiguous, as it is used in two senses: first, to refer to the public benefit in the purpose itself; and, secondly, to refer to the section of the community that must be capable of benefiting. It is clear that, in *Gilmour v Coats*, the testatrix's purpose was accepted as being for the advancement of religion, and so satisfied public benefit in the first sense; but, as the purported trust was restricted

---

[32] *Pemsel's* case [1891] AC 531, 583.
[33] [1948] AC 31, 42 (Lord Wright).
[34] [1949] AC 426.

to members of an enclosed order who never left the convent, it was not for the public benefit in the second sense[35]. When the case had been in the Court of Appeal, Lord Greene MR had been of similar opinion[36]:

> The gift may be a most beneficial one, it may tend to the advancement of religion: yet if it appears that the benefit is a private and not a public one, the gift fails to satisfy the conditions requisite in the case of a valid charitable gift. A gift for the religious instruction of a man's grandchildren tends to the advancement of religion: it is beneficial; but on the face of it the gift is a private one and any *prima facie* assumption is displaced.

Once it is appreciated that public benefit in the law of charities is used in these two senses, we are on the way to understanding the development of the law in this area, and the earlier quoted statement of Lord Wright in the *National Anti-Vivisection Society* case[37]. In his reference to the presumption of public benefit in the first three heads of *Pemsel*[38], Lord Wright was referring to public benefit in the first sense: in other words, it is presumed that, for instance, the advancement of religion, as a concept, is for the public benefit. He was not laying down any presumption as regards public benefit in the second sense, namely that a sufficient section of the community must be capable of benefiting. In *Re Hetherington*[39], Browne-Wilkinson J did not distinguish between the two types of public benefit, and he evidently treated the presumption as applying to public benefit in the second sense as well. It is submitted that the cases do not support any presumption of public benefit in the second sense[40]. What is crucial, however, is to analyse precisely what is meant by stating that there is a presumption of public benefit in the first sense.

Although Lord Wright referred to the presumption of public benefit in the first three heads of *Pemsel*, the presumption seems to have been the subject of rather more judicial consideration in cases involving the

---

[35] In *Cocks v Manners* (1871) LR 12 Eq 574, which was applied in *Gilmour v Coats* [1949] AC 426, Wickens V-C held that a trust for a Dominican convent was not charitable because its purpose did not fall within the letter or the spirit of the Preamble. His Lordship did not refer to public benefit, but the absence of public benefit in the second sense is implicit in his reasoning, as he commented: 'A voluntary association of women for the purpose of working out their own salvation by religious exercises and self-denial seems to me to have none of the requisites of a charitable institution'.

[36] *Re Coats' Trusts* [1948] Ch 340.

[37] [1948] AC 31, 42.

[38] [1891] AC 531.

[39] [1990] Ch 1; see Browne-Wilkinson's proposition (2) at 12.

[40] See the interesting analysis by A Sanders, 'The Mystery of Public Benefit' (2007) 10(2) *CL&PR* 33 (especially at 35).

advancement of religion than in cases concerned with the relief of poverty or the advancement of education[41]. The explanation probably lies in the fact that the courts will make a value judgment on whether a particular purpose is meritorious when determining whether it is capable of being educational; whereas the courts are not willing to adjudicate on the merits of different religions, the long-stop being only faiths whose tenets are 'adverse to the very foundations of all religion' or 'subversive of morality'[42]. Equity's stance being thus one of toleration, it is not surprising that this attitude of neutrality as between different religions and sects is often equated with the presumption of public benefit.

Indeed, it is easy to see how the trusts to publish harmless but essentially unmeritorious religions writings in *Thornton v Howe*[43] and in *Re Watson*[44] might appear to be illustrations of the presumption of public benefit in the advancement of religion. Adopting that construction, it might be thought that trusts falling under the advancement of religion are treated as charitable merely because their public benefit is presumed – the implication being that many such trusts would not be charitable if public benefit had to be shown.

The central thesis in this chapter is that public benefit in the first sense in inherent in the concept of the advancement of religion. To explain this, a useful comparison can be made with the advancement of education. It would appear that, as concepts, the relief of poverty and the advancement of education are self-evidently for the public benefit in the first sense[45]. This can be illustrated by supposing a gift for a school for pickpockets[46]. The reason why this would be denied charitable status, it is submitted, is that such purpose is not for the public benefit and so cannot rank as the advancement of education. It would be odd to treat such a gift as *prima facie* for the advancement of education and only then to go on to deny it charitable status on the grounds of absence of

---

[41] A discussion of the presumption of public benefit in cases involving the advancement of religion is contained in the judgements in *Re Watson* [1973] 3 All ER 678 *Holmes v A-G* (1981) The Times 12 February, *Re Hetherington* [1990] Ch1, and in *Re Le Cren Clarke* [1996] 1 All ER 715.

[42] i.e. within the criteria in *Thornton v Howe* (1862) 31 Beav 14, 19.

[43] (1862) 31 Beav 14.

[44] [1973] 1 WLR 1472.

[45] For an analysis of this in relation to the advancement of education, see P Luxton, 'Public Benefit and Charities: The Impact of the Charities Act 2006 on Independent Schools and Private Hospitals', in M Dixon and G Griffiths (ed) *Contemporary Perspectives on Property, Equity and Trusts Law* (Oxford, Oxford University Press, 2007) 181.

[46] One of Harman LJ's illustrations in *Re Pinion* [1965] Ch 85, 105; a similar example had been used by Rigby LJ in *Re Macduff* [1896] 2 Ch 451, 474.

public benefit[47]. The same might be said of purported gifts to teach poodles to dance[48], or to compile lists of Derby winners[49]. If a trust can be fitted within the category of the advancement of education it is *prima facie* presumed to be for the public benefit. There is, however, no presumption that any particular form of words contained in a will or other governing instrument is for the public benefit. In many instances, therefore, where it is sought to argue that a particular purpose is charitable for the advancement of education, the question is whether the particular purpose described can be properly considered to fall within what charity law means by the advancement of education, and, unless public benefit is clear, evidence of it will need to be adduced[50]. There is, in other words, no presumption of public benefit at an evidential level; the presumption operates only at the conceptual level.

Does the presumption of public benefit operate in a different way in the advancement of religion: could it, in other words, be argued that a trust, whilst for the advancement of religion, is nevertheless not for the public benefit in the first sense? At first blush, it might appear that Lord Simonds referred to this possibility in *Gilmour v Coats*, when he commented:

> even if the simple argument that, if education is a good thing, then the more education the better, may appear to be irrefutable, to repeat that argument substituting "religion" for "education" is to ignore the principle which I understand to be conceded that not all religious purposes are charitable purposes[51].

However his Lordship then proceeded to discuss *Cocks v Manners*[52], which shows that he had in mind that a gift for the advancement of religion might fail to be a charity because of absence of public benefit in

---

[47] See Rigby LJ in *Re Macduff* [1896] 2 Ch 451, 474: 'I think it is true that when you say: "Gifts to the poor, trusts for the advancement of education, trusts for the advancement of religion, are charities", that does not mean that in every conceivable case where you can bring a gift under one or other of those general words it is necessarily a charity. It means nothing of the kind. It means, as in the case of "for the general benefit of the community", that these are heads or categories under which actual and valid charities may be implied. No one will suggest, for instance, to take only one illustration, that "education" meant the education of pickpockets in a thieves' kitchen to make them fit for their profession.'

[48] Russell J's example in *Re Hummeltenberg* [1923] 1 Ch 237, 242.

[49] An example supplied by Brunyate, (1945) 61 *LQR* 268, 273.

[50] e.g. *Re Shaw* [1957] 1 WLR 729, *Re Dupree* [1945] Ch 16, *Re Pinion* [1965] Ch 85.

[51] [1949] AC 426, 449.

[52] (1871) L R 12 Eq 574.

what this chapter has called the second sense. His words do not therefore refute the proposition that the advancement of religion is necessarily for the public benefit in the first sense.

Does the Charities Act 2006 Affect the Presumption?

With Part I of the Charities Act 2006 in force, it becomes vital to know whether, as a concept, the advancement of religion remains for the public benefit in the first sense. Section 2(1) makes it explicit that public benefit is a separate requirement from the statutory list of purposes in section 2(2), and section 3(2) states that it is not to be presumed that any particular description of charitable purposes is for the public benefit. Might it be now argued that a gift, trust, or institution may be *prima facie* for the advancement of religion within paragraph (c), but still be denied charitable status because, in the absence of any presumption, public benefit in the first sense cannot be established? If that were so, then it might indeed seem that, in the advancement of religion, the effect of section 3(2) is to reverse the conceptual presumption of public benefit. At this juncture it is necessary to pause to note to serious consequences that ensue if this is indeed the effect of section 3(2). If the sub-section reverses the conceptual presumption of public benefit, it must inevitably lead to the courts' having to inquire into whether particular faiths are for the public benefit – something that the courts have, understandably consistently refused to do, as the assessment of the merits of different religious doctrines is hardly a suitable subject for judicial pronouncement[53]; the sub-section might also have human-rights implications[54].

In its recent draft guidance on public benefit and the advancement of religion, the Charity Commission accepts the view, which certainly pertained under the previous law[55], that, as between different religions

---

[53] *Craigdallie v Aikman* (1813) 1 Dow 1, HL (Sc); *General Assembly of Free Church of Scotland v Lord Overtoun* [1904] AC 515, HL (Sc); *Varsani v Jesani* [1999] Ch 219. See also R Atkinson, 'Problems with Presbyterians: Prolegomena to a Theory of Voluntary Association and the Liberal State' in C Mitchell and S Moody (ed) *Foundations of Charity* (Oxford, Hart Publishing, 2000) 125.

[54] See A Sanders, 'The Mystery of Public Benefit' (2007) 10(2) *CL&PR* 33, 37, referring to Articles 9 and 14 of the European Convention on Human Rights, and Human Rights Act 1998, s 13. See also F Quint and P Hodkin, 'The Development of Tolerance and Diversity in the Treatment of Religion in Charity Law' (2007) 10 (2) *CL&PR* 1, at 15.

[55] *Gilmour v Coats* [1949] AC 426, 457 (Lord Reid); *Neville Estates Ltd v Madden* [1962] Ch 832, 853 (Cross J).

the law is neutral[56]. Yet to accept that the law is neutral is necessarily to accept that, despite the new Act, there is a continuing presumption that the advancement of religion is for the public benefit in the first sense. However, the Commission then goes on to contradict itself by stating that[57]:

> whether a religious organisation's aims are for the public benefit is a question of judgement based on factual evidence. This means that there must be an assessment of whether the aim is for the public benefit.

In other words, whilst the Commission effectively accepts that the presumption of public benefit (necessarily in the first sense) does not affect the principle of neutrality as between different religions, it nevertheless regards the presumption as otherwise reversed. This contradiction reveals the conceptual confusion at the core of the Commission's guidance on public benefit.

The Commission's draft guidance goes on to state[58]:

> It will no longer be sufficient to simply say that the religious beliefs are not immoral or are not of any harm for it to be concluded that they are for the public benefit.

In some instances, the Commission consider that, under the new law, the benefit might need to be balanced against any detriment or harm: if it is a fundamental aspect of a faith that adherents must withhold consent to medical treatment to children or other vulnerable people, the Commission states that it would need to consider whether the general benefit of freedom of religion would be outweighed by any possible damage to health[59]. The problem with this approach, however, is that is seeks to consider under public benefit an issue that is properly one of charitable purpose. What the Commission should instead be considering is whether a faith with a fundamental tenet such as that could be denied charitable status as coming within the dicta in *Thornton v Howe* that exclude religions or sects whose tenets are subversive of all morality.

It would appear that, contrary to the view taken by the Commission, the *dicta* in *Thornton v Howe* go to describe one aspect of what is meant by 'the advancement of religion' in charity law; they do not go to the

---

[56] Charity Commission, *Public Benefit in the Advancement of Religion: Draft supplementary guidance for consultation*, E2 (page 23) (February 2008).

[57] Ibid.

[58] Ibid, E2 (page 24).

[59] Ibid, E4 (pages 26-27).

second issue of public benefit. In other words, if the tenets of a religion or a particular sect are against religion or immoral, the reason a gift to promote such religion or sect will not be charitable is that it will not fall within the concept of the advancement of religion: the claim to charitable status falls at the first hurdle, without the second, the issue of public benefit, even needing to be addressed[60]. This is so because, once the purpose is shown to be for the advancement of religion, it is necessarily for the public benefit in the first sense. This is consonant with Plowman J's view in *Re Watson*[61]:

> that having regard to the fact that the court does not draw a distinction between one religion and another or one sect and another, the only way of disproving a public benefit is to show, in the words of Romilly MR in [*Thornton v Howe*[62]], that the doctrines inculcated are "adverse to the very foundations of all religion, and that they are subversive of all morality".

The Commission rejects this analysis, asserting that such *dicta* are not a complete or accurate statement of the law[63]; yet the examples that the Commission supplies of instances where public benefit is disproved in other ways all relate to public benefit in the second sense[64]. It is clear, however, that Plowman J's *dicta* relate to public benefit in the first sense, and are therefore still good law.

The Fourth-Head Fallacy

It remains to explain how it has come about that the Commission is proposing, in the advancement of religion, to look for public benefits and to weigh benefits and detriments beyond what they were able to do under the previous law. To justify its new stance, the Commission points to

---

[60] Romilly MR's dicta in *Thornton v Howe* (1862) 31 Beav 14, 19, are treated as an aspect of the definition of 'the advancement of religion' rather than as an aspect of public benefit, both by H Picarda, *The Law and Practice Relating to Charities* (third edition, London, Butterworths, 1999), chapter 4 at 74 and by P Luxton, *The Law of Charities* (Oxford, Oxford University Press, 2001) chapter 4 (para 4.42 at 129).

[61] [1973] 3 All ER 678, 688.

[62] (1862) 31 Beav at 20.

[63] Charity Commission, *Analysis of the law underpinning* Public Benefit and the Advancement of Religion, February 2008, para 1.5 (pages 4-5).

[64] Thus the Commission (ibid) mentions that 'the beneficiaries may be insufficiently numerous or may be required to have some common characteristic determined by personal relationship or contract', and it places reliance on *Gilmour v Coats* [1949] AC 426, which also concerned public benefit in the second sense.

what it claims to be a statutory reversal of the presumption of public benefit, which, according to the Commission, thereby creates a new level playing field[65].

It is evident that the government's aim in introducing section 3(2) was to strengthen the test for public benefit in the first three heads of *Pemsel*, where, as Lord Wright said in the *National Anti-Vivisection Society* case[66], public benefit is presumed, so as to equate it with the test in the fourth head, where public benefit must be proved[67].

Thus, just as in the *National Anti-Vivisection Society* case the House of Lords needed to be satisfied that the promotion of anti-vivisection was for the public benefit, which involved its weighing the merits and detriments of such purpose, so, the Commission argues, the courts or the Commission would need to be satisfied that any of the purposes previously falling within the first three heads of *Pemsel* is for the public benefit – hence their view that public benefit must still be shown even where the purpose is accepted as being the advancement of religion.

The Commission appears, therefore, to be endeavouring to carry into practice what the government intended. There is, however, a fundamental flaw in the attempt to draw an analogy with public benefit under *Pemsel's* fourth head. The problem is that, whereas the first three heads of *Pemsel* identify specific charitable purposes, the fourth head does not describe any particular purpose. The fourth head is qualitatively different from the first three, in that it is describes a quality that any purpose must have in order to be admitted as charitable, namely that of being beneficial to the community. Lord Upjohn once likened the fourth head to a portmanteau into which are placed purposes that satisfy the quality of being beneficial to the community[68].

The status of the first three heads can be understood if the analogy is reversed: if descriptions of purposes that are beneficial to the community (and so for the public benefit) can be regarded as having been removed from the portmanteau, then it can be seen that Lord Macnaghten listed three descriptions of charitable purposes only (these being his first three heads), leaving his fourth head as the portmanteau itself. He had already

---

[65] See Charity Commission, *Public Benefit and the Advancement of Religion*, February 2008, Foreword (page 3), B2 (page 4) and B6 (pages 6-7); and see Charity Commission, *Analysis of the law underpinning* Public Benefit and the Advancement of Religion, February 2008, Introduction, para 3 (page 3).

[66] [1948] AC 31, 42.

[67] Strategy Unit Report, *Private Action, Public Benefit*, 2002, para 4.18 (page 40).

[68] *Scottish Burial Reform and Cremation Society Ltd v IRC* [1968] AC 138, 150.

identified the first three heads as purposes that were beneficial to the community and then left his fourth head as 'other' purposes that were (also) for the public benefit, but without specifying them. Every purpose that the court has over the centuries identified as a charitable purpose, and which can be regarded as falling within the fourth head, has, in effect, been removed from the portmanteau and now rests on a par with the first three heads. The list of purposes held charitable within the fourth head is too long to list here; but it includes the relief of the aged, the disabled, and those in distress[69]; the provision of public works[70]; the relief of rates and taxes[71]; the provision of national and local defence and the preservation of public order[72]; the welfare of animals[73]; the promotion of agriculture[74]; the promotion of public health[75];the relief of unemployment[76]; the promotion of mental or moral improvement[77]; and faith-healing in a secular context[78]. At a conceptual level, all the specific purposes held to fall within the fourth head are for the public benefit because that is the quality they needed to possess in order to qualify as such in the first place. Such purposes have already satisfied the public-benefit test. The level playing field has therefore been present all along. When it was sought to bring new purposes within the ambit of charity, it might be said that they were merely seeking admission to the pitch.

It should now be clear that there are two different means by which an attempt can be made to show that the particular words in a governing instrument specify a charitable purpose. First, it might be argued that the words used indicate a purpose that, whilst not previously considered to be charitable, should now be treated as charitable within the residual category, which used to be the fourth head of *Pemsel* and is now the final paragraph in the list contained in section 2(2) of the Charities Act 2006. If this argument is to succeed, the court or the Commission must consider whether the purpose is for the public benefit; and (as in the *National Anti-Vivisection Society* case) the court or the Commission

---

[69] The relief of the aged and the 'impotent' is within the letter of the Preamble.

[70] *A-G v Heelis* (1824) 2 Sim & St 67.

[71] The Preamble expressly mentions 'the aid or ease of any poor inhabitants concerning payment of fifteens ... and other taxes.'

[72] The 'setting out of soldiers' is a purpose specified in the Preamble.

[73] *Re Wedgwood* [1915] 1 Ch 113.

[74] *IRC v Yorkshire Agricultural Society* [1928] 1 KB 611.

[75] *Re Resch's Will Trusts* [1969] 1 AC 514 (PC).

[76] *IRC v Oldham TEC* [1996] STC 1218.

[77] *Re Scowcroft* [1898] 2 Ch 638; *Re Hood* [1931] 1 Ch 240; *Re Price* [1943] Ch 422; *Re South Place Ethical Society* [1980] 1 WLR 1565.

[78] *Re Le Cren Clarke* [1996] 1 All ER 715.

will, in determining this, weigh (where appropriate) any perceived benefits against any perceived detriments. Secondly, it might be argued instead that the words used (in the will or other governing instrument) indicate a purpose that can be fitted into one of the recognised categories of charitable purposes[79]. If the latter approach succeeds, public benefit in the first sense is satisfied because all the recognised categories contain descriptions of purposes that have already been held, conceptually, to satisfy the public-benefit test[80]. This is why the attempt to apply the same so-called 'strong test'[81] to the first three heads of *Pemsel* (or to any of the first twelve descriptions of purposes in section 2(2)) is impossible: it is an attempt to apply for a second time the very test that has necessarily already been satisfied. Furthermore, as public benefit means the same under the Charities Act 2006 as it did immediately before 1 April 2008[82], it cannot be argued that the courts or the Commission are now entitled to look for further or additional benefits. It is already apparent that commentators are puzzling over what such benefits might be, and are revealing that there is plenty of scope for disagreement over what ranks as a benefit, how much benefit needs to be established, and how ascertained benefits are to be weighed against possible detriments[83]. To attempt to apply the public-benefit requirement as the Commission proposes to do simply because it is apparently what the government intended is

---

[79] Before 1 April 2008, the recognised categories included the first three heads of *Pemsel* and all other purposes previously held to fall within the fourth head. From that date, the recognised purposes include the purposes specified in the first twelve paragraphs of s 2(2) of the Charities Act 2006, together with all other purposes that have already been held charitable.

[80] A particularly interesting instance of where both arguments were used (successfully) was *Re Le Cren Clarke* [1996] 1 All ER 715, where charitable status was sought under both the fourth head (namely that secular faith healing should be held charitable in its own right) and under the third head, as being faith-heading in a religious context and so charitable for the advancement of religion (*Re Kerin (decd)* (1966) Times, 24 May).

[81] Referred to as such in a report from the NCVO (prepared by the charity barrister Francesca Quint) whose public-benefit recommendations the government adopted: NCVO, *For the public benefit? A consultation document on charity law reform*, NCVO, London, 2001, para 4.2.1 (page 30).

[82] Charities Act 2006, s 3(2).

[83] See, for instance, the comment of Professor Albert Weale at the Bircham Dyson Bell forum on public benefit in March 2008, reported in *Third Sector*, 2 April 2008, 28-29: 'The commission will have to take sides on what is beneficial, which, in a sense, nobody can do.' For an attempt to establish some general rules, see J Warburton, 'Charities and Public Benefit – from Confusion to Light?' (2008) 10(3) CL&PR 1. See also M Harding, 'Trusts for Religious Purposes and the Question of Public Benefit' (2008) 71 *MLR* 159.

rather like trying to build in reality one of those impossible pictures where people appear able to walk up staircases for ever without reaching the top.

The proper interpretation of section 3(2) is that it operates, in every category of charity, at an evidential level only. It refers to there being no presumption that 'any particular description' of charitable purposes is for the public benefit. The 'particular description' does not refer to the descriptions of purposes in section 2(2), but to the words of any individual will, trust instrument, or other governing document. What section 3(2) makes clear is that there is no presumption that such particular descriptions are for the public benefit. This does not, however, change the law one jot, because there has never been any evidential presumption that any particular description used in the words of any particular document is for the public benefit. As Russell J said in *Re Hummeltenberg*:

> no matter under which of the four classes a gift may *prima facie* fall, it is still, in my opinion, necessary (in order to establish that it is charitable in the legal sense) to show ... that the gift will or may be operative for the public benefit[84].

As the presumption of public benefit operates only at the conceptual level, it is untouched by section 3(2), which merely puts the position before 1 April 2008 into statutory form, and so makes no difference to public benefit in the law of charities. The conclusion must be that the Charity Commission's stance on public benefit in the advancement of religion is unsustainable. A challenge in the courts can surely be only a matter of time.

---

[84] [1923] 1 Ch 237, 240-241.

HUMAN RIGHTS AND THE CHRISTIAN TRADITION:
A QUAKER PERSPECTIVE

Frank Cranmer[1]

Introduction: Are Human Rights 'Christian'?

If people of a religious bent think systematically about human rights at all, they tend to regard them as self-evident. Moreover, if they are adherents of a faith-community within the broadly Judaeo-Christian tradition, they tend to assume that modern notions of human rights are rooted in that tradition. But even the most cursory examination of the New Testament evidence reveals attitudes that are impossible to reconcile with current thinking on human rights. 'Slaves [*douloi*], be obedient to those who are your masters according to the flesh, with fear and trembling, in the sincerity of your heart, as to Christ'[2] is only one of a number of New Testament references in a similar sense[3].

What Rowan Williams has called 'Christianity's confused and uneasy relationship with the institution of slavery'[4] was reflected in the fact that those texts were still being used to justify slavery at the time of the American Civil War. The first and only President of the Confederacy, Jefferson Davis, supported slavery as sanctioned by Scripture[5], while one of the leaders of the Southern Baptists, Dr Furman, argued that:

---

[1] An earlier and much shorter version of this paper was prepared for the Quaker Public Affairs Group in 2006. I should like to thank Michael Bartlet and Russell Sandberg for commenting on earlier drafts and Victoria Hale for casting an eye over the section on Aquinas. Any remaining defects are my responsibility. It goes without saying (but I'll say it anyway) that no single individual has any authority whatsoever to speak on behalf of the Religious Society of Friends collectively and that I take sole responsibility for the opinions expressed.

[2] Ephesians 6:5.

[3] Most obviously, the whole of Philemon; but see also, for example, Matthew 10:24–25; Colossians 3:22; 1 Timothy 6:1–2; Titus 2:9–10.

[4] R Williams, 'Religious Faith and Human Rights' – Lecture given at the London School of Economics, 1 May 2008, available at <http://www.archbishopofcanterbury.org/1780>.

[5] D Rowland, *Jefferson Davis, Constitutionalist; His Letters, Papers And Speeches* (Jackson MS, JJ Little & Ives Company, 1923) v 1 286.

> [t]he just and humane master who rules his slaves and provides for them,
> according to Christian principles, [may] rest satisfied that he is not, in hold-
> ing them, chargeable with moral evil nor with acting in this respect, con-
> trary to the genius of Christianity[6].

The fact that as late as the mid-nineteenth century anyone could seriously argue that enslaving a fellow human being might be in any way
compatible with the commandment in both the Old and New Testaments
to love your neighbour 'as yourself'[7] merely casts doubt on the suggestion that the expression 'human rights' in the modern understanding of
the term has very much at all to do with the Christian tradition.

And, perhaps surprisingly, this equivocal attitude to slavery dies
hard among those who believe in the inerrancy of Scripture. In 2003
the religious journalist Andrew Brown reported a piece in the Calvinist/
Evangelical *English Churchman* that said:

> When an institution such as slavery was abused it was eventually banned.
> However, the form it took in the Old Testament was not permanent and was
> a form of social security for which many starving people today would be
> grateful. It was never the best but an emergency help to enable those who
> had lost all they possessed to get back on their feet again[8].

So that's all right then: the slave-owners were just providing a very
early welfare-to-work scheme. Paul Sieghart suggests that:

> ... the movement for 'freedom of belief' precedes every other in the history
> of the struggle for human rights and fundamental freedoms: in Europe, for
> example, it goes back to at least the sixteenth century, if not the Roman
> Empire[9].

Not so: the various protagonists in the Reformation may have been
claiming the right to obey their own consciences but, far from there being
any general movement for 'freedom of belief', the tendency was for each
competing religious group to attempt to impose its own particular view
on everyone else. Almost all the major protagonists in the Reformation
believed that heretics would endure everlasting damnation and concluded

---

[6] Quoted in WS Jenkins, *Pro-Slavery Thought in the Old South* (Chapel Hill NC,
University of North Carolina Press, 1935) 211–212.

[7] Leviticus 19:18; Matthew 22:39.

[8] See <http://www.thewormbook.com/helminthology/archives/2003/06/16/a_truly_
reformed_social_securi.html>, and G Fraser, 'The Church of England faces a struggle
with its own Militant Tendency' (2003) *The Guardian* 14 July.

[9] P Sieghart, *The International Law of Human Rights* (Oxford, Clarendon Press, 1984)
324.

that torture in this life was but a small price for avoiding eternal misery in the next. Even after making due allowance for the fact that, as James Lloyd Carr so memorably observed, 'the Middle Ages were not us in Fancy Dress... they believed in Hellfire and the Everlasting Pit'[10], their brutality makes very uncomfortable reading for the modern student of human rights law. Rex Ahdar and Ian Leigh come to the same conclusion: 'The contemporary acceptance of religious freedom owes comparatively little to Christian theology. The historical record is a regrettable testimony to that'[11].

Even as late as the eighteenth century, the stance of the Roman Catholic Church on the issue of freedom of religion was, to put it at its most charitable, equivocal. In *Quod Aliquantum*, an Apostolic Brief of 10 March 1791 directed to the French bishops taking part in the *Assemblée Nationale*, Pius VI condemned the *Déclaration des Droits de l'Homme et du Citoyen* and the principles of freedom of religion and of expression as contrary to divine law. In a passage that is surprisingly difficult to translate, he seemed to be arguing that, in order for people to join together in civil society, a form of government was necessary under which freedom was circumscribed by the law and the supreme power of rulers; and that:

> ...from this there follows directly what St Augustine teaches, in saying, "It is a general agreement of human society to obey their own Kings". Therefore, this power does not derive as much from the social contract as from God himself, author of what is right and what is just[12]

– which looks suspiciously like Bossuet's Divine Right of Kings and certainly nothing like the modern juridical understanding of human rights.

But that is not to say that the record of many other Christian communities is any better. In Scotland, repeated attempts by the Stuarts to reimpose episcopacy led, ultimately, to the 'killing times' and the persecution of the Covenanters. In 1670 attendance and preaching at the Covenanters' dissident open-air conventicles were banned; and many died resisting

---

[10] J L Carr, *The Harpole Report* (Harmondsworth, Penguin, 1984) 131.

[11] R Ahdar and I Leigh, *Religious Freedom in the Liberal State* (Oxford, Oxford University Press, 2005) 36.

[12] '... da ciò consegue direttamente ciò che insegna Sant'Agostino dicendo: "È un patto generale della società umana ubbidire ai propri Re". Pertanto, questa potestà non deriva tanto dal contratto sociale, quanto da Dio stesso, autore del retto e del giusto.' I should like to thank The Revd Dr Robert Ombres OP for his help. His conclusion was, 'What a troubling few words: but then 18th-century constitutional vocabulary is not going to have ready modern equivalents'!

Government troops sent to suppress their worship[13]. For Presbyterians, the situation was not finally resolved until the ejection of James VII & II and the subsequent enactment of the Claim of Right in 1689[14]; but Episcopalians then suffered periods of disability in their turn, not least because they were suspected of Jacobite sympathies. At about the same time in England, the so-called Clarendon Code[15] imposed considerable disabilities on Puritans and Dissenters, while Catholic emancipation did not finally come about until the enactment of the Roman Catholic Relief Act 1829. Even then, not all disabilities on Roman Catholics – or indeed on Dissenters – were removed: the requirement of the Universities of Oxford, Cambridge and Durham for conformity to the Church of England was not abolished until the enactment of the Universities Tests Act 1871[16]. In post-Reformation Sweden, Roman Catholics were simply forbidden to profess their faith at all and converts were obliged to leave the country[17]: most notably Queen Kristina, who on becoming a Roman Catholic abdicated on 5 June 1654 and departed for Rome. The authorities also pursued a policy of enforced conformity against Dissenters through such vehicles as the Conventicle Edict [*konventikelplakat*], enacted as late as 1726, which forbade worship in private groups.

Human Rights as a Secular Construct

The Roman Catholic scholar Roger Ruston begins his study of the relationship between human rights and 'the creation of human beings in

---

[13] It is estimated that at the battle of Bothwell Bridge in 1679 Government troops killed between three and four hundred Covenanters and took over a thousand prisoner: see, for example, JG Miall, *Footsteps of Our Forefathers* (Boston MA, Gould & Lincoln, 1852) 305 and S Leathes *et al*, *Cambridge Modern History* Vol 5 (Cambridge, Cambridge University Press, 1907) 286 – both no doubt relying on Bishop Gilbert Burnet's estimate in *A History of his Own Time*.

[14] Which declared that he had 'Invaded the fundamentall Constitution of the Kingdome and altered it from a legall limited monarchy To ane arbitrary despotick power and hath Exercised the same to the subversione of the protestant religion and the violation of the lawes and liberties of the Kingdome'.

[15] Corporations Act 1661, Act of Uniformity 1662, Conventicles Act 1664, Nonconformists Act 1666 (commonly known as the Five Mile Act), Test Act 1673: JRH Moorman, *A History of the Church in England* (2nd edition, London, A & C Black, 1967) 252–253.

[16] And even after the abolition of the religious test, as late as 1910 undergraduates at Durham were still obliged to attend Sunday service in the Galilee Chapel of the Cathedral in order to 'keep term' to fulfil the residence requirements for a degree: E Jones, *University College Durham: A Social History* (Aberystwyth, Edgar Jones, 1996) 132.

[17] See, for example, N Hope, *German and Scandinavian Protestantism 1700–1918* (Oxford, Clarendon Press, 1995) 468.

the image and likeness of God'[18] by declaring that, in reality, in the two thousand years since the time of Jesus,

> ... universal human rights appears to be a novel teaching with dubious origins. The phrase, after all, has only been in popular use since the end of World War II. Certainly, the substance of the doctrine has been around for some time longer... But, in whatever form, it remains a characteristically modern idea... Christianity and other biblical religions have traditionally expressed morality in terms of doing the will of God, which does not easily translate into a language of rights[19].

Nor, it should be said, does it translate easily into a language of 'freedom of belief'; and Lord Bingham of Cornhill has argued very strongly that, far from being a product of religious sensibility, human rights are essentially secular in nature, pointing out that the freedom of thought, conscience and religion guaranteed by Article 9 of the European Convention on Human Rights (ECHR) and Article 18 of the UN Universal Declaration of Human Rights (UDHR)

> ... is a right which, historically, established religions have found it very hard to accommodate and in some places still do. The reason is not far to seek. Those who believe... that the religion to which they adhere has an exclusive perception of the truth and offers an exclusive path to salvation also tend to believe, naturally enough, both that they should resist any attempt to weaken or challenge that faith and also that they should convert others to it[20].

The Anglican theologian Nicholas Sagovsky would go even further than Bingham, suggesting that, far from being part of the Christian tradition, the notion of human rights arose

> ... in opposition to the public practice of Christianity, against oppressive notions of divine order and "divine justice"... It was only... with the publication in 1891 of *Rerum Novarum*, that the Roman Catholic Church began to promote such "rights" as an expression of human dignity, and only after the Second World War, with the founding of the World Council of Churches in 1948, that the Protestant and Orthodox Churches found a common voice in support of human rights[21].

[18] R Rushton, *Human Rights and the Image of God* (London, SCM Press, 2004) v.

[19] Ruston, *Human Rights and the Image of God* 3. Note, incidentally, his expression 'other biblical religions': does he really mean 'religions founded on sacred texts'?

[20] Lord Bingham, 'Endowed by their Creator?' (2005) 8 *Ecc LJ* 173, 181.

[21] N Sagovsky, 'Human rights, divine justice and the churches' in M Hill (ed) *Religious Liberty and Human Rights*: (Cardiff, University of Wales Press, 2002) 46 – emphasis in original.

The stance adopted by Pius VI in *Quod Aliquantum* would tend to support Sagovsky's view.

Sagovsky suggests, moreover, that in moral terms a simple declarative approach to human rights does not go far enough. He appears to adopt the argument of liberation theologians that 'the justice of God is exercised in support of those who are socially marginalized' and links this with the Jesus of Luke/Acts, who 'reaches out to the marginalized and reintegrates them within the kingdom that celebrates God's jubilee': in short, he is arguing that Christianity's bias to the poor overrides a strictly egalitarian philosophy of rights. He concludes, however, that for the churches simply to turn away from the pursuit of human rights in pursuit of an alternative agenda 'seems... little short of a betrayal of humanity in the name of religion...'[22]

It should be said that the views of Ruston, Bingham and Sagovsky are by no means undisputed. Robert McCorquodale, for example, argues that

> ... much of the legal and social discourse of human rights is grounded in Biblical material and... the language of human rights is a contemporary discourse that is consistent with the discourse and practice of Christ[23].

Of course, there is a great deal of truth in what he says, if by 'the discourse and practice of Christ' he means 'the ethical content of the teachings of Jesus as we read them today through our twenty-first century moral and cultural perceptions'. But the problem with McCorquodale's approach is that on issues such as slavery and the position of women in society he seems to accept, perhaps unconsciously, a dissonance between the message of the Jesus of the Gospels and the teaching and practice of the first-century Church. That dissonance would come as no surprise to the majority of Quakers (nor, indeed, to many on the Liberal wing of the mainstream Trinitarian churches) who would regard it as axiomatic that some aspects of the early Church, at any rate as manifested in the Epistles, were culturally-determined and seem to have only the most tenuous relationship with what we understand to be Jesus' ethical teaching. Equally, however, very many mainstream Christians, particularly (but not exclusively) those whose theology is broadly Evangelical, would firmly reject any such suggestion.

---

[22] Sagovsky, 'Human rights, divine justice and the churches' at 58, 61, 65.

[23] R McCorquodale, 'Contemporary Human Rights and Christianity' (2005) 154 *Law & Justice* 6 at 8.

Perhaps a more workable approach to grounding human rights in religious values is that of Richard Harries, who would argue that human rights are discovered in Creation itself:

> God creates and at once recognises the value of what He has created. Here is the foundation for a consciously Christian – and I would suggest also religious – approach to human rights. God makes man in His own image and respects the value of what He has created. He makes man – makes humanity, I should say – in His own image and respects its worth and dignity[24].

Human Rights, the Enlightenment and Natural Law

Bingham suggests that the key documents in the evolution of human rights are the American Declaration of Independence 1776, the *Déclaration des Droits de l'Homme et du Citoyen* 1789 and the first ten Amendments to the US Constitution adopted in 1791[25]. In short, 'human rights' are a product not of religion but of the Enlightenment.

The proponents of the Enlightenment view rested their case, at least implicitly, on a natural law approach to rights: that by the exercise of reason it could be established that human beings had certain inalienable rights as human beings. Perhaps because of that, much modern discourse on natural law and natural rights continues to be derived, to a surprising degree, from the writings of Thomas Aquinas, who believed that natural reason would direct us towards right ends because human nature is rational nature[26]. Aquinas appears to be thinking in terms of four types of law:

i.   the eternal law that is God's plan for us all and which only God can know[27];

ii. the natural law derived from the eternal law through the exercise of right reason by the rational person[28];

---

[24] R Harries, 'The Complimentarity between Secular and Religious Perspectives of Human Rights' in N Ghanea-Hercock, A Stephens and R Walden (eds), *Does God Believe in Human Rights? Essays on Religion and Human Rights* (Leiden, Martinus Nijhoff, 2007) 21.

[25] Bingham 'Endowed by their Creator?' at 183. Somewhat surprisingly, he does not mention Tom Paine's *The Rights of Man* published in 1791–92.

[26] See, for example, J Finnis, *Natural Law and Natural Rights* (Oxford, Clarendon Press, 1980).

[27] *The Summa Theologica of St Thomas Aquinas translated by the Fathers of the English Dominican Province* (London, Burns, Oates & Washburne Ltd, 1912–1936) *Prima Secundae Partis* Q 93 Art 1.

[28] *Summa Theologica Prima Secundae Partis* Q 93 Art 3.

iii. the law derived from natural principles: for example, that one must not kill because one should do no harm[29]; and

iv. general principles for the guidance of legislators: that law should foster religion, that it should be helpful to discipline, and that it should further the common good[30].

The problem with the scholastics' approach, however, is that even when considered on its own terms it is open to two objections.

The first is purely theological. As Richard Harries observes, 'Protestants have been suspicious of [natural law] because they believe that, unaided by God's grace, we haven't a real capacity to discern right from wrong'[31]. But even considered in its own terms, there seems to be a fundamental problem here: if, as Aquinas seems to suggest, rational humanity tends to pursue right ends, then to what purpose was the Incarnation? And the obvious counter-argument – that human nature is, at root, morally sound – comes dangerously close to the Pelagian heresy about the perfectibility of humanity that Aquinas himself would have immediately rejected. In short, there seems to be something of a mismatch between the concept of 'natural law' and the concept of 'original sin'.

The second is this: if the natural law can be deduced by the exercise of reason alone, why is there so much evidence to suggest that, in the real world, rational people disagree about legal principles? For example, while it is a basic principle of the English law of contract that (unless executed under seal) a contract is only enforceable if it includes an element of consideration on each side, the concept of consideration is alien to the Scots law of obligations and under certain circumstances a unilateral promise can be binding. If the governing principle of contractual obligations in England is quid pro quo, in Scotland it is 'my word is my bond.'[32] One cannot help wondering how two mature – and adjacent – jurisdictions can have arrived at quite such opposite conclusions. At a much more fundamental level, while there is probably a majority consensus that adultery is socially undesirable, different jurisdictions categorise

---

[29] Ibid Q 95 Art 2.

[30] Ibid Q 95 Art 3.

[31] Harries, 'The Complimentarity between Secular and Religious Perspectives of Human Rights' at 22.

[32] The binding nature of a unilateral promise that is not conditional on acceptance by the other party was reiterated by Lord President Hamilton (relying on Stair's *Institutions*) in *Ilona and Ors v Vaughan* 2007 CS IH 3 at para 15: 'It is undoubted that the law of Scotland will recognise as obligatory a promise duly made. Delivery to or acceptance by the promisee is not necessary to the constitution of a promise'.

it in different ways: as a criminal offence (for example, in Saudi Arabia), as a civil wrong (the position in Ireland until 1996[33]), or as an activity which, while not unlawful per se, is adequate evidence of marital breakdown for the purpose of divorce proceedings (England and Wales). And on what are generally regarded as matters of morality it is possible for different communities even in the same state to come to quite different conclusions: genital activity in private between consenting males over the age of twenty ceased to be an offence in England and Wales in 1967 while remaining a crime in Northern Ireland for a further fifteen years[34].

Human Rights as a Product of Moral Norms?

If human rights are not based on traditional Biblical teaching or natural law, on what can they be based? The most obvious answer would seem to be that they are founded on current moral norms. But the difficulty with this approach is that different societies have developed moral norms that are sometimes so different from each other as to be almost completely contradictory. Jacqueline Laing suggests that though the language of rights is as familiar now in common parlance as it is to academic lawyers, '...at the same time, in the post Judaeo-Christian West there has never been less belief in or acceptance of moral objectivity'[35].

It requires very little effort to find evidence to support her view: compare and contrast, for example, Malta (where there is no provision for civil divorce) with Sweden or the United States (which still executes those convicted of murder) with Canada. Moreover, even within the same society moral norms will change over time. Perhaps most starkly, when the American Founding Fathers averred that 'all men are created equal, that they are endowed by their Creator with certain unalienable Rights, that among these are Life, Liberty and the pursuit of Happiness' it simply did not occur to them that their Creator might have intended to bestow those blessings on Native and Black Americans as well as on white Anglo-Saxon Protestants.

---

[33] 'No fault' divorce was introduced by the Family Law (Divorce) Act 1996; but that Act could only be put on the statute book after the Constitutional prohibition on divorce had been lifted by the Fifteenth Amendment of the Constitution Act 1995.

[34] Sexual Offences (Amendment) Act 1967 s 1: Homosexual Offences (Northern Ireland) Order 1982.

[35] J Laing, 'A certain kind of moral scepticism and the foundations of human rights' (2006) 157 *Law & Justice* 39.

In a sermon in Durham Cathedral in 2006, Joseph Cassidy, a Canadian Anglican social ethicist, offered what seems to be a useful insight into the issue of changing moral norms[36]. He suggests that the story of the encounter between Jesus and the Syro-Phoenician woman in Mark 7:25–30 and Matthew 15:21–28 shows us that:

> ... we must sometimes change our minds on ethical issues because the good keeps changing on us... the moral good is not set in stone. The moral good, what I really and truly ought to do, this changes in time, across cultures, within religions, even within a communion of autonomous local churches, and not necessarily at the same rate or in the same way everywhere.

This, suggests Cassidy, is because we can only see as far as we can see and imagine what we are capable of imagining. New 'goods' emerge as we become capable of discerning them:

> The real moral challenge is not just to do the eternally preordained right thing, but to set up the conditions, the structures, so that new and better things become imaginable, become conceivable, and so become do-able. This is the key to the 'common good' tradition, the justice tradition, which was so strong in twentieth-century Roman Catholic social teaching.

It is precisely because we are capable of imagining 'new and better things' that moral norms change over time. Even Western liberal democracies like England, Scotland and the Nordic countries that once regarded themselves as 'Christian' have moved away from – or at least reinterpreted – what might have been regarded fifty years ago as 'Christian principles'. In the United Kingdom, corporal punishment in schools has been outlawed; previous generations held to the principle 'spare the rod, spoil the child' which they derived from Proverbs 13:24 and 23:13–14. As noted above, homosexual acts between consenting adult males were a criminal offence in England and Wales until 1967; we now have the Civil Partnership Act 2004 which, though controversial in some quarters, reflects the majority view that same-sex couples should not be disadvantaged in matters such as tax and succession[37]. On the other hand, the enactment of the Company Securities (Insider Dealing) Act 1985 in response to a series of major financial scandals criminalised an activity

---

[36] J Cassidy, 'Who's in and who's out?' in MD Chapman (ed), *Living the Magnificat: Affirming Catholicism in a Broken World* (London, Darton, Longman & Todd, 2007) 105–106,108. A text is available at <http://prodigal.typepad.com/prodigal_kiwi/files/joseph_cassidy_whos_in_and_whos_out_a_sermon.pdf>.

[37] See Mark Hill's contribution to this volume.

that had been previously regarded simply as prudent business practice and (possibly) as the exercise of one's unrestricted right to use one's personal property.

A British Bill of Rights?

It has been assumed that in order to be fully effective, rights need to be enshrined in some kind of basic law that binds public authorities – which is why the ECHR has been a relatively useful tool for enforcement. However, in 2006 it was proposed that United Kingdom adherence to the ECHR should be supplemented, or even possibly replaced, with a 'British Bill of Rights'; and that proposal has attracted a certain amount of support from across the political spectrum.

The original proposal was made by the Leader of the Opposition, David Cameron, who argued for domestic legislation to:

> ... protect the fundamental rights set out in the European Convention ... in clearer and more precise terms. Greater clarity and precision would allow those rights to be enforced more easily and effectively in circumstances where they ought to be protected but it would become harder to extend them inappropriately as under the present law. Greater clarity and precision in the law, as opposed to vague general principles, which can be interpreted in many different ways, is more in accordance with this country's legal tradition[38].

Cameron's theme was then taken up by his Shadow Attorney-General, Dominic Grieve, who suggested that a new Bill of Rights, while remaining compliant with the ECHR, would offer an opportunity to define Convention rights more clearly and precisely and would provide guidance to the judiciary and government in their application. He also believed that it would stimulate a national debate on the core values in the area of civil liberties that need to be protected and that it could provide a definition of common values of which all British citizens, from whatever background, could feel ownership[39].

---

[38] 'Balancing freedom and security – a modern British Bill of Rights (London, 26 June 2006); available at <http://www.cps.org.uk/search/default.asp>. When Cameron talked of 'this country's legal tradition', I wonder whether he was mindful of the fact that the legal tradition of Scotland is rather different from the legal tradition of England? Answers on a postcard...

[39] 'Liberty and community in Britain' (London, 2 October 2006), available at <http://www.dominicgrieve.org.uk/record.jsp?type=speech&id=67>.

It should be said that, initially, the Cameron-Grieve proposal was not greeted with total unanimity even among members of the Conservative Opposition – Kenneth Clarke, Chairman of the party's Democracy Task Force, dismissed the idea as 'xenophobic and legal nonsense'[40] – but many others felt that it represented a serious and thoughtful attempt to grapple with the inevitable uncertainties of a jurisprudence that operates on very general principles. The problem, however, is that it is difficult to see how, realistically, one *can* go much beyond broad statements of principle in defining Convention rights, since it would be quite impossible to provide a series of detailed prescriptions directed at every conceivable circumstance in which a right might be traversed.

To return to Article 6: whether or not a particular court judging a particular set of facts on a particular day constitutes 'a fair and public hearing within a reasonable time by an independent and impartial tribunal established by law' does not depend entirely on the court's powers and constitution but, at least in part, on whether its members are perceived as behaving fairly and impartially in the instant case. It was precisely that consideration which led the (Scottish) Court of Criminal Appeal, in *Hoekstra and Ors v HM Advocate (No 2)*[41], to exercise the *nobile officium* to set aside an interlocutor of a differently-constituted bench of the same court and direct a retrial. After the diet at which the original interlocutor had been pronounced Lord McCluskey, one of the judges at that hearing, had published an article in Scotland on Sunday in which he described the ECHR as 'a field day for crackpots, a pain in the neck for judges and legislators, and a goldmine for lawyers'[42]. This, the bench at the subsequent hearing concluded, might have led the accused to believe that his Lordship was biased against claims based on Convention rights and the hearing was therefore unsatisfactory in terms of Article 6. As to the more general matter of public perceptions of impartiality, in *Starrs and Chalmers v Ruxton*[43], the Court of Criminal Appeal held that the practice whereby the Lord Advocate appointed temporary sheriffs for a term of one year under section 11 of the Sheriff Courts (Scotland) Act 1971 was not compatible with Article 6(1) of the Convention because

---

[40] R Sylvester, 'Has Cameron thought it through or is he just thinking aloud?'(2006) *Daily Telegraph* 27 June <http://www.telegraph.co.uk/opinion/main.jhtml?xml=/opinion/2006/06/27/do2701.xml>.

[41] 2000 SCCR 367; 2000 SLT 605: see especially Lord Justice General Rodger at SLT 610–611.

[42] In *Scotland on Sunday* (2000) 6 February.

[43] 1999 GWD 37.

those so appointed did not present a sufficient appearance of judicial independence from Government[44].

While Cameron makes an entirely reasonable point about the need for 'greater clarity and precision', whether a new Bill of Rights would provide a more secure basis for the European Court of Human Rights to give a similar margin of appreciation to decisions of the United Kingdom courts as it gives to decisions of the German courts is at least arguable. There is a crucial difference between the two jurisdictions: rights are firmly entrenched in Chapter 1 of the German Basic Law [*Grundgesetz*], while the United Kingdom has no completely tamper-proof method of entrenching legislation – though it should be said that in *Jackson and Ors v HM Attorney General* Lord Steyn seemed to be willing to contemplate the idea of foundational constitutional principles 'which even a sovereign Parliament acting at the behest of a complaisant House of Commons cannot abolish'[45].

Where 'greater clarity and precision' are undoubtedly needed, however, is in the interpretation that individual officials place on the Act and the Convention in their day-to-day dealings. In his Harry Street Lecture in February 2007, the then Lord Chancellor, Lord Falconer of Thoroton, launched a Government campaign entitled 'Human Rights: Common Values, Common Sense'. Commenting on a report that a man evading arrest by taking refuge on the roof of a house had apparently been supplied by the Gloucestershire Police with cigarettes, drink and food, he ridiculed the alleged remarks of a spokeswoman for the force that 'although he's a nuisance, we still have to look after his wellbeing and human rights'. Whether or not meeting the man's demands would make it easier to end the stand-off, said Falconer, was a matter for the professional judgment of the police – but the idea that the suspect had any such human rights was 'nonsense'[46].

Falconer's answer was 'common sense':

---

[44] On the other hand, an Extra Division of the Inner House of the Court of Session held that the fact that Lady Cosgrove was a member of the International Association of Jewish Lawyers and Jurists did not give rise to any real possibility that she might be biased in determining the application of the petitioner (a Palestinian) for leave to appeal against the decision of an Immigration Tribunal: *Helow v Advocate General for Scotland & Anor* [2007] CS IH 5 (16 January): <http://www.bailii.org/scot/cases/scotcs/2007/csih_5.html>.

[45] [2005] UKHL 56 at para 102.

[46] 'Human rights and common sense' (Manchester, 9 February 2007) para 38, available at <http://www.dca.gov.uk/speeches/2007/sp070209.htm>.

[F]rom time to time, in any area, a human rights problem will occur. When it does, those dealing with it need to adopt a common sense approach. Yes, they need to apply the law. But my argument is that the law, the Human Rights Act, is common sense. So when they do apply the law, they must then be applying common sense. And coming up with a common sense answer to their human rights problem[47].

Well, up to a point, Lord Falconer, if we take it as axiomatic that people can always recognise a 'common sense solution' when they see one; but even if they can, an appeal to 'common sense' can sometimes prove of very little practical help in resolving an argument about the Act or the Convention.

In *Aston Cantlow*[48] the conclusion of the Court of Appeal that an Anglican Parochial Church Council was a public authority for the purposes of the Act might have seemed 'common sense'; but the House of Lords took the opposite view – and in doing so, suggests Augur Pearce, overturned 'basic assumptions which have characterised England's religious constitution since, if not from before, Tudor times'[49]. Similarly, 'common sense' might suggest that in a democratic country governed by the rule of law a properly-constituted criminal court of senior judges would be a fair and impartial tribunal for the purposes of Article 6 of the Convention – but that is not what was decided in *Hoekstra*. Or turning specifically to Article 9, two disputes over the wearing of religious dress in schools[50] have involved careful appraisal by the courts of the dress-code of the schools in question, their degree of accommodation to the religious requirements of students and how all that related to the wider interests of the school community. Neither case was simple; indeed, in *Begum* the House of Lords reversed the Court of Appeal – which had, in turn, reversed the trial judge.

The argument about a new domestic Bill of Rights has been taken up once more and this time by the Government, though in a rather different form from the original proposal by David Cameron. In a lecture in 2007 in Cambridge, the Lord Chancellor, Jack Straw, dismissed any suggestion

---

[47] Falconer para 61. In the course of a 5,000-word lecture he used the expression 'common sense' 21 times.

[48] *Parochial Church Council of the Parish of Aston Cantlow and Wilmcote with Billesley, Warwickshire v Wallbank and Anor* [2003] UKHL 37; [2004] 1 AC 546.

[49] A Pearce, '*Aston Cantlow*: Chancel Repairs and the Status of Church of England Institutions' (2003) *Law & Justice* 151.

[50] *R (On the application of Begum) v Headteacher and Governors of Denbigh High School* [2006] UKHL 15 (relating to the *jilbab*) and *R (On the application of X) v Y School* [2007] EWHC 298 (Admin) (relating to the *niqab* veil).

that simply repealing the Human Rights Act 1988 and enacting a new domestic Bill of Rights in its place would lead to a greater margin of appreciation in Strasbourg. However, he suggested that there was a danger that rights

> ... become commoditised, yet more items to be "claimed". This is demonstrated in how some people seek to exercise their rights in a selfish way without regard to others – which injures the philosophical basis of inalienable, fundamental human rights. Alongside that, some people resent the rights that are afforded to fellow humankind: we see this is in the media uproar around human rights being a terrorist's charter or there for the benefit of minorities alone[51].

He told his audience that he would be working closely with the Review of Citizenship being conducted by the former Attorney General, Lord Goldsmith, to look at how British Bill of Rights and Responsibilities might help to foster a stronger sense of citizenship by establishing and articulating the balance between rights and the obligations.

Straw returned to the theme in a speech in Washington DC during which he pondered the desirability of a written Constitution. Reiterating his unhappiness at the idea of rights as commodities, he noted that there could not be:

> ... an exact symmetry between rights and responsibilities. In a democracy, rights tend to be "vertical": guaranteed to the individual by the state to constrain the otherwise overweening power of the state. Responsibilities, on the other hand, are more "horizontal": they are the duties we owe to each other, to our 'neighbour' in the New Testament sense. But they have a degree of verticality about them too, because we owe duties to the community as a whole[52].

He also emphasised that, in seeking to clarify relations between the citizen, the state and the community, legislators had to be careful about the scope and extent of their justiciability, agreeing with Lord Bingham that the importance of predictability in the law precluded 'excessive innovation and adventurism by the judges'. Justiciability was not the only purpose of human rights legislation:

> If, for instance, economic and social rights were part of our new Bill, but did not become further justiciable, this would not in any way make the exercise

---

[51] 'Mackenzie-Stuart Lecture' (Cambridge, 25 October 2007), available at <http://www.justice.gov.uk/news/sp251007a.htm>.

[52] 'Modernising the Magna Carta' (Washington, DC, 13 February 2008) available at <http://www.justice.gov.uk/news/sp130208a.htm>.

worthless... As the jurist Philip Alston described, Bills of Rights are "a combination of law, symbolism and aspiration". What he makes clear is that the formulation of such a Bill is not a simple binary choice between a fully justiciable text on the one hand, or a purely symbolic text on the other. There is a continuum. And it is entirely consistent that some broad declarative principles can be underpinned by statute. Where we end up on this continuum needs to be the subject of the widest debate.

On the following day, in a speech at Lincoln's Inn, Straw's Junior Minister, Michael Wills, reiterated much of what his boss had said, made reference to the Government's proposal for a Constitutional Renewal Bill and added a third element: 'the formulation of a British Statement of Values... to find a way to express who we believe ourselves to be in a way that is inclusive and commands broad support'[53].

Rights, Duties and Community: a 'Neighbour Principle'?

As suggested by Straw, rights normally imply duties; and even though rights and duties are not always symmetrical, common law jurisdictions tend to assume that, in practice, a right inhering in one legal person will usually imply a corresponding duty on another – even if is a duty to refrain from doing something rather than a positive duty to act in a particular way. So if, for example, I have an easement/servitude in respect of someone else's land, the occupier of that land has a duty not to obstruct me in the exercise of my right of way.

In a common law context it is almost inevitable that individuals will conflict with each other in the exercise of private rights and it is ultimately for the courts to adjudicate those conflicts. But the dichotomy between rights and duties is not necessarily absolute. Significantly, the Roman Catholic *Codex Iuris Canonici 1983* always speaks of 'duties and rights' rather than 'rights and duties'[54]. The Roman Catholic model does not proceed exclusively from the common law assumption that if A has a right, B has a corresponding duty since, in addition, the *Codex* assumes that a right may imply a duty subsisting in the same person. In the social theology of *Pacem in Terris*, for example,

---

[53] 'The constitutional reform programme' (London, 14 February 2008), available at <http://www.justice.gov.uk/news/sp120208a.htm>.

[54] For example, Canon 96: 'By baptism one is incorporated into the Church of Christ and constituted a person in it, with the duties and the rights [*officiis et iuribus*] which, in accordance with each one's status, are proper to Christians...'.

... man's awareness of his rights must inevitably lead him to the recognition of his duties. The possession of rights involves the duty of implementing those rights, for they are the expression of a man's personal dignity[55].

So, for example, the right to free speech implies the duty to speak truth rather than falsehood and to do so with circumspection[56]. This linking of duties and rights is rather different from the common law idea of 'playing your hand': 'I'll give you a right if you'll give me a duty'. Moreover, many of the world's major religions seem to lay more stress on the duties of the faithful than they do on rights: for example, the Christian commandment to love your neighbour, the obligatory nature of almsgiving [*zakat*] in Islam and the multiplicity of rules for the relief of the poor in Judaism[57]. If there is a dichotomy between law and religion on the question of human rights it is because, in pursuing them, law and religion have different ends in view.

For British Quakers the ultimate authority is Britain Yearly Meeting in session, responsible *inter alia* for setting the direction of the central work of the Society, one of the four strands of which is:

> ... raising awareness and developing understanding within and without Britain Yearly Meeting about the basic tenets of Quaker faith and practice, such as spirituality, peace and human rights[58].

Friends, on the whole, tend to give systematic theology a fairly wide berth: birthright Friends because most of them have never been exposed to it and Friends who came into the Society from other religious communities because they frequently joined the Society to get away from it. Perhaps as a result of this, they are possibly more inclined than some other religious groups to seek agreement with each other over the broad range of issues facing them rather than conducting internal arguments based on *a priori* theological positions. But Friends are by no means monochrome in their views and what 'human rights' might mean for them in practice is by no means self-explanatory. Not only might a human rights

---

[55] AG Roncalli [Pope John XXIII], *Pacem in Terris* para 44 (1963) *Acta Apostolicae Sedis* 55 257–304.

[56] For example, Canon 218 declares that 'Those who are engaged in the sacred disciplines enjoy a lawful freedom of inquiry and of prudently expressing their opinions on matters in which they have expertise, while observing a due respect for the teaching [*magisterium*] of the Church.'

[57] As well as almsgiving the obligation, for example, to leave the corners of fields [*peah*] and gleanings for the poor.

[58] *Quaker Faith and Practice* (London, Britain Yearly Meeting of the Religious Society of Friends, 2005) para 8.02: hereinafter *QF&P*.

lawyer and a Quaker take different views of what might be included in a definitive list of 'human rights', a random selection of Friends might not necessarily find themselves in total agreement either.

Though, perhaps surprisingly, the expression 'human rights' occurs very rarely in *Quaker Faith and Practice*, there are many passages in which rights provide the underlying theme. London Yearly Meeting's *Foundations of a True Social Order*, adopted during the First World War, contains more than a hint, if not of utopianism, then at least of Christian Socialism:

i. The Fatherhood of God, as revealed by Jesus Christ, should lead us toward a brotherhood which knows no restriction of race, sex or social class.

ii. This brotherhood should express itself in a social order which is directed, beyond all material ends, to the growth of personality truly related to God and man.

iii. The opportunity of full development, physical, moral and spiritual, should be assured to every member of the community, man, woman and child. The development of man's full personality should not be hampered by unjust conditions nor crushed by economic pressure.

iv. We should seek for a way of living that will free us from the bondage of material things and mere conventions, that will raise no barrier between man and man, and [that] will put no excessive burden of labour upon any by reason of our superfluous demands.

v. The spiritual force of righteousness, loving-kindness and trust is mighty because of the appeal it makes to the best in every man, and when applied to industrial relations achieves great things.

vi. Our rejection of the methods of outward domination, and of the appeal to force, applies not only to international affairs, but to the whole problem of industrial control. Not through antagonism but through co-operation and goodwill can the best be obtained for each and all.

vii. Mutual service should be the principle upon which life is organised. Service, not private gain, should be the motive of all work.

viii. The ownership of material things, such as land and capital, should be so regulated as best to minister to the need and development of man[59].

---

[59] *QF&P* 23.16. London Yearly Meeting was the predecessor to Britain Yearly Meeting.

Although the majority of Friends would probably support most of its sentiments, this statement reads very much as the child of its time. A more modern Quaker formulation – and one that almost every Friend would accept without question – is simply this: 'People matter. In the end human rights are about people being treated and feeling like people who matter'.[60]

Part of the role of religion is to locate rights in the context of relationships: not as an impersonal, prescriptive code but as a moral imperative towards the recognition of what Quakers would claim to be 'that of God in every person' – a position that is not a million miles away from the scholastics' *imago Dei* approach to human rights that Roger Ruston traces back at least to Augustine of Hippo and which, he suggests,

> ... owes little to secular Enlightenment sources and everything to an enduring religious tradition shared by both Catholics and Protestants, even though not consistently practised by them[61].

Moreover, in practical terms the majority of Friends would probably wish to locate rights as much in community relationships as in individual ones, which is why they have been very active over such issues as the cancellation of Third World debt, the Make Poverty History campaign and, though less well-known, the Ecumenical Accompaniment Programme in Israel-Palestine[62].

In *Donoghue v Stevenson*[63] Lord Atkin, referring back to the parable of the Good Samaritan[64], answered the question 'Who then in law is my neighbour?' as:

> persons who are so closely and directly affected by my act that I ought reasonably to have them in contemplation as being so affected when I am directing my mind to the acts or omissions which are called in question[65].

Has this anything to say to us in the context of how we seek to exercise our rights? In asserting our own rights, how far may we go before we begin to conflict with the rights of others? Does the principle enunciated

---

[60] *QF&P* 24.49.

[61] Ruston, *Human Rights and the Image of God* at 270 – emphasis added.

[62] For which the UK coordinator is Quaker Peace and Social Witness.

[63] [1932] AC 532.

[64] Luke 10:25-37.

[65] At 580. This was subsequently modified by *Caparo Industries Plc v Dickman and others* [1990] 1 All ER 568; [1990] 2 WLR 358 into a three-stage test: that the damage is foreseeable, that there is a relationship of proximity or neighbourhood and that the situation is such that it would be fair, just and reasonable that the law should impose a duty of a given scope on one party for the benefit of the other.

by Lord Atkin imply, potentially at least, an element of the 'duties and rights' approach of the *Codex*? For example, is there (or should there be?) some moral limitation on the right to the peaceful enjoyment of possessions under Article 1 of the First Protocol to the ECHR, if unrestricted 'peaceful enjoyment' means that the rich flourish at the expense of the poor? Or consider the issue that probably causes the greatest degree of contention within the Society of Friends, albeit contention of a very polite, Quakerly kind: the continued existence of fee-charging Friends' Schools. Does the right of parents under Article 2 of the Protocol (on the right to education) '... to ensure such education and teaching in conformity with their own religions and philosophical convictions' include the right to run fee-paying, independent faith-schools that, coincidentally, tend to confer a degree of social privilege on their pupils?

Even more challenging are some of the rights espoused by the UDHR, for example: 'the right to work, to free choice of employment, to just and favourable conditions of work and to protection against unemployment' (Article 23), 'the right to rest and leisure including reasonable limitation of working hours and periodic holidays with pay' (Article 24) and 'the right to a standard of living adequate for the health and well-being.., including food, clothing, housing and medical care and necessary social services, and the right to security in the event of unemployment, sickness, disability, widowhood, old age or other lack of livelihood...' (Article 25). Clearly, the only means by which every person on the planet could have the faintest hope of enjoying any of these rights, even at the most modest level, would by the rich acquiescing in a massive shift of resources to the poor: the 'neighbour principle' carried over into affirmative action on a grand scale.

In 2007 the Government experienced intense internal conflict over the refusal of Roman Catholic adoption agencies to place children with same-sex couples and the right of those couples to equal treatment under the Equality Act 2006[66]. Cabinet ministers weighed in on both sides of the argument, until the then Prime Minister announced on 29 January 2007 that the forthcoming Regulations under the Act would not give any exemption on religious grounds to faith-based adoption agencies but that there would be a transitional period until the end of 2008, coupled with a statutory obligation on any publicly-funded agency that would not process applications from same-sex couples to refer them to and agency

---

[66] See further Pauline Robert's contribution to this volume.

that would do so[67]. There appeared to be two conflicting rights here: the right to respect for private and family life[68] and the right to freedom of thought, conscience and religion[69].

Most of the discussion centred on the conflict between the view of same-sex couples hoping to adopt and the adoption agencies; but relatively little was said about the position of the children hoping to be adopted. Taking a 'rights in community' approach, Friends would probably want to put the greater degree of emphasis on the position of those children; and many would draw attention to the statement in the Preamble to the UN Convention on the Rights of the Child that 'the child, for the full and harmonious development of his or her personality, should grow up in a family environment, in an atmosphere of happiness, love and understanding'. But, that said, by what mechanism might a child who is currently looked after by a local authority assert that right in practice?

Similarly, the approach adopted by Lady Hale in *ex parte Williamson* was a carefully-argued attempt to balance the right of parents to administer 'carefully controlled, mild and loving discipline' to their children 'in the context of a clear moral code'[70] against a huge body of opinion, both among human rights specialists and educationalists, that corporal punishment in schools was neither an effective deterrent to bad behaviour nor without attendant psychological harm to the child. On that occasion she opted for something very much like a 'rights in community' approach, concluding that the rights of individual parents had to be subordinated to the views of 'the bodies charged with monitoring our compliance with the obligations which we have undertaken to respect the dignity of the individual and the rights of children'[71]. Lady Hale took a similar stance in *R (On the Application of Begum) v Headteacher and Governors of Denbigh High School*[72], preferring the interests of the community as a whole – in this case, the school – to the individual preference of a Muslim pupil

---

[67] See <http://www.pm.gov.uk/output/page10869.asp>. The Equality Act (Sexual Orientation) Regulations 2007 (SI/2007/1263) as finally made provided in Regulation 14 a religious exemption for organisations the purpose of which is to practice a religion or belief; but the Roman Catholic adoption agencies could not rely on this, since under Regulation 14(8) in combination with Regulations 4 and 8 the religious exemption was lost if the organisation contracted with a public authority.

[68] ECHR Article 8.

[69] ECHR Article 9.

[70] At para 77.

[71] At para 84.

[72] [2006] UKHL 15.

who wanted to wear the long *jilbab* coat. She stressed the importance of a uniform school dress-code in fostering a sense of community and cohesion within the school and 'smoothing over ethnic, religious and social divisions'[73], while noting that strict dress codes might be imposed upon women by others, denying them the freedom to choose for themselves[74].

Conclusion: A Quaker Positivism?

The problem with broad appeals to morality and to common humanity is that it is axiomatic that you cannot make people 'good' by legislation and, in any case, legal systems seek largely to regulate behaviour in terms of outcomes – acts or omissions – rather than in terms of moral intent. Some actions of animal rights activists, for example, have been undertaken for reasons that the perpetrators regarded as entirely moral: but they have nevertheless resulted in criminal sanctions because in English law criminal damage is criminal damage, largely irrespective of motive. Similarly, as the Revd Clive Blake found out when he told a court that it was on the instructions of God that he had written an anti-war slogan on a concrete pillar, saying 'God made me do it' is no defence[75].

That there has been a decisive shift in public policy-making from Judaeo-Christian ethics to a common moral paradigm should certainly not present Friends with any particular problem – whatever difficulties it may cause for certain other religious groups. But for all of us, religiously-inclined or not, whether or not the concept of human rights is rooted in the Christian tradition is largely irrelevant *because there is no going back*. Surely no right-thinking person would want, for example, tribunals that were not 'fair and impartial' within the terms of Article 6 of the Convention. And if, for some obscure reason, someone did want tribunals that were partial and unfair, to what conceivable Judaeo-Christian principle could that person appeal for support? The result of the paradigm shift is that, in practice, human rights in the United Kingdom are those rights enshrined in the Human Rights Act 1988 and the ECHR: no more, no less. In United Kingdom law, human rights are essentially positivist; and I would contend that this is both reasonable and proportionate, for three reasons.

---

[73] At para 97.
[74] At para 95.
[75] *Blake v DPP* [1993] Crim LR 586. See also R Sandberg and N Doe, 'Religious exemptions in discrimination law' (2007) 66 *CLJ* 302–312.

First, society can only recognise rights when it has agreed what those rights are and, in a society governed by the rule of law, that agreement is often then expressed in legislation of some kind. So, for example, Article 40 §3 (3) of *Bunreacht na hÉireann* [the Constitution of Ireland] declares that the State:

> ... acknowledges the right to life of the unborn and, with due regard to the equal right to life of the mother, guarantees in its laws to respect and, as far as practicable, by its laws to defend and vindicate that right.

However, in a society where there are deep divisions between those who assert 'the woman's right to choose' and those who hold that the destruction of human life is in all cases wrong it is simply not possible to create an all-embracing 'right to life'.

Secondly, in any particular set of circumstances individuals may claim rights that conflict with each other. How their competing claims are to be resolved is certainly a matter for the courts – but the broader contextual issue is also a matter for the wider community. Unless the exercise of religion is to be given primacy over every other right, society as a whole needs to take a view as to how far the right freely to exercise one's religion can be unfettered. Malcolm Evans has suggested that in Western liberal democracy religious liberty, rather than being seen as inviolable, is subordinated to a pluralist human rights framework, with the result that 'religious belief becomes acceptable only to the extent that it poses no challenge to the accepted orthodoxies of that framework'[76]. From a Quaker perspective, the exercise of religion within a more general framework of rights and duties would seem to be perfectly proper: so, for example, when the Farm Animal Welfare Council's recommended that slaughter without prior stunning should be banned, it seemed entirely reasonable to most Friends that the Government should reject the proposal because 'we respect the rights of communities in Britain to slaughter animals in accordance with the requirements of their religion'[77].

However, it is almost impossible to be totally consistent about what kinds of behaviour should be regarded as acceptable in the name of religion and what should not. Unless the exercise of religion is to be given primacy over every other right, society as a whole needs to take a view as to how far the right freely to exercise one's religion can be unfettered.

---

[76] M Evans, 'Religion, law and human rights: locating the debate' in P W Edge and G Harvey (eds), *Law and Religion in Contemporary Society* (Aldershot, Ashgate, 2000) 182.

[77] HC Deb (2004–05) c 837W.

Rowan Williams observes that fundamental issues of human rights

> ... blend with reasonable contractual expectations in a confusing way, and the idea of a list of entitlements dropped, as it were, into the cradle of each individual is deeply vulnerable to the charge of arbitrariness[78].

Unfortunately, the act of deciding whether or not a particular religious obligation should be recognised is itself somewhat arbitrary. The provision of *sharia*-compliant financial instruments in order to meet the needs of observant Muslims would be regarded by most people as a perfectly acceptable accommodation to Islamic religious requirements, while a proposal to exempt Rastafarians from the ban on the possession or use of marijuana might be regarded as less so, given the debate about its possible effects on mental health. Ill-informed though many of his critics might have been, the furore over Archbishop Rowan's lecture in February 2007 in which he suggested, very tentatively, that there might be a place for a limited recognition of *sharia* in respect of marriage and the law of succession highlighted the enormous sensitivities around the relationship between religious and secular law[79]. It is self-evident that just because something is done in the name of religion that does not mean that it is necessarily right, still less that it should be normative for everyone else: as stark an example as any of religion gone horribly wrong was the fate of the Branch Davidians in Waco, Texas, in 1993. But equally, it is not difficult to understand why different faith-groups might wish to challenge the liberal secular consensus.

Thirdly, the primary purpose of human rights legislation is normally to give the citizen redress against public authorities rather than against each other; and it is against public authorities specifically that the 1998 Act provides a remedy for breach of Convention rights[80]. Precisely what constitutes a 'public authority' for the purposes of enforcement can sometimes be open to question[81]; and in 2007 the Ministry of Justice held a consultation on the extent to which the provisions of the Freedom of Information Act 2000 might be extended to non-Government bodies that undertake quasi-public functions[82]. But except as an aspiration, the

---

[78] RD Williams, 'Religious Faith and Human Rights'.

[79] 'Civil and religious law in England: a religious perspective' (London, 7 February 2008) available at <http://www.archbishopofcanterbury.org/1575>.

[80] S 6(1): 'It is unlawful for a public authority to act in a way which is incompatible with a Convention right'.

[81] See *Aston Cantlow*.

[82] Ministry of Justice: *Freedom of Information Act 2000: Designation of additional public authorities* (London, Ministry of Justice, 2007) <http://www.justice.gov.uk/docs/cp2707.pdf>.

concept of 'human rights' is often simply not very relevant to the day-to-day operation of private law. If my neighbour erects a new fence that encroaches on part of my garden or if someone owes me money and refuses to pay, my most obvious remedy is to sue at common law. On the other hand, if the local authority appropriates my land *ultra vires* and without due process or if Her Majesty's Revenue and Customs overestimates my tax liability and refuses to refund the excess, it may be more effective for me to rely on the right to peaceful enjoyment of possessions under Article 1 of the First Protocol to the ECHR than to bring an action in tort or delict.

Much maligned though it may be, positivism has its uses: a right that is not clearly set out in a justiciable document is, for most practical, day-to-day purposes, hardly a right at all. That said, however, as Jack Straw implied in his speech at George Washington University, the aspirational element in human rights should not be dismissed out of hand. Even a non-justiciable right may still have considerable moral force; and when Jeremy Bentham, in the famous passage from *Anarchical Fallacies*, ridiculed 'natural and imprescriptible rights' as 'rhetorical nonsense, nonsense upon stilts'[83] he may have underestimated the power of human rights to change behaviour by persuasion rather than by coercion. The comparative success of the Fair Trade movement, for example, has not been the result of governmental or judicial action but the outcome of a growing awareness that if you pay Third World producers a pittance for their coffee beans or bananas, you are not treating them as 'people who matter'.

In conclusion, one cannot but wonder whether some of the criticisms of the operation of the Human Rights Act 1998 after almost ten years of its operation have simply been symptomatic of a more general decline in politicians' enthusiasm for the human rights agenda, fuelled at least in part by the tendency since the commencement of the Act for the courts to elevate Convention rights above the administrative preferences or convenience of Government. In the same way, there is a suspicion that the proposal for a British Statement of Values might be driven almost as much by concerns about the electoral successes of the Scottish National Party and Plaid Cymru in the 2007 elections for the Scottish Parliament and the National Assembly of Wales as by a desire to promote social cohesion in a multi-faith, multi-racial society.

---

[83] P Schofield, C Pease-Watkin and C Blamires (eds), *Rights, Representation and Reform − Nonsense upon stilts and other writings on the French Revolution.* (Oxford, Oxford University Press, 2002) 330.

If such doubts about the motivations of politicians are well-founded, then it cannot but make one slightly wary of those who propose an alternative Act. It should be remembered that the United Kingdom was already a signatory to the ECHR when the Human Rights Act 1998 was put on the statute book: what the Act did was to make Convention rights immediately justiciable in the domestic courts. And if the subtext of at least some of the Act's critics is that there should be some degree of derogation from the Convention, that is a different issue again: is it unfair to ask whether, except in the direst emergency, a modern Western liberal democracy at the beginning of the 21st century could seriously contemplate pursuing such a course and at the same time hope to retain any international credibility?

Perhaps in developing a response to broader questions of rights and responsibilities we might usefully explore two themes. The first is how human rights might be related to the traditional Quaker testimony to 'that of God in every person': an approach to human rights issues that is both echoed in McCorquodale's assertion that the contemporary discourse is consonant with the teachings of Jesus and not very far removed from some kind of neighbour principle. The second is particularly timely in view of the Lord Chancellor's remarks on the problem of balancing rights with responsibilities: whether the Roman Catholic canonical concept of duties and rights subsisting together in the same person, as two sides of the same coin, might have anything helpful to say to us.

STRUCTURES OF RELIGIOUS PLURALISM IN ENGLISH LAW

David Harte

Introduction

Until recently, multiculturalism and social diversity were in fashion[1]. Now, politicians vie to promote, instead, 'integration' of all individual citizens into society.'[2] Underlying this unanimity seems to be an assumption that the first allegiance of the citizen is to the State. The dangers of this approach were addressed by the Archbishop of Canterbury, Dr Rowan Williams, in a Foundation Lecture at the Royal Courts of Justice on 7 February 2008 which touched a raw nerve in secular sensitivities, promoting much controversy in the media:[3]

> The danger arises not only when there is an assumption on the religious side that membership of the community (belonging to the *umma* or the Church or whatever) is the only significant category, so that participation in other kinds of socio-political arrangement is a kind of betrayal. It also occurs when secular government assumes a monopoly in terms of defining public and political identity. There is a position – not at all unfamiliar in contemporary discussion – which says that to be a citizen is essentially and simply to be under the rule of the uniform law of a sovereign State, in such a way that any other relations, commitments or protocols of behaviour belong exclusively to the realm of the private and of individual choice.

By contrast, a plural approach calls not just for integrating individuals into the host society but also a recognition that faith traditions play a vital role in providing the foundation of common principles which the

---

[1] Recognition of the pluralistic and multicultural nature of modern British society may be found in *R (on the application of Williamson) v Secretary of State for Education and Employment* [2005] UKHL 15, per Lord Nicolls of Birkenhead at paras 15-19, and is echoed by Lord Bingham in *R (on the application of Begum) v Denbigh High School Governors* [2006] UKHL 15.

[2] E.g speech to the Runnymede Trust by the then Prime Minister Tony Blair on 'Our Nation's Future – Multiculturalism and Integration' 8 December 2006, <http://www.number10.gov.uk/output/Page10563.asp> and key note speech in Birmingham by David Cameron, leader of the opposition on, 'The Challenge of Cohesion' <http://www.conservatives.com/tile.do?def=news.story.page&obj_id=134759&speeches=1>.

[3] R Williams, 'Civil and Religious Law in England: a Religious Perspective', <http://www.archbishopofcanterbury.org/1575>.

law expresses and by which society functions. Dr Williams' lecture was controversial particularly because he suggested the possibility of 'a delegation of certain legal functions to the religious courts of a community'. This conjured up nightmares of a parallel system of Islamic *Sharia* law being introduced to the United Kingdom; allotting an inferior place to women and with a barbaric set of criminal penalties. However, what Dr Williams clearly envisaged was no whole scale abdication of authority by the State courts but a structured framework within which particular religious authorities are given a recognised role where that is appropriate and always subject to the oversight of the State courts. As Dr Williams pointed out, such systems are in fact already recognised under English law. The ecclesiastical law of the Church of England is a fully integrated example[4]. A major aspect of this is the delegation to the faculty jurisdiction of responsibility for parish churches which are State listed buildings[5]. In a different context, State law on marriage takes account of religious traditions by delegating to ministers of religion responsibility for formalising legally recognised marriages in England where the parties to a marriage wish to have a religious ceremony[6].

At a deeper and more general level, religion can provide an underlying source of authority for a liberal and democratic political order. Because religious traditions make claims to absolute truth which are necessarily incompatible, the secular approach is to drive all religion into the private sphere. However, this involves imposing a secular conformity which

[4] The range of Ecclesiastical Law as part of the general law of England is demonstrated in M Hill, *Ecclesiastical Law* (Third edition, Oxford, Oxford University Press, 2007).

[5] This 'ecclesiastical exemption' is provided under Planning (Listed Building and Conservation Areas) Act 1990 s 60. For the interrelation between the general and ecclesiastical systems see Charles Mynors, *Listed Buildings and Conservation Areas and Monuments* (Fourth edition, London, Sweet & Maxwell, 2006) chapter 16. Such delegation is also made in respect of other major Christian denominations which are responsible for important historic religious buildings; Ecclesiastical Exemption (Listed Buildings and Conservation Areas) Order 1994, SI No 1771.

[6] Most obviously, under the Church of England system of marriage in a parish church, preceded by reading of banns under Marriage Act 1949, section 12. The Act also recognises Church of England marriages authorised by Episcopal licences and provides for the delegation to celebrate a marriage to the minister of any building which is registered as a place of worship licenced for the celebration of marriages. In respect of divorce, Jewish religious courts are afforded special recognition where a wife who is being divorced may obtain a stay on making the decree absolute until a *get*, a religious divorce, has been obtained from the *Beth Dinn*, the religious court. Family Law Act 1996, section 9. See further M Freeman, 'Is the Jewish *get* any business of the State?' in R O'Dair and A Lewis (ed) *Law and Religion* (Oxford, Oxford University Press, 2001) 365 and Mark Hill's contribution to this volume.

may be just as intolerant and oppressive as those previously demanded by religious authorities. By contrast, a plural approach will both enable religious believers to operate in accordance with their principles of faith as fully as possible, openly in the public domain, and will pay serious regard to religious principles and arguments in public debate over developments in the law[7].

The possibility of a genuinely plural model has been recognised in recent legal scholarship[8]. As Dr Williams put it in his lecture, the question is, 'whether there should be a higher level of attention to religious identity and communal rights in the practice of the law'. This chapter aims to discuss some aspects of the extent to which English law represents such a model and how religious pluralism could be more fully expressed in legal terms. The scope of religion and its legal definition are problematic but, for present purposes, the essence of a religion is that it provides an absolute source of authority outside the positivist framework used for identifying and making law[9]. The chapter argues that the aim of a neutral system of law should not be to promote secularism but rather to provide a structured framework for religious pluralism.

First, public decision makers need to take particular account of the teaching of the major religious traditions in weighing claims to religious rights. This is necessary both to ensure fair treatment for believers and also so as to enhance social cohesion and the authority of the law itself. Because it recognises no ultimate authority other than itself, an avowedly secular State may impose a conformity which subordinates the aspirations and the liberties of all religious believers.

Second, the chapter stresses the importance of identifying the different legal and social levels at which disputes involving claims to religious liberty arise. Exceptions and conscience clauses provide legal instruments for accommodating different and opposed beliefs.

---

[7] Such an approach is explored from a philosophical perspective in R Trigg, *Religion in Public Life: Must Faith be Privatised?* (Oxford, Oxford University Press, 2007).

[8] Notably by Julian Rivers: e.g. J Rivers, 'From Toleration to Pluralism: Religious Liberty and Religious Establishment under the United Kingdom's Human Rights Act' in R Ahdar, (ed) *Law and Religion* (Aldershot, Ashgate, 2000) 133, and J Rivers, 'In Pursuit of Pluralism: The Ecclesiastical Policy of the European Union' (2004) 7 *Ecc LJ* 267. The significance of a plural model for the debate over liberalism and religious liberty has been recognised in the major study: R Ahdar and I Leigh, *Religious Freedom in the Liberal State* (Oxford, Oxford University Press, 2005) 84.

[9] For religious traditions this external source of authority is usually expressed in terms of divine revelation.

Third, the chapter argues that the measure of how far society is religiously plural, rather than secular, depends on the extent to which the general law accommodates religious beliefs on an axis from the private to the public, through the personal and the corporate.

Religious Pluralism and the Importance of Taking Religious Beliefs Seriously

Western liberal democracies are inherently plural in that they are based on principles which include tolerance of religious diversity. However, the degree of tolerance can vary significantly[10]. Some States define themselves as secular. Secularism, like religion, poses problems of definition. However, for present purposes, its essential characteristic is that it seeks to exclude religious faith from public life[11].

The problem of containing behaviour based on dramatically different theological beliefs is an intractable one. It has notoriously disfigured the history of Christianity[12]. Today, however, from the perspective of many Christians, the achievement of tolerance, if not harmony, between such conflicting views has been one of the great achievements of the Christian faith and is hard won evidence of its validity. Whatever alternative uses may have been made and still are made of scriptural authority, it certainly does provide a source for validating principles of mutual respect for human beings and also respect for the natural world. By contrast, a liberal human philosophy which is simply human depends upon consensus which is unstable, because it is ultimately relativist. As Professor Trigg has written:

---

[10] Some states give particular recognition to one or more religions. The very different models of establishment of Christianity in England and Scotland are obvious examples. The special status of both the Orthodox and the Lutheran churches in Finland is also striking. Some states with an established religion may be very restrictive as to others and loath to recognise new expressions of religious belief. Thus the Orthodox Church in Greece has very much a favoured relationship with the State, whereas other Christian bodies are marginalised e.g *Valsamis v Greece* (1997) 24 EHRR 294.

[11] Very different approaches are illustrated by the French doctrine of *laïcité*, and by secularism in Turkey and on the other hand by the United States' concept of the separation of state and religion which appears to represent a more genuinely plural model. The tensions over differing attitudes to religion within the European Union are examined, by Rivers, 'In Pursuit of Pluralism' and by Gerhard Robbers, 'Diversity of State-Religion Relations and European Unity' (2004) 7 *Ecc LJ* 304.

[12] This aspect of the notoriously difficult dilemma for liberalism of how to tolerate the intolerant has recently been explored by Ahdar and Leigh, *Religious Freedom in the Liberal State*.

Relativism can appear to offer a foundation for toleration and respect, but it can not demand that we ought to be tolerant, since that is an appeal to a non-relative standard. It simply demands the acceptance of whatever standards people happen to have, and if they are intolerant and prone to oppression of others they can not be criticised[13].

(1) Religious authority for key principles of general law

Tolerance may be drawn from Judeo-Christian teaching through principles expressed in the Ten Commandments, summarised by Jesus in two passages from the Old Testament which he brought together[14]. The second part of this summary, 'Thou shalt love thy neighbour as thyself', remains generally acknowledged as a touch stone for civil behaviour. It is embedded in the sacred texts of the other major World religions apart from Judaism and Christianity. It was, famously, the starting point for Lord Atkins' seminal opinion which was the fountain of the English law of negligence[15]. This principle is the foundation for a plural system of law, even though its application differs as between faith traditions and it is too general to be used as a practical tool in applying the law[16].

(2) The importance of religious discernment for the law

Different understandings of divine truth may require accommodating theological propositions which some find deeply uncomfortable. Major religious traditions which share the practical principle of loving one's neighbour may take exclusive positions about the relationship of the individual with God, about salvation and about the destination of the

---

[13] Trigg, *Religion in Public Life*, 2-3.

[14] Deuteronomy 6:5 and Leviticus 18:19, brought together in Matthew 22:37-39.

[15] *Donoghue v Stevenson* [1932] AC 562.

[16] For the religious believer, the law is dependent on loving God first. For Jews and Christians this is expressed in the group of Commandments, comprising the first table of the Decalogue 'Thou shalt love the Lord thy God with all thy heart and with all thy soul and with all thy might'. The conflicts in human history attributed to religion may be seen as a result of attempts by one group of believers to impose their particular views of God on others without taking proper account of the relationship between the two basic commandments. For the consequences see e.g. K Armstrong *The Battle for God* (London, Harper Collins, 2000) on fundamentalism in Judaism, Christianity and Islam. Against this background, the Human Rights Act 1998, through Article 9 of the European Convention on Human Rights which purports to guarantee freedom of religion, has implications for the religious obligation to love God. From a human rights perspective, as much as a religious one, enabling one's neighbour to fulfil the command to love God according to his or her own conscience is an essential aspect of loving one's neighbour as one's self.

individual after death. It was the importance attached to such beliefs which led to the horrors of religious persecution in the past. They lie behind religious terrorism today, justifying mass slaughter and suicide. The dilemma of liberalism is how to be tolerant of those who are themselves intolerant of others.

The secular fundamentalist, even one claiming liberal credentials, may respond by seeking to repress or at least marginalise all religion[17]. The pluralist, by contrast, will be careful to distinguish religious traditions which support the liberal democratic order from those which are opposed to it[18]. The challenge for the general law is to take religion into account in a manner which respects and values the different and sometimes conflicting principles of religious citizens. This may extend to recognising religion as positively contributing to a free and diverse political and social culture. It will at least involve recognising the importance for citizens of their particular beliefs. Both levels demand understanding of what those beliefs entail and an assessment of how they relate to common principles which the law seeks to promote.

This process invites discrimination between different associations of believers. A plural society will avoid penalising believers who are supportive of society even when it is impelled to penalise others who pose a threat. It will not be inhibited in actively promoting believers who support civil society and will welcome the general public benefit which a religious tradition can bring. 'Discrimination' has become a negative concept, expressing prejudiced judgement. It is seen as oppressive of those negatively discriminated against. Supposedly positive discrimination is distrusted because it tends to involve indirect negative discrimination against others. Thus, a policy for employing adherents of a particular faith

---

[17] The New Atheism is associated, particularly, with C Hitchens, *God is not Great* (New York, Grand Central Publishing, 2007) and R Dawkins, *The God Delusion* (London, Bantam 2006). Cf A McGrath, *The Twilight of Atheism: The Rise and Fall of Disbelief in the Modern World* (New York, Doubleday, 2004) and, A McGrath and J Collicutt McGrath, *The Dawkins Delusion? Atheist Fundamentalism and the Denial of the Divine* (London, SPCK, 2007).

[18] The challenge for religious communities is to separate the internal religious law concerned with protecting doctrinal belief from the external application to the general law of moral and social principles taught by the faith. Religious precepts provide motivation for influencing the general law. They also provide a critique based on religious teaching which could be made far more explicit than it is. However, to carry weight in the modern public forum, proposals as to the scope and content of the general law must be based on reasons which can be argued independently of any external religious authority; See J Rawls 'The Idea of Public Reason Revisited' (1997) 64 *U Chicago L Rev* 765 and discussion by Ahdar and Leigh *Religious Freedom in the Liberal State*, especially 46-52.

is a policy against employing those of other faiths or unbelievers. The word 'discrimination' is therefore now difficult to use so as to mean the drawing of justified distinctions. The concept of 'discernment' is a candidate for filling the gap[19].

Traditionally, judges have been reluctant to discern the differences between religious belief, treating them as simply matters of private conscience. It is generally assumed that it would be inappropriate and indeed dangerous for judges to be asked to answer theological questions[20]. The classic judicial discussion of the meaning of religion in the case of *Segerdaal*,[21] illustrated the reluctance of the courts even to define the concept of religion. There, the Divisional Court and the Court of Appeal upheld the assessment of the Registrar General that a meeting place of the Church of Scientology was not a place of religious worship. In particular, Winn LJ, stressed how the meaning of religion, which he called 'a chameleon word', varies with the context. He professed that he did not feel well qualified 'to discuss religion or religious topics' and was wary of any such attempt, since there were two reasons why observers were likely to be disqualified: 'The one is if one is particularly religious in the sense of being particularly observant of the processes and rituals of a particular current religion. The other is if one is preconditioned by a certain amount of study of pre-Christian religions or religious superstitions towards thinking of religion in a very general and wide.'

Reluctance to take sides does not mean being dismissive of the content of belief. Judicial diffidence in addressing the content of religion is shown, typically, in *R v Chief Rabbi ex parte Wachmann*, where the High Court was asked to overturn the doctrinal assessment by an internal Jewish court of the fitness of a rabbi. Simon Brown J stated that, 'the court

---

[19] Bishop Geoffrey Rowell, 'As we outlaw discrimination, so we need discernment' *Times* 17 February, 2007. In a rather different manner, the concept of judgment has been debased in the word 'judgmental,' which implies judging detached from the fairness and balance which are characteristic of justice.

[20] 'When the genuineness of a claimant's professed belief is an issue in the proceedings the court will inquire into and decide this issue as a question of fact. This is a limited inquiry. The court is concerned to ensure an assertion of religious belief is made in good faith… But, emphatically, it is not for the court to embark on an inquiry into the asserted belief and judge its "validity" by some objective standard such as the source material upon which the claimant founds his belief or the orthodox teaching of the religion in question or the extent to which the claimant's belief conforms to or differs from the views of others professing the same religion': *R (on the application of Williamson) v Secretary of state for Education and Employment* [2005] UKHL 15, per Lord Nicolls of Birkenhead, para 22.

[21] *R v Registrar General, ex parte Segerdal* [1970] 2 QB 697.

would never be prepared to rule on questions of Jewish law', and that, in relation to the determination of whether someone is morally and religiously fit to carry out the spiritual and pastoral duties of his office, the court, 'must inevitably be wary of entering so self-evidently sensitive an area, straying across the well-recognised divide between church and state'.[22] There, the Chief Rabbi's disciplinary functions were treated as essentially internal religious procedures and the Chief Rabbi did not perform public functions in the sense that he was regulating a field of public life where, but for his offices, the government would impose a statutory regime. On the contrary, his functions were essentially intimate, spiritual, and religious ones which there was no question of the government discharging in his place were he not to exercise them. Simon Brown stated as a reason for not intervening in unsatisfactory procedures that it would not always be easy to separate out procedural complaints from consideration of substantive principles of Jewish law which may underlie them. However, with increasing governmental intervention in private employment law the reality is that such activities may increasingly be brought within the ambit of the courts in any event, in which case there will be an increasing need for employment tribunals and the courts to be conversant with religious principles[23].

Nevertheless, judges can not always ignore the content of belief. Where belief is crucial for parties to litigation it is essential for its content to be taken seriously and a judge should be as capable of understanding theological positions coherently presented by expert witnesses as of understanding the arguments of other specialist disciplines – even if the judge is then careful to avoid taking sides over the correctness of a particular doctrine. If a judge can demonstrate understanding of a religious point of view, that may assist in reaching a reasoned judgment and may make the judgment more acceptable to the parties[24].

---

[22] [1992] 1 WLR 1036 1042G–1043A.

[23] See further, M Hill 'Judicial Approaches to Religious Disputes' in O'Dair and Lewis, *Law and Religion* 410. For some argument that religious bodies may more satisfactorily be addressed as subjects of the general public law rather than being treated like ordinary employers, see D Harte 'Defining the Legal Boundaries of Orthodoxy for Public and private Religion in England' in O'Dair and Lewis, *Law and Religion* 471. However, the danger of the approach suggested in the latter discussion is that treating religious organizations as public bodies could make them subject to the Human Rights Act 1998 whilst denying them standing as potential victims themselves, on which see the decision of the House of Lords in *Aston Cantlow v Wallbank* [2004] 1 AC 546.

[24] The approach was well illustrated in *In re A (Children) (Conjoined Twins: Surgical Separation)* [2001] Fam 147 where, exceptionally, the Court of Appeal allowed evidence

A court may be called on to adjudicate between coreligionists who are at loggerheads on matter of doctrine, typically because they also claim property. This may involve examining particular beliefs and assessing whether or not they are consistent with one another. Notably, in *General Assembly of Free Church of Scotland and others v Lord Overtoun*[25], the House of Lords held that because the doctrines of the majority of the members of the Free Church of Scotland did not conform with the foundation documents of that church the majority were debarred from changing those doctrines and merging with another church[26].

In drafting legislation, even more than in litigation, a plural approach will seek to understand and explicitly accommodate religious concerns through the processes of consultation and Parliamentary debate. Conflicts where both legislators and judges may be expected explicitly to take into account religious views in society include, particularly, those concerned with issues of life and death and of sexual morality. Where the general law differs from well recognised religious moral views, the authority of legislation and policy may be severely weakened unless the religious position is understood and appropriate provision made for exceptions and conscience clauses.

The issue of same sex relations is a major current area of dispute both between religious people and secularists and within the Christian Church[27].

---

to be presented by the Cardinal Archbishop of Westminster and by the Pro Life Alliance to help the court resolve the intense moral dilemma of whether to authorise an operation which would result in the immediate death of one of two conjoined twins so that the other might survive.

[25] *General Assembly of Free Church of Scotland and others v Lord Overtoun; Macalister v Young and others* [1904] AC 515 (1042G–1043A). In that case the House of Lords grappled with double predestination and held that it was a foundation doctrine of the Free Church. The need to define what constitutes a religion gave rise to the instructive decisions in, *R v Registrar General, ex p Segerdal* which was concerned with whether a Scientologist 'church' could be registered as a place of religious worship.

[26] Compare, the dissenting opinion of Lord Mcnaghten at 630, 'The question, therefore, seems to me to be this. Was the Church thus purified – the Free Church – so bound and tied by the tenets of the Church of Scotland prevailing at the time of disruption that departure from those tenets in any matter of substance would be a violation of that profession or testimony which may be called the unwritten charter of her foundation, and so necessarily involve a breach of trust in the administration of funds contributed for no other purpose but the support of the Free Church – the Church of the Disruption? Was the Free Church by the very condition of her existence forced to cling to her subordinate standards with so desperate a grip that she has lost hold and touch of the supreme standard of her faith? Was she from birth incapable of all growth and development? Was she (in a word) a dead branch and not a living Church?'

[27] For discussion of the legal issues here see: J Humphreys, 'The Civil Partnership Act 2004, Same-Sex Marriage and the Church of England' (2006) 8 *Ecc LJ* 289; C Falconer, 'Church, State and Civil Partners' (2007) 9 *Ecc LJ* 5-9; J Rivers, 'Law, Religion and

It provides a particularly instructive test of the differences between a secular and a plural approach in the law. In this area, regulations against discrimination on the grounds of sexual orientation have posed problems for religious believers who consider physical same sex relations inherently wrong. Concessions are made in the regulations for the activities of religious associations but not where the relevant activities of the believers are of a commercial nature[28]. Believers who choose to comply with the dictates of both the general law and religious principle may feel obliged to give up occupations which they can no longer conduct in accordance with their conscience[29]. A more plural approach would allow further exceptions, for example in respect of the provision of services by individuals or small organisations, provided there are adequate alternatives open to those whom they have scruples about serving.

(3) Weighing religious significance in practical situations

The diffidence which judges have in being seen to assess the seriousness of religious belief has led to the development of a complex series of filters for restricting claims based on rights to freedom of religion. Courts may exclude religious interests at various stages and this may risk a confusing lack of consistency where different judges weigh religious interests against other interests, even though they reach the same conclusion[30]. Thus, a belief may not be recognised at all; or a court may consider that a particular act motivated by belief is not a manifestation of that

Gender Equality'; M Scott-Joynt, 'The Civil Partnership Act 2004: Dishonest Law?' (2005) 7 *Ecc LJ* 92; A Opromolla, 'Law, Gender and Religious Belief in Europe: Considerations from a Catholic Perspective' (2007) 9 *Ecc LJ* 61 and Mark Hill's contribution to this volume.

[28] Equality Act (Sexual Orientation) Regulations 2007, SI No 1263. The problems for believers posed by anti-discrimination laws are discussed further below and also in Pauline Roberts' contribution to this volume.

[29] Thus a Christian photographer who feels unable to attend civil partnership ceremonies for same sex couples or a couple running a bed and breakfast establishment unwilling to let a double bedroom to a pair of civil partners may simply close their businesses. Others may choose to break the law as a matter of principle. Thus the photographer may openly turn down work associated with civil partnerships. However, a middle way which stays within the law may be to decline any sort of photographic work concerned with marriages or partnerships. The couple with the bed and breakfast establishment could confine themselves to offering single beds.

[30] The concept of filters is discussed, e,g, in Ahdar and Leigh, *Religious Freedom in the Liberal State*, at 123. The confusion which can arise from different judges using different filters is discussed in R Sandberg, 'Recent Controversial Claims to Religious Liberty' (2008) 124 *LQR* 213.

belief; or the court may find that the manifestation has not actually been interfered with. Finally, even if the right to belief is engaged, the court may decide that it is overruled by other interests, public or personal, under the margin of appreciation provided by paragraph 2 of Article 9 of the European Convention on Human Rights.

A court may go so far as to discount certain forms of belief as not worthy of serious consideration because they are incoherent or, even, because they are positively harmful[31]. Lord Nicolls has stated the test in these terms:

> The belief must be consistent with basic standards of human dignity or integrity. Manifestation of a religious belief, for instance, which involved subjecting others to torture or inhuman punishment would not qualify for protection. The belief must relate to matters more than merely trivial. It must possess an adequate degree of seriousness and importance... it must be a belief on a fundamental problem .... The belief must also be coherent in the sense of being intelligible and capable of being understood[32].

However, even an initial assessment of the seriousness of a belief and its coherence and intelligibility will require a judge to address its content, if not to assess is its truth[33].

In some circumstances, a court may be prepared to declare whether a particular belief or practice is religious at all. Thus, in the asylum case of *Omoruyi v Secretary of State for the Home Department,* the Court of Appeal rejected the applicant's argument that he was at risk from religious persecution where, as a Christian, he had stood up to a Nigerian

---

[31] A judge who aims at as complete neutrality as possible rather than a discerning pluralism will be reluctant to draw distinctions between religious beliefs; See the Australian case concerned with Scientology, *Church of the New Faith v Commissioner for Pay-Roll Tax (Vic)* (1983) 49 ALR 65, discussed by G Watt 'Giving unto Caesar; Rationality, Reciprocity and Legal Recognition of Religion' in O'Dair and Lewis *Law and Religion* 46-53.

[32] *Williamson,* at para 23.

[33] This first filter was emphasised in the Court of Appeal by Arden LJ, [2003] QB 1300, see para 258. By contrast, in the House of Lords, Lord Walker of Gestingthorpe, who was sceptical of a rigidly analytical approach in any event, considered, 'rather alarming', the qualifications it involved which could exclude certain beliefs from protection (para 60). As Lord Nicolls pointed out , it may rarely be necessary for courts to consider whether a belief is, 'religious', since Article 9 protects all seriously held beliefs and their manifestation (para 16). Nevertheless, where a believer relies upon a well known belief of a major religion or philosophy it may be easier to convince a court of personal sincerity in espousing it. Furthermore, even though they are not exclusive, the specific examples of manifestation of belief given in Article 9 are for the most part distinctively religious; that is 'worship, teaching, practice and observance'.

cult which had demanded his father's body, so as to perform unmention-
able rituals upon it.[34] In the view of Simon Brown LJ, the practices of
the cult were not worthy of consideration as the subject of belief at all[35].
This sits uneasily with the principle of human rights that the individual
has an unqualified right to belief. The beliefs of the cult were not actually in issue, but whether or not they were 'religious', under Article 9 of
the Convention, the right to hold even such beliefs should be sacrosanct.
Similarly, on a literal approach, even horrific beliefs, such as a commitment to cannibalism, would seem to be engaged if the State interferes
with them.

A purely theological belief concerned with the nature of God or of life
beyond the present material world, whether it is the bizarre invention of
a disordered mind or the dogma of an ancient religion, developed over
centuries by intellectual giants, may properly be out with the jurisdiction
of a court established under the general law. However, matters of religious order and worship and questions as to personal morality involve
manifestation of belief. They are therefore qualified and are subject to
State intervention under Article 9(2) of the Convention. The forms of
manifestation for which rights may be claimed are palpably not all equal.
An example which has caught the judicial imagination is the throwing
of rice or confetti, traditionally associated with weddings. This seems
clearly not a serious candidate for protection, in the way that the right to
celebrate a marriage in a church service may be[36].

Even if there is a genuine and serious belief, a claim based on it may
be excluded because the claimant has not shown that the belief is engaged.
Thus in *Arrowsmith v United Kingdom*, the European Commission on
Human Rights ruled that the right to practice a belief 'does not cover

---

[34] *Omoruyi v. Secretary of State for the Home Department* Case No: C/2000/0025/
IATRF, unreported, per Simon Brown LJ, 'The notion that a "devil cult" practising pagan
rituals of the sort here described is in any true sense a religion I find deeply offensive.
Assume opposition to such practices on the part of a secular state; is that to be regarded
as a religious difference? I hardly think so. It seems to me rather that these rites and rituals of the Ogboni are merely the trappings of what can only realistically be recognised
as an intrinsically criminal organisation – akin perhaps to the voodoo element of the Ton-
Ton Macoute in Papa Doc Duvalier's Haiti'. As for Omoruyi's belief, it was held that he
was not at risk because of his Christian belief but simply because he was the target of a
criminal gang.

[35] Cf the attitude of Murphy J in *Church of the New Faith v Commissioner for Pay-
Roll Tax*.

[36] Taken from a footnote to the judgement of Scalia J in a US case from Oregon (1990)
494 US 872 at 888, footnote 4, the example is quoted by Lord Walker of Gestingthorpe in
Williamson, at para 63.

each act which is motivated or influenced by religion or belief'[37]. In *Playfoot* a Deputy High judge held that a pupil's rights to manifest her belief were not engaged where she was prohibited from wearing a silver ring which symbolised her profession of chastity as a Christian[38]. The ring was treated as merely an item of jewellery, which was not allowed under school rules. The judge held that wearing the ring was not 'intimately linked' to the pupil's belief in chastity because it was not a requirement of her faith, that she should wear the ring.

Ahdar and Leigh criticise such decisions as *Arrowsmith* and argue persuasively that courts should be generous in recognising where there is an issue of belief and in accepting that the belief has been engaged[39]. If a right to freedom of belief and its manifestation is to be overridden that should be on the clear basis of superior public interest or of other private rights. From a civil liberties point of view, a religious belief should not be overridden on general grounds of public disapproval but only if it poses a real threat to the rights of others. Ahdar and Leigh give, as an example, the punishment of Rastafarian cannabis users where the need to protect society from drug abuse would not necessarily be compromised by making an exception. That could be provided by means of an express defence or under an appropriate licensing system.

It seems likely that decisions as to whether Article 9 has been infringed would be more consistent if attention were confined much more rigorously to the single question of whether the State is justified under Article 9 (2) in overriding them. In answering that question, the coherence of the belief and whether it is supported by a serous religious authority would seem important factors for striking the necessary balance.

Thus, preaching and proselytising are key forms of manifestation of belief. They may appear provocative. However they can not be properly weighed unless the judge understands their theological significance. A preacher who believes that those who practice certain behaviour, such as

---

[37] *Arrowsmith v United Kingdom* (Application 7050/75) (1978) 3 EHRR 218. There, a peace campaigner had been convicted under the Incitement of Disaffection Act 1934 for handing out literature which called on soldiers not to serve in Northern Ireland. She failed in her claim to Strasbourg that her conviction contravened her human right to manifest her pacifist beliefs.

[38] *R (on the application of Playfoot) v Millais School Governing Body* [2007] EWHC Admin 1698, criticised in Sandberg, 'Recent Controversial Claims to Religious Liberty'.

[39] Ahdar and Leigh, *Religious Freedom in the Liberal State* see generally 160 – 189. A similar conclusion, that the emphasis in deciding claims that Article 9 has been breached should concentrate far more on the qualification of such rights allowed for in paragraph 2, is also reached by M Hill and R Sandberg, 'Is Nothing Sacred? Clashing Symbols in a Secular World' [2007] *PL* 488.

sexual activity with members of their own sex, are at risk of eternal damnation cannot justly be considered a peddler of hatred if he attacks such behaviour with the desire of saving his audience from an appalling fate. If he is expressing a seriously held theological position this should be acknowledged and afforded respect, even if the manner in which he expresses himself causes offence[40].

Even an unusual subjective belief must properly be understood if its genuineness is to be judged and if it is to be balanced against other interests. However, in the balance, it is suggested that the considered support of a major religious tradition should add weight to a belief. This is the point at which human rights moves from the dimension of personal autonomy to religious pluralism. The secularist may see no difference between the claim of the Rastafarian and the ordinary cannabis user who claims that he or she genuinely believe that they should be free to take drugs. Similarly, the secularist may see no difference between the Moslem woman demanding the right to wear a head scarf at work or in a place of education and any person claiming the right to wear some unusual item of personal clothing. In respect of a horizontal clash between those in same sex relations and religious believers who see such relations as inherently sinful, the secularist may simply write off the latter position as one of outmoded prejudice. From a plural perspective, the Rastafarian, the Moslem woman and the religious objector to same sex relations all have religious rights which are particularly worthy of respect because they are part of a coherent package of beliefs which are central to their identity.

One objection to giving added weight to the teaching of major religious traditions is that it raises the question of how significant a particular

---

[40] Believers may categorise such preaching as prophecy. Preaching which offends others may be an offence under Public Order Act 1986, section 5; *Hammond v Director of Public Prosecutions* [2004] EWHC Admin 69, [2005] *Crim LR* 851. But preaching which is not offensive may be protected by the courts if efforts are made to stop it when it attracts attention. Cf *Beatty v Gillbanks* (1892) 9 QBD 308 and, more recently, *Redmond-Bate v Director of Public Prosecutions* [1999] Crim LR 998. Cf also *The Church of Jesus Christ of Latter Day Saints and others v Price* [2004] EWHC 3245 (QB), even aggressive evangelists may be victims of harassment by others with different religious views! Toleration of views with which one strongly agrees may include developing a framework for a dialectic which involves understanding those with whom one disagrees, even if one does not accept their views. For John Locke, *A Letter Concerning Toleration* emphasises that toleration does not preclude seeking to change the views of the person who is tolerated. See JH Tully (ed) *A Letter Concerning Toleration* (Indianapolis, Hackett Publishing, 1983). The concept of 'understanding' is developed by L Green 'On Being Tolerated' (a seminar paper presented at Newcastle University, April 2008). See also *supra*, note 12 and related text.

belief is to the religious tradition which holds it. It also raises questions as to whether one such group is more significant than another. These are real dilemmas[41] but if freedom of religion is to be taken seriously, particular care must be given to limiting legislation and public decision making which conflict with the teaching of recognised religious authorities and organisations. That is not to downplay the importance of the individual conscience but simply to underline the need for the State to respect coherently articulated views which are held by substantial numbers of citizens and are based on an authority which in their view is greater than that of the State. To override such views simply because they are not shared by a majority in Parliament may be potentially damaging to social stability. What appear to be needed are more general ground rules for consistency in weighing conflicting rights.

Contexts for Conflicting Principles

There is said to be no hierarchy of human rights. Rather, conflicts between competing rights fall to be judged against the context in which they arise, applying the principle of proportionality. Nevertheless, the weight to be given to religious beliefs where they conflict with other rights may hopefully become clearer in the light of developing case law[42]. A rudimentary framework may be emerging for their evaluation[43]. One dimension, which relates particularly to the importance of the interests affected for those asserting them, is the level where decision making is located.

(1) The location of decision making

A religious interest may be overridden by the general law, either for the general public benefit or to protect the specific rights of others. The guiding principle in balancing such interests is the relativist one that the

---

[41] See Ahdar and Leigh, *Religious Freedom in the Liberal State* 168 on 'The Core/Peripheral Beliefs and Practices Distinction'.

[42] The manner in which the Human Rights Act 1998 might impinge on religious liberties was anticipated in D Harte 'The Development of the Law of Employment and Education' in M Hill (ed) *Religious Liberty and Human Rights*, (Cardiff, University of Wales Press, 2002), 159. For actual developments see M Hill and R Sandberg, 'Is Nothing Sacred?'

[43] Ahdar and Leigh provide a useful table of points where clashes have emerged, Ahdar and Leigh, *Religious Freedom in the Liberal State* 157-8.

balance must be proportionate. However, there are several general points which may be made.

If there is a conflict between the general law and the internal laws of one or more major religious traditions, it would seem particularly desirable for the matter to be fully debated at a national level and for consideration to be given as to whether exceptions or conscience clauses may be provided in the general law. How the exceptions are to be applied will need to be determined in specific cases. Where there are differences involving simply the sincerely held religious belief of an individual, these must be taken seriously but decisions will normally be made at a local level. The two leading House of Lords decisions on Article 9 of the European Convention on Human Rights illustrate the two approaches.

In *R (on the application of Williamson and others) v Secretary of State for Education and Employment and others*[44], a statutory instrument which extended a ban on corporal punishment to private schools was challenged on an application for judicial review by parents and teachers from a group of Christian schools who considered that corporal punishment administered in a moderate manner was a practice required by Biblical authority. The claim was that an exception to the ban was needed to satisfy the consciences of believers such as the applicants. The claim was not supported by a large religious constituency. However, the decision to make no exceptions for Christian schools was taken expressly at governmental level. The court of first instance, the Court of Appeal and finally the House of Lords were all satisfied that the balance of interest had been properly struck.

By contrast, in *R (on the application of Begum) v Denbigh High School Governors*,[45] the conflict was between a school which had banned the wearing of a particular form of religious clothing and a pupil who considered this an interference with her right to religious freedom. There was no national ban on religious clothing in schools but decisions on school uniforms were made by individual schools. The pupil sought judicial review of the school's decision. This was unsuccessful before Bennett J, in the Administrative Court, but succeeded in the Court of Appeal, which unanimously held that the school had failed to give adequate weight to the pupil's religious sensitivities. In their judgement, '[n]obody who

---

[44] In the House of Lords, [2005] UKHL 15. In the Court of appeal see *R (on the application of Williamson) v Secretary of State for Education and Employment* [2002] EWCA Civ 1926 and at first instance [2001] EWHC Admin 960.

[45] In the House of Lords [2006] UKHL 15, on appeal from the Court of Appeal [2005] 1 WLR 3372.

considered the issues on its behalf started from the premise that the claimant had a right which is recognised in English law, and that the onus lay
on the school to justify its interference with that right'[46]. The Court of
Appeal accepted that the school authorities might well have been able to
justify their decision but the onus lay upon them to do so and the relevant
issues were, from a legal aspect, 'approached from the wrong direction'[47].
In passing, Scott Baker LJ commented significantly that '[t]he United
Kingdom is not a secular state'[48].

The House of Lords, also unanimously, overturned the decision of the
Court of Appeal on the basis that it had wrongly applied the traditional
judicial review approach and had focused on the procedure followed
by the school and its failure to apply a particular form of reasoning[49].
The court should, instead, have concentrated on the proportionality of
the school's interference. Given the Court of Appeal's recognition that
the school could well have justified its decision if required to remake it,
the original decision could not properly be condemned as disproportion-
ate[50]. The outcome was that the House of Lords upheld the right of the
particular school to override the religious claims of a pupil, where it did
so for legitimate reasons.

In effect, the principle of subsidiarity was applied, allowing the school
to make its decision in the light of local circumstances. As Lord Bingham
acknowledged, '[i]t would in my opinion be irresponsible of any court,
lacking the experience, background and detailed knowledge of the head
teacher, staff and governors to overrule their judgement on a matter as
sensitive as this'[51]. Most pertinently, as Lord Hoffmann said, 'a domestic
court should accept the decision of Parliament to allow individual schools
to make their own decisions about uniforms'[52]. Nevertheless, although

---

[46] Per Brook LJ at para 76.

[47] Per Mummery LJ at para 88.

[48] Para 94.

[49] HL para 29, per Lord Bingham and para 68, per Lord Hoffmann. The House of
Lords took its cue from academic criticism of the Court of Appeal; T Poole 'Of headscarves and heresies: *The Denbigh High School* case and public authority decision making
under the Human Rights Act' [2005] *PL* 685; T Linden and T Hetherington, 'Schools and
Human Rights' (2005) 6(4) *Educational Law Journal* 229 and G Davies 'Banning the
Jilbab: Reflections on Restricting Religious Clothing in the light of the Court of Appeal
in *SB v Denbigh High School*' (2005) *European Constitutional Law Review* 511.

[50] HL paras 30 and 32.

[51] Para 34.

[52] Para 64. See too, *R (on the application of X) v Headteachers and Governors of
Y School* [2007] EWHC Admin 298, where the High Court refused judicial review of
another school which had changed its school rules in a manner that prevented a pupil

the House of Lords was concerned that such local decisions should not
be subjected by the courts to a formalistic straightjacket, they made clear
that on matters of substance the courts are there to oversee dispropor-
tionate exercise of power which fails to recognise the significance of
religious rights.

(2) Types of conflict

Conflicts between law and conscience may occur in a range of situations. The intensity of the dilemma for a religious person caught up in
such a conflict will depend on how their belief is affected. The problem
may be a general legal prohibition against something required by the
religion or a positive order to do something forbidden by the religion[53].
Frequently, however, even in avowedly secular States, both religion and
the State agree in forbidding certain acts and in requiring others. In some
cases, one authority either forbids or permits whilst the other is neutral.
Cases of direct conflict are rare. However, if religious rights are to be
respected, an exception or a conscience clause is essential where an individual would otherwise be absolutely required to do something prohibited by their religion or to refrain from something which their religion
requires. Thus a Roman Catholic priest in a country where alcohol was
forbidden would effectively be forbidden to celebrate the Mass unless
the law provided an exception.

More often, one authority limits the manner in which it is possible
to observe requirements imposed by the other but does not prohibit or
prevent observance altogether. Thus, the general law may impose con-
scription in time of war, but it may allow those with conscientious objections to fighting to fulfil their obligations to the State in other ways which
are religiously acceptable, such as by working on the land or in hospitals.
In some cases, the only means of performing an activity permitted by
one authority is impermissible for the other but there is a choice to
opt out altogether. Thus, if *kosher* or *halal* meat were prohibited on
grounds of animal welfare, Jews and Muslims would not have to break

---

already there from assuming a full veil which covered her face, when she reached puberty,
even though her sisters who had previously been at the school had been allowed to do
this.

[53] A full range of permutations was identified in Bruce (ed) *Obeying Christ in a
Changing World* vol 3 (Glasgow, Fontana,1977) see chapter 3, 'Education and the Law'.
A similar analysis is used by Ahdar and Leigh *Religious Freedom in the Liberal State* at
156-158.

the commandments of their religions because they could become vegetarians[54]. A Christian employee unwilling to follow a new shift system which requires him to work on a Sunday may be expected to resign and find work elsewhere.[55]

For the secularist, that may be sufficient to satisfy the Convention right to religious liberty. However, from a pluralist perspective, it is contrary to the spirit of human rights that individuals should be restricted in such a manner. Unless there is an overriding reason, a conscience clause should be provided under the general law giving space for the believer. Such provision was made for shop workers when Sunday trading was generally permitted by the Sunday Trading Act 1994[56]. Greater use of conscience clauses is desirable where without one the believer can only comply with his or her conscience by opting out altogether. Thus, the Abortion Act 1967, section 4, protects medical staff from taking part in abortions against their conscience, but the concession is not extended to those in lesser or more peripheral rolls such as a secretary who feels morally compromised by sending out appointment letters for abortion operations[57].

Generally, preventing a believer doing something permitted but not actually required by their religion is less likely to be a problem than preventing or requiring them to do something on which there is a definite rule. However, major religious belief systems may teach that an individual believer must be free to follow his or her conscience in certain circumstances, even if the religious tradition does not itself lay down an absolute rule[58]. If the State prevents such believers following the dictates of their conscience, that may alienate a far wider constituency. The debates over abortion and same sex relations provide examples[59]. A related and

---

[54] Or they might be able to buy in meat from another country: *Jewish Liturgical Association Cha'ar Shalom v Tsedek* (2000) 9 BHRC 27.

[55] *Copsey v WWB Devon Clays Ltd* [2005] EWCA Civ 932. See too *Ahmad v Inner London Education Authority* [1978] QB 36 and *X v United Kingdom* (1981) 22 Decisions and Reports of the European Commission 27. A similar attitude was taken by the English courts in *Begum* and in the similar case of *R. (on the application of X) v Headteachers and Governors of Y School*, discussed above.

[56] Section 4 and Schedule 4.

[57] *R v Salford Health Authority, ex parte Janaway* [1989] AC 53

[58] See discussion by Ahdar and Leigh *Religious Freedom in the Liberal State* 163 on 'The Religiously Motivated/Compelled Distinction'.

[59] The Equality Act (Sexual Orientation) Regulations 2007, SI No 1263,which were approved by both Houses of Parliament in March 2007, after heated opposition from outside but relatively little debate within, prohibit discrimination in the provision of goods and services against persons on the grounds of sexual orientation.

much publicised example was the refusal of the government to exempt
religious adoption agencies from the obligation to consider same sex couples as potential parents for adoption along with heterosexual couples.
Even where religious people have no problem with the principle of civil
partnerships or 'gay' adoption they may have considerable concerns if
others, who take a stricter view, are penalised for advocating those stricter
views and are restricted in observing them themselves. Thus, a genuinely
plural society would permit those who have conscientious problems with
same sex relations to run businesses and non commercial agencies which
withhold services where those involved have conscientious reasons for
doing so[60].

The Embedding of Legal Instruments of Pluralism

Conflicts of varying intensity may be generated by legislation or may
arise because issues have been left for resolution at a local level. Thus, as
Williamson illustrates, the general law has determined that no school may
practice corporal punishment even to satisfy the religious beliefs of certain parents. By contrast, as the *Begum* case illustrates, decisions on clothing with religious implications are delegated to local schools. A further
dimension to a framework for distinguishing different sorts of conflict
over religious belief depends on the context in which a right is claimed
and may be seen as an axis from the private to the public, through the
personal and the corporate. Conflicts which arise in a commercial context
seem to be particularly significant in identifying to what extent the law
is plural.

(1) Private and Personal

The first part of Article 9 of the European Convention on Human
Rights purports to guarantee an absolute right to freedom of belief. This
is somewhat disingenuous. The beliefs of any individual are shaped by
events and influences over which he or she may have little or no right
of control. Furthermore, as soon as a belief is acted on, even simply by

---

[60] For a positive appraisal of the law on civil partnerships from a Christian perspective
see J Humphries 'The Civil Partnership Act, Same-Sex Marriage and the Church of England' (2006) 8 *Ecc LJ* 289. A Biblical principle supporting the concern discussed here is
provided in 1 Corinthians 10:28. This advised abstinence in eating meat which had been
used in non Christian sacrifices, so as not to upset the consciences of others. See also
Mark Hill's contribution to this volume.

being stated to someone else, it ceases to be immune from interference, since the manifestation of belief is only a qualified right for the purposes of Article 9. What can be said is that the right to freedom of belief does support the qualified right to privacy in Article 8. The State may claim a margin of appreciation to examine a person's papers or their computer and prosecute them for what is found there but this may be strictly limited[61]; in the famous phrase of Elizabeth I, the State is restrained from 'making windows into men's minds'. When it is simply in the mind, religion may be seen as a purely personal matter, with no legal basis for distinguishing between highly developed systems of belief and the bizarre or grotesque.

As soon as belief is expressed, it may conflict with the enjoyment of belief by other individuals or with public policies upheld by the general law. Here, the difference between a plural and a secular approach may be sought in the delineation between private and public. Those religious traditions which are suspicious of any partnership between religion and the State may, nevertheless, unite with liberal secularists in claiming as wide a private sphere as possible. However, an essentially secular law may restrict freedom to personal privacy; that is, to activities in private by individuals or by small numbers in consensual relationships. As the law is expected to turn a blind eye to such activity, no distinction will be drawn, for example, between sexual activity which many would find abhorrent and small prayer meetings or sessions to study sacred texts[62]. Against this, the traditional place of religion in English public life may enable a more plural approach. This may be equally liberal in not interfering with personal choices in private but it will allow and may encourage public manifestation of personal religious belief at both a personal and a corporate level.

(2) Personal but Public

A religiously plural system of law will allow a public dimension to the personal manifestation of faith. This is well illustrated by the use of oaths in legal and other public proceedings. The Oaths Act 1978 begins by prescribing the norm that the Oath is to be taken by Christians on the

---

[61] R (Daly) v Secretary of State for the Home Department [2001] UKHL 26.

[62] The liberal acceptance of what would long have been considered obviously aberrant behaviour is shown for example in academic reaction to the notorious case of R v Brown and others [1994] 1 AC 212.

New Testament and Jews on the Old Testament[63]. However, other forms may be used for those who are not Christians or Jews[64]. Similarly, a court may permit a witness to affirm rather than swear any religious oath[65]. The crucial requirement today is that, 'The efficacy of an oath must depend on it being taken in a way binding, and intended to be binding, upon the conscience of the intended witness.'[66] Thus, in *R v Kemble*[67], a Muslim was held to have given reliable evidence where he had considered himself morally bound to tell the truth after taking the oath on a New Testament. Lord Lane CJ stressed that the oath must both appear to the court administering it to be binding on the witness and the witness must in fact consider it binding on his or her conscience.

The law, therefore, respects the religious beliefs represented by oaths but, pragmatically, it focuses on what the individual witness believes rather than on its formal validity under the internal law of the witness' religion[68]. Although the Oaths Act does affirm religious pluralism, it could be objected that it gives primacy to the Judeo-Christian tradition. Those wishing to use other religious oaths or to affirm are required to take the initiative in requesting their preference. This could be justified on the basis that Christianity is still recognised by the majority of the population as the religion of choice[69]. However, a more fully plural practice would be to invite witnesses to choose whether to take a religious oath or to affirm and if they opted for an oath to ask which form of oath they considered binding.

Oaths are legal instruments for personal manifestation of faith in the most public of circumstances. Although they are public, they can not be said to harm the rights of any one of a different belief. Rather, they benefit the legal process by playing to factors which, at least in some cases, are likely to make witnesses treat the proceedings more seriously.

---

[63] Oaths Act 1978, section 1(1).

[64] Section 1(3). An early example of religious pluralism in the courts was the acceptance of evidence taken on commission in India in 1745 from a Hindu witness, 'in a form recognised as binding by a member of that religion': *Omychund v Barker* [1745] 1 A & K 21. Twenty years later an oath taken on the Koran by an English convert to Islam was recognised in an English criminal court: *R v Morgan* [1764] 1 Leach 54.

[65] Section 5.

[66] *R v Chapman* [1980] Crim LR 42.

[67] *R v Kemble* [1990] 1 WLR 1111.

[68] Thus, in *Kemble*, the Court of Appeal (Criminal Division) discounted evidence by an expert in Islamic law that an oath on the New Testament was not binding under *Sharia* law.

[69] The census figures for 2000 showed over 72% of respondents in England and Wales identifying as Christians. <http://www.statistics.gov.uk/census2001/>.

Similarly, the wearing of religious dress or symbols, such as the cross, is essentially personal. In practice, this also may be permitted in the most public of contexts, as where a Sikh judge wears a turban when sitting in an English court.

Religious dress appears to be a touchstone for pluralism. There are circumstances where particular clothing may pose practical difficulties which justify restriction, as where a full veil hides the face and muffles the voice, making difficult identification of the person and hampering communication. Unlike the secular approach, a plural law would only impose restrictions on religious clothing in public for specific reasons of this sort and then only when the restrictions were proportionate in addressing the relevant problem. Also, in achieving a balance, a plural law may be expected to discern the real reason for the religious require-ment. Here, Sikhs have been treated with particular respect as a group with clear religious requirements as to dress, including the obligations for men not to cut their hair but to cover it with a turban and also always to carry a ceremonial sword or knife. Thus, concessions are made in road traffic regulations requiring the wearing of helmets by motor cycle riders which permit a turban to be worn instead[70].

Religious dress may give rise to particular controversy where it is per-ceived to threaten the monopoly of other beliefs. Female Muslim clothing in particular has been censored in avowedly secular jurisdictions and, despite Article 9 of the Convention, this has been justified by the Stras-bourg jurisprudence to safeguard the secular ethos of those societies[71]. *R (on the application of Begum) v Denbigh High School Governors*, which has been discussed above in respect of the location for decision making on religious rights, demonstrates a more nuanced approach. Miss Begum refused to return to her school at the beginning of a new school year, unless she was permitted to wear a *jilbab* (a long dress) rather than a *shalwar kameez* (a short dress over trousers). Both were forms of female Muslim dress but only the latter was available as a version of the school uniform. It was considered by Miss Begum to be less modest but it was approved by the mosques consulted by the school. The school itself had a high proportion of Muslim pupils and staff. The school's decision to

---

[70] Road Traffic Act 1988, s 16. As to turbans instead of hard hats on building sites see Employment Act 1989, sections 11 and 12; Employment Equality (Religion or Belief) Regulations 2003/1660, regulation 26.

[71] *Sahin v Turkey* (2004) ECHR 44774/98, ECt HR. See too the French ban on religious clothing in schools, Assemblée National, LOI no 2004-228 du 15 Mars 2004, JO no 65 du 17 Mars 2004, 5190.

exclude the pupil was eventually vindicated by the House of Lords as a proportionate exercise of discretion.

However, one of the underlying reasons why the school's actions were accepted as proportionate was the opportunity for Miss Begum to transfer to another school which would allow her to wear the *jilbab*. The decision was made against the background of other schools being available in the public sector to satisfy her religious rights[72]. Indeed, Lord Scott argued that a pupil who voluntarily chose to enter a faith school on the basis that this would involve participation in a daily act of worship would not be able to claim that her freedom of belief under Article 9 had been infringed if she became an atheist but was compelled to continue attending worship 'unless, perhaps, the institution offered an essential service not obtainable elsewhere'[73].

In other situations, the freedom of religious believers to manifest their faith is significantly determined by where the legal boundary is drawn between the public and the private spheres[74]. Here, the state has increasingly encroached on what was previously considered the private domain by regulating commercial relations between citizens, effectively drawing them from the private into the public domain. The regulation of contracts, particularly contracts of employment, has significant effects on freedom of religion for individuals. It is here that the struggle for a plural rather than a secular society may become increasingly evident.

If one seeks an underlying ethos for modern law, materialism and the promotion of economic productivity rival the protection of individual human rights. Certainly, the economic demands of employers may be given priority over personal religious rights of employees. Thus, religious people may be denied redress where they are indirectly discriminated against by an employer who imposes working practices which it is harder for them to comply with than it is for other employees. Where a Christian employee has claimed the right not to work on a Sunday, the response of the Strasbourg court, tamely accepted by English judges, has been that he is free to find a job elsewhere[75].

---

[72] By contrast, religious corporations may provide, in a private enclave, a place for activities which elsewhere would be seen as essentially public. Thus, faith schools may not be permitted in an avowedly secular state education system but private religious schools may still flourish in the same State.

[73] At para 88.

[74] See D Oliver *Common Values and the Public-Private Divide* (London, Butterworths 1999).

[75] See the case of *Copsey,* this reviews the Strasbourg case law and, although applying it, is not wholly uncritical.

Shops provide an exception where workers are specifically protected by statute from being required to work on a Sunday[76]. A more general right to opt out of Sunday working, except where this is necessary for specific reasons such as protecting life, would doubtless have economic consequences but it would be more consistent with a plural society. It would not prevent work being carried out on Sundays by non religious employees who were happy to do it. In the meanwhile, as we shall next consider, the law appears to be out of balance, because it can cause difficulties for religious associations which wish to operate on their own terms in the commercial field.

(3) Private but Corporate

Freedom of association for religious adherents brings together the Convention right of freedom of religion and belief in Article 9 with that of freedom of association in Article 11. Whether their numbers are large or small, if they are to be accorded genuine individual autonomy, believers must be free to regulate their working lives according to the moral principles taught by their religion. If they can not do this whilst working for secular employers who find religious practices obstructive, believers need to be free to carry out the same work with people of similar views. Therefore, exceptions may be required from the general law, so as to allow religious associations to operate on their own terms. This is particularly necessary where the general law seeks to privilege the individual autonomy of those whose morality conflicts with the group values of others[77].

However, the general law may make it difficult for believers to act corporately. This is strikingly illustrated by anti discrimination legislation. Here, the early anti discrimination case of *Mandela v Dowell Lee*[78] contrasts with that of *Begum*. In *Mandela* a private Christian school was held to have committed racial discrimination by refusing to accept a Sikh pupil unless he agreed not to wear a turban. Mandela was able to rely on specific legislation against racial discrimination because the Sikh religion coincides with a cultural group. Jews would similarly be protected as a racial and cultural group but members of most major world religions

---

[76] Sunday Trading Act 1994.

[77] See here generally R Ahdar, 'Religious Group Autonomy, Gay Ordination and Human Rights Law' in O'Dair and Lewis *Law and Religion* and P W Edge, 'The Employment of Religious Adherents by Religious Organisations' in P W Edge and G Harvey (eds) *Law and Religion in Contemporary Society*' (Aldershot, Ashgate 2000).

[78] [1983] 2 AC 548.

would not, because their members are drawn from all races and cultures. Today, if a private Christian school sought to ban turbans or other religious dress, so as to emphasise its Christian nature, a pupil affected could claim a breach of the law prohibiting both racial and religious discrimination[79] and could call in aid Article 9 of the European Convention on Human Rights. On the other hand, those running and using the school could claim that preventing it from imposing rules on dress, designed to protect its own religious ethos, was a breach of their right to religious freedom. How the relationship between the *Mandela* and *Begum* cases would be played out must be left to future litigation. But what is striking is that, in *Mandela,* a faith school in the private sector was afforded less leeway in organising its affairs than the state non faith school in *Begum.*

Anti discrimination legislation, partly driven by the European Union, ostensibly promotes many of the specific rights provided in the European Convention on Human Rights, but it inevitably promotes certain rights at the expense of others[80]. As the rules are set in legislation, the balance may need to be adjusted by making exceptions if account is to be taken of interests which conflict with those which the relevant legislation is designed to protect. These exceptions are particularly important for believers who have moral qualms about working with people holding conflicting beliefs and for believers who positively wish to work with coreligionists. Anti discrimination law now generally prohibits religious beliefs or practices being used as a criterion in selection. However, religious organisations may require a particular religious commitment from employees in certain circumstances.

The Employment Equality (Religion or Belief) Regulations 2003, Regulation 7(2)(a) makes an exception, whether or not the employer has an ethos based on religion or belief, where, 'having regard to the nature of the employment or the context in which it is carried out being of a particular religion or belief is a genuine and determining occupational requirement'. By paragraph (3) there is a further exception where an employer has an ethos based on religion or belief and, 'having regard to that ethos and to the nature of the employment or the context in which it is carried out, (a) being of a particular religion or belief is a genuine occupational requirement for the job'. In each case it must be shown that (b) it is proportionate to apply that requirement in the particular case; and (c) either

---

[79] Race Relations Act 1996, Equality Act 2006, Part II and Employment Equality (Religion or Belief) Regulations 2003, SI No 1660.

[80] See further Pauline Roberts' contribution to this volume.

– (i) the person to whom that requirement is applied does not meet it, or (ii) the employer is not satisfied, and in all the circumstances it is reasonable for him not to be satisfied, that that person meets it.

Although the regulations against discrimination in employment do make some exceptions for religious sensitivities of employers, it is not clear to what extent a religious association, such as a group of professional practitioners or a manufacturing or service business, can insist on all its employees being co religionists. Generally, the law seems likely to protect employees who oppose a religious employer applying, in the workplace, beliefs they do not share. By contrast, as we have seen, it may be less protective of religious employees whose faith conflicts with the demands of an ordinary, commercial employer[81].

There appears, therefore, to be an imbalance between the liberty of commercial employers to override the religious sensibilities of their employees and the prohibitions on discrimination which prevent people with specific religious principles from functioning, commercially, within a market of those who share their beliefs. There appears to be a similar imbalance with regard to legislation designed to establish equality for persons of a homosexual orientation[82]. In a case between *Amicus* and other Trade Unions, in which the Christian group, *Christian Action Research Education* was allowed to intervene[83], the Trade Unions challenged exceptions to regulations banning discrimination against employees on the grounds of their sexual orientation. The exceptions were designed to protect religious sensitivities[84]. Richards J upheld the validity of an exception on the basis that it was proportionate in balancing the rights of those with a same sex orientation against those who believed that homosexuality is morally wrong. He quoted at length the speech of Lord Sainsbury, the

---

[81] See *Copsey*.

[82] Equality Act 2006, Part III.

[83] *R (on the application of Amicus -MSF section and others) v Secretary of State for Trade and Industry and Christian Action Research Education and others* [2004] IRLR 430.

[84] One exception permits discrimination on the grounds of sexual orientation based on the proportionate application of a genuine and determining occupational requirement; Employment Equality (Sexual Orientation) Regulations 2003, regs 7(2), 7(3), 20(3) and 25. A second, wider, exception is provided in favour of organised religions which discriminate (i) so as to comply with the doctrines of the religion or (ii) because of the nature of the employment and the context in which it is carried out, so as to avoid conflicting with the strongly held religious convictions of a significant number of the religion's followers. This second exception applies where (i) the person to whom the requirement is applied does not meet the requirements of the organisation, or (ii) the employer is not satisfied, and in all the circumstances it is reasonable for him not to be satisfied, that that person meets it.

Minister presenting the legislation, to show the limited scope of the exception: Lord Sainsbury anticipated that a nurse in a care home, a teacher in
a faith school, a cleaner, a gardener a secretary or a librarian would not
be able to rely on the exception.[85]

The regulations prohibiting discrimination against those with a same sex
orientation in employment are seen by a vocal group of religious believers
as a major interference with their religious freedom to choose employees
who conform with their moral standards. This has been even more striking
with the regulations prohibiting discrimination in the provision of goods
and services[86].

The point made in this section is that the law has been adapted in a
manner which intrudes into the corporate lives of believers by treating
what were, previously, the subject of private contract as matters for public concern. This may be seen as imposing a new public morality which
is the opposite of that which used to prevail. In fact, the new morality
may actually be acceptable to and indeed partly driven by people with
Christian beliefs. However, it is indisputable that others with strong religious convictions believe that the changes are morally wrong. If the
guiding principle of human rights law is personal autonomy, it is difficult
to see how it can be proportionate to override the consciences of such
individuals. Realistically, those discriminated against will readily be able
to find the employment, goods and services they require, elsewhere. If
what they object to is the offensiveness of their treatment, they are effectively seeking to trump the freedom of expression of their religious opponents. A plural approach would allow corporate associations in the private
sphere to follow their members' conscience even if it meant offending
others.

The present law is slanted in favour of those with a same sex orientation. Employers and those providing goods or services who are conservative religious believers are obliged to change their practices or withdraw from the market. Their predicament contrasts sharply with that of
the employer who requires employees to work in a manner contrary to
their religious principles for example by working on a Sunday. There,
it is the believing employee, rather than the commercially motivated
employer, who is likely to be required to go elsewhere.

---

[85] See further Pauline Roberts' contribution to this volume.
[86] Equality Act 2006 s 81 and Equality Act (Sexual Orientation) Regulations 2007,
SI 1263.

(4) Corporate and Public

In a plural society, public recognition of religion may involve the incorporation of organisations with a faith basis in some degree of partnership with the State. Such partnership may be beneficial to society in material terms. Faith schools and the management of historic buildings which comprise a significant part of the national heritage, religious care homes for the elderly and other groups with special needs, or religious provision of social services, such as adoption agencies can, in part, shift financial burdens off the state to private donors. They can channel state funding efficiently through volunteers. It may be that much of this benefit could be achieved through voluntary associations which do not recognise any underlying authority outside the State. However, religious bodies[87] offer a particular depth of enthusiasm and dedication because they tap into what their members see as fundamental moral principles.

If religious individuals are restricted as to what they are allowed to do through religious associations, they may redirect their energies to activities which are of no social benefit even if they are not harmful to the wider community[88]. Alternatively, they may vent their frustration by opposing the State, in extreme cases even with violence. By contrast, if religious organisations are integrated with the state it may be easier to monitor them and to ensure that they inculcate shared values, particularly of toleration, which make for social stability and cohesion. Resistance to such arrangements may be posed by those within the religious community who fear that their beliefs will be compromised by pressure to conform to the values of wider society. A telling example is, again, the problem which some traditional religious believers have with tolerating same sex relationships. Conversely, those with a secular perspective may resist the corporate integration of religion with similar fundamentalist objections. This may involve stereotyping all religious traditions as somehow irrational and obscurantist. Here the underlying objection may really be the recognition that a religion refers to a source of authority beyond the state.

The point to be made here is that if the law is truly plural it will accept different religious associations as partners in providing public services. On the other hand, the State may in return demand fuller conformity with a common public ethic. A religious association may be

---

[87] This may include quasi religious organisation, such as humanist associations.

[88] *Cocks v Manners* (1871) LR 12 Eq 574 and *In re Coats Trust, Coats v Gilmour* [1948] Ch 1.

formally characterised as a public body or its functions may be deemed
public in the sense that it is itself bound to observe Convention rights[89].
However, whether it is public in this sense or not, more conformity may
be required of a religious association the more its activities are public,
rather than simply corporate, as where Roman Catholic adoption agencies will be unable to continue operating unless they accept same sex
adoptive parents[90].

Conclusion

The separation of religion from the State is a principle inherited from
the Enlightenment which has become a dogma for Western liberal democracy. However, it is a principle which can take a secular or a plural form.
This chapter has pointed to evidence that in many respects English law
today provides a plural model, although it is squeezed by secular pressures to marginalise religion. Whether the law will become more secular
or more coherently plural could simply be left to the vagaries of democratic governance. However, whether one favours a secular or a plural
model, a more principled and structured approach would seem both possible and desirable. In the light of the discussion in this paper five general
principles are suggested for developing instruments to ensure that the law
is plural.

First, the contribution of faith traditions to the stability of society, as
well as their disruptive capacity, needs to be addressed in a more informed
manner. Religious belief can only be taken seriously if it is recognised as
more than a matter of individual liberty. The importance of major religious traditions as sources of authority beyond the Positivist institutions
of national law need to be accepted and points of conflict taken into
account as a matter of course in formulating legislation. Article 9 of the
European Convention of Human Rights and the traditional establishment
of religion by law in England reflect different but not necessarily incompatible approaches[91].

Second, where there are likely to be conflicts between beliefs, mechanisms are needed for ensuring that the balance is struck at the most
appropriate level. Both religious and secular fundamentalists may seek

---

[89] Cf *Aston Cantlow v Wallbank* [2003] UKHL 37. There, Church of England Parochial Church Councils were held not be public bodies or even performing a public function
in their role of caring for historic church buildings.

[90] Equality Act (Sexual Orientation) Regulations 2007, SI 1263, regulation 15.

[91] See further Charlotte Smith's contribution to this volume.

to control decision making. Where there is sufficient choice for those whose views are suppressed to go elsewhere, controversial decisions may best be dealt with at a lower level. However, major areas of conflict or ones where a particular belief appears to be inconsistent with a major shared social principle such as preventing discrimination require clear guidance at a higher level, preferably in Parliamentary legislation.

Third, more attention should be given to how much space is allowed to religious believers to live in accordance with their beliefs. The manner in which the general law hampers the freedom of religious believers needs to be clearly recognised, especially where changes in the general law are likely to involve new restrictions. A plural approach will follow the emphasis of the Human Rights Act 1998 on individual autonomy by emphasising the freedom of individuals to manifest their faith in the public sphere in such personal matters as dress. In the border lands between public and private, notably in employment law and other areas where the focus is on commercial interests, particular leeway should be allowed for the conscience of organised religious believers. Where services such as education are provided within the public system, significant religious interests need to be safeguarded and may be extended, notably in the provision of faith schools and chaplaincies.

Fourth, in an avowedly plural law, policies will be actively promoted to provide more public space for religious believers. More exceptions and conscience clauses will be built in to enable religious believers to live lives which are as fully integrated as possible with their neighbours'. More partnerships will be encouraged between the State and religious bodies in the provision of social goods, such as schooling. More effort will be made to ensure that the general law accommodates religious sensitivities in the way social life is organised, for example by maintaining a time structure, particularly with Sunday as a protected day of rest, which accords with major religious traditions. By comparison, a more secular approach may lead to the marginalisation of believers. Even so, rudimentary recognition of their rights should ensure that they are not forced to do acts prohibited by their religion or prevented from doing what their beliefs positively require. Where a minister certifies whether new legislation is compatible with the Human Rights Act, this should expressly take into account whether religious principles are affected and if these are overridden should justify doing so, unless appropriate exceptions or conscience clauses are provided[92].

[92] Human Rights Act 1998, section 19.

Fifth, for their part, religious believers need to develop clearer principles for relating to the State and these may need to be expressed in their own internal laws. They must acknowledge that full participation in civic society needs to be qualified by respect for its diversity. This will require a clearer distinction between the parts of religious law which may appropriately be expressed in the general law and those which may not. In arguing for reform of the general law, the priorities of believers may be determined by their faith but they must use arguments which carry weight on their own, apart from any underlying religious authority. The more secular the general law, the more difficult it may be for believers to participate fully with a clear conscience. However, there is an essential difference between thwarting those with different beliefs and demanding freedom not to be compromised by having to submit to those beliefs.

Developing laws which enable religious pluralism will, thus, include a new understanding of the respective spheres of God and Caesar appropriate for democratic governance in a society of mixed beliefs[93]. From a religious perspective this involves identifying common criteria of what constitutes good of the neighbour. It then means criticising the law prophetically and seeking reform against those shared criteria. On its part, a plural State will recognise the claim and indeed the social benefit of integrating believers, not simply as individuals but on the basis of their religious commitment to shared social aims. Religious believers may need to be less diffident about claiming rights for themselves, but both they and their secular opponents need to be clearer as to what is genuine freedom of action for a particular person and what is the unnecessary restriction of another.

---

[93] The classical Biblical texts include, notably, Romans 13:1-7.

A COLLECTION OF STATES OR A STATE OF MIND? THE RELIGIOUS AND SPIRITUAL DIMENSION OF EUROPEAN CITIZENSHIP*

Alexandra Pimor

Introduction

The EU is primarily a union of States and not of peoples, it is a construct of governments and not of citizens; as such, there is an arguable lack of emotional and human bonding between the Union and its citizens[1]. This has led some to ask whether the ideological support for the common market and economic rights accorded by the founding Treaties are a sufficient incentive to maintain affective support for the Union[2], to which the French and Dutch 'no' vote on the former draft Constitutional Treaty seems to answer in the negative.

It has been argued that for a society to survive it must have meaning, including values, attitudes, and assumptions, coupled with 'an understanding of the present reality and a vision of the future'[3]. Therefore, in order for the Union to develop into more than an economic community and become a truly social, political and cultural entity, it must capture the hearts and imagination of its peoples[4], and ensure their support by encouraging a sense of belonging and ownership. The European Commissioner Margot Wallström thus asserts that 'a political integration project, such as the EU, can only work if people are part of writing the

---

* Please note that the chosen title for this chapter was spotted on an airport advert billboard whilst on a trip to France in May 2008.

[1] A Coughlan, 'A Critical Analysis of the EU Draft Constitution' *TEAM Working Paper* No.10, 2003 <http://teameurope.info/wp-analysisconstitution.nr10.pdf>.

[2] B Nelsen and J Guth, 'Religion and Attitudes toward the European Union: the New Member States, A Research Note' [2005] <http://aei.pitt.edu/3053/01/EUSA_2005_1.5.pdf>.

[3] B Reynolds and S Healy, 'The Practice of Spirituality and Social Engagement' [2002] <http://www.cori.ie/Justice/Spirituality/45-Spirituality/196-the_practice_spirituality_social_engagement?format=pdf >.

[4] F Amedeo, *Les Fossoyeurs de l'Europe – Diatribe Politique* (Bourin Éditeurs, 2005).

"script" [and] if it is possible for them to relate to and identify with the project as a commonly agreed venture'[5]; a view which is echoed by the Union's efforts to get closer to its citizens by promoting a holistic conception of citizenship that, beyond the purely legalistic, would also include political, social and cultural components for the advancement of a common European identity and a more active citizenship.

Given that religion is said to constitute a 'fundamental part of people's preoccupations, reactions and behaviour'[6] and is a source of value-, identity- and meaning-making processes, it is deemed to be an essential element of European integration and development, as suggested by the modified preamble of the Treaty on the European Union (TEU)[7], which asserts that the latter draws inspiration from 'the cultural, religious and humanist inheritance of Europe'. Furthermore, given the long-held search for Europe's soul and spirituality [8] and the increasing popular interest in spiritual affairs over the last two decades[9]; and considering that the preamble of the EU Charter on Fundamental Rights[10] states that the Union is 'conscious of its spiritual and moral heritage', it is apparent that spirituality may also have a key role to play in the European venture.

Therefore, on the premise that religion and spirituality occupy a significant position in peoples' individual and collective lives, as well as in the European private and, increasingly, public spheres, the chapter aims to explore the possibility that a holistic Union citizenship could encompass distinct religious and spiritual dimensions. This reflection is two-fold: whilst the first part covers the convoluted nature of Union citizenship and its holistic aspiration; the second part addresses the potential spiritual and religious dimensions of EU citizenship.

---

[5] M Wallström Vice President of the European Commission responsible for Institutional affairs and communication strategy, 'Bridging the Gap; How to bring Europe and its Citizens Closer Together?' (speech/05/668).

[6] R Rémond, *Religion and Society in Modern Europe* (Oxford, Blackwell Publishers, 1999) 5.

[7] As amended by the Treaty of Lisbon (2007).

[8] The call for Europe's soul searching and spirituality was initially given by Jacques Delors in an address to European church leaders in 1993.

[9] Ford argues that over 70% of Europeans believe either in a 'god', spirit or life force, reinforcing the view that Europe faces a 'crisis of secularism'; see P Ford, 'In a Secular Ocean, Waves of Spirituality' [2005] *The Christian Science Monitor* <http://www.csmonitor.com/2005/0223/p01s03-woeu.htm>.

[10] The scope of which is yet to be determined once it is given legal force following the Lisbon Treaty ratification.

Union Citizenship: Towards a Holistic Conception

The idea of a European Union citizenship was broached as early as the 1960s, and received further support in the 1970s with former Belgium Prime Minister, Leo Tindemans reporting to the European Council that a technocratic Europe is undesirable. Europe, he argues, is not merely a collaborative project that is the sole custody of the Member States but is also a *rapprochement*[11] of the peoples', whose values 'are their common heritage'[12]. Tindemans recalls that, as was the intention of the founding fathers and as is reflected in the Treaties, the Union must be brought closer to its citizens, so as to create a 'new type of society', with greater legitimacy, democracy, solidarity and humanity. Consequently, he emphasises the necessity for a 'human dimension' to the European project, whereby EU citizens should not merely feel the effects of Union policies, but should also 'experience the European Union in their daily life'[13].

A legal and political conception of union citizenship

In 1992, the Maastricht Treaty formally recognised European citizenship within the Union's constitutional and legal framework, amending the Treaty of Rome to incorporate Article 17(1) of the Treaty Establishing the European Community (ECT) which established the Citizenship of the Union. The provision asserts that 'Every person holding the nationality of a Member State shall be a citizen of the Union', and that Union citizenship is complementary and not a replacement to national citizenship[14]. The European Parliament describes Union citizenship as 'a dynamic

---

[11] A 'bringing together'.

[12] L Tindemans, 'European Union. Report to the European Council (The Tindemans Report)' *Bulletin of the European Communities*, Supplement 1/76, at 26.

[13] Tindemans, 'The Tindemans Report' at 12.

[14] This citizenship provision, as amended by the Treaty on the Functioning of the European Union (TFEU), is now contained in article 20 TFEU, which describes Union citizenship as 'additional' and no longer simply as a 'complement' to national citizenship. This new wording choice has led some to wonder whether there is a new hierarchal relationship between national and Union citizenships, rather than just complementary one; a particularly relevant question regarding the citizenship status of the Queen of England as the Queen of Australia and other Realms (see A Mote MP, 'Australian Concern over the Enforced Citizenship of the Queen' 2008 <http://www.wewannado.com/?p=344<). What would be the implications when this 'additional', also termed 'double' EU citizenship involves obligations, and these conflicts with national citizenship duties? As EU law prevails over domestic law, should EU citizenship eventually prevail over national citizenship in given EU-specific situations where Union matters would override national concerns?

institution, a key to the process of European integration [and] for the citizen, the guarantee of belonging to a political community under the rule of law'[15]; a view further supported by the statement of the European Court of Justice[16] that Union citizenship is deemed to become 'the fundamental status of nationals of all the Member States'[17].

So, originally a legally engineered concept, the source and substance of European citizenship are to be found in Articles 17 to 22 ECT which clarify the rights inherent to the citizenship status. As stated by David Edward[18]:

> Citizenship confers positive, albeit limited, rights. The limits must be stated expressly and are not subject to the discretion of the Member States (MS). To that extent, European citizenship is not a myth, and is no longer just a hope or political idea. It constitutes a new and significant legal category or status[19].

The legal definition of European citizenship, contained in the current Article 17 ECT, provides that it is dependant on the individual being a citizen of a Member State; therefore EU citizenship is based on a pre-existing Member State nationality criterion, which does not supersede or replace national citizenship, but instead supplements or enhances the latter by providing it with additional Union rights. The substance of EU citizenship is based on four key principles, including freedom of movement and settlement[20], election rights[21], diplomatic and consular protection rights[22], and finally petition and contact rights[23]. Edward further states that, besides the exercise of free movement and economic rights Union citizenship also ensures equal treatment of citizens across the Union. It follows that components of Union citizenship are not solely found in

[15] European Parliament, *Resolution on the Second Commission report on Citizenship of the Union* (COM(97)0230 – C4-0291/97) A4-0205/1998.

[16] European Court of Justice (ECJ).

[17] ECJ C-184/99 *Grzelczyk v Centre public d'aide sociale d'Ottignies-Louvain-la-Neuve*.

[18] ECJ judge.

[19] D Edward 'European Citizenship – Myth, Hope or Reality? The Interpretation of Article 18 of the EC Treaty' in A N Sakkoulas (ed), *Problemes D'interpretation: A la Mémoire de Constantinos N Kakouris* (Bruxelles, Bruylant, 2004) 123-134 at 131.

[20] Article 18 ECT, now Article 21 TFEU.

[21] Article 19 ECT, now Article 22 TFEU, the right to right to vote for and stand as a candidate to municipal and EP elections.

[22] Article 20 ECT, now Article 23 TFEU.

[23] Article 21 ECT, right to petition the European Parliament and to complain to the EU ombudsman, now Article 24 which also includes the Citizen's initiative right (current Article 11 TEU).

Articles 17-22 ECT, but are in fact scattered across the *acquis commun-autaire*, making Union citizenship 'a very uncentred notion' whereby

> the relevant provisions in EU law lack transparency as they are spread throughout the treaties, secondary legislation and case law – like a scattering of jigsaw pieces which at first glance do not seem capable of fitting together into any articulated notion of citizenship[24].

Consequently, in addition to the four primary rights the Union also guarantees, for instance, non-discrimination[25], equality[26] and the protection of fundamental rights[27] for its citizens. This, however, is not an exhaustive list of rights, as Article 22(2) ECT[28] also provides that Union institutions may take measures to 'strengthen and add to' the primary rights as contained in Article 18 ECT[29], thus suggesting that the legal nature of Union citizenship allows for a fluid and organic growth of its parameter and scope, for it is not a notion explicitly defined by the Treaties nor corseted within a rigid legal framework. Following a traditional conception of citizenship[30], EU citizenship is thus infused with at least two dimensions: a formal one, which provides a membership status to its citizens; and a substantial one, which guarantees an array of citizens' rights and duties[31].

Exploring EU citizenship from a legal perspective is often the obvious approach, since EC legislation generated the concept, and the latter is

---

[24] S Douglas-Scott *Constitutional Law of the European Union* (London, Pearson Longman 2002) at 485.

[25] Article 12 ECT on non-discrimination on grounds of nationality, now Article 18 TFEU.

[26] Article 13 ECT, now Article 10 TFEU on non-discrimination based on sex, racial or ethnic origin, religion or belief, disability, age or sexual orientation; Article 19 TFEU also provides the Council with the power to take measures towards combating discrimination.

[27] A protection offered by the intricate web constituted of EU Treaty provisions, including Article 6 TEU; ECJ case law; the European Charter of Fundamental Rights; and references to the European Convention of Human Rights and Member State's constitutional traditions.

[28] Now Article 25(2) TFEU.

[29] Although Shaw argues that this developmental potential is limited by the fact that the main impetus for going forward with EU citizenship lies mainly in the hands of MS, see J Shaw, *The Transformation of Citizenship in the European Union* (Cambridge, Cambridge University Press, 2007) 9.

[30] D Dunkerly, L Hodgson, S Konopacki, T Spybey and A Thompson, *Changing Europe – Identities, Nations and Citizens* (London, Routledge, 2002) 9-22.

[31] Despite a mention in the Charter that the rights attached to European citizenship also entail responsibilities and duties (to other person, the human community and future generations), there is no clear information on what these entail. Therefore, this aspect of European citizenship remains rather vague, if not empty of practical meaning so far.

often described as a rights-based citizenship[32]. However, though its substantial character is anchored in market-based mobility rights[33], Union citizenship is nevertheless also a political conception attached to political rights, and was initiated for political purposes, having evolved from a legal to a political theory of European integration since the early 1970s[34]. Therefore, some view a purely legal analysis of the concept of citizenship as a restrictive and minimalist methodology, which runs the risk of 'repeating a normative discourse on citizenship' and ignoring its political and historical implications[35]. Others have coined the minimalist approach to defining citizenship 'the legal-participatory approach', arguing that a rights-based European citizenship is operable or active only when citizens actually participate in the development of European governance and policy, or by exercising the substantive rights provided under EC law[36]. In other words, those individuals who do not exercise their right to freely move across the Union to seek employment or for educational purposes, or who do not exercise their right to vote at European Parliament elections may not necessarily experience the practical benefits of that status, and therefore be unable to give it meaning or even contemplate its value in their personal life.

Either way, the criticism here is that a narrow legal and economic view of European citizenship does not provide an accurate picture of the concept of citizenship, and would unfortunately prevent citizens from developing a deeper attachment to the European project. Indeed, a primarily market-based citizenship, and a Union allegedly founded on a 'materialistic-utilistic ideology of economic growth'[37], cannot emulate the kind of support and attachment that citizens pledge to their nation-State; consequently, people are unlikely to 'ever risk their lives for such nasty

[32] G Delanty, 'European Citizenship: A Critical Assessment' (2007) 11(1) *Citizenship Studies* 63-72.

[33] R Bellamy, 'The "Right to Have Rights": Citizenship Practice and the Political Constitution of the EU' in R Bellamy and A Warleigh (ed), *Citizenship and Governance in the European Union* (London, Continuum, 2001) 40-70; M Poiares Maduro, 'Europe's Social Self: "The Sickness Unto Death"' School of Politics, International Studies and Philosophy, QUB, ConWEB, No.2/2000 <http://www.qub.ac.uk/schools/SchoolofPolitics-InternationalStudiesandPhilosophy/FileStore/ConWEBFiles/Filetoupload,38364,en.pdf>.

[34] Shaw, *The Transformation of Citizenship in the European Union* at 96-101.

[35] Y Déloye, 'Exploring the Concept of European Citizenship: A Socio-Historical Approach' (2000) 14 *Yearbook of European Studies* 197-219.

[36] MA Becker, 'Managing Diversity in the European Union: Inclusive European Citizenship and Third-Country Nationals' (2004) 7 *Yale Human Rights & Development Law Journal* 132-183.

[37] A Zijlstra, 'The Soul of Europe. A search for Meaning and Identity' [2005] *Key-note lecture Intensive Programme 'The Soul of Europe: Worldviews and Identities in a Changing Continent* 1 at 3.

things as consumerism and hedonism'[38]. Therefore, despite the contestations of Euro sceptics, it is increasingly advocated and even acknowledged that the Union cannot progress any further as a merely economic entity, and must fully embrace its political endeavour in order to gain popular support and inspire its citizens[39]; the promotion of Union citizenship is therefore essential to the Union's aspiration to becoming a political, cultural, social and democratic constitutional polity[40].

An unfulfilling citizenship

The political nature of Union citizenship is therefore essential from the onset, as a legal-economic conception would be counter-productive to achieving the aim of bringing the Union and its citizens closer to each other. Still, what value individuals attach to their citizenship status is debatable: Union citizenship seems to go unnoticed by many ordinary citizens[41], as its political scope is said to lack any emotional meaningfulness, experiential value, and practical impact on citizens' lives for they do not generally exercise their political rights. This view is further evidenced by recent empirical research, which suggests that EU citizens are more likely to exercise their free movement and other socio-economic rights, rather than their political rights, of which they in fact seem to be rather oblivious or simply uninterested about[42]. This has led a former CFI judge[43] to state that it was difficult to speak of citizenship in the context of the Community Treaties:

> since this concept deals mainly with rights of political participation and of public nature, that is, rights that imply the participation of the individual in the construction of a political entity in which he is inscribed[44].

This statement quite accurately points out the main weakness inherent to EU citizenship: the lack of active citizen participation in the construction

---

[38] Ibid.

[39] F Amedeo, *Les Fossoyeurs de l'Europe – Diatribe Politique* (Bourin Éditeurs 2005).

[40] S Besson and A Utzinger, 'Future Challenges of European Citizenship – Facing a Wide-Open Pandora's Box' (2007) 13(5) *European Law Journal* 573-590.

[41] Bellamy and Warleigh, *Citizenship and Governance in the European Union.*

[42] A Favell, 'European Citizenship in Three Eurocities' paper presented at the European Union Studies Association Conference, Austin (TX) <http://aei.pitt.edu/3096/02/austin2.doc>; J Painter, 'European Citizenship and the Regions' *Queen's Papers on Europeanisation* (7/2003), <http://www.qub.ac.uk/schools/SchoolofPoliticsInternationalStudiesandPhilosophy/FileStore/EuropeanisationFiles/Filetoupload,38407,en.pdf>.

[43] Professor Rui Manuel Gens de Moura Ramos, former judge at the European Court of First Instance of the European Communities from 1995 to 2003.

[44] RMG de Moura Ramos, European Union Citizenship (2003).

of the Union polity, which may be explained by the particular nature of Union citizenship, as opposed to the traditional nation-State paradigm. As traditional citizenship describes and determines the nature of the relationship between the individual and the State, a relationship which is characterised by a *demos* who lends allegiance to their government, such key components as a common people, a shared national identity, and a popular affective attachment to the State would therefore appear necessary to the development of Union citizenship. However, the Union does not embody a common people, but is a Community of communities, joining a multiplicity of peoples and cultures together under one roof. This diversity of peoples, characterised by the lack of ethnic, cultural and linguistic homogeneity, indicates that the Union cannot claim to have a single common identity. It has been argued that people gel together through the recognition of a common identity bolstered by mutual support, which is seen as:

> the basis of a shared citizenship that people feel is real to them. This solidarity is also the basis of a stable political democracy [which] underpins a people's allegiance to a government as "their" government[45].

This kind of bonding solidarity, tough mainly found 'within national communities alone', is not present in the European venture, leading to the conclusion that there is no *demos*, no 'we' as Europeans[46]. Furthermore, since the nation is 'the object of intense emotional and psychological investment' from individuals who derive from their national allegiance a sense of identity and civic commitment[47], it follows that a lack of a common European identity may be the source of citizens' disinterest in and disengagement with Union affairs. Despite its efforts, the Union has failed to unravel and define a specific European identity, as the latter cannot be imposed by the state or government, least of all by Union institutions, but must come from the ground root up[48]. However, EU citizenship is a 'top-down constructed character'[49] and not the product of a grassroots movement or popular will. Instead, it is the conception of an artificial process of economic unification through intergovernmental negotiations,

---

[45] Coughlan, 'A Critical Analysis of the EU Draft Constitution' at 9.

[46] Ibid.

[47] Déloye 'Exploring the Concept of European Citizenship: A Socio-Historical Approach' at 212.

[48] K Biendenkopf, 'United in diversity: What Holds Europe Together?' in K Michalski (ed), *What Holds Europe Together* (Budapest, Central European University Press, 2006) Vol. 1, 13-29.

[49] Shaw, *The Transformation of Citizenship in the European Union* at 9.

and emerged 'as a result of a series of bargains among leaders of putatively sovereign states'[50]. As the concept developed alongside the evolving European project and the creation of individual rights through successive founding and amending treaties, the absence of a real popular impetus to come and stick together implies that the Union is unable to guarantee the allegiance of its citizens, who, it is argued, 'will never be willing to die for the EU, and will only notionally live for it'[51].

Following a basic functional definition, citizenship provides the following: membership into a political community; legal status, rights and obligations; a model of good conduct; criteria of origin; and an identity denominator fostering belonging and social cohesion[52]. Whilst Union citizenship provides the membership card[53]; legal status[54]; a model of good conduct[55]; and a criterion of origin[56]; it nevertheless misses an arguably essential (and controversial) element that is the common identity (or emotive) factor. In other words, European citizenship lacks the affective element which assures individuals' attachment to a collective identity and their commitment to a political community.

The Union recognises this deficiency and aims to remedy it by promoting active citizenship through education in a bid to bring the Union closer to its citizens, and to ensure that they have the means to shape its future. The European Commission, entrusted by the Amsterdam Treaty to develop the citizenship of the Union, thus states in its mission statement on Education and Active Citizenship in the European Union that:

> Having the right to participate in economic, political and social life is not equivalent to doing so in practice, nor indeed being equipped to do so on equal terms. [...] The practice of active citizenship is therefore a question

---

[50] W Maas, 'Challenges of European Citizenship', Paper presented at the 102nd annual meeting of the American Political Science Association, Philadelphia PA, 1 September 2006 <http://www.yorku.ca/maas/Maas-APSA06.pdf>.

[51] Coughlan, 'A critical analysis of the EU draft Constitution' at 9.

[52] C Birzea 'European Citizenship as a Cultural and Political Construct' (2005) *Online Journal für Sozialwissenschaften und ihre Didaktik*, <http://www.sowi-online.de/journal/2005-se/birzea_european_citizenship.htm>.

[53] Only EU citizens are entitled to exercise the Citizens' rights as contained in chapter 5 of the Charter.

[54] With the four primary rights and additional rights contained throughout the *acquis communautaire*.

[55] Through various schemes aimed at developing awareness and a sense of European citizenship with, for instance, the European capital of culture; citizenship education in school across Europe; and European citizens' web forum for open communication & discussions.

[56] As EU citizenship is automatically granted to a Member State citizen/national.

of being empowered to handle the practice of democratic culture, and feeling that one has a stake in getting involved in the communities in which one lives, whether by choice or force of circumstance. The concept of active citizenship ultimately speaks to the extent to which individuals and groups feel a sense of attachment to the societies and communities to which they theoretically belong, and is therefore closely related to the promotion of social inclusion and cohesion as well as to matters of identity and values. These are the affective dimensions of active citizenship.[57]

The Union therefore considers that providing better information, guidance and opportunities for the practice of citizenship would contribute to educating its citizens; an approach seemingly validated by recent empirical research, which finds that the reason behind the low levels of citizenship rights usage are to be explained by individuals' lack of awareness of these rights, or by their inability to exercise them effectively[58]. Accordingly, better citizenship awareness means empowered citizens who have a clearer understanding of their rights and political environment. However, to make Union citizenship meaningful 'it should also be reflected *sociologically* in the choices, experiences and behaviour of European citizens'[59]. Therefore, as highlighted in the European Commission statement above, attachment and belonging would enhance the probability of citizens' engagement in Union affairs if they can identify with, and see their values reflected in the European community. The way forward therefore appears to be towards adopting a holistic model of EU citizenship.

Towards a meaningful conception of Union citizenship

> An effective and just economic order must also be embedded in the morals, customs, and expectations of human beings, as well as in their social institutions[60].

This implies that the Union needs to become a political entity which reflects, pursues and protects the values of its citizens, thus ensuring its legitimacy; consequently, in order for its institutions to function effectively,

---

[57] European Commission, *Learning for Active Citizenship: A Significant Challenge in Building a Europe of Knowledge*, 1998 DGXXII at 2.1(2) <http://ec.europa.eu/education/archive/citizen/citiz_en.html>.

[58] Favell, 'European Citizenship in Three Eurocities'.

[59] Ibid.

[60] K Biedenkopf, B Geremek, K Michalski & M Rocard, 'What Hold Europe Together? Concluding Remarks' in Michalski *What holds Europe together?* at 96.

democratically and legitimately, the Union should 'involve itself more with [EU citizens] particular concerns'[61] and place them 'at the heart of its activities'[62]. Literature on EU citizenship abounds, as does the material attempting to define the concept, which from whatever vantage point, whether political, legal, sociological or other, is seen as ambiguous, difficult, elusive, complex, contested and fragmented[63]. The concept of citizenship itself is contingent, circumstantial and contextual, and 'is not an eternal essence but a cultural artefact [that] is what people manage to derive from it'[64].

This is particularly true of Union citizenship, which, as previously stated, is not a static and finite notion with clear delineation, nor is it fixed within a rigid theoretical conceptualisation. Instead, the European Court of Justice's jurisprudence in the development of citizenship law[65], and academic commentaries demonstrate that European citizenship is a dynamic process of integration, an evolving phenomenon, a practice or 'lived experience'[66], which responds to the Union's needs and to citizens' meaning and value-making endeavour. EU citizenship is thus a convoluted notion characterised by a multifaceted nature reflecting its diverse peoples and as evidence by its various conceptions; including, for instance, legal, political, market/economic, youth, social, gender and sexual citizenships[67]. It appears therefore that Union citizenship has clear holistic ambitions, and whilst 'holistic' will mean different things to different people in different contexts, it is argued that defining holistic as 'emphasizing the importance of the organic, interdependent relationship between

---

[61] Laeken Declaration 2001.

[62] Preamble of the Charter of Fundamental Rights of the Union.

[63] Bellamy, 'The "Right to Have Rights": Citizenship Practice and the Political Constitution of the EU' in Douglas Scott *Constitutional Law of the European Union*.

[64] C Birzea, 'European Citizenship as a Cultural and Political Construct' quoting H van Gunsteren, *A Theory of Citizenship: Organizing Plurality in Contemporary Democracies* (Oxford, Westview Press, 1998)11.

[65] For instance, the development of Union citizenship beyond the boundaries of economic activities to include social rights, see Poiares Maduro 'Europe's Social Self: "The Sickness Unto Death"'.

[66] Bellamy, 'The "Right to Have Rights": Citizenship Practice and the Political Constitution of the EU'; G Moro, 'The "Lab" of European Citizenship: Democratic Deficit, Governance Approach and Non-Standard Citizenship' 2001 <http://www.activecitizenship. net/citizenspolitics/The_Lab_of_European_Citizenship.pdf>; S Douglas-Scott *Constitutional Law of the European Union*.

[67] Bellamy, 'The "Right to Have Rights": Citizenship Practice and the Political Constitution of the EU'; CF Stychin 'Disintegrating Sexuality: Citizenship and the EU' in R Bellamy and A Warleigh (Eds), *Citizenship and Governance in the European Union* (London, Continuum 2001) 107-121.

the whole and its parts'[68] is an apt description of the Union's efforts to develop a relationship with its citizens. According to the European Commission:

> A more holistic conception of citizenship is more appropriate to modern European society, which can incorporate legal, political and social elements as well as working critically with a foundation of diverse and overlapping values and identities. It is this very complexity and fluidity that enables the maintenance of a negotiated social integration that can adequately encompass all those who live in today's Europe and hence have a stake in its shape and future. This is a demanding agenda, because it requires that European citizens are able and willing to negotiate meanings and actions and to do so with a reflectively critical spirit; and it presupposes that no value or behaviour is *prima facie* excluded from scrutiny in that process. The practice of active citizenship is thus focused on the process of critical reflection, and is not automatically prestructured by a fixed list of norms and values. It is evident that under these circumstances, learning for citizenship is not an optional extra but is an integral part of the concept and practice of modern citizenship altogether[69].

Accordingly, it can be inferred that the negotiation of meaning within the concept of citizenship does not strictly require that it is based on national identity[70], but that it can instead be based on a notion of personal identity. Furthermore, in addition to legal and social rights, issues of difference and diversity appear as core elements of EU citizenship, as the concept shifts 'to a broader based notion, in which legal and social rights and entitlements continue to furnish an essential element, but in which negotiated and culturally-based understandings of citizenship are becoming more prominent[71]. So beyond its market and political uses, exploring Union citizenship is thus an exercise in meaning-making, whereby each of the previously mentioned conceptions forms a facet of European citizenship and a different angle from which to develop a line or layer of understanding in the quest for meaningful citizenship. This multifaceted nature can be said to constitute a holistic European citizenship, which increasingly integrates 'questions of attachment, identity and participation'[72]

---

[68] Pranazone, 'Definitions' <http://www.pranazone.com/defin.htm>.

[69] European Commission, *Learning for Active Citizenship: A Significant Challenge in Building a Europe of Knowledge* at 2.1(6).

[70] Moro, 'The "Lab" of European Citizenship'.

[71] European Commission, *Learning for Active Citizenship: A Significant Challenge in Building a Europe of Knowledge* at 2.1(4).

[72] Painter, 'European Citizenship and the Regions'.

within its model. As such, Union citizenship is more than a mere tool of the Community institutions and becomes an opportunity for citizens to develop a concept with which they can identify at various levels.

To conclude this section on the evolving nature of Union citizenship towards a holistic model, it is noted that:

> A vision of citizenship which conceives of individuals only as instruments of the market will not capture the hearts and minds of Europeans. [...] It is important for EU law to develop and embrace a complex notion of citizenship which is capable of capturing the different identities, attachments, and aspects of their personhood which individuals adopt in a multicultural supranational community. As Lacey and Frazer write: "[o]nce we recognise the complexity of human subjectivity – the way in which we can hold multiple commitments, relationships, views, desires, and roles together without collapsing under the weight of incoherence – the idea of the unitary subject becomes less attractive"[73]. These particular tensions may lead us in the EU context to a richer conception of citizenship. But we must recognise that this will bring difficulties and double binds, and even perplexity[74].

Nothing brings more perplexity than the issue of spirituality, or stronger emotional responses than a mention to the religious question. Yet, in considering Union citizenship as a meaning-making process and tool for encouraging popular belonging and affective support, it is posited that the controversial notions of religion and spirituality may provide additional layers of understanding in the construction of a holistic conception of Union citizenship; especially so given the fairly recent events regarding religion-related issues trickling onto the European public scene and political agenda[75]; as well as the long-held attempt at identifying a Soul for Europe.

Religious and Spiritual Dimensions of Union Citizenship

> Europe brings together opposite extremes: the secular world and transcendence, science and faith, material technology and religion[76].

---

[73] E Frazer and N Lacey, *The Politics of Community* (Hemel Hempstead, Harvester Wheatsheaf, 1993) 199.

[74] Douglas-Scott, *Constitutional Law of the European Union* at 514.

[75] E.g. the debate on the reference to a deity or Christian heritage in the Draft Constitutional Treaty; religious terrorism; controversy over the Islamic scarf; the ban on Christian Unions in some UK universities.

[76] B Geremek, 'Thinking about Europe as a Community' in Michalski, *What holds Europe together?* at 9, quoting Karl Jaspers, speaking on the European spirit in Geneva in 1946.

In 1993, Jacques Delors stated that Europe could not succeed solely on a legal and economic basis, and that if we could not 'give a soul to Europe, to give it spirituality and meaning, the game [would] be up'. This bold statement has led to much debate over the so-called 'spirit or soul for Europe' and its meaning; spirituality itself is not an easily definable concept and the spirituality of the Union even less so. Still, it appears from various EU official sources that envisioning a soul for Europe means considering its peoples, from which it can be inferred that the soul of Europe is the coming together of the human souls of the Union. Incidentally, talks of spirituality have also raised questions over the role of religion in the construction of the EU, and although spirituality and religion are distinct concepts, they are often confounded.

Whilst an extreme secular or *laic* approach would consider religion as extraneous to the European project, it is nevertheless increasingly acknowledged as a pertinent and topical issue on the European public and political scenes; recent research also suggests that religion, as a determinant of European attitudes is an influencing factor of European people's opinions and position on the Union and its integration process[77]. Though it might be dismissed by some as irrelevant to serious politico-legal debates on the future of the EU, whether on grounds of secularism or lack of EU competence on religious matters, the growing relevance of European self-reflection, soul searching and religious awareness is compounded by the constitutional recognition of the role of religion and spirituality in the development of the European idea.

The significance of religion and spirituality in the European context

Despite an ever increasing secularised Europe, whereby religion is dissociated both from the State and civic society, the religion question is still an issue of great importance for people, irrespective of whom, why and in which form. Traditionally confined to the private sphere within a secular society, the concern for religion related issues is often publicly

[77] Nelson and Guth state that 'Christian religious traditions... have contributed to the ideological and cultural support of the European Union... [i]f in fact this contribution is now diminishing, the question for European elites is whether or not ideological support for the market and individual cost-benefit analyses will be enough to maintain *affective support for the Union* in both the East and the West', see B Nelsen and J Guth 'Religion and Attitudes toward the European Union: the New Member States, A Research Note' [2005] <http://aei.pitt.edu/3053/01/EUSA_2005_1.5.pdf >; B Nelsen and J Guth, 'Exploring the Gender Gap: Women, Men, and Public Attitudes Toward European Integration' (2000) 1(3) *European Union Politics* 267-291.

expressed through media controversy, social conflict, or political upheaval. More recently, religion became an item on the European political debate, particularly with the controversies surrounding the mention to a deity and Europe's Christian roots within the former Draft Treaty on the Constitution of the European Union. Indeed, despite a generally secularised Europe, religion still plays a role both in the life of citizens across the Union Member States and in the relations between the state and confessional institutions. It can also be said that, regardless of the official secular nature of a State, certain countries retain a close relation with religious organisations and dogmas, such as Italy, Greece and Ireland. The importance of such a connection between a State and its religious background is not to be taken lightly, as shown by the nature of the debates on the Draft Constitutional Treaty.

In 2004, several Member States, including Italy, Ireland, Spain, Slovakia, Latvia, Lithuania and Poland submitted a proposal to the European Irish presidency that the Constitutional Treaty should include a reference to 'Europe's Christians roots'. Poland Foreign Minister, Wlodzimierz Cimoszewicz, argued that 'it is the Christian faith that has shaped European culture and is inseparably linked with its history'[78]. This move was backed by a petition signed by more than a million Union citizens asking for the inclusion within the text of a reference to 'God' or to Europe's Christian heritage.

For the supporters of such an inclusion, the question is not one of religious militancy, but rather of historical accuracy[79]: the point is not to profess Europe to be Christian but merely to acknowledge the pivotal role played by Christianity in the history of Europe, and as the source of its values. In response to these concerns, a ratified Lisbon Treaty would amend the preamble of the Treaty on the European Union to read that it draws inspiration from the 'cultural, religious and humanist inheritance of Europe', the values of which are still present in its heritage. This approach has been welcomed by many, whose view is that specific references to 'God' and Christian values in the constitutional text would have been a 'huge' and 'serious mistake', 'absurd', as well as offensive to those of other faiths and to non-believers; and that any 'reference to God would have created unnecessary barriers in Europe which has to be secular for it to be really united'[80].

---

[78] I Black, 'EU Members in Unholy Row', (03.10.03) *The Guardian*.

[79] L Barthelemy, 'Europe's Christian heritage Proves Source of Division' (22.06.03) <http://www.eubusiness.com/imported/2003/06/113103>

[80] BA Robinson, 'Do "God" and "Christianity" have a Place in the European Union Constitution?', (20.05.2003) <http://www.religioustolerance.org/const_eu.htm>.

Indeed, the secular nature of Europe is seen by left-wing convention members and humanist partisans as essential to the Union's future; and as such, it has been contented that any reference to religious, spiritual and moral values in the Treaty should be shunned. Still, the Treaty recognition of the broadly spiritual roots of Europe, including religious and humanist beliefs, indicates that the Union directly endorses a spiritual potential and human experience within its reality in a bid to strengthen its efforts to become more accessible and closer to its citizens.

Nevertheless, whilst reference to a deity or religious denomination in a constitutional text would undoubtedly raise legal concerns, despite a sigh of relief expressed by advocates of its non-inclusion, the profound implications attached to it arguably still remain though from a different angle. Indeed, the Lisbon Treaty still gives religious, spiritual, humanist and moral values a prominent place in what is to be a legally binding document once ratified by all Member States. As it stands today, a reference to Europe's religious and spiritual heritage still poses some questions as to how this will be formulated in ensuing European and national legislation, and how it will be addressed by the European Court of Justice when interpreting and reviewing the application of Treaty provisions across the Union.

Although the preambles have been said not to bear legal effects, it is believed that the mentions are not deprived of significance and of future potential legal implications. The preambles are contained in foundational and constitutional legal documents, implying that mentions to Europe's religious and spiritual inheritance may have some bearing beyond the purely symbolic. In France, for instance, the preamble of the 1946 Constitution, which only has mention in the current fifth Republic Constitution, has nevertheless been given the status of a principle of constitutional value. In other words, the 1946 preamble has constitutional authority, whereby the legislator and the courts must take it into consideration when either enacting or interpreting legislation. As EC legal principles are also developed and inspired from the constitutional traditions of Member States, it is not impossible to imagine that the ECJ may one day consider the preambles of the TEU and EU Charter of Fundamental Rights to determine and develop new legal rules and principles of EC law.

At this stage, it is difficult to speculate on the scope of these value-laden references; however, it is safe to say that there will be consequences, whether at the social, political or judicial level. Indeed, the focus might be off Christian values and 'God'; however the odds for controversies may have increased with the apparently inclusive, yet more elusive and debatable reference to 'spiritual, moral, cultural, religious and humanist' heritage of Europe within the Union's Treaties. Consequently, the religious and spiritual mentions in the preambles may arguably raise some very interesting, if not tricky, questions in the future.

Considering the concepts of religion and spirituality and how they may be translated in the European context would therefore be a pertinent exercise. Though spirituality and religion are frequently used interchangeably, they are two distinct notions, with religion often used to refer to dogmatic institutional religious organisations, and spirituality used to describe affairs of the spirit or the soul, which relate to a more personal experience of the transcendental or divine. The following sections therefore address spirituality and religion as separate dimensions.

Conceptions of a spiritual dimension of Union Citizenship

> If we consider that the constitutional treaty must not only introduce more clarity, transparency and efficiency into the workings of the European institutions, but also bring the European Union closer to its citizens, we need to introduce a bit of "European metaphysics". We need to talk about the European idea and the European spirit so that the text can encourage the citizens of Europe to think about how we came together, why we are staying together and what we want to do together[81].

Mentions to spirituality often seem to imply a reference to religion; so in attempting to understand the concept, it is essential to determine some elements of definition and distinction. From a psychology of religion perspective, spirituality is described as a 'fuzzy' notion, mostly used as 'a generic and politically correct alternative for religion'[82]. Although the two terms are used interchangeably, it appears that the relationship between religion and spirituality is highly debated, as spirituality may not always mean religion although it is said to be an essential part of the latter. Whilst religion denotes a commitment to external manifestations of beliefs or religious observance, spirituality focuses primarily on the internal realm of human experience[83]. It is advocated that 'spirituality is

---

[81] Geremek, 'Thinking about Europe as a Community' at 10.

[82] D Helminiak, 'The Role of Spirituality in Formulating a Theory of the Psychology of Religion' (2006) 41(1) *Zygon* 197–224.

[83] C Daly, 'Definitions of Terms: Spirituality versus Religiousness' (2005) 98(12) *Southern Medical Association* 1238; AC Robertson, *Spirituality and Depression: A Qualitative Approach*, <http://etd.unisa.ac.za/ETD-db/theses/available/etd-05212007-093323/unrestricted/thesis.pdf >.

a product of human capacity' and is thus separable from 'theist belief and metaphysical speculation'; as such, it may become 'an empirically grounded science'[84]. Spirituality deals with people's visions of meaning, sense of purpose and values to foster transcendence; and is described as:

> a relatively new term that refers to the nearly universal human search for meaning, often involving some sense of transcendence; ... and that it is a broader concept than religion and is therefore more appropriate for plural-istic contexts[85].

Different concepts of spirituality have been summarised in three cat-egories. Firstly, spirituality can be understood as the ultimate belonging or connection to the transcendental ground of being; secondly, as a rela-tionship to god, fellow humans, the Earth; and thirdly, as a devotion and commitment to a particular faith or form of practice[86]. It appears that these attempted definitions cannot steer away from reference to the religious, a deity, god-like attributes or the sacred. However, empirical research on the definition of 'spirituality' reveals that it deals with peo-ple's 'interior and subjective lives' leading to conclusions that emerging forms of spirituality are in fact forms of private preference[87], and sug-gesting that spirituality is a notion associated with very individualistic connotations. Furthermore, from a semantic analytical perspective, the meaning of a word is said to be both contextual and experiential: its definition is thus dependant both on the source of the experience in which it is lived, and on the context in which it is used. With regards to spiritu-ality, this suggests that the word encompasses 'a range of religious and non-religious experiences that are based on perceived sources of sacred and secular nature'[88]. Therefore the notion of spirituality can either be sacred or secular, it may or may not relate to the divine or the transcend-ent; and its particular nature would be dependent upon a situation or an individual's perception of the spiritual experience, and of the source of

---

[84] Helminiak, 'The Role of Spirituality in Formulating a Theory of the Psychology of Religion'.

[85] D Hall, AM Catanzaro, MO Harrison and H Koenig, 'Religion, Spirituality, and Mysticism' [2004] 161(9) *American Journal of Psychiatry* 1720.

[86] F Vaughan, 'What is Spiritual Intelligence?' (2002) 42(2) *Journal of Humanistic Psychology* 16-33.

[87] S Speers, 'Secularity, Spirituality, and Liberal Arts Education' [2007] *Social Science Research Council* <http://religion.ssrc.org/reforum/Speers.pdf>.

[88] KL Todd, 'A Semantic Analysis of the Word *Spirituality*', <http://web.nwe.ufl.edu/~jdouglas/spiritual.pdf>.

that experience, which can equally be religious or secular. Therefore it has been argued that the meaning of the word depends on the use we make of it, based on our personal experience and individual understanding of that word, be that from a religious or secular perspective[89]. It is therefore possible to create a meaning of spirituality which is associated with the concept of European citizenship and the European project at large, and which could encompass notions of a religious, humanist/secular and cultural nature.

Still, there is a word of caution over its use as attention is drawn towards the distinction between the human spirit, spiritual and spirituality. Whilst the *human spirit* is 'a structured, open-ended, dynamic dimension of the mind', allowing for self-reflection and transcendence but still grounded in the human mind and not the divine; *spiritual* encompasses 'any human functioning that involves experience, understanding, judgement or decision', which is the application of the human mind. Finally *spirituality* is said to refer to 'a particular usage of the human spirit', which implies an individual commitment to engage on a path or journey for positive growth[90].

The distinction between these three aspects may apply to the Union venture. The human spirit is what the Union is trying to reach in getting closer to its citizens, as it seeks a new impetus and popular legitimacy. The spiritual heritage of Europe, which could arguably cover religious, humanist and cultural values under a neutral and pluralist-friendly appellation, refers to the lessons learnt by the various peoples of Europe in their long history, and displays the human functioning of a Community who developed and enshrined fundamental principles such as human dignity, freedom, the rule of law, democracy and equality in its founding treaties. Finally, spirituality could be described as the new phase in European development, whereby the Union and its citizens are bound to reflect some more on the next step or new direction of the project, as its current status cannot sustain the consequences of European enlargement. Consequently, the Union must embark on a path for positive growth in order to evolve and be able to address effectively such issues as demographic ageing, immigration and ensuing inequalities, and the preservation of peace in a globalised world[91].

[89] Ibid.

[90] Helminiak, 'The Role of Spirituality in Formulating a Theory of the Psychology of Religion' at 211-214.

[91] K Biedenkopf, B Geremek, K Michalski and M Rocard, 'What Holds Europe together?' at 96.

These are but some personal and tentative reflections on the potential meaning of the spiritual dimension of the Union; what is interesting, though, is how this spirituality concept is formulated by the Union itself, with references to the European spirit and soul appearing in various EU officials' speeches. The EU Commissioner Benita Ferrero-Waldner[92], for instance asserts that the Union has an 'inner compass', a soul, which makes the Union 'a spiritual and cultural' entity beyond its mere economic being[93]. 'Spirit' and 'Soul' though are two distinct notions. It is understood that, from a Christian perspective, the soul refers to how one relates to oneself and to others, implying questions of identity and self understanding. By contrast, the spirit is described as the 'immaterial facet of man' and fosters the idea of a relationship with 'god', the sacred or the divine. Whilst a person *is* a soul, one *has* spirit[94]. Therefore whilst the soul is about one's self; the spirit is about what drives us; and for the EU, it is therefore a question of identity and direction. Put even more simply:

The human mind comprises the brain and all its workings – memory, perception, reason, the stew of hormones that results in our emotions. It is, in other words, the 'hardware' of human existence. The human soul is what governs the human hardware – the 'software' of human existence, our very own 'operating system', unique to each of us. The human spirit is the 'electricity' that animates us[95].

Despite their distinctiveness, 'spirit' and 'soul' tend to be used interchangeably in the European context, and it appears that the meaning of Europe's soul/spirit is associated to concepts of culture, identity, values and diversity[96]. This is further confirmed by the preambles to the TEU and the EU Charter of Fundamental Rights, which both affirm in the same breath that the Union is based on fundamental values whose sources originate from the spiritual, religious, humanist and cultural roots of Europe's diverse traditions and peoples. The Union's soul is indeed described as

---

[92] Commissioner for External Relations and European Neighbourhood Policy.

[93] B Ferrero-Waldner, Speech at the Berlin Conference 'A Soul for Europe', 17-19 November 2006 <http://www.berlinerkonferenz.eu/uploads/media/Speech_Ferrero-Waldner_061118.pdf>.

[94] Got Questions Ministries, 'What is the difference between the soul and spirit of man?', last accessed June 2008 <http://www.gotquestions.org/soul-spirit.html>.

[95] M Matthews, 'The Difference Between Soul and Spirit' [2005] <http://www.extremelysmart.com/insight/theology/soul&spirit.php>.

[96] J M Barroso, 'A Soul for Europe' speech/06/706; B Ferrero-Waldner A Speech at the Berlin Conference 'A Soul for Europe'; A Merkel, 'Speech to the European Parliament in Strasbourg' 2007 <http://www.eu2007.de/en/News/Speeches_Interviews/January/Rede_Bundeskanzlerin2.html>.

cultural[97] and the embodiment of tolerance[98]; a 'living and sharing soul'[99], which is founded on a culture of respect, tolerance, and intercultural dialogue. It is also based on the protection of core shared non-negotiable values, such as freedom, the rule of law and human dignity, in order to maintain peace and unity in Europe. Conversely, the fundamental values underpinning the European edifice are also said to constitute what is termed the 'European spirit'[100].

Some might wonder how a spiritual dimension can be reconciled with a rights-based conception of Union citizenship. This chapter does not aim to provide an answer, but merely to consider the possibility, for it is argued that 'rights alone may be insufficient to create a meaningful European citizenship'[101]. The undeniable link between the European and human soul's characteristics is further emphasised by a statement from the EU Commissioner Ján Figel[102] that such values as human dignity and solidarity are 'the functions, the products of a responsible, emphatic human soul', and so 'to give a soul for Europe is very important, hence – as Jean Monnet said very wisely – "*we are not building an alliance of States, we integrate people*".'[103] It follows that to envisage Europe's soul and the European spirit is therefore to envisage what it is to be European; and consequently, what it is to be a European citizen. It is thus argued that Europe's soul searching is intrinsically linked to the understanding and development of the concept of citizenship and of the Union as a whole. Furthermore, it is believed that the question is not whether the Union and its citizenship have a spiritual dimension because they clearly do, but rather how this dimension is formulated into a concrete idea and realised in the long run.

The religious dimension of Union citizenship

In 1993 the European Parliament stated that:

the European message must concern Europeans both in their professional dimension, in terms of new opportunities and better living standards, but

---

[97] Barroso 'A Soul for Europe'.
[98] Merkel, 'Speech, to the European Parliament in Strasbourg'.
[99] J Figel, Speech at the Berlin Conference 'A Soul for Europe' 17-19 November 2006, at 8 <http://www.berlinerkonferenz.eu/uploads/media/Speech_Figel_061117_02.pdf>.
[100] Barroso 'A Soul for Europe'.
[101] Stychin, 'Disintegrating Sexuality: Citizenship and the EU' at 107.
[102] Commissioner for Education, Training, Culture and Multilingualism.
[103] J Figel, Speech at the Berlin Conference 'A Soul for Europe' at 8.

also in their historical and cultural dimension, in terms of values, outlook and a commonly shared identity.

The argument from observers is that the European citizenship discourse is essentially rooted in an ethno-cultural perspective, which may find its basis in a principle or idea of common history[104]. To that effect, it has been acknowledged, both by academic commentators and Community institution officials, that Europe was built on Greek rationalism and culture; Roman concepts of justice, law and State organisation; and Judeo-Christian values and principles[105]. The interrelation between Christianity and European cultural identity is a historical fact also observed and confirmed by social science research, which showed that 'a shared religious heritage based on Christian value may be seen as one formative cultural influence at the heart of and giving substance to "European civilisation".'[106] Consequently, religion is perceived as a potential key player in the social cohesion of Europe[107], and is it further argued that the 'shared religious heritage of Western Europe' may be crucial to the continent's future development[108].

However, the Union is often described as secular, the meaning of which can be many-fold: secularism can refer to the institutional separation between State and church; to the disappearance of religion altogether; or to the displacement of religion in the public sphere. It can indicate a state of neutrality between religion and the State, and between religions within the State; and it can also place itself as the rival of religion. As such, this has led many to argue that secularization, though for a long time considered a truth and an inevitability of modernity and progress, is but another theory, 'a kind of substitute religious conviction' and an 'ideology in the service of power politics'[109]. Therefore, the secularization of the political and economic public spheres does not necessarily imply the secularization

---

[104] P Hansen, 'European Citizenship, or Where Neoliberalism meets Ethno-Culturalism: Analysing the European Union's Citizenship Discourse' (2000) 2(2) *European Societies* 139-165.

[105] K Blei, *Freedom of Religion and Belief: Europe's Story* (Royal Van Gorcum, International Association for Religious Freedom, 2002).

[106] G Davie, *Religion and Modern Europe: A Memory Mutates* (Oxford, Oxford University Press 2000) 7.

[107] D Hervieu-Léger, 'The role of religion in establishing social cohesion', 2003 EUROPA <http://europa.eu.int/comm/research/social-sciences/pdf/michalski_210503_contribution01_en.pdf>.

[108] Davie, *Europe: The Exceptional Case.*

[109] T Halik, 'The Public Role of Religion in a United Europe: A central-European Perspective' [2005] <http://www.st-edmunds.cam.ac.uk/vhi/fis/fpr/halik.pdf>.

of peoples' lives and beliefs systems, nor does it equal to the death of religion in Europe; instead, it is argued that religion is in fact in a phase of transformation[110] in which it must redefine its place and nature within society.

Though secular fundamentalist would deny the reality of religion in the lives of many people, as previously mentioned religion is increasingly acknowledged as constituting an essential part of European integration and individual identity. Religion, like the citizenship concept, is a 'social construct', a component of the processes in which individuals engage to make sense and give meaning to their lives[111]. It follows that, although religion tends to be relegated to the private sphere, and that religious dogma may not rule public institutions anymore, politics however are influenced by people; in turn, people are influenced by their beliefs systems, including religious, secular or humanist values. It has also been advanced that Europe should not define itself as a '*laic*' entity, for it denotes anti-religious feelings; instead, the Union should rather take a neutral approach to the religious issue, and foster a 'religious openness' in order to facilitate the integration progress further[112].

> While the European Union cannot escape from religion if it wants to further its cultural base, become truly European, neither can it minimalize religion as a mere purveyor of values. Religion is not the ancilla in ethics of the state. It is not the handy dupe for purely economic and political interests, and it is not a cultural history museum. Religion must have space for its own sake.

It is therefore contented that there is a link between European citizenship, identity and religion, and that exploring a religious dimension of Union citizenship would fit within the favoured holistic model. The first step towards defining a religious dimension is to establish its meaning and parameters. The Latin root of religion is *religio*, meaning obligation or reverence. The concept of *religio* is defined as 'as a collection of State-sanctioned symbols and rituals' and 'a matter of ritual contact with the sacred foundations of society, the symbolic expression of a common identity, of what holds a society together'[113]. In that respect, it is argued that Christianity is no longer seen as 'the religion of present-day Europe',

---

[110] G Davie *The Sociology of Religion* (London, Sage, 2007).

[111] Davie *The Sociology of Religion* at 53.

[112] G Robbers, 'Religious Freedom in Europe', October 2002, paper presented at the International Congress on Religious Freedom, Mexico City.

[113] Halik, 'The Public Role of Religion in a United Europe: A Central-European Perspective'.

nor is European Christianity a religion any longer, but is rather a philosophy of life or an ideology. If *religio* personifies the common language of
a given civilisation, then it is further contented that religion, as well as
science do not fulfil this role anymore. Instead the role of modern *religio*
in Western society is said to be fulfilled by the mass media, which impact
on people's thinking and behavioural attitudes, create communication,
mediate symbols and network patterns, and which determine what is of
importance and relevance in society according to what is covered in
the news or not, and how[114]. So, in this context, religion is relegated to
the level of a cultural factor in determining identity not as common language, but as a perspective. In addition, religion can include the idea of
collective gathering, where people share common beliefs and tradition,
and join together to practice their faith or worship; as well as providing
an institutional framework for its followers, leading adherents to the faith
to apply its principles in their daily lives.

In the European context, a religious dimension could therefore encompass the following conceptions: a perspective, life style or philosophy;
an institutional and organised system of beliefs; and a collective expression or experience of that belief. By comparison with the spiritual dimension, the religious dimension would imply a more outward and collective
nature, and would also be much more linked to the protection of rights.
Given the existing provisions for the protection of religious freedom,
equality and non-discrimination under EC law, it is argued that Union
citizenship already has a religious dimension. Some could even describe
the religious dimension more boldly and call it religious citizenship.
Religious citizenship can take five forms, such as:

> The citizenship that the nation allows individuals to exercise in religious
> matters; the citizenship which citizens exercise as religious persons in the
> civic sphere; religious citizenship in terms of the rights of the persons;
> citizenship as defined by legal positivities; and a reflexive account of reli-
> gious citizenship according to which persons can acquire such citizenship
> by adopting specific discursive positions[115].

In light of these different conceptions of religious citizenship, the
Union version could encompass the rights-based and reflexive account
approach. As stated before, citizens do benefit from specific rights which
protect their religious freedom. The reflexive account would, in turn, fit

---

[114] Ibid.
[115] W Hudson, 'Religious Citizenship' (2003) 49(3) *Australian Journal of Politics and History* 425 at 426-427.

within the holistic model whereby differences, diversity and identity are negotiated features of citizenship. In relation to the citizenship exercised by religious persons in the public sphere, this would be most relevant to the provisions of Article 52 ECT[116], whereby the national status of religious and nonconfessional associations is recognised and respected; and a continued dialogue between the Union and these protagonists is guaranteed; thus ensuring a protected public role and participation in the Union affairs for religious, philosophical and nonconfessional organisations.

Conclusion

Concepts of European citizenship, Europe's soul/spirit and religion are complex and controversial; so why should the Union citizenship encompass spiritual and religious dimensions? All three are symptomatic of the apparent (and also contested) desire and need for the Union to redefine its direction, purpose and identity. All are engaged in a quest for meaning, and meaning is everything. Meaning gives substance, direction, and purpose to an experience, a moment, a project, a life. Meaning shapes what is important and what is of worth. It is contextual, circumstantial, and subject to interpretation. Meaning is subjective, variable and boundless.

As previously mentioned, wondering whether there exist any spiritual and religion dimensions within the Union is moot: the Union has a spirit and a soul, and religion is a key player in its history and evolution. The question is therefore how these dimensions are to be articulated and developed within the holistic model of citizenship. This chapter has dealt with the spiritual and the religious as two distinct approaches.

It is possible to talk about a European religious citizenship as a concrete notion, since it involves the protection of religious freedom and the provision of rights which consider or impact at some level on religious matters[117]. Religious citizenship would thus be an additional conception of Union citizenship, in the same vein as economic citizenship (mobility rights), social citizenship (welfare rights), political citizenship, gender citizenship (equality rights), and so on. Though multifaceted, this citizenship remains European in essence and is the common denominator which

---

[116] Now article 17 TFEU.

[117] For more details regarding EU legislation affecting and/or addressing religion-related issues, see: G Robbers (ed.) *Religion-Related Norms in European Union Law*, 2007 <http://www.uni-trier.de/fileadmin/fb5/inst/IEVR/Arbeitsmaterialien/Staatskirchenrecht/ Europa/EU-Bestimmungen/Englisch/EnglischVolltext.pdf>.

allows and recognises the expression of differences and diversity of its many peoples. Religious citizenship would thus remove the need for individuals to define themselves as either citizens or believers, and reconcile their different allegiances in a holistic outcome.

By contrast, there would be some reluctance in talking of a spiritual citizenship, as it is believed that the spiritual concept is too complex and still too vague. It is therefore more apt to talk of a spiritual dimension, which denotes a more symbolic, emotive and affective nature and suggests common values and a shared vocation. Spirituality ensures that the realisation of the self is nested in the realisation of the whole or bigger entity. Acknowledging and embracing spiritual values may also contribute to determining individual identity and developing a sense of belonging to a wider community. Spirituality also enables the revelation of meaning and purpose of the physical and material life, it is the driving force underpinning the direction of that life at individual, European and global levels; so a spiritual dimension may therefore cover religious as well as non-religious matters, including secular and humanist ideology, and spiritualities expressed in different other ways, such as arts and culture. The proposed view is that the uncovering of a spiritual dimension in a holistic conception of Union citizenship is a quest for the meaning of a European idea and entity, which encompasses and recognises the diversity of the human spirit across the Union. Consequently, a spiritual dimension is not necessarily linked to individual rights, and instead can be a source of inspiration for further political, social and cultural development, and could inform the formulation of legal principles. The idea is that the perspectives taken would not be grounded solely on a given theory to the detriment of another, for example, secularist versus religious, economic versus social. It would instead reflect the diversity of perspectives of its various peoples, and would be anchored in a culture of openness.

A holistic citizenship which embraces spiritual and religious dimensions considers the citizen as a whole, as it acknowledges the intricacies and complexity of individuals' internal and external lives, and enhances the interconnectedness between the spiritual, religious and secular, as well as the social, cultural, and political. This approach would be even more important for Union citizens who do not exercise their mobility rights, as it can inspire them to get interested in exercising their political rights: mobility would not be the sole element to engage and raise awareness of Union citizenship rights; citizens would have a more relevant and pertinent stake in political affairs if they can identify with the Union holistic dimension.

It is suggested though that it is not necessarily the role of the Union to define its spiritual and religious dimensions, as it is in fact an opportunity of the people to get involved and write the script. The EU should instead provide the opportunity and support for this development, as the inspiration and impetus should come from the bottom up in order to encourage engagement, a sense of ownership and belonging in its citizens. By putting the citizens at the heart of its activities, the Union aims to build a peoples' and citizens' Europe, and not just a mere collection of states. It aims to embrace peoples' differences and diversity, reflected in a holistic active citizenship which would contribute, besides technocratic manoeuvring, to steering the Union in a direction determined by its citizens. The Union project is therefore beginning a new phase in its development by attempting to engineer a meeting of the minds and realising a Europe inspired and envisioned by its peoples.

REGIONAL ECCLESIASTICAL LAW:
RELIGION AND DEVOLUTION IN SPAIN AND WALES

Javier García Oliva and David Lambert[1]

Introduction

Traditionally law and religion scholarship has focussed on Church-State relations. This is particularly true of comparative accounts[2]. However, this focus is becoming increasingly out-dated as the nation State is challenged by competing authorities from both above and below. International law, both global and regional, can be found above the nation State. In the European context, the importance of the Council of Europe and the European Convention on Human Rights (ECHR) for religious believers and groups is self-evident. Also, important in this respect, but less appreciated is the role of the European Union (EU)[3].

The EU – established by the Treaty of Maastricht in 1992 – has gone through an impressive transformation in the course of the last few years, especially with the two most recent enlargements, in 2004 and 2007. This international organization, by far the most developed in the world in terms of legislative powers and mechanisms of enforcement, is now composed of twenty seven members and Croatia and Turkey, for instance, are queuing to join this very attractive club. Although Euro-scepticism is a fact in countries such as the United Kingdom, Sweden and Denmark, Europe seems to be facing a brighter future after the signature of the Reform Treaty in Lisbon in December 2007. Moreover, religion is increasingly on the EU's agenda[4].

---

[1] We would like to thank Professor Norman Doe, Director of the Centre for Law and Religion, who kindly provided us with his unpublished article on 'Executive Devolution and Religious Organisations in Wales', Dr Alex Seglers for his invaluable assistance in relation to the Catalan legal framework and Marie Navarro, for her very helpful research with regard to the Welsh settlement.

[2] See, for example, G Robbers (ed) *State and Church in the European Union* (Second edition, Baden Baden, Nomos 2005) and, for a critique, see R Sandberg and N Doe, 'Church-State Relations in Europe' (2007) 1(5) *Religion Compass* 561.

[3] See Alexandra Pimor's contribution to this volume.

[4] Membership of the EU entails acceptance of religious diversity and the prohibition of discrimination on grounds of religion: see, e.g. Treaty of Amsterdam, Appendix:

The EU also increasingly recognises authorities below the Nation State. Since the 1990s, it has also looked at the regional and national dimensions within its Member States and in 1994 the Committee of the Regions was established[5]. This is an advisory body to the legislative institutions[6] of the European Union, which aims to provide regions and municipalities with a voice in the legislative process. The creation of the Committee of the Regions was an acknowledgment of the pluralistic nature of some Member States[7].

This approach is justified. It is undeniable that several States[8] in the European Union are comprised of different regions or nations[9] and this sociological fact has been followed by a process of devolution of powers to the territories within those States. Both Spain and the United Kingdom fit into this category and a joint analysis of their models of devolution could not be timelier. Both countries are experiencing ongoing processes of devolution. Moreover, in both countries, aspects of the regulation of religion are being devolved to the regional level. This chapter seeks to explore recent developments in both Spain and Wales chronologically to explore to what extent it is now possible to talk about a 'regional ecclesiastical law' existing in these jurisdictions[10].

A few words of caution, however, are required at the outset. Any attempt to make a comparison without taking into consideration the very different natures of their legal frameworks is bound to fail and so we have not attempted to create an artificial uniformity in the explanation of their devolution settlements. Furthermore, it would have been unrealistic to make a plain comparison between the British and the Spanish models,

---

Declaration on the Status of Churches and Non-confessional Organisations and see Council Directive 2000/78/EC.

[5] Consolidated Version of the Treaty Establishing the European Community, Arts 263-265.

[6] The Commission, the Council and the European Parliament.

[7] Although this pluralism may have become less obvious from 2004 onwards due to the very centralist nature of the majority of the countries which joined the Union at that stage.

[8] Alongside the United Kingdom and Spain, other European States have strong national voices within their territories. Belgium is a very important example. In 2007/08 the composition of the Federal Government became extremely complicated and there were serious concerns about the future of Belgium as a sole country.

[9] For its interest, see M Guibernau, *Nations without States: Political Communities in a Global Age* (Cambridge, Polity Press, 1999).

[10] For a discussion of the opposite point, the extent to which it is possible to talk about an 'European law on religion', see N Doe, 'Towards a Common Law on Religion in the European Union (2009) *Religion, State and Society* (forthcoming). See also Alexandra Pimor's contribution to this volume.

without bearing in mind that there are at least three different responses in the United Kingdom, as far as devolution of powers is concerned (Scotland, Wales and Northern Ireland) and at least seventeen in Spain, as this is the number of *Comunidades Autónomas*[11] ('Autonomous Communities') which the State comprises of. Therefore, in relation to the United Kingdom we have restricted our analysis to devolution in Wales. In the case of Spain, since there are some features which all different Spanish territories share we have decided to look at them, before focusing on Catalonia, as a very advanced *Comunidad Autónoma*.

Devolution of Powers and Religion in Spain

In order to determine whether or not the *Comunidades Autónomas* hold or exercise any powers on religious matters, the model contemplated by the 1978 Constitution should be properly explained. Alongside the religious question (confessionalism / separatism)[12] and the dichotomy between monarchy and republic[13], the territorial structure of the State was undoubtedly one of the most controversial matters which the drafters of the Constitution had to face and deal with.

The distribution of powers between the State and the Comunidades Autónomas in the Spanish Constitution

The 1978 Constitution presents a system based on the principles of unity, autonomy and solidarity, recognized by Article 2. The first principle

---

[11] Article 137: The State is organized territorially into municipalities, provinces, and the Autonomous Communities which may be constituted. All these entities enjoy autonomy for the management of their respective interests. The Autonomous Communities will enjoy legislative powers and can be set up by either *nacionalidades* or regions. The meaning of these two realities will be explained below.

[12] In the process of elaboration of the Constitution there was tension between those who preferred the maintenance of the status quo: the confessional nature of the State and those who would have liked to see a separatist model similar to the French system. The solution is provided by Art 16 of the Spanish Constitution, which recognises a hybrid or cooperationist system (that is, a system characterised by a simple separation of State and Church coupled with the recognition of a multitude of common tasks which link State and Church activity). Art 16 is discussed further below.

[13] The left-wing political parties were clearly favourable of a Republican system, but the two republican experiences in Spain, especially the Second Republic (1931-1936) caused an outstanding rejection on the part of many social sectors. The compromise solution was the recognition of a Parliamentary monarchy, with Juan Carlos I, Alfonso XIII's grandson as the King of Spain. The monarchy is regulated in Arts 56-65 of the Spanish Constitution.

becomes essential to make sure that the system is consistent: there is only one nation in Spain; the Spanish nation. As a result of this explicit pronouncement, any future attempts on the part of different Spanish territories to regard themselves as nations would be rejected by the legal framework. Indeed, this has happened with the recent amendments of the *estatutos de autonomía* ('regional laws of autonomy') in Catalonia[14] and Andalucía[15], which struggled to find the partial approval of their national identities.

Furthermore, the same Article emphasizes the right of autonomy – or the establishment of *Comunidades Autónomas* – of *nacionalidades* and regions. The terminology used by the Spanish *constituyente* in order to identify the different territories is fascinating. The drafters of the Constitution made up the term *nacionalidades* in a clear attempt to meet the expectations of certain territories which on the one hand, could never have accepted to be regarded as mere regions and on the other, found their aspirations unduly curtailed by the recognition of a sole nation by the Constitution. It is a hybrid concept. This very crafty approach was sufficiently wide to be accepted by the electorate, but as a sign of the unavoidable ambiguity which fundamental documents are bound to embrace, the 1978 Constitution did not list what territories were *nacionalidades* and which others were regions.

Finally, alongside the principles of unity and autonomy Article 2 emphasized solidarity as a mechanism of cohesion amongst different *Comunidades Autónomas*.

As far as the access to autonomy is concerned, the Constitution differentiated between those regions with a more limited range of powers (*vía lenta* – 'slow path')[16] and those others (*vía* rápida – 'fast path')[17] which were allowed to embrace some of the powers listed in Article 149 from the outset. The territories within the first category were expected to wait for five years[18] in order to start enjoying these competences. This distinction, now historically outdated, has however had an important influence on the way the autonomy of the different Spanish territories has been developed throughout the last thirty years as there have been

[14] Ley Orgánica 6/2006, de 19 de julio, de Reforma del Estatuto de Autonomía de Cataluña.

[15] See S Fernández Ramos and JM Pérez Monguió, *Ley Orgánica 2/2007, de 19 de marzo, de Reforma del Estado de Autonomía para Andalucía* (Instituto Andaluz de Administración Pública, 2008).

[16] Art 143.2 and Disposición transitoria primera.

[17] Art 151 and Disposición transitoria segunda.

[18] Art 148.2.

undeniable tensions between those *Comunidades Autónomas*, which held a wider degree of powers, due to their idiosyncrasy and special historical position (e.g. Catalonia and the Basque Country) and all other territories. Ongoing attempts have been made by the latter regions to 'catch up' with the powers held by the former, leading to the uniformity of the legal position of all different territories and the inevitable frustration of *nacionalidades* such as Catalonia or even Andalucía.

In compliance with the provisions of the Constitution, the legal framework of the different *Comunidades Autónomas* is provided by their *estatutos de autonomía*[19], which are laws that despite being initiated by the regional authorities, must receive the final endorsement of the Spanish Parliament in Madrid and on some occasions the previous support of the electorate. All *Comunidades Autónomas* must have a legislative assembly – which will be known as Parliament in most cases – and a Government, which should include the President and his/her regional Cabinet. However, the *Comunidades Autónomas* do not have their own judicial structure and the highest judicial bodies in each territory are simple branches of the State framework. This explains why Spain cannot be regarded as a federal State, despite having evolved so clearly from centralist positions.

The traditional view of religion as an area within the powers of the State

In the Spanish context, it can be questioned whether Ecclesiastical Law – regarded here as simply the law on religious matters –[20] belongs to the State, the *Comunidades Autónomas* or both. In principle, the response is very simple: traditionally Ecclesiastical Law has been regarded as the law of the State concerning religious bodies[21]. This emphasis has been upon the role of the State is underlined by the fact that the subject which law students study in their degree is called 'Ecclesiastical Law of the State' in most Spanish universities[22].

---

[19] Art 147.

[20] This can be compared with the definition of the term in England. On which, see N Doe, *The Legal Framework of the Church of England* (Oxford, Clarendon Press, 1996) 12-16 and Augur Pearce's essay in this volume.

[21] However, leading commentators of Ecclesiastical Law have for a while used a different terminology to refer to this subject. See J A Souto Paz, *Comunidad Política y Libertad de Creencias: Introducción a las libertades públicas en el Derecho comparado* (second edition, Marcial Pons, 2003) and D. Llamazares Fernández, *Derecho de la Libertad de conciencia I: Libertad de conciencia y laicidad* (second edition, Civitas, 2002).

[22] Ecclesiastical Law of the State is a compulsory module in Spanish universities. See, for instance, Universidad Complutense de Madrid.

Article 16 contains the basic constitutional provisions affecting religion. After recognising ideological and religious freedom[23] and the protection of the privacy of the ideology and beliefs of the individual[24], the third paragraph of this Article declares that no denomination will have an official status and that public authorities, taking into consideration the beliefs of the Spanish Society, will cooperate with the Catholic Church and other religious bodies.

Such fundamental rights, in accordance with Article 81 of the Constitution[25], must be developed by organic laws and so the implementation of Article 16 was carried out by the *Ley Orgánica de Libertad Religiosa* 7/1980 de 5 de julio. This law hardly affects the position of the Roman Catholic Church, as four comprehensive international agreements[26] between the Holy See and the Spanish State had been signed a year before, on 3 January 1979. The Law 7/1980 was therefore applicable to other religious bodies, which were enabled by its Article 7 to sign agreements with the State, provided that the specific religious body were registered in the Registry of Religious Entities and were deeply rooted. A few years later, in 1992 the Spanish Government signed three agreements with three minority federations: the Protestant Federation[27], the Islamic Commission of Spain[28] and the Jewish Federation[29]. Unquestionably the executive adopted a very generous approach here as strictly speaking the only deeply rooted denomination in the Spanish society in 1992 was the Catholic Church and this may well still be the same in 2008, with the only exception of Islam. However, the Government took sociological and historical factors into account in order to put forward these agreements.

---

[23] Art 16.1.

[24] Art 16.2.

[25] Art 81: (1) Organic laws are those relative to the exercise of fundamental rights and public liberties, those approved by the Statutes of Autonomy and the general electoral system, and the others provided for in the Constitution.(2) The approval, modification, or repeal of organic laws shall require an absolute majority of the House of Representatives in a final vote on the entire bill.

[26] Agreements of 3 January 1979, between the Spanish State and the Holy See, concerning legal affairs, educational and cultural affairs, economic affairs and religious attendance of the Armed Forces and the military service of clergymen and members of religious orders.

[27] Agreement of cooperation between the State and the Federation of Evangelical Religious Entities in Spain.

[28] Agreement of cooperation between the State and the Islamic Commission of Spain.

[29] Agreement of cooperation between the State and the Federation of Israelite Communities of Spain.

The main difficulty of the current framework is the establishment of a distinction between the Catholic Church, on the one hand, and other denominations, on the other[30]. The former is regulated by international treaties and consequently the State is prevented from modifying its legal framework on a unilateral basis. The latter are regulated by agreements with the Spanish State, which have been subsequently recognized by internal laws of the Parliament and as a result of that, this could modify them unilaterally. With the principle of equality in mind, this situation is far from ideal and the fact that it is a common pattern in other jurisdictions such as Italy[31] is not really a justification.

The emerging Derecho Eclesiástico autonómico: the Catalan model

Thus, although the legal framework of religious freedom has traditionally been considered a State matter, some discussion on the existence of a legal branch known as Derecho Eclesiástico autonómico ('regional ecclesiastical law') has taken place. To understand this further, a proper analysis of the powers of the State and the Comunidades Autónomas is necessary. This exercise requires a study of both Articles 149 and 148 of the Constitution, which refer to the powers of the State and the Comunidades Autónomas, respectively.

In principle, all powers listed in Article 149 seem to belong exclusively to the State, but a deeper interpretation of the Constitution shows that there are a good number of competences, which, despite being considered powers of the State, could also be exercised by the Comunidades Autónomas, as they are concurrent powers. The religious competence, if something as such exists, is not included in the list of Article 149, but traditionally commentators have nevertheless considered that the powers concerning religion belong to the State and they have used Article 149.1.1 to support their position. This states that:

> The State holds exclusive competence over the following matters: 1) the regulation of the basic conditions which guarantee the equality of all Spaniards in the exercise of their rights and fulfilment of their constitutional duties.

---

[30] For further information about the different treatment of the Catholic Church and other religious bodies, see J García Oliva, 'Religious Freedom in Transition: Spain' in P Walters (ed), RSS Journal (forthcoming)

[31] For a comparison between the Italian and the Spanish models of Ecclesiastical Law, see J García Oliva, 'Public Authorities and Religious Denominations in Italy and Spain' in R Morris (ed), Church and State: Some Reflections on Church Establishment in England (University College London, The Constitution Unit, 2008) 41-50.

This Article has been interpreted as meaning that religious competence is a matter exclusively for the State since Article 16 of the Spanish constitution protects freedom of ideology, religion and worship. However, this conclusion is questionable as Article 149.1.1 should be studied in the light of the distribution of powers recognized by Articles 148 and 149[32]. Just because the central authorities hold the competence on the basic framework of the principle of religious freedom, the powers of the *Comunidades Autónomas* should not be underestimated. Commentators such as Goti have highlighted that the *Comunidades Autónomas* can assume powers on this area because religious matters are not listed in Article 149[33]. Castro Jover, who states that in the Spanish Constitution there is no exclusion of either the State or the *Comunidades Autónomas* on these areas[34], shares Goti's views. In this context, the provisions of Article 149 would enable the State to be in charge of the basic regulation whilst the different *nacionalidades* and regions could assume the legislative development and implementation. These powers may refer to important areas such as education and organization of the press, radio and television.

Furthermore, Article 148 of the Spanish Constitution lists the powers of the *Comunidades Autónomas,* which all of them could assume from the outset. Some of these competences may certainly have an effect on religious matters. These areas will include: town and country planning and housing[35]; museums, libraries and music conservatories of interest to the self-governing community[36]; the promotion and planning of tourism within its territorial area[37]; social assistance[38]; and health[39]. For instance, religious observance in hospitals can vary from one region to another and teachers of Catholic religion in different *Comunidades Autónomas* may well be paid by the educational representatives of that region or *nacionalidad*, as opposed to the Ministry of Education.

Bearing this in mind, it seems pointless to argue whether or not the *Comunidades Autónomas* could assume powers on religious matters

---

[32] For an extremely thorough analysis of the powers of the State and *Comunidades Autónomas* concerning religion see A Seglers Gómez-Quintero, *Libertad Religiosa y Estado autonómico* (Comares, 2005) and with regard to this specific issue see 25-26.

[33] J Goti, *Sistema de Derecho Eclesiástico* (Zarautz, 1994)330-331.

[34] A Castro Jover, 'El Derecho Eclesiástico Autonómico en España', *Laicidad y Libertades,* n 1, December 2001, 67.

[35] Art 148.1.3.

[36] Art 148.1.15.

[37] Art 148.1.18.

[38] Art 148.1.20.

[39] Art 148.1.21.

through the enactment of their *estatutos de autonomía*. Undoubtedly they can do so unless they had been prevented from doing it by Article 149. Competence[40] is therefore the leading principle in the Constitution, which has recognized a horizontal – as opposed to hierarchical – distribution of powers between the State and the *Comunidades Autónomas*. In the Spanish context, Barcelona or Sevilla could, before the Constitutional Court, oppose the assumption of powers which Madrid does not possess. As the distribution of powers described above is far from clear, the Constitutional Court has developed a very detailed jurisprudence and the Spanish model has been known as *Estado autonómico jurisprudencial*.

As *Comunidades Autónomas* can hold powers on religious matters, it follows that they will also be entitled to sign agreements with religious bodies. However, this possibility has not been explicitly acknowledged by the Spanish legal framework. On the contrary, Article 7 of the *Ley Orgánica de Libertad Religiosa* provides the State with the exclusive powers to sign agreements with religious bodies. However, in the view of some commentators[41], the 7/1980 organic law has gone clearly beyond its powers and has assumed competences which the Parliament in Madrid did not possess. Stating that those agreements must necessarily be signed by the central authorities blatantly ignores the distribution of competences between the State and the religious bodies, as contemplated by the Title VIII of the Constitution. The Spanish Parliament, in 1980, overlooked the territorial structure of the State, which could not be regarded any longer as a centralist one, whilst creating a reservation of law in favour of the State, which is not contemplated by the Constitution at all[42]. Indeed, this development by Article 7 of the 1980 *Ley Orgánica* is at odds with Artcle 16.3 of the Constitution, which speaks about cooperation between public authorities and the Catholic Church and other religious bodies. This reference to 'public authorities' is a sufficiently wide term which may comprise regional bodies. Consequently, there are no reasons to prevent *Comunidades Autónomas* from subscribing agreements with religious bodies and the 1992 agreements signed between the State and the three Federations could be further developed by other regional agreements.

[40] For a detailed analysis of the principle of competence, see L López Guerra, E Espín, J García Morillo, P Pérez Tremps and M Satrústegui, *Derecho Constitucional Volumen II: Los poderes del Estado. La organización territorial del Estado* (Seventh edition, Tirant Lo Blanch, 2007) 327-345.

[41] See Seglers Gómez-Quintero, *Libertad religiosa y Estado autonómico*, 42-43.

[42] Ibid 44-45.

Moreover, cooperation is not at the same level as the right of religious freedom and therefore it can be differently treated, not necessarily by *Leyes Orgánicas*. By way of example, the laws which recognize the 1992 Agreements with the three Federations are ordinary, as opposed to organic laws. Therefore, this is a different field from the one contemplated by Article 149.1.1, which refers to the basic conditions of fundamental rights such as religious freedom.

Under the current Spanish socialist Government there has been a major increase of the powers exercised by different *Comunidades Autónomas,* especially those which had access to their model of autonomy through the so-called *vía rápida* ('fast path'). Catalonia and Andalucía, for example, modified very recently, in 2006 and 2007 respectively, their *estatutos de autonomía.* Both of them were subject to their electorates and finally approved by the Spanish Parliament. Catalonia is a very clear example of the remarkable transformations which *Comunidades Autónomas* have recently experienced. Although seventeen *Comunidades Autónomas* were created as a result of the territorial model suggested by the Spanish Constitution, for comparative purposes, only Catalonia will be studied more in depth. This is a *nacionalidad* which has achieved an ambitious level of powers in the last few years and being the existence of *Derecho Eclesiástico Autonómico* almost symbolic in many other parts of Spain, Catalonia is somehow an exception as Seglers[43] has carried out an extensive study of different aspects of this ongoing Catalan Ecclesiastical Law. It reveals the following:

(i) The *estatuto de autonomía* of Catalonia, in its Article 161, explicitly recognizes, for the first time, the relations with religious entities as one of the powers of the *Generalitat de Catalonia,* its regional legislature. The importance of such a pronouncement cannot be emphasized enough.

(ii) Protection is afforded for religious freedom[44]: for instance, the second clause of the *Convenio Marco de Colaboración entre la Generalitat de Catalunya y el Consell Islamic I Cultural de Catalunya*

---

[43] See A Seglers Gómez-Quintero, 'El convenio marco de colaboración entre la Generalitat de Catalunya y el Consell Islamic i Cultural de Catalunya (CICC)', (2004) 5 *iustel. com, RGDCDEE* p 3. Seglers has carried out a commendable analysis of different minor agreements signed by the *Generalitat* of Catalonia with different religious bodies, but he personally favours the strengthening of a coherent policy for the whole of the State, which would bring the General Direction of Religious Affairs and the *Comunidades Autónomas* together, based on institutional trust and loyalty.
[44] Ibid 2.

declares that the latter will cooperate with the former in all those questions concerning religious freedom affecting the Muslim Community of Spain.

(iii) Catalonia is the first *Comunidad Autónoma* which has created a *General Direction of Religious Affairs* in order to discuss matters of common interests with religious bodies based in its territory. There is a General Direction of Religious Affairs at State level which is part of the Ministry of Justice.

(iv) Clearly related, the transfer of some of the powers of the *General Register of Religious Entities* to autonomous Registers has been frequently requested by some territories, especially Catalonia[45]. It seems recommendable and more than that, practical, for regional bodies to make decisions concerning the Registry as they have a more direct contact with religious bodies located in that *Comunidad Autónoma*. In principle, the organization of the different Registers is, in compliance with Article 149, in the hands of the State. However, there are instruments provided by the Constitution, such as *leyes orgánicas de transferencia o delegación* and *encomienda de funciones* which could enable the different regions and *nacionalidades* to create their regional registers.

(v) Economic cooperation was recognized by the above agreement and also by the *Convenio Marco de Colaboración entre la Generalitat de Catalunya y la Comunitat Israelita de Barcelona*[46]. In this agreement the Catalan Government only commits itself to facilitating the means to promote the participation of the Jewish community in Barcelona in order to achieve and apply for the necessary financial support.

(vi) In relation to education, different religious bodies[47] have subscribed agreements with the legislative Catalan authorities under the umbrella of Article 27.3 CE.

(vii) Numerous powers are enjoyed in relation to social support[48].

---

[45] See Moció 115/VI del Parlament de Catalunya, sobre la política envers les confessions religioses, in A. Seglers Gómez-Quintero, 'La descentralización autonómica del Registro de Entidades Religiosas (RER), (2003) 2 *iustel.com, RGDCDEE*, 1.

[46] For an analysis of this agreement see A Seglers Gómez-Quintero, 'El convenio marco de colaboración entre la Generalitat de Catalunya y la Comunitat Israelita de Barcelona (CIB)' (2003) 3 *iustel.com, RGDCDEE*, 3.

[47] For example, the Israelite Community.

[48] See A Seglers Gómez-Quintero, 'El convenio marco de colaboración entre la Generalitat de Catalunya y la Comunitat Israelita de Barcelona' (CIB), 3.

(viii) The regulation of religious observance in hospitals is devolved[49]. The significance of this assistance should not be underestimated due to the extremely complicated position of the individuals who are in those premises. The agreement with the local Baha'i Community of Barcelona focuses on this area.

(ix) The regulation of religious observance in prisons is likewise devolved[50]: although the legislation on penal establishments belongs to the State, the Constitution declares that the development of these provisions can be assumed by the *Comunidades Autónomas*. In compliance with these provisions, the *Secretaria de Serveis Penitenciaris, Rehabilitació I Justicia Juvenil*, a branch within the Department of Justice of the *Generalitat* of Catalonia, have recently approved the Instruction 1/2005, the main scope of which is to guarantee that inmates enjoy the religious observance which they deserve. This instruction includes the signature of agreements with the Catholic Church and the religious bodies who are members of the three Federations which signed agreements with the State in 1992. With regard to other religious bodies, the petition will have to be made by the inmates of that specific denomination.

(x) It seems to be a common pattern[51] that the *Generalitat* of Catalonia recognizes the history and cultural patrimony donated to society by different religious bodies and consequently cooperates and assists them in the organization of different cultural events.

(xi) Different agreements signed with religious bodies[52] emphasize the importance of bilingualism in Catalonia and request from the latter an effort to adapt Catalan in their day to day life.

For all the above reasons, Catalonia is a very important example of the growing nature of this branch known as *Derecho Eclesiástico Autonómico*, which does not refer exclusively to religious bodies. Indeed, the

---

[49] See A Seglers Gómez-Quintero, 'El convenio de colaboración entre la Generalitat de Catalunya y la Comunitat Local Baha'í de Barcelona'(2005) 9 *iustel.com, RGDCDEE*, 3. Very recently, in April 2008, the 1997 agreement between the Catholic Church and the *Comunidad Autónoma de Madrid*, has been renewed. Due to this agreement, the former will have a much more important role as far as the treatment of patients with incurable diseases. This is another important example of the powers of the *Comunidades Autónomas* on religious matters.

[50] See A Seglers Gómez-Quintero, 'Comentario a la nueva regulación autonómica sobre asistencia religiosa penitenciaria' (2005) 9 *iustel.com, RGDCDEE*, 1.

[51] See agreement with the Jewish Community.

[52] For instance, *el convenio marco de colaboración entre la Generalitat de Catalunya y el Consell Islamic I Cultural de Catalunya (CICC)*.

Generalitat of Catalonia has recently signed an agreement with *la Liga por la Laicidad*[53], raising questions about the social role of agnostics, atheists and other secular movements and whether or not they receive protection beyond the provisions of the fundamental right of association.

It is obvious that all different agreements signed between religious bodies and the *Generalitat* of Catalonia show that the Catalan society has become increasingly pluralistic and the old responses are not valid any longer. The same could be said about other parts of Spain[54]. These transformations have also had an effect on our model of Ecclesiastical Law and maintaining that the legal framework concerning religion is an exclusive competence of the State is no longer a defensible stance.

Devolution of Powers and Religion in Wales

The model of devolution of powers in Wales[55] was part of a wider commitment of the Labour Government, which in its manifesto for the 1997 general election, promised to deliver referenda on devolving powers to Scotland and Northern Ireland, alongside Wales. Those in favour of devolution in Wales won the referendum[56] by a very small margin and the support was somewhat muted as shown by the low turnout of the Welsh electorate (about 50%).

However, although devolution itself is a fairly recent phenomenon in the United Kingdom, divergent Church-State relations have existed for considerably longer. Although it is often said that both England and Scotland have established churches, the nature of their establishment differs greatly[57]. In the case of Wales, the Welsh Church Act 1914 brought about the 'forced abdication by the Church of England of all responsibility for the church in Wales'[58] by repealing the laws concerning the 'established' relationship between the Church and Monarch and the

[53] See A. Seglers Gómez-Quintero, 'El convenio de colaboración entre la Generalitat de Catalunya y la Liga por la Laicidad' (2005) 8 *iustel.com, RGDCDEE*.

[54] See J A Alberca de Castro and J Oliva, 'Sociology, Law and Religion in Italy and Spain' (2004) 152 *Law and Justice,* 44-67.

[55] For its interest and thorough explanation of the development of the Welsh legal framework, see T G Watkin, *The Legal History of Wales* (Cardiff, University of Wales Press, 2007).

[56] In compliance with the Government of Wales Act 1998.

[57] For a discussion of establishment in the English context, see Charlotte Smith's contribution to this volume.

[58] T G Watkin, 'Disestablishment, Self-Determination and the Constitutional Development of the Church in Wales' in N Doe, Ed) *Essays in Canon Law – A Study of the Church in Wales* (Cardiff, University of Wales Press, 1992) 32.

Church and Parliament: the Monarch lost all rights of appointment, Welsh Bishops could no longer sit in the House of Lords and ecclesiastical law ceased to exist as law[59]. However, vestiges of establishment have remained such as the right to marry in the Parish church[60] and certain burial rights[61].

This means that it is difficult, if not impossible, to speak of a Welsh ecclesiastical law[62]. However, it is possible to talk of the law of the Church in Wales[63] and also of a Welsh Law on Religion[64]. This part of the chapter will focus upon the extent to which this Welsh law on religion varies from the English law on religion and the extent to which the devolution process in Wales has caused this difference. The Government of Wales Act 1998 created a system of executive devolution. This has been buttressed by the Government of Wales Act 2006 which creates a legislative system of devolution. The effect of both of these Acts upon the Welsh law on religion will now be analysed in turn before looking at how this impacts upon the Church in Wales and other religious bodies in Wales:

Executive devolution and its impacts on religious matters

The Government of Wales Act 1998 gave the National Assembly for Wales powers which were generally the same as given to central government Ministers in relation to England[65]. This was achieved in Acts[66] following the precedent of the Transfer of Functions Orders 1999[67]. Consequently, the Assembly could do in Wales, either on its own or

---

[59] Welsh Church Act 1914, sections 1-3.

[60] Welsh Church (Temporalities) Act 1919, section 6; Marriage Act 1949, section 78 (2).

[61] Welsh Church (Burial Grounds) Act 1945.

[62] Section 3(1) of the Welsh Church Act 1914 states that: 'As from the date of disestablishment ecclesiastical courts and persons in Wales and Monmouthshire shall cease to exercise any jurisdiction, and the ecclesiastical law of the Church in Wales shall cease to exist as law.' In the context of England the term 'ecclesiastical law' has taken on a technical meaning exclusively 'the law of the Church of England to the exclusion of all other law applicable to other churches' see N Doe, *Legal Framework of the Church of England* (Oxford, Clarendon Press, 1996) 14 and M Hill, *Ecclesiastical Law* (Third edition, Oxford, Oxford University Press, 2007) 1-2.

[63] See N Doe, *The Law of the Church in Wales* (Cardiff, University of Wales Press, 2002).

[64] For a discussion on the difference between English ecclesiastical law and the English law on religion, see Augur Pearce's contribution to this volume.

[65] Government White Paper, *A Voice for Wales*, (Cm.3718), para. 1.1.

[66] See Wales Legislation Online available at <http://www.wales-legislation.org.uk>.

[67] SI.1999/672.

jointly with central government, whatever Ministers in England could do, within in the list of Fields included in Schedule 2 to the Government of Wales Act 1998. However, the Assembly was never fully responsible for making executive decisions, including making subordinate legislation within any Field listed in the Act.

Nevertheless within its *devolved competencies,* the Assembly could exercise separate and different powers to those given to central government in England. This meant that the Assembly, over the eight years of the existence of the Government of Wales Act 1998, made up to a thousand separate pieces of subordinate legislation of which possibly up to 50%[68] were in some way different to the subordinate legislation made by central government under the same powers in relation to England. The result was that, unlike the situation between 1966 and 1999 when there was a decentralisation of powers exercisable by the Secretary of State for Wales, there were differences made by the Assembly in policy and subordinate legislation in relation to up to 18 subject fields[69].

Matters of interest to religious bodies in Wales were more likely to be affected in ways which were different to such matters in England than had occurred during the time that the Secretary of State for Wales was part of the UK central government system. Executive devolution could impact directly or indirectly on various religious matters. In particular, it could affect religious matters relating to education, child care, health care, public health and the management of property.

In relation to education, for example, the Assembly had considerable powers under the Education Acts 1996 and 2002 which consolidated many of the provisions in previous statutes dealing with education in both secular and church schools. Examples in the 1996 Act include requirements that religious education must be part of the basic curriculum and must mainly be Christian but take into account other religions[70], as well as legal requirements concerning agreed religious syllabuses[71], daily acts of collective worship which were to be of a broadly Christian character[72] and the right of both parents[73] and teachers[74] to opt out of religious education and worship.

---

[68] M Navarro, 'The Evolution of Welsh Devolution' (Cardiff University, doctoral thesis, forthcoming).
[69] See Schedule 2 to Government of Wales Act 1998.
[70] Education Act 1996, s 352(1)(a).
[71] S 375(3).
[72] Ss 385-386.
[73] S 389.
[74] S 146.

Under the solely executive system of devolution the Assembly could not change these provisions because they are in primary legislation. They could regulate their administration and the way in which the powers were exercised by advising on the scope and meaning of the provisions in issuing circulars, in making regulations[75] or issuing directions. The maintenance of church schools[76] would have to be continued but they could be inspected[77] and education development plans[78] affecting possible closure of individual schools and the creation of new church schools[79] were devolved under the executive competencies.

With regard to child care, executive powers could be exercised by the Assembly in relation to eight major statutes[80] which deal with both the religious rights of children in care and the activities of religious organisations in providing child care. Such executive functions cover areas relating to adoption, fostering, children homes, day care, and religious care homes.

As far as health care was concerned, the Assembly could provide for the spiritual care of patients and staff in hospitals. This was achieved through health service guidelines[81]. Under the guidelines patients and staff should have reasonable facilities for religious observance and a chapel or rooms. Chaplains from the main Christian denominations should be appointed in consultation with the appropriate church authorities. In relation to public health, executive powers could be exercised in relation to the activities of non-Christian religious bodies. There were executive powers to regulate the religious methods used in the slaughter of animal and poultry and this includes the licensing of persons carrying out Jewish and Muslin method's of killing for food[82].

With regard to ecclesiastical property, executive powers could control through planning legislation the construction or substantial alteration of

[75] See for example Assembly SI: No: 1069 (W 109) Education (Pupil Referral Units) (Application of Enactments) (Wales) Regulations 2007; No: 3562 (W 312) Education (Information about Individual Pupils) (Wales) Regulations 2007.

[76] School Standards and Framework Act 1998.

[77] Schools Inspection 1996 s11.

[78] School Standards and Framework Act 1998 ss 6 and 7.

[79] School Standards and Framework Act 1998 s 69.

[80] Children and Young Persons Act 1933; the Adoption Act 1976, Adoption and Children Act 2002, Children Act 1989, Registered Homes Act 1984, Children (Leaving Care) Act 2000, Carers and Disabled Children Act 2000, Children Act 2004.

[81] These guidelines are non-statutory and therefore very difficult to find as there is no central database maintained by the Welsh Assembly Government for this purpose.

[82] Slaughterhouses Act 1974, Part II; Slaughter of Poultry Act 1967; Welfare of Animals (Slaughter or Killing) Regulations 1995 (SI 1995/731).

any religious buildings[83]. Burials in Church in Wales' burial grounds are subject to rules approved by the Welsh Assembly Government in relation to rights of burial and payment of burial fees[84]. Through its agency CADW, the Assembly gave grants to the maintenance of ecclesiastical buildings which are listed as historic buildings[85]. A system of ecclesiastical exemptions was also operated whereby certain religious bodies in Wales were given exemptions from the necessity to obtain listed building consent and conservation area consent before they carry out works on their ecclesiastical buildings[86].

As far as retained powers are concerned, the executive powers of the Assembly never extended to certain matters which were retained by the central government even within devolved fields. Examples include teachers' pay in the field of education and many other areas within the field of health and safety at work. Outside the devolved fields are retained fields under which all the executive powers are exercisable by central government in relation to Wales. These include religious charities, marriage, licensing of public places of worship, exemption from rates in relation to public places of worship, and criminal offences relating to religion.

A general proviso in the Government of Wales Act 1998 to the exercise of all executive powers in Wales, which continues under the Government of Wales Act 2006, is that the Assembly, and now the Welsh Assembly Government, cannot violate the rights contained in the European Convention on Human Rights[87] which are set out in Schedule 1 to the Human Rights Act 1998, which include the Article 9 right to freedom of thought, conscience and religion. All executive decisions continue to be subject to challenge as to their legality in the courts as a devolution issue[88].

Legislative Devolution and its impact on religious matters

The Government of Wales Act 2006 introduced a division between the Assembly which becomes a mainly primary legislative body and the Welsh Assembly Government, the executive body which exercises all devolved

---

[83] Town and Country Planning 1990, Part III.

[84] Welsh Church (Burial Grounds) Act 1945 s 2.

[85] Town and Country Planning 1990, Part V.

[86] Ecclesiastical Exemptions (Listed Buildings and Conservation Areas) Order 1994, SI 1994/1771.

[87] Government of Wales Act 1998, s 107; Government of Wales Act 2006, ss 81 and 94(6).

[88] Government of Wales Act 2006 Schedule 9.

functions and reports to the Assembly on the exercise of its functions[89]. The powers of the Welsh Assembly Government continue to be exercised both through powers already granted in Acts of Parliament[90] and Transfer of Function Orders and in post 2007 Acts. The Welsh Assembly Government also derives powers from laws made by the Assembly[91].

The Government of Wales Act 2006 provides two different systems of legislative devolution. Part III of and Schedule 5 to the Act provides an interim system, which is currently in force. Part IV of and Schedule 7 to the Act provides the final system whereby which the Assembly could make Acts by reference to lists of powers comprehensively set out in Schedule 7. This final system is subject to Parliament's prior agreement, a two thirds majority vote of Assembly Members and a favourable referendum of Welsh electors[92].

The difference between the Schedule 7 powers and the Schedule 5 interim system is that the Assembly would be fully aware of the extent of all of its legislative powers by reference to the list of enabling powers in Schedule 7. Under the interim system of Schedule 5 there is a continuous piecemeal addition by Parliament to the legislative powers of the Assembly. Such powers can change day by day. Schedule 7 would be a settled list, though the list could be extended by Orders in Council. For current purposes, we will focus upon the interim system.

Part III of the Government of Wales Act 2006 introduced new powers which enable the Assembly to make laws called Measures within the twenty Fields defined in Schedule 5. Under each Field the Assembly can bid for Matters. Once a Matter is inserted by Parliament into a Field in Schedule 5 then the Assembly can create a Measure on that Matter. These laws can create the same provisions as in an Act of Parliament[93]. The unique nature of these new powers of the National Assembly to make laws means that within its competencies the Assembly can make considerable changes to Acts of Parliament and including some of those relating to religious matters.

As the White Paper – *Better Governance for Wales*[94] – states these powers include the ability of the Assembly to add to, amend, or repeal both existing Acts of Parliament and those enacted in the future. Legislative

---

[89] Government of Wales Act ss 1 and 44.
[90] Schedule 3.
[91] S 94.
[92] Government of Wales Act 2006, s 103.
[93] Government of Wales Act 2006, s 94(1).
[94] Government White Paper, *Better Governance for Wales*, 2005 (Cm.6582), para 3.16.

provision can also be made where there are no Acts of Parliament governing the particular objective. Potentially therefore much primary legislation affecting religious matters can be changed by the Assembly in relation to Wales. Such changes cannot be made without the consent of Government Ministers in relation to functions which in Wales continue to be exercised by UK Ministers[95]. With this proviso and the overriding condition that no law made by the Assembly can be contrary either to EU law or the European Convention of Human Rights[96], as contained in the Human Rights Act 1998, major legislative changes can be effected.

The twenty Fields in Schedule 5 indicate the areas where a distinctively Welsh law on religion could develop. Religious believers and groups would be affected by new laws affecting 'Ancient monuments and historic buildings'[97],'Education and training'[98], 'Food'[99], 'Health and health services'[100], 'Housing'[101], 'Local government'[102], 'Social Welfare'[103], 'Tourism', 'Town and country planning'[104] and 'the Welsh Language'[105].

At the time of writing, the Assembly either has or is bidding for 47 Matters, of which 29 are already in force[106]. Under the field of 'Social Welfare' there are 9 proposed Matters[107]; in the Field of 'Education',

---

[95] Government of Wales Act 2006, Schedule 5, Part 2.

[96] Schedule 5, Part 2 paras 1, Part 3, para 7.

[97] There could be a fundamental change in the system of classifying ecclesiastical buildings and their grant aid.

[98] In education the change could affect the financing of church maintained schools to the extent that they cease to be maintained by the state, the role of religion in State schools, inspections of church schools, training of teacher, the curriculum etc.

[99] Measures could be made relating to the slaughtering of animal for human consumption, provisions relating to food safety and hygiene which would have a general affect on all church schools and religious bodies which prepare and supply food.

[100] Laws relating to the recognition of the medical beliefs of non-Christian religious bodies could be altered but not laws relating to abortion (a retained matter).

[101] This could affect religious groups and their associations who own property.

[102] Measures could alter the number of local authorities, adversely affecting the relationship that religious bodies had formed with their local government organisations.

[103] Social Welfare Measures could impact on the activities of religious bodies in carrying out function of adoption, children homes, fostering, day care and residential care home.

[104] Planning law relating to religious buildings and the extent of the exemption that certain religious bodies have from existing planning legislation could be altered

[105] For example the Assembly could impose a duty on religious bodies to carry out their activities in both the England and Welsh language

[106] See Wales Legislation Online under the new Constitution section.

[107] Field 15- Matters 15.1 to 15.9. Eight of these draft Matters could have wide effects on the care of children and could therefore change the responsibilities of religious bodies in their work of adoption, fostering, care homes and the social welfare of children by religious bodies.

there are 17 Matters[108] so far in force which relate to Education and which include wide powers applying to primary and secondary education (11 Matters) and further education (6 Matters); in 'Housing' there is currently one draft Matter and this could affect housing associations managed by religious bodies[109]; 'local Government' has 5 Matters[110] in force which could affect the relationship which religious bodies presently have with existing local authorities; in' Town and Country Planning' there are 3 proposed Matters[111] relating to development and use of land which could affect new religious buildings or extensions to current ones. Moreover, the law relating to the duty of religious bodies to maintain disused burial grounds and, in relation to the Church in Wales, to allow any person within an ecclesiastical parish to be buried in vacant areas of the parish church burial ground could be affected by Assembly Measures.

It is therefore possible for a body based in Wales, for the first time since well before the Act of Union of 1535, to make primary laws within its legislative competence which are different in substance to laws applying in England. The procedures for making such legislation are also different in that they reflect a new participative approach in law making.

Participation in the Assembly's law making and the Assembly Government Executive work

It is necessary for religious bodies which have any interest in Wales to realise that it is no longer necessary only to seek to influence UK central government Departments and Parliament. Although attaining such influence remains an important part of their work (because a federal system has not been created by the Government of Wales Act 2006 and therefore central government and Parliament continue to play in important part in Wales), nevertheless, as we have seen, the Assembly's laws can be different to those in England and where the Welsh Assembly

---

[108] Field 5- Matters 5.1 to 5.17. It seems possible within these powers to change, amend or repeal Acts which define the place of religion in the State education system. Consequently it would seem that church schools could have their state funding remove by Assembly legislation. The duty relating to daily acts of worship of a Christian nature could be changed or repealed. In fact any aspect of religion in schools could be changed or excluded but always subject to Article 9 ECHR.

[109] Field 11- Matter 11.1.

[110] Field 1- Matters 12.1 to 12.5.

[111] Field 18- Matters 18.1 to 18.3.

Government has executive powers, these can be exercised separately and differently to those exercisable in England[112].

Consequently it is necessary for machinery to be established for religious bodies operating in Wales to seek to influence the legislative output of the Assembly and the executive work of the Assembly Government. An example is the Church in Wales which has established a Committee of Senior Officials working with the Bench of Bishops to analyse the proposals of the Assembly and the Assembly Government and to work to reflect the interests of the Church and religious bodies as a whole. Meetings are held on a regular basis with Assembly Ministers, Assembly Members and officials. It is also possible for any religious body to make representations to Assembly Committees including Subject Committees as well as Committees dealing with proposed Assembly legislation[113]. With legislative Matters in existence or being bid for by the Assembly, these representations become a very important area of the work of religious bodies in Wales. The exercise of executive powers by the Welsh Assembly Government continues to be widely based and their use can be subject to representations from outside bodies. This is an exciting development which involves all persons and bodies in Wales who will be subject to Assembly laws and executive decisions and it requires religious bodies to be fully aware of the implications of each of these dramatic powers and to play a full part in their evolution[114].

For the first time religious bodies can legally challenge the validity of primary laws. This means that the Supreme Court will play the role of a constitutional court at least as regards having jurisdiction in relation to deciding whether the Assembly's laws are within the Assembly's legislative competence[115]. In addition, any court or tribunal will be able to decide whether the executive actions of the Assembly Government are within its powers and whether such actions are incompatible with the ECHR as set out in the Human Rights Act 1998[116]. For this purpose it is important that religious bodies understand the boundaries of the legislative and executive powers of the Assembly and of the Assembly

---

[112] Government of Wales Act 2006, s 84.

[113] The Assembly Standing Orders enable persons and bodies to make representations under a variety of provisions, e.g. Standing Order 10.44 where persons and bodies can attend Committee meetings and give oral and written evidence if invited.

[114] This includes the right to petition under Standing Order 28.

[115] Government of Wales Act 2006, s149 and Schedule 9 'Devolution Issues' Para 1. Part 1.

[116] Government of Wales Act 2006, s 81.

Government so that if their interests are adversely affected they can decide whether and how to challenge such laws or decisions.

Religious bodies should also be aware that Schedule 5 is an interim system. The Archbishop of Wales heads a wide ranging body *Cymru Yfory- Tomorrow's Wales*[117] which was established in 2004 seeking to inform the Welsh public about the future of devolution. Similarly in autumn 2007, the Assembly government established the *All Wales Convention*[118] to ascertain the views of the Welsh Electorate as to the possibility of implementing the Schedule 7 powers. Religious bodies could play an important part in the work of the Assembly's Convention by representing to it the views of their members.

Conclusions

Until relatively recently, Spain and the United Kingdom were both very centralist States[119]. In both countries, moves towards decentralisation have been characterised by compromise[120]. The central authorities in both Madrid and London created blatant differences amongst the territories within their States with a view to appease those with a stronger national identity[121]. These compromises have led to further legislation and tensions[122] as the

---

[117] See their website available at: <http://www.tomorrow-wales.co.uk/>.

[118] See <http://new.wales.gov.uk/about/strategy/allwalesconvention>.

[119] In Spain, the 1978 Constitution broke a period of sheer centralism under General Franco's regime (1939-1975). The dictator had fiercely opposed any recognition of national identities within the State and following his death, under the period known as the democratic transition, one of the major concerns of the drafters of the Constitution was to acknowledge in its new territorial model the pluralistic nature of the Spanish State. The devolution settlement for Wales, alongside Scotland and Northern Ireland, took place many years later, in 1998 as one of the policies of the Blair government.

[120] The Spanish Constitution of 1978 has not tried to give a response to very diverse social groups, with outstandingly different needs and expectations. Although this highest source of law is to be praised for having provided Spain with stability and peace after many years of dictatorship, the ambiguity is obvious as far as the territorial model of the State is concerned as discussed above. In relation to Wales, the current interim period of legislative devolution is the product of unease felt by Labour politicians at Westminster.

[121] Evidence of these differences can be found the *vía rápida/vía lenta* dichotomy in Spain and the Scotland Act 1998, Northern Ireland Act 1998 and Government of Wales Act 1998 in UK.

[122] For example, as discussed above, in Spain there is a clear conflict between 16 of the Constitution, which states that the power to cooperate with religious bodies belongs to public authorities and Article 7 of the General Act 7/1980 of 5 July of Religious Liberty which has enabled the State to sign agreements with those religious bodies registered in the General Register of Religious Entities and deeply rooted in the Spanish society.

process has deepened and moved towards uniformity[123]. In both States, decentralisation has been a process rather than a one-off event and this process remains on-going[124].

Decentralisation clearly has ramifications for religious believers and groups. However, these are too often ignored. In Spain, the Constitution fails to give an explicit recognition of the treatment of religion as a competence of the central authorities, and by misinterpreting the religious dimension, narrowing it down to the principle of religious freedom and focusing exclusively on the wording of Article 149.1.1, commentators have traditionally regarded it as a power of the State. A clear symbol of this approach is the fact that one compulsory subject which Law students must study in their degrees is usually entitled 'Ecclesiastical Law of the State'. This overlooks the fact that many of the powers such as health and social assistance – listed in Article 148 of the Constitution – and which can be assumed by the *Comunidades Autónomas*, may have an important effect on the religious element. With regard to the UK, a country where until relatively recently law and religion generally received scant attention, it is imperative that those who do work in this field note the important effect that Schedule 5 will have in creating a distinctively Welsh law on religion. Although final legislative devolution in Wales, when and if it comes, will attract more attention, it is vital to note the already considerable consequences of the interim system of legislative devolution as well as the system of executive devolution.

By reference to Catalonia and Schedule 5 to the Government of Wales Act 2006, we have sought to list some examples of the current powers that sub-State authorities may have which effect religious matters. The list is not comprehensive, but aims to illustrate the extent to which a 'regional ecclesiastical law' (in a continental European sense) exists. Under these circumstances, it is essential that religious bodies engage with bodies below the level of the State in a productive dialogue and in a fruitful cooperation. It is also vital that law and religion writers do not get so entangled in the phraseology of 'Church and State' that they forget that there are other levels that impact on and can be impacted by religious matters.

---

[123] From the early eighties, Spain has witnessed an ongoing process of 'catching up' between *Comunidades Autónomas*. Although the model of devolution in Britain, remains very young, the Government of Wales Act 2006 can be seen in this light.

[124] The reform of the *estatutos de autonomía* in Catalonia (2006) and Andalucía (2007) and the enactment of the Government of Wales Act in 2006 clearly symbolise the ongoing and evolving nature of the models of devolution in Spain and the United Kingdom, which is far from being definite.

THE CONCEPT OF CHRISTIAN LAW – A CASE STUDY: CONCEPTS OF 'A CHURCH' IN A COMPARATIVE AND ECUMENICAL CONTEXT

Norman Doe[1]

Introduction

The renewed interest in the study of religious law in recent years has led to increasingly sophisticated accounts with a move towards interdisciplinary and comparative studies[2]. It has been suggested that it may be possible to construct a category 'Christian law', analogous to Islamic law, Jewish law and Hindu law by means of the comparative study of the internal laws and regulatory instruments of Christian churches[3]. This chapter seeks to build upon that analysis by means of a case study on a topic of interdisciplinary importance, the concept of 'a Church'.

Ecclesiology does not generally deal with the nature of 'a church'[4]: its principal focus is discourse on doctrines of the church universal[5], and doctrines commonly proposed as images or models[6]. However, some ecclesiologists do treat the relationship between, for example, 'the church', as 'Spiritual Community', one and undivided, and 'churches', disunited human organisations. The former is not an organised body but 'a mystical reality latent in and behind the visible churches'; the spiritual community is indivisibly one and the visible churches are not and need not be one[7]. The use of the words 'the' and (commonly) 'of' in the official titles

---

[1] I am grateful to Revd Dr Timothy Bradshaw, Regents Park College, Oxford, for invaluable assistance with this study. The study is based upon a presentation to the Seventh Colloquium of Anglican and Roman Catholic Canon Lawyers held at Rome in April 2005.

[2] See Russell Sandberg and Rebecca Catto's contribution to this volume in relation to the merits of interdisciplinary work.

[3] N Doe, 'Modern Church Law' in J Witte and F S Alexander, *Christianity and Law* (Cambridge, Cambridge University Press, 2008) 271.

[4] See typically A V Dulles, *Models of the Church* (Second edition, Dublin, Gill and Macmillan, 1988).

[5] The one, holy, catholic and apostolic church.

[6] Such as 'people of God', 'Body of Christ', 'Community of the Holy Spirit', 'Mystical Communion', 'sacrament', 'servant', 'herald' and 'institution'.

[7] P Tillich, *Systematic Theology*, Vol. 3 (Chicago, Chicago University Press, 1963) 162-172.

of churches[8] presupposes the concept of 'a church' as distinct from 'the church' universal. It is that concept of 'a Church' which will be explored in this chapter to illustrate how religious law may inform ecclesiological analysis.

This chapter seeks to identify and examine: (1) the concept of 'a church' in Anglican self-understanding and to compare this with self-understandings of 'a church' in the Roman Catholic, Orthodox and Lutheran traditions; (2) the respective unilateral conditions which Anglicans, Roman Catholics, Orthodox and Lutherans require to be satisfied before a body is recognised as 'a church'; (3) ecumenical understandings of 'a church' in Anglican dialogues with Roman Catholics, Orthodox and Lutherans; and (4) how these understandings of ecclesiality might be applied, to an idea of the Anglican Communion as 'a church', a question particularly timely given recent ongoing developments in Anglican law at a global level. The conclusion will reflect on the merits of this comparative approach and the use of the category 'Christian law'.

1 – Ecclesiology in Self-Understanding and Identity

For some it is almost universally accepted as a foundation principle of ecclesiology, that 'a church must be a community of people', in 'a place', because it is only in community that the elements of church can be present and operative[9]. Such approaches to the idea of 'a church' are in part based on New Testament texts, which employ the Greek *ekklesia* (commonly understood to translate the Hebrew *qahal*, assembly) to refer to such communities[10], as distinct from the church universal[11]. From this emerges the notion that 'a church is an ecclesially complete whole in which the means of grace are present and in which the Christian may know himself or herself to be a member of the body of Christ'; and that a local church is therefore a 'microcosm' or 'image' of the universal church[12], a 'provisional', 'specific or local expression of the relationship of individual persons in Christ which is the Church'[13]. The English word 'church'[14] is

[8] Such as 'The Church of England': see Canon A1.
[9] G R Evans, *The Church and the Churches: Toward an Ecumenical Ecclesiology* (Cambridge, Cambridge University Press, 1994) 48.
[10] E.g. in geographical places 1 Corinthians. 1.2; 2 Corinthians1.1), as a house (Philippians. 2; Romans 16.3-5), as a city (Acts 8.1) or a region (Acts 9.31,15.3).
[11] 1 Corinthians.10.32; Galatians 1.13; Ephesians. 1.22; Colossians 1:18, 24: E P Clowney, *The Church: Contours of Christian Theology* (Illinois, Intervarsity Press, 1995) 111f.
[12] *Lumen Gentium* (hereafter LG), 23a.
[13] Evans, *The Church and the Churches* 49, 113, 293.
[14] OE *cirice*, Teutonic *kirika*.

said to derive from the Greek *kuriake*, 'belonging to the Lord'[15], and over time was used not only for the church universal[16], but also for particular local communities of Christians with a visible outward organisation distinct from other such communities or 'churches'[17].

1.1 – Anglican self-understanding

The distinction between 'the church' (universal) and 'a church' (local) appears in classical Anglicanism[18]. Today, at the global level of its forty-four member churches, the Anglican Communion employs numerous images of 'the whole Church' (universal)[19]. Moreover, in turn at the local level, each autonomous Anglican church spells out in official texts (doctrinal, catechetical and constitutional) not only its own identity but also its own understanding of the church universal, as, for example, 'the family of God and the Body of Christ through which he continues his reconciling work'[20], and commonly these texts define each of the elements of the one, holy, catholic and apostolic church[21].

Contemporary Anglican ecclesiology has been described as 'the activity in which the churches of the Anglican Communion engage when they explain what they are *as churches*'[22]. It is proposed that there are six main

[15] E.g. in post-apostolic tradition as the Christian house of worship: Apostolic Constitutions, c. 300 (II.59); Council of Ancyra (can. 15).

[16] This can be seen in the Oxford English Dictionary (OED) entry for 'church' eg 1382, Wyclif, Eph v.23: 'Crist is heed of the chirche'; R Field, *Of the Church* (1628): 'This glorious Society of men and angels whom the most high God made capable of felicity and blisse is rightly named the Church of the living God'.

[17] This can be seen in the OED entry for 'church': 1564 Becon, New Catechism: 'What meanest thou by this word 'church?...Nothing else than a company of people gathered together, or a congregation'; 1692, Locke, *Toleration*, Wks 1727, II.i.235: 'A Church then, I take to be a voluntary Society of men, joining themselves together of their own accord, in order to the publick worshiping of God, in such manner as they judge acceptable to him'; 1726 Ayliffe, *Parerg*, 167: 'The word Church is also taken for any particular Congregation or Assembly of Men, as the Church which was at Corinth'.

[18] 'The visible Church of Christ is a congregation of faithful men, in the which the pure Word of God is preached, and the Sacraments be duly ministered according to Christ's ordinance in all those things that of necessity are requisite to the same' which may be contrasted with 'the Church of Jerusalem, Alexandria, and Antioch and the Church of Rome': Thirty-Nine Articles of Religion, Art. 19.

[19] See Lambeth Conference (hereafter LC) 1897, Resolution 24.

[20] Wales, Catechism, III.15.

[21] New Zealand, Constitution, Preamble: the Church is one 'because it is one body, under one head, Jesus Christ', holy 'because the Holy Spirit dwells in its members and guides it in mission', catholic, 'because it seeks to proclaim the whole faith to all people to the end of time' and apostolic 'because it presents the faith of the apostles and is sent to carry Christ's mission to all the world'.

[22] P Avis (ed) *The Christian Church: An Introduction to the Major Traditions* (London, SPCK, 2002) 132 (italics added).

characteristics of 'a church' in Anglicanism: territoriality (geographical); sociality (community and membership); polity (autonomy); relationality (being in communion with Canterbury); universality (relationship to the church universal); and loyalty (to catholicity and apostolicity). The following examines each characteristic in turn.

First, for Anglicans a church is characterised by territoriality: geographical unity. At the level of its global fellowship, the Anglican Communion describes each of its members variously as: 'particular Church[es]'[23], 'local Churches'[24], 'national Churches'[25], and 'regional churches'[26]. They have also been described as 'colonial Churches'[27], and 'native Churches[28]. Needless to say, the official titles of individual institutional Anglican churches express the geographical dimension of their ecclesial being[29], by reference variously to the secular territory in which they function (such as 'The Church of Ireland'), or to their ecclesiastical territory (as in 'The Church of the Province of Southern Africa')[30]. It is possible to suggest, therefore, that for Anglicans a church is a spatial (or geographical) entity which promotes within its territory a national (or regional) expression of Christian faith, life and worship[31].

Secondly, individual Anglican churches see themselves as a constituted and unified community (in a geographical area) with a (reasonably distinct) membership: 'a community to exemplify in the world the good news of Jesus Christ'[32], or, perhaps more temporally, as 'the Community which is associated under the provisions' set out in its constitution[33]. The

---

[23] LC 1897, Res. 25.

[24] LC 1908, Res. 25.

[25] LC 1908, Res. 8.

[26] LC 1930, Res. 49.

[27] LC 1897, Res. 10.

[28] Churches which are 'their own and not a foreign Church', 'adapted to local circumstances': LC 1897, Res. 18, 19; LC 1908, Res. 21.

[29] Evans, *The Church and the Churches* 82: 'Anglican provinces as they have evolved historically have continued to see themselves as "churches" of the Anglican Communion, with something of the same pattern of autonomy as obtains among the Orthodox'.

[30] The territorial boundaries of national churches may correspond to those of the secular state in which they exist, a single province (e.g Sudan) or many (e.g ECUSA: Protestant Episcopal Church in the USA); they may also correspond to secular jurisdictional territories within a single state (a province in Wales, two provinces in England). Regional churches may cover a number of secular states, as a single province (e.g West Indies) or more (e.g Ireland), or as non-provincial (e.g Jerusalem and the Middle East): see N Doe, *Canon Law in the Anglican Communion* (Oxford, Clarendon Press, 1998) 9.

[31] LC 1930, Res. 49: the particular and national churches 'promote within each of their territories a national expression of Christian faith, life and worship'.

[32] Hong Kong, Constitution, Preamble.

[33] Southern Africa, Constitution, Art. XXIV.1.

community is sometimes understood as having 'constituted herself into the Church of [X]' which 'shall remain one indivisible Church under God'[34], a constituting occasionally presented as an independent act 'in a spirit of self-reliance'[35]. Alternatively, the ecclesial community may have been formed by an external act (for example, by a declaration of the Archbishop of Canterbury)[36], or see itself as 'derived' from another institutional church[37]. This is close to the idea of a community being a church because it is so seen by its founders. This self-perception is verifiable, so to speak, through the perceptions of others, for example, by the wider Anglican Communion (when the church is 'duly constituted' as such)[38], and even by its host State[39], the laws of which may recognise Anglican communities as 'churches'[40]. Indeed, with the exception of England[41], key to Anglican identity is that churches are not established by State law[42]. A church as a distinct community is also reflected in its membership, which may be based variously on baptism, confirmation, communicant status, or entry of names on membership rolls and registers[43].

Thirdly, a church is a community in a particular place with a unified autonomous provincial and/or diocesan polity or institutional structure. Sometimes Anglicans equate 'church' with 'province': for instance, '"Church"…means the Province of the Episcopal Church of the Sudan'[44]; indeed, some churches see themselves as 'provinces of *the Church*'[45], or (even) as 'a Province of *the Anglican Church* in communion with

---

[34] Nigeria, Constitution, Preamble and I.2.

[35] Korea, Constitution, Preface.

[36] E.g the Church in Wales, disestablished by Parliament (Welsh Church Act 1914) was formed as a province by declaration of the Archbishop of Canterbury 10 February 1920. See, generally, N Doe, *The Law of the Church in Wales* (Cardiff, University of Wales Press, 2002).

[37] 'This Church…derived from the Church of England' (Australia, Constitution, I.I.II.4).

[38] LC 1930, Res. 49.

[39] 'The constitution of the Anglican Church…came into existence formally on the enactment of the Church of England in Australia Constitution Act 1961': *Scandrett v Dowling* [1992] 27 NSWLR 483.

[40] Eg Barbados: Anglican Church Act 1969; Grenada: Church of England Disestablishment Act 1959.

[41] On which see generally N Doe, *The Legal Framework of the Church of England* (Oxford, Clarendon Press, 1996) and M Hill, *Ecclesiastical Law* (Third edition, Oxford, Oxford University Press, 2007).

[42] Southern Africa, Constitution, Preamble: this church is 'not by laws established'.

[43] See Doe, *Canon Law in the Anglican Communion* 160ff.

[44] Sudan, Constitution, I.1(1)(xi). See also Tanzania, Constitution, s.1.2: '"Province' means the Church of the province of Tanzania".

[45] Evans, *The Church and the Churches* 78; *quaere*: Of which church: the church universal or the 'Anglican Church'?

the Anglican Communion'[46]. A province is 'a self-governing church composing of several dioceses operating under a common constitution and having one supreme legislative body' and 'a fully autonomous member within the Anglican Communion having independent ecclesiastical authority vested in the General Synod'[47]. Many Anglican churches define themselves as a provincial composite of dioceses: '[a] provincial union of dioceses'[48]; 'the entire Church, which comprehends the five aforesaid Dioceses', is 'a combination under Metropolitical and Synodical Authority...of the several Dioceses'[49]. Consequently, though a province is 'a church', a church is not just a province: an extra-provincial diocese may be a church[50], and 'a church' may be a grouping of 'churches': for example, '"The Church of Nigeria" is...the Churches associated under the provisions of this Constitution and known in full as Church of Nigeria', and each diocese, gathered around its bishop, has its own polity (and constitution)[51]. Indeed, within the diocese, for some a parish 'is in a limited sense a local church in its own right, but it is not, in an episcopal system, regarded as a complete church' in so far as it lacks, for instance, the capacity to ordain[52]. That autonomy is a mark of being 'a church' is buttressed by prohibitions against one church from interference in the domestic affairs of other individual churches[53].

Fourthly, for Anglicans a community with an autonomous provincial (and/or diocesan) polity in a particular geographical area is 'a church' by virtue of its relations of unity with other member churches of the Anglican Communion. Membership of the Anglican Communion is critical in the self-understanding of its constituent churches. One the one hand, sometimes communion is represented as a *bipartite* relationship between one institutional church only and Canterbury[54]: '[t]o be Anglican it is necessary to be in communion with that See'[55]. Some churches

---

[46] Hong Kong, Constitution, Preamble.

[47] Hong Kong, Constitution, Preface, 1, 2.

[48] Hong Kong, Constitution, Preamble.

[49] Southern Africa, Constitution, Res. 1870 (whilst 'called the Church of the Province of South Africa; this title not being intended to exclude other titles (such as English or Anglican Church), under which this Church, or any portion of it, may be known') and Art. XXIV.2.

[50] Eg Bermuda, Costa Rica, Puerto Rico.

[51] Constitution, XVI.75(5); see Ch. IX for diocesan constitutions.

[52] Evans, *The Church and the Churches* 79.

[53] LC 1897, Res. 24; LC 1878, Res, 1; LC 1968, Res. 63; LC 1978, Recommendations 1.

[54] LC 1930, Res. 49: '[t]he Anglican Communion is a fellowship of...dioceses, provinces and regional Churches *in communion with the See of Canterbury*'.

[55] *Virginia Report*, 37.

declare themselves in 'full communion with the Church of England'[56], or in 'communion with the sister Church of England'[57]. On the other hand, communion surfaces as a *multipartite* relationship. A church considers itself in 'communion with all churches of the Anglican Communion', or 'with the See of Canterbury and with all...Churches...in full Communion with the See of Canterbury', or as 'a...member of the Anglican Communion, a Fellowship of...Churches in communion with the See of Canterbury'[58]. In turn, occasionally geographical identity is mixed with Anglican identity: churches see themselves as 'a Province of the Anglican Church'[59], or as a 'Church of the Anglican Communion in these parts'[60], or, in their official titles, as 'The Anglican Church in South East Asia', 'The Anglican Church of Chile', 'The Anglican Episcopal Church of Brazil'. Similarly, geographical identity may be mixed with historical religious identity[61] or national identity[62]. Some churches see themselves 'a Province of the Anglican Church in communion with the Anglican Communion'[63]. As well as political autonomy, episcopal leadership, synodical governance (lay participation in governance), and common traditions of liturgy, spirituality and openness to theological exploration are what makes churches distinctively Anglican[64].

Fifthly, member churches of the Anglican Communion see themselves as intimately related to the church universal: 'We are what we are *as a Church* (italics added) and as members of the Church by reason of what we have received from Him through and in the Holy Catholic Church'[65]. Different images are used to convey the relationship of a church to the church universal. Some churches see themselves as 'being *a branch* of the One Holy Catholic and Apostolic Church of Christ, [which] retains inviolate in the sacred ministry the three orders of Bishops, Priests and Deacons, as of Divine Institution'[66], others as 'a partner ... in the universal

[56] Canada, Declaration.

[57] Ireland, Constitution.

[58] Korea, Nigeria, ECUSA, Constitutions.

[59] Hong Kong, Constitution, Preamble.

[60] Southern Africa, Constitution, Preamble.

[61] For instance, 'The Church in Wales is the ancient Church of this land, catholic and reformed': Wales, Catechism, III.25.

[62] See, for example, '[t]he Church in Papua New Guinea [is] a National Church' Papua New Guinea, Constitution, Preamble.

[63] Hong Kong, Constitution, Preamble.

[64] Avis, *The Christian Church*, 135.

[65] The Church of India, Pakistan, Burma and Ceylon, Constitution, Prefatory Statement, 1.

[66] Scottish Episcopal Church, Can. 1.1. For others: 'We declare this Church to be... an integral *portion* of the one Body of Christ composed of Churches which [are] united under the One Divine Head and in the fellowship of the one Holy Catholic and Apostolic Church': Canada, Constitution, Declaration of Principles, 1.

Church'[67]. Whereas most employ the English word 'church' in their titles, some use words of their native languages more closely related on their face to the Greek *ekklesia* and Latin *ecclesia*[68].

Finally, then, integral to this relationship with the church universal is loyalty to the marks of the church universal in terms of catholicity and apostolicity in faith, sacraments and ministry[69]. At the global level, Anglican churches have 'characteristics in common' in that 'they uphold and propagate the Catholic and Apostolic faith and order'[70]. Catholicity and apostolicity, and loyalty to them as effecting ecclesial identity, commonly surface in the texts of individual churches[71]. At the same time, however, each church is provisional in character, a pilgrim community: this too is part of Anglican self-understanding[72], particularly in ecumenical duties to maintain fellowship, to seek unity, or to restore unity between churches[73].

1.2 – Roman Catholic self-understanding

The Roman Catholic Church also uses the terms 'the church' and 'churches' in its own self-understanding. First, as to the church universal:

[67] Anglican Church of Canada, Mission Statement. The understanding of the Church of England is that it '*belongs* to the true and apostolic Church of Christ' (Canon A1). Indeed, in the eucharist Anglicans 'are brought into closer communion, not only with the Lord and with fellow worshippers, but with the whole Church, made up on earth of local churches...that are episcopally ordered': *The Eucharist: Sacrament of Unity*, An occasional paper of the House of Bishops of the Church of England (London, 2001); A McGrath, '*Communicatio in sacris*: An Effort to Express the Unity of Christians or an Exercise in Politeness' (2001) 63 *Canon Law Society of America Proceedings*, 173.

[68] e.g: *eglwys* (Welsh: *Yr Eglwys yng Nghymru – the Church in Wales*); *église* (*L'Eglise de la Province de L'Océan Indien*) or *iglesia* (*Iglesia Anglicana de Mexico*).

[69] Indeed, it has been understood in civil law that: 'the identity of a religious community described as a Church must consist in the unity of its doctrines', which 'bind them together as one Christian community': *Free Church of Scotland (General Assembly) v Overtoun (Lord)* [1904] AC 515.

[70] LC 1930, Res. 49.

[71] Typically: 'The Anglican Church of Australia, being a part of the One Holy Catholic and Apostolic Church of Christ, holds the Christian Faith', receives the scriptures, and 'will ever obey the commands of Christ, teach His doctrine, administer His sacraments, follow and uphold His discipline and preserve the three orders of bishops, priests and deacons in the sacred ministry': Australia, Constitution, I.I.1-3.

[72] LC 1930, Res. 49: the Lambeth Conference prays for and eagerly awaits 'the time when the Churches of the present Anglican Communion will enter into communion with other parts of the Catholic Church not definable as Anglican...as a step towards the ultimate reunion of all Christendom in one visibly united fellowship'.

[73] Eg South India, Constitution, II.2; Southern Africa, Res. 1 (1973); Korea, Fundamental Declaration.

'The Church in Christ is in the nature of a sacrament...a sign and instrument of communion with God and union among all people'; The church, 'the community of faith, hope and charity', is also 'a visible organization through which [Christ] communicates truth and grace to all'. Yet, 'the society structured with hierarchical organs and the mystical body of Christ, the visible society and the spiritual community...are not to be thought of as two realities', but 'form one complex reality which comes together from a human and a divine element'. The people of God represent the visible church: incorporated by baptism, bound by confirmation, and taking part in the eucharist; and marriage is 'the domestic church'[74].

Secondly, whilst for Pius XII 'the Mystical Body of Christ and the Roman Catholic Church are one and the same'[75], today the Roman Catholic position is that 'the church' (universal) 'established and ordered in this world as a society, subsists (*subsistit*) in the catholic Church, governed by the successor of Peter and the bishops in communion with him'[76], not wishing to identify the Church of Christ with the Roman Catholic Church in a way which excluded other churches and communities[77]. Ecclesial sociality is also expressed in clear ideas about membership: 'Christ's faithful are those who, since they are incorporated into Christ through baptism, are constituted the people of God'[78], and '[t]hose baptised are in full communion with the catholic Church here on earth who are joined with Christ in his visible body, through the bonds of profession of faith, the sacraments and ecclesiastical governance'[79].

Thirdly, in Roman Catholicism '[p]articular churches, in which and from which the one and only catholic Church exists, are principally dioceses'[80]; larger groupings of dioceses are understood to be 'not "Church" in the theological sense'[81]. Particular churches are characterised by their: *foundation* (they may be erected as such by the apostolic see)[82]; *territoriality* (dioceses have fixed boundaries which should have a demographic

---

[74] LG, 1, 11, 48.

[75] *Humani generis* (1950).

[76] LG, 8; Code, c.204(2).

[77] *The Canon Law: Letter and Spirit – A Practical Guide to the Code of Canon Law*, The Canon Law Society of Great Britain and Ireland (Dublin, Veritas, 1995) para. 428.

[78] Code, c. 204(1); LG, 10, 11.

[79] LG, 14-15; Code, c.205.

[80] Code, c.368: a territorial prelature (eg) is also a particular church, being equivalent to a diocese.

[81] J Ratzinger,, *Church, Ecumenism and Politics* (Slough, St Paul Publications, 1988), 115: they are simply useful 'organisational forms of Christian congregations'.

[82] Code, c.373; for the idea of the local church as a community, see D M Doyle, *Communion Ecclesiology: Vision and Versions* (New York, Orbis Books, 2000) 15.

unity)[83]; *polity* and *autonomy* (bishops govern them as vicars of Christ not 'as vicars of the Roman Pontiff for they exercise the power which they possess in their own right')[84]; *universality* (they 'are constituted after the model of the universal Church; it is in these and formed out of them, that the one and unique Catholic church exists')[85]; *sociality* (a diocese is a 'portion of the people of God, entrusted for pastoral care to a bishop, with the cooperation of the presbyterate, so that, adhering to the pastor and by him gathered (*congregata*) in the Holy Spirit through Gospel and Eucharist, it constitutes (*constituat*) a particular Church in which the one, holy, catholic and apostolic Church of Christ is truly present and operative')[86]; *relationality* (headed by bishops in communion with each other, they form 'a corporate body of Churches')[87]; and *provisionality* (perfected in the glory of heaven)[88]. Having 'their ecclesiality in her and from her'[89], '[t]he church of Christ is truly present in all legitimate local congregations of the faithful, where the faithful are gathered together (*congregantur*) in the preaching of the Gospel and in the celebration of the mystery of the Lord's Supper'[90]. A person 'does not belong to the universal Church in a mediate way', but 'through belonging to a particular Church'; 'entry into and life within the universal Church are necessarily brought about within a particular church'[91].

1.3 – Orthodox self-understanding

Whilst sometimes said that the Orthodox are reluctant to formulate a system of ecclesiology ('the Church is her own life')[92], Orthodoxy employs concepts of 'the church' and 'churches'. First: 'the Church of

---

[83] *Christus Dominus*, 23.

[84] LG, 27.

[85] LG, 23.

[86] Code, c.369; they are 'one of the same kind': LG, 26a.

[87] LG, 23.

[88] LG, 48-49.

[89] *The Church as Communion*, Letter to the Bishops of the Catholic Church from the Congregation for the Doctrine of the Faith, *Catholic International*, 3 (1992) (hereafter CDF, *Communion* (1992)) para. 9, 10.

[90] LG, 26; for the local church as a realisation of the church universal, see eg L Boff, *Ecclesiogenesis: The Base Communities Reinvent the Church* (Maryknoll, New York, Orbis Books, 1986) 9.

[91] CDF, *Communion*, para. 10.

[92] N A Nissiotis, 'The main ecclesiological problem of the Second Vatican Council and the position of the non-Roman Catholic Churches facing it' (1965) 2 *Journal of Ecumenical Studies* 32 at 38.

Christ is...a new life in Christ moved by the Holy Spirit'[93], a *'creatura Christi* and *creatura Spiritus*, created by the redemptive work of Christ the Son of the Father, instituted at Pentecost by the sending of the Holy Spirit who proceeds from the Father and rests in the Son'; whilst the church is not of itself an institution it has an 'institutional dimension', which must be 'true to the deep, essential nature of the Church'[94].

Secondly, Orthodox speak of 'The Orthodox Church', and in several senses: 'The Orthodox church is the one true church of Christ, which as his body is not and cannot be divided'[95]; 'the Holy Orthodox Church alone has preserved in full and intact "the faith once delivered unto the saints"'[96]; and '[t]he Orthodox Church is the Church of the Seven Ecumenical Councils'[97]. Official texts speak of 'the common mind of the Orthodox Church...an organic member of the World Council of Churches'[98], and some civil laws of 'the Oriental Orthodox Church of Christ'[99]. The Orthodox Church is also understood to be 'a family of self-governing Churches', held together 'not by a centralized organization...a single prelate wielding absolute power', but 'by the double bond of unity in the faith and communion in the sacraments'[100].

Thirdly, when Orthodox 'speak about "our Churches" what we have in mind is the local Churches, each having its own jurisdiction, and this being held in respect'[101]; Orthodox churches are 'local Most Holy Orthodox Churches'[102]. Local churches are characterised by their: *locality* (the (Pauline) notion of the Church of God which is at one place or another 'provides the basic principle of the Orthodox territorial approach to ecclesiology')[103]; *polity*, as autocephalous (one which elects its own primate), or autonomous (one which elects its primate with the participation of the primate of an autocephalous church) churches; *relational sorority* (local churches, in full communion with one another, are 'sister

[93] S Bulgakov, *Pravoslavie* (Paris, YMCA Press, 1935) 1.
[94] N Lossky, 'The Orthodox Churches' in Avis, *The Christian Church* 1.
[95] Dublin Agreed Statement (1984) 100.
[96] Statement of Delegates to 2nd Assembly of WCC (1954): G Limouris (ed), *Orthodox Visions of Ecumenism* (Geneva, World Council of Churches, 1994) 29.
[97] Lossky, 'The Orthodox Churches' 9,13.
[98] Fourth Pan-Orthodox Conference, Chambésy, 1968, Ress. 1 and 2.
[99] Greek Constitution 1975, Art. 3.
[100] T Ware, *The Orthodox Church* (London, Penguin Books, 1963) 15.
[101] Address of Patriarch Dimitrios (1973): E J Stormon (ed), *Towards the Healing of Schism* (New York, Paulist Press, 1987). 239.
[102] Message: Primates of the Most Holy Orthodox Churches (Phanar, 1992): Limouris, *Orthodox Visions of Ecumenism* 195-6.
[103] Lossky, 'The Orthodox churches' 2.

Churches'[104]; 'a local Church, in order to be not just local but also Church, must be in full communion with the rest of the local Churches in the world')[105]; episcopal and eucharistic *community* nature ('the Christians of a given place are gathered in one Eucharistic community'[106]; but '[t]he local community is a true and eucharistic manifestation of the Church of God only if it is catholic in its composition and structure', and it is 'in the episcopal diocese through which each eucharistic gathering acquires its catholic nature')[107]; *universality* ('the Church is fully present in a local Eucharistic gathering', so 'the local Church is the Church universal' with 'fullness of ecclesial reality')[108]; sometimes *nationality*[109] and constitutional *foundation* (as with the autocephalous Greek Orthodox Church[110], 'united... to the Great Church of Constantinople'[111], and 'indissolubly bound by the dogma of...Constantinople and all other Orthodox churches'[112], and the autonomous Orthodox Church of Crete)[113].

---

[104] Ibid, 6.

[105] J Zizioulas, *Being as Communion* (New York, St Vladimir's Seminary Press, 1985) 257.

[106] Lossky, 'The Orthodox Churches' 6.

[107] Report of an Inter-Orthodox Consultation: The Ecumenical Nature of Orthodox Witness (New Valamo, 1977): Limouris, *Orthodox Visions of Ecumenism* 66f.

[108] Lossky, 'The Orthodox Churches' 3-5.

[109] Ware, *The Orthodox Church* 15.

[110] I M Konidaris, 'The Legal Parameters of Church And State Relations in Greece' in TA Couloumbis, *et al* (ed), *Greece in the Twentieth Century* (London, Frank Cass, 2001) 223, 225. Royal Decree 1833: the Orthodox Church of Greece is composed of the Dioceses (Metropleis) of the Autocephalous Church of Greece according to the Patriarchal Tome 1950, Patriarchal and Synodal Acts 1866 and 1882, and those of the 'New Territories' based on the Patriarchal and Synodal Acts of 1928; their members are all Orthodox Christians who inhabit these Dioceses (Statutory Charter 1977, Art 1.3). Each diocese is divided into parishes (Statutory Charter 1977, Art 1.3). 'The Church of Greece, its Dioceses (Metropoliteis) and the parishes are public law entities' (Statutory Charter 1977, Art 1).

[111] Greek Constitution 1975, Art. 3; Konidaris, 'The Legal Parameters of Church And State Relations in Greece' 225: 'Thus when we speak of the Orthodox Church of Greece, we mean the Church formed from: First the Autocephalous Church of Greece as it was constituted canonically in 1850 and enlarged later through its union with the Dioceses of the Ionian islands in 1866, part of Epirus and Thessaly in 1882. And secondly the Dioceses of the annexed New Territories, meaning the rest of Epirus, Macedonia, Thrace and the Aegean islands, which were formally ceded to it in 1928 by the Ecumenical Patriarchate'.

[112] Statutory Charter (1977), Art. 1.1.

[113] Founded in 1900 on the basis of an agreement between the Ecumenical Patriarchate of Constantinople and the former Cretan State, after Crete and Greece united in 1913, the church retained its independence from the Greek Church which status was enshrined in Greek State Law in 1961: it is governed by the Holy Provincial Synod of Crete, which consists of its eight diocesan bishops under the chairmanship of the Archbishop of Crete (who is elected by the Synod of the Patriarchate of Constantinople on a nomination by the Greek government and three bishops of he Church of Crete (Statutory Charter 1967)).

1.4 – Lutheran self-understandings

Lutherans too employ concepts of 'the church' and 'churches' in their self-understanding. First, they 'confess and affirm the unity of the one universal church, which is the body of Christ in this world'[114]. According to the Augsburg Confession, 'the church is the assembly of all believers in which the gospel is preached purely and sacraments are administered rightly'; gospel and sacrament are 'the means the Holy Spirit employs to create the church as the community of faith', whose members 'are called as justified sinners into communion with the triune God and with one another as Christ's sisters and brothers', a communion experienced in baptism and the Lord's supper[115]. The church, constituted as an assembly[116], is not invisible, but hidden[117]: its true membership (the justified) is 'hidden within its apparent membership' (which may include those who hear the gospel and receive the sacraments without faith)[118].

Secondly, whilst Lutherans today speak of 'The Lutheran Church'[119], historically Lutheran churches developed at the Reformation variously as confessional and independent folk, territorial or state churches (*cuius regio eius religio*)[120]. Whilst some remain national churches[121], emigration has meant that beyond Europe they are one amongst many denominations[122]. Nevertheless, Lutheran ecclesial identity is based on their common confession as set out in the authoritative Reformation texts[123]:

[114] *Lutheran World Federation as a Communion of Churches* (LWF, Geneva, 2003) 8.

[115] CA, Arts 4,7,10,11; LWF, 2003, 14.

[116] That is: a group of persons, a society (*societas*, Apology of the Augsburg Confession 1531 (Ap) 7.5), a people (*populus*, Ap 7.14), or a folk (*Volk*, Luther, LW 41:145); the people includes all and only those who can be described as saints, as faithful, or as believers; the church is not 'a physical assembly', but an assembly of 'hearts in one faith' (Luther, LW 39:65). It will assemble in the strict sense only eschatalogically – the universal church of all times and places; it is 'an association of faith and of the Holy Spirit in persons' hearts' (Ap 7:5).

[117] Luther, LW 41:211: 'The church is a high, deep, hidden thing which one may neither perceive nor see, but must grasp only by faith, through baptism, sacrament and word'; Ap 7.5: '[t]hose in whom Christ is not active are not members of Christ'.

[118] Avis, *The Christian Church* 191.

[119] Lutheran World Federation, Constitution, Art. II.

[120] Evans, *The Church and the Churches* 59.

[121] Danish Constitution, Art. 4: 'The Evangelical Lutheran Church is the Danish National Church and as such is to be supported by the State in its economic, legal and political relations'.

[122] J Gros, et al (ed), *Growth in Agreement: Reports and Agreed Statements of Ecumenical Conversations on a World Level 1982-1998* (WCC, Geneva, 2000) 168.

[123] Including: the Augsburg Confession (1530), Luther's Small Catechism (1529), the Formula of Concord (1577) and the collection of the confessions in the Book of Concord

'[t]he acceptance of some or all of these confessions still today defines the Lutheran churches'[124]. For example, the Evangelical Lutheran Church of America (ELCA) sees itself as 'a church body', its roots 'deep in the soil of the Lutheran Confessions and...our biblical foundations', which accepts, *inter alia*, 'the Augsburg Confession as a witness to the Gospel...[and] the Book of Concord'[125].

Thirdly, for Lutherans '[e]very local church gathered around the preaching of the gospel and the celebration of the sacraments is a realization of the universal church of all God's people'. Consequently, '[t]hrough word and sacraments every local church is bound to the wider communion of churches'[126], and in 'all congregations where [the] proclamation of Christ takes place effectually, the prerequisite for church fellowship is already present'[127]. Lutheran churches see themselves 'as integral to the church as the body of Christ, the unity of which is stated as participating in the unity of the Holy Trinity and given in the gospel through Word and sacrament'[128].

Fourthly, key to the identity of individual Lutherans churches is their relationship one to another[129], particularly as members of the Lutheran World Federation: 'a communion of churches which confess the triune God, agree in the proclamation of the Word of God and are united in pulpit and altar fellowship'[130]. The federation is not, however, 'a church'[131],

---

(1580) which consists *inter alia* of the Apostles, Nicene and Athanasian Creeds: R Kolb and T J Wengert (ed), *The Book of Concord: The Confessions of the Evangelical Lutheran Church* (Minneapolis, 2000).

[124] Avis, *The Christian Church* 188. A full listing of Lutheran churches: E T Bachmann and M B Bachmann, *Lutheran Churches in the World: A Handbook* (Minneapolis, Augsburg, 1989)

[125] ELCA, Constitution and Foundational Texts (2003) Chapters 1, 2.

[126] LWF 2003, 14.

[127] LWF Assembly, Evian 1970, *Sent into the World*, Proceedings of the Fifth Assembly of the LWF, 1970, 5, p.72,76; see also Augsburg Confession (CA) VII.

[128] LWF 2003, 8. The Evangelical Lutheran Church of America, for example, is a particular gathering of people known as the Evangelical Lutheran Church of America; as 'part of the whole Church of Christ, we announce and declare the teachings of the prophets and apostles and seek to confess in our time the faith once delivered to the saints'. The church 'exists both as an inclusive fellowship and as local congregations gathered for worship and Christian service. Congregations find their fulfilment in the universal community of the Church, and the Church universal exists in and through congregations'.

[129] ELCA allows 'exchangeability of ordained ministers with member churches of the LWF'.

[130] LWF Constitution (1997), Art. III; see also LWF 2003, 27.

[131] The LWF as a Communion of Churches (2002) 21: 'If [the LWF] is a communion as such, the LWF would itself be a church'; rather it is 'a communion of churches'.

but 'the collective identity of its member churches'[132]. The federation may act for member churches[133], and membership is open to churches which accept its doctrinal basis (including scripture, the creeds and 'the Confessions of the Lutheran Church'), but may be terminated by withdrawal or suspension[134].

Finally, however, organisation or polity is not as such constitutive of the ecclesiality of a local community as these are conceived of as of human not divine institution[135]. Apostolicity lies in continuity in the doctrine and preaching of the apostles, rather than in any structural succession[136]. Thus, for instance, whereas baptism and preaching are divinely instituted, forms of ministry, church organisation or worship are of human institution[137], their arrangement a matter for the local church[138].

Nevertheless, the autonomy of the local church and its synodality are fundamentals of Lutheran polity: although 'The member churches of the [LWF] are autonomous, with their own structures of ministry and governing bodies. Normally, church governance is carried out by synods in which the ordained ministers and bishops/presidents have their part'[139], 'no church is completely autonomous, since all churches live from traditions and spiritual sources that are not their own, but are shared gifts' (such as ordination)[140]. The Lutheran 'principle of governance' is that

---

[132] LWF 2003, 15.

[133] LWF may take action in maters committed to it by the member churches. 'It may act on behalf of one or more churches in such specific tasks they commit to it. It may request individual churches to assume tasks on behalf of the entire Communion' (Art. IV).

[134] LWF, Constitution, Art. V; the LWF 'confesses the Holy Scriptures of the Old and New Testaments to be the only source and norm of its doctrine, life and service. It sees in the three Ecumenical Creeds and in the Confessions of the Lutheran Church, especially in the unaltered Augsburg Confession and the Small Catechism of Martin Luther, a pure exposition of the Word of God' (Art. II).

[135] Melanchthon, apology for the Augsburg Confession (XIV.1ff).

[136] Avis, *The Christian Church* 192: Lutherans have never claimed any particular polity: 'The church is defined without reference to such historical arrangements' (congregational, presbyterian, episcopal, patriarchal, papal).

[137] CA, Art V: LWF, 2003, 8.

[138] Many constitutions of the German regional churches give the bishop a veto over decisions of synod.

[139] LWF, 2003, 32: 'The LWF does not have decision making power over the member churches'; ibid., 19: 'The Lutheran Church Missouri Synod has adopted a strongly congregational understanding of what it means to be church. At the same time, there [are] also Episcopal trends within this synod'.

[140] 'Ordination to the ministry, in the Lutheran understanding, is not carried out simply for the particular church in which it takes place. Ordination is in principle an ecumenical action, since it is an authorization to preach the gospel and to administer the sacraments, which are gifts to the universal church': LWF, 2003, 32.

'the Spirit guides the church through the interaction of...an ordained ministry, called by God to proclaim the gospel with authority and...a larger community whose baptism authorises and empowers it to judge the exercise of the ordained ministry'[141].

2 – Unilateral Conditions for Status as a Church

Anglicans, Roman Catholics, Orthodox, and Lutherans employ unilaterally a number of conditions which must be satisfied before another body is recognised as a church (having ecclesiality) capable of being in a relationship of communion with them[142].

2.1 – Anglicanism

The establishment of communion with another church is a matter for determination by each Anglican Church individually[143]. Anglican churches are clear which authorities, within them, may determine whether another church may be recognised for the purposes of ecclesial communion: for example, its synod, episcopal assembly, archbishops, or episcopal assembly with synodical consent[144]. However, the conditions for recognition of ecclesiality vary as between Anglican churches. Requirements include: recognition of the catholicity and sacramental integrity of the other (but not 'the acceptance of all doctrinal opinion, sacramental devotion or liturgical practice characteristic of the other')[145]; the other to subscribe to Trinitarian doctrine and administer the sacraments of baptism and eucharist[146]; or to be 'a congregation of Christian people, holding the... faith as set forth in the Catholic creeds and recognising the Scriptures as containing all things necessary to salvation'[147].

---

[141] Avis, *The Christian Church* 201: Initially, Lutherans saw episcopacy as an ideal (Smalcald Articles 1537), II.4,9); e.g. Finland and Sweden claim episcopal succession. In ELCA (e.g) the 'congregations, synods and churchwide organisations' are 'interdependent partners sharing responsibility in God's mission'. ELCA, Constitution, Chapters 1 and 5.

[142] Evans, *The Church and the Churches* proposes that a united church must display the following marks: the presence of Christ in its midst; apostolic origin; it must show salvation at work; confession of the apostolic faith; baptism and the Lord's Supper; a pastoral ministry; order (in life and worship); discipline; separateness from the world; an ecclesial intention; see also Stormon *Towards the Healing of Schism* 241 and H Fries, 'The Ecclesiological Status of the Protestant Churches from a Catholic Viewpoint' (1964) 1 *Journal of Ecumenical Studies* 198.

[143] LC 1968, Res 47.

[144] See respectively (e.g), New Zealand, Central Africa, England, Scotland.

[145] E.g New Zealand, General Synod Standing Res 1952.

[146] Church of England (Ecumenical Relations) Measure 1988, s 5(1).

[147] ECUSA, Cans. I.16.1.

2.2 – Roman Catholicism

The Roman Catholic Church has settled criteria for recognition of ecclesiality[148]. The church recognises that: 'All the baptized...though not professing the full Roman Catholic faith and not in full communion with the See of Rome, are seen as "joined to the Church in many ways"' (that is, in shared faith, sacramental and spiritual life, liturgy, devotion and virtue)[149]. However, 'a Church outside of communion with the Roman Pontiff lacks more than just the visible manifestations of unity with the Church of Christ which subsists in the Roman Catholic Church'[150]. Many 'communities of Christians' proclaim the gospel, announce the kingdom, and celebrate baptism and other sacraments, through which 'we know that God saves and sanctifies them'; but it is difficult to determine their relationship with the Catholic Church and to describe them (differing as they do in origins and convictions)[151]. Consequently, in Roman Catholicism: '"Churches", "other Churches", "other Churches and ecclesial communities"...refer to those who are not in full communion with the Catholic Church'[152].

On the one hand, there are 'churches' which 'possess true sacraments, above all – by apostolic succession – the priesthood and the eucharist, whereby they are still linked with us in closest intimacy'[153]. A church is a community which 'retains a certain communion with the Catholic Church'[154]. The Eastern Churches[155], while not 'in perfect communion with the Catholic Church, remain united to her by means of the closest bonds, that is, by apostolic succession and a valid eucharist, [and] *are true particular Churches*'[156]; the Church of Christ 'is present and operative' in them but 'they lack full communion...since they do not accept the

---

[148] Ratzinger, *Church, Ecumenicalism and Politics* 114-115.

[149] LG, 15; but: 'Christ...founded one church...yet many Christian communities present themselves as the true inheritors of Jesus Christ...such division openly contradicts the will of Christ' (UR).

[150] Official Response of the Roman Catholic Church to *The Final Report* of the First Anglican-Roman Catholic International Commission, printed in *The Tablet* (December, 1991).

[151] *Unitatis redintegratio* (UR) 3,19.

[152] Directory for the Application of Norms and Principles of Ecumenism (CTS 1993) (hereafter Ecumenical Directory (1993)), 17; 18: 'sects and new religious movements' must be distinguished from churches and ecclesial communities': see also Sects or New Religious Movements: A Pastoral Challenge, Interim Report, SPCU, IS 1986.

[153] UR, 15; see also 13: churches as 'Christian bodies'.

[154] Ecumenical Directory (1993), 17, 18.

[155] OE, 1-4.

[156] *Dominus Iesus* (DI), Declaration of the CDF (2000) 17.

Catholic doctrine of Primacy, which, according to the will of God, the Bishop of Rome objectively has and exercises over the entire Church'[157].

On the other hand, 'the ecclesial communities which have not preserved the valid Episcopate and the genuine and integral substance of the Eucharistic mystery, *are not Churches in the proper sense*; however, those who are baptised in these communities are, by Baptism, incorporated in Christ and thus are in a certain communion, albeit imperfect, with the Church'[158]. Eucharistic communion and ecclesial communion are 'considered inseparable'[159], since the eucharist is a 'church-making' sacrament: for the Catholic Bishops' Conference of England and Wales, Anglican communities fall into this category[160]. Yet such communities commemorate the Holy Supper and 'profess it signifies life in communion with Christ'; their worship 'displays notable features of a liturgy once shared in common'; their way of life 'is nourished by faith', and for them the Word is a 'source of Christian virtue'[161]. While 'these separated churches and communities...suffer from defects', they have not been 'deprived of significance and importance in the mystery of salvation'; 'the spirit of Christ has not refrained from using them as means of salvation which derive their efficacy from the very fullness of grace and truth entrusted to the Catholic Church'[162]. Indeed, they 'derive their efficacy from the fullness of grace and truth entrusted to the Catholic Church'[163].

[157] DI, 17.

[158] DI, 17.

[159] Ecumenical Directory (1993) 129.

[160] Catholic Bishops' Conference of England and Wales, Ireland and Scotland, *One Bread, One Body* (London, 1998) 53. See House of Bishops, Church of England response to *One Bread, One Body* (2001): '[T]he Church of England is not correctly referred to as one of those "Christian communities rooted in the Reformation". The Church of England traces its origins back to the beginnings of Christianity in England and is continuous with the Church of the Apostles and Fathers. The particular churches of the Anglican Communion belong to the one holy catholic and apostolic Church of Christ, reformed and renewed at the Reformation (though not, of course, only then)'. 'Anglicans look for clarification of the unresolved ambiguities in the official stance of the Roman Catholic Church towards various "ecclesial communities", as Vatican II calls them'.

[161] UR, 23.

[162] DI, 17: the Christian faithful are therefore 'not permitted to imagine that the Church of Christ is nothing more than a collection – divided yet in some way one – of Churches and ecclesial communities'; nor 'hold that today the Church of Christ nowhere really exists, and must be considered only as a goal to which all Churches and ecclesial communities strive to reach'; see also UR, 3.

[163] DI, 16. For Pope John Paul II, their members were 'brothers and sisters', and 'the elements of sanctification and truth' in them, varying from one to the other, constituted 'the objective basis for communion, albeit imperfect, which exists between them and the Catholic Churc'; '[t]o the extent that these elements are present in the other Christian

2.3 – Orthodoxy

The Orthodox refer to other Christian communities in various ways: for example, as 'holy Churches of God', the 'Church of the Protestants', the 'Anglican Church, and as 'Christian Churches'[164]. Their ecclesiality is found 'in the past in their common history, in their common ancient and apostolic tradition, from which all of them derive their existence'[165]. However, if reluctant to 'pass judgment upon those of the separated communions', Orthodox do not accept the idea of a 'parity of denomination' (or 'equality of confessions')[166]. Rather, 'in these communions certain basic elements are lacking which constitute the reality of the fullness of the Church', namely: 'the Faith of the ancient, united, and indivisible Church of the Seven Ecumenical Councils'[167]. The church (universal) 'is not necessarily present in every eucharistic assembly but in the episcopal diocese through which each Eucharistic gathering acquires its catholic nature'; a local community is 'a true manifestation' of the church 'only if is catholic in its composition and structure'[168]. As the Orthodox Church confesses its faith in the oneness of the church, so 'there can be no churches (in the plural) except as manifestations of the one true Church'[169]. Other churches may thus be pilgrim communities[170], not 'self-sufficient' realities[171].

Communities, the one Church of Christ is effectively present in them'. *Ut unum sint* (1995) 11; see 52 for 'canonical communion'.

[164] Limouris, *Orthodox Visions of Ecumenism* 2,3,4,7,9.

[165] Orthodox Statement, 3rd Assembly of WCC (New Delhi, 1961): Limouris, *Orthodox Visions of Ecumenism* 31.

[166] Limouris, *Orthodox Visions of Ecumenism* 191.

[167] Statement of Orthodox Delegates, 2nd Assembly of WCC (Evanston, 1954): Limouris, *Orthodox Visions of Ecumenism* 29: Return 'to the pure and unchanged and common heritage of the forefathers of all divided Christians, shall alone produce the desired reunion of all separated Christians'.

[168] Report of an Inter-Orthodox Consultation: The Ecumenical Nature of Orthodox Witness (New Valamo, 1977): Limouris, *Orthodox Visions of Ecumenism* 66f.

[169] Orthodox Contribution to 6th Assembly WCC (Vancouver, 1983): LIMOURIS (1994) 103: 'The unity of the Church does not mean creating a worldwide organization, often called structural unity. The one Church cannot be created by putting all the local churches and individual denominations into one worldwide structure'.

[170] Limouris, *Orthodox Visions of Ecumenism* 228: *Paroikia* as 'a community of sojourners or pilgrims' (*paroikos*: pilgrim) reflects a self-understanding of the church, as 'a stranger to the world'.

[171] Ibid: *Communio ecclesiarum* is the description of the real nature of the church. The universal (catholic) church is not a worldwide organization but a koinonia of local churches: 'There can be no churches (in the plural) except as manifestations of the one true church (in the singular)' (*Signs of the Spirit*, Official Report WCC 7th Assembly (Canberra, 1991)). '[I]f we conceive ourselves as churches and act as such, and not as manifestations

2.4 – Lutheranism

In the development of full ecclesial communion with 'sister churches', which exist in 'reconciled diversity'[172], Lutherans (with their ecumenical partners), have employed a methodological paradigm for seeking unity by stages: in this ecclesiality is recognised by agreement as to the goal of full visible unity on the basis of shared faith and common order; declaration of mutual acknowledgment (of authenticity of ministries, sacraments and oversight); and mutual commitments[173].

3 – Ecumenical Understandings of a Church

A key difficulty for ecumenism is recognising the ecclesiality of the communities' party to it[174]. Christians have not found 'the transformation of the plural of confessional Churches separated from one another into the plural of local churches that are in their diversity really one Church'[175]. The following presents some ideas of 'a church' in ecumenical dialogues (mainly those involving Anglicans).

3.1 – World Council of Churches

The WCC is 'a fellowship of churches which confess the Lord Jesus Christ as God and Saviour according to the scriptures and therefore seek to fulfil together their common calling to the glory of the one God, Father, Son and Holy Spirit'[176]. The term 'church' may include an association, convention or federation of autonomous churches[177]. 'Applicant

of the *una sancta*, we become merely a federation of churches'. The following are requirements of full koinonia: mutual recognition of baptism, common confession of faith, Eucharistic communion, mutual recognition of ministries, common diakonia and witness, establishment of decision-making structures.

[172] LWF VI, 201.

[173] For the Meissen Agreement (1991) see Avis, *The Christian Church* 150.

[174] Evans, *The Church and the Churches* 19: 'It remains a central difficulty that "churches" which are...not quite sure of the fullness of one another's ecclesiality cannot in any visible sense, and often in their own self-understanding, see themselves as together constituting "one Church"'. Another difficulty, of course, is the model to be adopted for a united church: for the models see ibid. 2ff.

[175] Ratzinger, *Church, Ecumenicalism and Politics* 120.

[176] WCC Const., Art I (Basis). Functions and Purposes: Art. III: 'to call the churches to the goal of visible unity in one faith and in one Eucharistic fellowship expressed in worship and in common life in Christ, and to advance towards that unity in order that the world may believe'.

[177] A group of churches in a country/region, or in the same confession, may determine to participate in the World Council of Churches 'as one church...to respond to their

churches" are required 'to express their agreement with the Basis on which the Council is founded and confirm their commitment to the Purposes and Functions of the Council'[178]. To be 'churches' for the purposes of membership, applicants must satisfy two tests: theological[179] and organisational[180].

3.2 – Anglican-Lutheran dialogue

Agreeing on the nature of 'the church'[181], the Reformation as 'a renewal movement within the church catholic' (not 'a beginning of a new church'), their 'common root', and that 'both our churches have been separated from communion with the Roman Catholic Church'[182], Anglicans and Lutherans 'acknowledge each other as true churches of Christ preaching the same gospel, possessing a common apostolic ministry, and celebrating

common calling, to strengthen their joint participation and/or to satisfy the requirement of minimum size' (Rules I, (3(b)(iii)).

[178] WCC Const. Art II.

[179] "1. In its life and witness the church professes faith in the Triune God as expressed in the scriptures and reflected in the Nicene-Constantinopolitan Creed. 2. The church maintains a ministry of proclaiming the Gospel and celebrating the sacraments as understood by its doctrines. 3. The church baptizes in the name of God, 'Father, Son, and Holy Spirit' and acknowledges the need to move toward the recognition of the Baptism of other churches. 4. The church recognizes the presence and activity of Christ and the Holy Spirit outside its boundaries and prays for the wisdom of all in the awareness that other member churches also believe in the Holy Trinity and the saving grace of God. 5. The church recognizes in the other member churches of the WCC elements of the true church, even if it does not regard them "as churches in the true and full sense of the word"'. See the Toronto Statement.

[180] '1. The church must produce evidence of sustained autonomous life and organization. 2. The church must be able to take the decision to apply for formal membership in the WCC and continue to belong to the fellowship of the WCC without obtaining the permission of any other body or person. 3. An applicant church must ordinarily have at least 50,000 members. The Central Committee may decide for exceptional reasons to accept a church that does not fulfil the criterion of size. ...5. Churches must recognize the essential interdependence of the member churches [of]...the WCC...and should make every effort to practise constructive ecumenical relations with other churches within their country or region. This will normally mean that the church is a member of the national council of churches or similar body and of the regional/subregional ecumenical organization': World Council of Churches, Central Committee, Minutes of 52nd Meeting, Geneva (2002) 210ff.

[181] The Diaconate and Ecumenical Opportunity (Hanover, 1995) II: see S Oppegaard and G Cameron (ed), *Anglican-Lutheran Agreements: Regional and International Agreements 1972-2002* (Geneva, Lutheran World Federation, 2004) 177.

[182] Cold Ash 1983, 15, 21: also, ibid: 'the church [is] a community constituted by Jesus Christ through his presence and action through the means of grace': see Oppegaard and Cameron *Anglican-Lutheran Agreements* 69.

authentic sacraments'[183]. Ecclesiality also lies in 'the witness of holy scripture as normative' and 'continuity with the apostolic faith and mission throughout the centuries'[184]. Full communion, 'a relationship between two distinct churches or communions', involves recognition of each other's catholicity, apostolicity, holding all the essentials of the Christian faith, autonomy and interdependence[185].

3.3 – Anglican-Orthodox dialogue

Orthodox and Anglicans refer to each other as 'our two churches'[186]. They 'agree in our fundamental understanding of the church as one, holy, catholic and apostolic', 'the marks of the church'[187], and share meanings of 'primacy' (Anglican) and 'seniority' (Orthodox) as 'not of coercion but of pastoral service'[188]. They recognise that '[t]he catholicity of the church is shown in the multiplicity of particular local churches, each of which, being in communion with all the other local churches, manifests in its own place and time the one catholic church'[189]. They also agree in regarding 'the church as a eucharistic community: the eucharist actualizes the church. In each local Eucharistic celebration the visible unity and catholicity of

[183] Helsinki Report 1982, 62 (Oppegaard and Cameron *Anglican-Lutheran Agreements*, 47). 'Our two churches are marked by a high esteem for sacramental life and liturgical worship' (Cold Ash Statement 1983, 15). 'The churches of the Lutheran tradition have received as the focus of God's faithfulness to them the creeds of the early church, the confessions of the 16th century, and the continuity of the ordained ministry through which the word of God has been preached and the sacraments and rites of the church have been administered' (Niagara Falls, Episcope 1967, 84); 'The churches of the Anglican Communion have received as the focus for God's faithfulness to them the creeds of the early church, the Book of Common Prayer from the 16th century (revised periodically and adapted regionally), and the continuity of the episcopal office through which clergy have been ordained for the preaching of the word of God and the administration of the sacraments and rites of the church' (ibid., 85); each church is being called to unity (ibid, 86).

[184] Cold Ash 1983, 15, 21: also, ibid: 'the church [is] a community constituted by Jesus Christ through his presence and action through the means of grace'.

[185] Cold Ash 1983, 25, 26: 'By full communion we here understand a relationship between two distinct churches or communions. Each maintains its own autonomy and recognizes the catholicity and apostolicity of the other, and each believes the other to hold all the essentials of the Christian faith (mutual recognition of ministry and sacraments)' (25); 'To be in full communion means that churches become interdependent while remaining autonomous' (26).

[186] Dublin Agreed Statement (1984) para 114; 9: Orthodox see Anglicans as 'brothers and sisters in Christ'.

[187] Ibid 96.

[188] Ibid 97.

[189] Ibid 12.

the church is fully manifested'[190]. However, whereas Anglicans consider full communion can be approached progressively, for the Orthodox '"communion" involves a mystical and sanctifying unity created by the Body and Blood of Christ'; there 'can be "communion" only between local churches which have a unity in faith, ministry and sacraments'; 'no ecclesial ruling can govern or partition such communion or make it a matter of "degree"'[191].

3.4 – Anglican-Roman Catholic dialogue

For Rome, amongst the communities of 'separated brethren' not in full communion with Rome, 'in which Catholic traditions and institutions in part continue to exist, the Anglican communion occupies a special place'[192]. No formal judgment has been issued by Rome recognising Anglican communities as 'a church or churches'[193]. In the common declarations of Rome and Canterbury reference is made only to 'the Roman Catholic Church and the Anglican communion' (small 'c' and not 'church' or 'churches') and to 'the union of our two communions'[194]. Indeed, the Catholic Bishops' Conference of England and Wales classifies Anglican bodies as Christian communities (not as churches)[195].

However, ARCIC refers to the constituent members of the Anglican Communion as 'churches'[196]. ARCIC sees 'the church' (universal) as communion[197], and speaks of 'Christian communities in which the essential constitutive elements of ecclesial life are present'[198]. These 'constitutive elements...are derived from and subordinate to the common confession

---

[190]   Ibid 109.

[191]   Ibid 20.

[192]   UR, 13.

[193]   J Coriden, T J Green, and D E Heintschel (ed), *The Code of Canon Law: A Text and Commentary* (New York, Paulist Press, 1985) 610. See also *Letter and Spirit*, para. 1659.

[194]   Common Declaration, Pope John Paul II and the Archbishop of Canterbury, 1982: GROS, 313; Common Declaration, Pope JP II and the Archbishop of Canterbury, Vatican, 1989.

[195]   *One Bread, One Body* (1998) 53. See refutation of this in House of Bishops, Church of England response to *One Bread, One Body* (2001).

[196]   ARCIC II, Preface: 'our own respective churches'.

[197]   ARCIC II, Church as Communion, 45: 'the confession of the one apostolic faith, revealed in the Scriptures, and set forth in the Creeds...one baptism...one celebration of the eucharist [as] its pre-eminent expression and focus...shared commitments to the mission entrusted by Christ to his Church...shared concern for one another in mutual forbearance, submission, gentleness and love...making room for each other in the body of Christ...solidarity with the poor and the powerless'.

[198]   ARCIC II, 44.

of Jesus Christ as Lord'[199]. First, communion in the local Christian community is necessary to be 'church': '[f]or a local community to be a
communion means that it is a gathering of the baptised brought together
by the apostolic teaching, confessing the one faith, celebrating the one
eucharist, and led by an apostolic ministry'[200]. Secondly, '[c]ommunion
with other local churches is essential to the integrity of the self-understanding of each local church, precisely because of its catholicity'[201].
Thirdly, then, 'this local church is in communion with all [those] Christian communities in which the essential constitutive elements of ecclesial
life are present'. Fourthly, in turn, '[f]or all the local churches to be
together in communion,...which God wills, it is required that all the
essential constitutive elements of ecclesial communion are present *and
mutually recognised* in each of them' (including ministerial communion).
Finally, '[t]his does not necessitate precisely the same canonical ordering:
diversity of canonical structures is part of the acceptable diversity which
enriches the one communion of all the churches'[202].

3.5 – Anglican-Reformed dialogue

The idea of denomination features in Anglican-Reformed dialogue:
"the denomination [is not] by itself 'the church', but [is] a family or fellowship of churches"; local communities are recognizable as 'church' in
'the proper sense' if they exhibit 'in each place the fullness of ministerial
order, eucharistic fellowship, pastoral care and missionary commitment
and which, through mutual communion and cooperation, bear witness on
the regional, national and even international levels'[203]. However, there is
no simple definition of 'local church', but it might refer to 'an area where
Christians can easily meet and form one committed fellowship in witness
and service. Every local church will normally gather in one Eucharistic
service'; and several communities can understand themselves 'as one
eucharistic fellowship'[204]. Whereas Anglican polity implies episcopal

---

[199] Ibid 43,44.

[200] Ibid 43; 36: '[a]t every eucharistic celebration of Christian communities dispersed
throughout the world, in their variety of cultures, languages, social and political contexts,
it is the same one and indivisible body of Christ reconciling divided humanity that is
offered to believers'.

[201] Ibid 39.

[202] Ibid 43.

[203] *God's Reign and Our Unity* (Woking, 1984) 110.

[204] Relying on WCC, *In Each Place: Towards a Fellowship of Local Churches Truly
United* (WCC 1977) 8-9.

structure, and Reformed a presbyterial or congregational one, in both traditions, in the local congregation ('the basic unit') 'the fullness of the catholic church is there in the Eucharistic celebration of the Sunday assembly of the people of God'[205].

3.6 – Lutheran-Roman Catholic dialogue

Similarly agreeing on the church as communion (in spirit, word, sacrament and ministry)[206], Lutheran-Catholic dialogue sees 'the church of God in local, regional and universal terms, but these different ways in which the church becomes a reality must be understood on the basis of the one, holy, catholic and apostolic church, the *una sancta* of the creed'[207]. However, 'for Lutherans the local congregation is church in the full sense; for Catholics it is the local church led by its bishop'[208]. Moreover, for Lutherans[209], local congregations are part of larger 'autonomous provincial or national churches'[210], and for Catholics, the church universal is 'the fellowship of local churches'[211].

---

[205] *God's Reign and Our Unity* (Woking, 1984) 111.

[206] *All Under One Christ* (1980) 16; *Church and Justification*, Wurzburg, 1993, 40: 'By church we mean the communion of those whom God gathers together through Christ in the Holy Spirit, by the proclamation of the gospel and the administration of the sacraments, and the ministry instituted by him for this purpose'; for the trinitarian dimension of the church see 48-50; and for the church as a pilgrim people, 51ff.

[207] *Church and Justification*, 80: *ecclesia* signifies the whole church (e.g. Matthew 16.18; Galatians 1.13) and the church of a region (e.g Galatians 1.2), the church of a city (e.g Acts 8.1; 1 Corinthians 11.18) or of a house (e.g Romans 16.5).

[208] Ibid 84.

[209] Ibid 85: 'Lutherans understand the *una sancta ecclesia* to find outward and visible expression wherever people assemble around the gospel proclaimed in sermon and sacrament. Assembled for worship the local congregation therefore is to be seen, according to the Lutheran view, as the visible church, *communio sanctorum*, in the full sense. Nothing is missing which makes a human assembly church: the preached word and the sacramental gifts through which the faithful participate in Christ through the Holy Spirit, but also the minister who preaches the word and administers the sacraments in obedience to Christ and on his behalf, thus leading the congregation'.

[210] Ibid 87: 'Lutheran congregations are part of larger fellowships which are themselves constitutionally structured. According to geographical, historical, national or political realities they form dioceses or juridically autonomous provincial or national churches. These larger communities are held together by communion in Christ, and that shows itself in their common understanding of the apostolic faith (confessional communion) in word and sacrament (pulpit and fellowship), and in a mutually recognised ministry' (87). First came the regional (North America and Europe) and finally worldwide (LWF 1947) Lutheran associations (88).

[211] Ibid: 'In Catholic ecclesiology the local church is essentially neither a part of the universal church nor an administrative or canonical district of it'. Rather, "the church of God is truly present and effective in the local church. ... The expression 'portion' (*portio*)

3.7 – Roman Catholic-Orthodox dialogue

It is agreed that '[t]he clearest human reflection of the Church's divine vocation is the Christian community united to celebrate the Eucharist, gathered by its common faith, in all its variety of persons and functions, around a single table, under a single president,...to hear the Gospel proclaimed and to share in the sacramental reality of the Lord's flesh and blood...and so to manifest those gathered there as "partakers of the divine nature"'[212]. Moreover, there are two conditions for a local church to be 'truly within the ecclesial communion': first and fundamentally, 'the identity of the mystery of the church lived by the local church with the mystery of the church lived by the primitive church'; and then, 'mutual recognition today between this local church and the other churches... Each should recognize in the others through local particularities the identity of the mystery of the church'. Thus mutual recognition depends on 'communion in the same kerygma, and so in the same faith', and on 'the will for communion in love and in service, not only in words but in deeds'[213].

3.8 – WCC-Roman Catholic dialogue

Whilst the Roman Catholic Church is not a member of the World Council of Churches, a Joint Working Group was established in 1965. For this Group, as to confession of the faith, proclamation of the Word, baptism, eucharist, presence of the Holy Spirit, announcement of the kingdom, and the ministry of authority: 'All these various features must exist together *in order for there to be a local church within the communion of the church of God'*. However, the local church is not free-standing and self-sufficient but part of 'a network of communion': 'the local church

is preferred to 'part' (*pars*) because a 'portion' contains all the essential features of the whole – which is not the case with 'part'. In other words the local church has all the qualities of the church of God, and one must not therefore look upon it as a branch office of the universal church" (92). In the diocese we find the presence of the church of God centred on the bishop who is in communion with the pope. 'Parishes set up locally under a pastor who takes the place of the bishop...in a certain way represent the visible church as it is established throughout he world' (SC, no. 42). 'The local church is not a free-standing, self-sufficient reality. As part of a network communion, the local church maintains its reality as church by relating to other local churches' (94); the universal church is the fellowship of local churches (97).

[212] Agreed Statement on Conciliarity and Primacy in the Church, Orthodox-Roman Catholic Consultation in the US: (1990) 35 *Greek Orthodox Theological Review* 217.

[213] Orthodox-Roman Catholic dialogue: *The Mystery of the Church and of the Eucharist in the Light of the Mystery of the Holy Trinity* (Munich, 1982) 3.3.

maintains its reality as church by relating to other local churches'[214]. Moreover, the local church 'is not an administrative or juridical subsection or part of the universal church'; in it 'the one, holy, catholic and apostolic church is truly present and active'[215]. The local church is 'the place where the church of God becomes concretely realized. It is a gathering of believers that is seized by the spirit of the risen Christ and becomes *koinonia* by participating in the life of God.'[216]

Indeed, according to the Group, 'All Christian world communities can, in general, agree with the definition of the local church as a community of baptised believers in which the word of God is preached, the apostolic faith confessed, the sacraments are celebrated, the redemptive work of Christ for the world is witnessed to, and a ministry of episcope exercised by bishops or other ministers is serving the community. Differences between world communions are connected with the role and place of the bishop in relation to the local church'[217]. For churches of the catholic tradition (Catholic, Orthodox and Anglican) the bishop is essential for the understanding and structure of a local church[218]. For churches of the Reformation and free-church traditions, with their variety of forms and self-understandings, the local church is generally represented in a parish or congregation or in 'communities of congregations (e.g. districts)'[219]. The universal church is 'the communion of all the local churches united in faith and worship around the world. However, the universal church is not the sum, federation or juxtaposition of the local churches, but all together are the same church of God present and acting in the world'[220].

4 – The Ecclesiality of the Anglican Communion

As has been seen, ecumenical partners not uncommonly speak of 'the Anglican Church', and many Anglicans include 'The Anglican Church' in the titles of their own churches. For some '[i]t is possible to speak

---

[214] *The Church: Local and Universal*, A Study Document Commissioned and Received by the Joint Working Group (1990) 13: 'it confesses the apostolic faith (with special reference to belief in the Trinity and the lordship of Jesus), it proclaims the word of God in scripture, baptizes its members, celebrates the eucharist and other sacraments; it affirms and responds to the presence of the Holy Spirit and his gifts; announces and looks forward to the kingdom; and recognizes the ministry of authority within the community'.

[215] *Christus Dominus*, 11.

[216] *The Church: Local and Universal*, 14.

[217] Ibid 15.

[218] Ibid 16.

[219] Ibid.

[220] Ibid 19.

of "the Anglican Church" although Anglicanism is really a communion of autonomous provincially based churches'[221]. For others, as it lacks a central governing authority and unified canon law, '[t]he Anglican Communion is not a global church; it is not a church at all in the proper sense of the word, though it has ecclesial characteristics'[222]. Whether the Communion is 'a church' is similar to debate about the ecclesial character of the WCC; whilst it has ecclesiality in its goal[223], it cannot hold its own eucharist, for example[224]. Employing the tests, so to speak, emerging from the foregoing sections, the following examines the possible ecclesiality of the Anglican Communion. This question is especially timely given two developments in relation to the Anglican Communion[225], namely the proposed Anglican Covenant[226] and the proposed Anglican *Ius Commune*[227].

4.1 – The territoriality test

On the one hand, the geographical dimension of understandings of 'a church', employed by Anglicans and shared by ecumenical partners around the concept of *locality* (Roman Catholic, Orthodox and Lutheran), suggest that the Anglican Communion is not 'a church': the Communion is not obviously 'the church in a place'; it is a global body. On the other hand, the globality of the Communion represents its territoriality, which may also be found in the sum of the ecclesiastical territorial boundaries of its constituent churches. In any event, lack of territoriality is not detrimental to ecclesiality: that their own local churches are dispersed around the globe is no bar to ecumenical partners considering themselves as The Orthodox Church or The Lutheran Church, as we have seen.

---

[221] Evans, *The Church and the Churches* 78, 215: Anglicans do not speak of the Church of Canterbury or the Church of York; the Anglican Communion, which is not coextensive with the Church'.

[222] Avis, *The Christian Church* 134.

[223] A Keshishian, 'Growing Together Towards a Full Koinonia', in Limouris, *Orthodox Visions of Ecumenism* 235 at 244.

[224] Evans, *The Church and the Churches* 301.

[225] On which see the essays in 'Communion, Covenant and Canon Law' a special edition (2008) 8(2) *International Journal for the Study of the Christian Church*, guest-edited by Mark Hill.

[226] On which see N Doe, *An Anglican Covenant: Theological and Legal Considerations for a Global Debate* (London, SCM Canterbury Press, 2008).

[227] On which see N Doe 'The Contribution of Common Principles of Canon Law to Ecclesial Communion in Anglicanism' (2008) 10 *Ecc LJ* 71.

4.2 – The sociality test of community

The social dimension of 'a church', employed by Anglicans and shared by ecumenical partners (Roman Catholic, Orthodox and Lutheran), that a church is a community (a local community or a community of churches), with a defined membership (and gathered at the eucharist) is clearly a feature of the Anglican Communion. This aspect of ecclesiality, when applied to the Anglican Communion, is found in its unity as a 'fellowship' of local churches[228]; or as 'the Anglican family of Churches'[229].

4.3 – The polity test

While not constitutive of ecclesiality in Lutheranism (but autonomy *is* associated with Lutheran identity), polity forms are constitutive of ecclesiality and identity in Anglicanism (autonomy, episcopal and synodical government are essential features of Anglican polity), Roman Catholicism (particular churches are episcopal) and Orthodoxy (local churches are episcopal). However, currently the Anglican Communion, as a global community, lacks an authoritative polity: Anglicans 'are bound together not by a central legislative and executive authority'[230], but by the moral authority of the instruments of unity: Archbishop of Canterbury, Primates Meeting, Lambeth Conference, and Anglican Consultative Council[231].

4.4 – The relationality test

Anglicans and their ecumenical partners propose that a community is 'a church' when its constituent parts (particular churches in Roman Catholicism, local churches in Lutheranism and Orthodoxy) are in a relation of communion one with another. On this basis, it is possible to suggest that the Anglican Communion is 'a church' *because* its member churches are in communion with each other.

[228] LC 1930, Res. 49; see also e.g New Zealand, Constitution, Preamble: it is 'a fellowship of duly constituted Dioceses, Provinces or Regional Churches in communion with the See of Canterbury, sharing with one another their life and mission in the spirit of mutual responsibility and interdependence'.

[229] West Indies: '"Anglican Communion" means the Anglican family of Churches and organised Churches, Provinces or extra-Provincial Dioceses which, being in communion with the Church of England, accept the Faith, Doctrine, Sacraments and Discipline of the One Holy Catholic and Apostolic Church according as that Church has received the same' (Constitution, Art. 4.1).

[230] LC 1930, Res. 49.

[231] LC 1998, Res. II.6.

4.5 – The universality test

Anglicans and their ecumenical partners agree that belonging to (Anglican), the realisation of (Lutheran), subsistence in (Roman Catholic) or the presence of (Orthodox) the church universal in the local church is critical for that community to be 'a church' in the fullest sense. It is possible to conceive of the Anglican Communion as 'a church' in this sense; Anglicans consider that the Anglican Communion is a fellowship of churches 'within the One Holy Catholic and Apostolic Church'[232].

4.6 – The loyalty test

Insofar as loyalty to catholicity and apostolicity are marks of 'the church' and 'a church' for Anglicans, Roman Catholics, Orthodox and Lutherans (even though, for example, Roman Catholics may not agree on whether Anglicans possess them in relation to eucharist and apostolic succession), in its own self-understanding the Anglican Communion may be classified as 'a church'. The Communion is 'church' because of its (perceived) loyalty to: catholic and apostolic faith and order; the normative record of Scripture; the sacraments (baptism and eucharist); the Creeds and the historic episcopate[233].

Conclusion

This exploratory study shows that, whilst it is difficult to construct a single definition of 'a church', a comparative approach examining the laws of different denominations may be instructive. Their own laws and regulatory instruments indicate their own self-understandings of their own tradition (both locally and globally) and also of other traditions (in relation to their ecumenical ventures together). From the materials examined here, the following definition may be proposed:

> "a church" is a community of Christians with a distinct membership in a particular geographical area possessing an institutional and autonomous polity by which it is identified and the local constituent parts of which exist in a relation of communion one to another each in turn provisionally associated with the church universal through loyalty to apostolicity and catholicity.

---

[232] LC 1930, Res. 49.
[233] LC 1930, Res. 49; and LC 1998, Res. III.6 and 8.

On this definition, the Anglican Communion would seem to bear the marks of 'a church' and it may be anticipated that this conclusion may become more definite as a result of ongoing developments in the Anglican Communion[234].

Furthermore, this definition of 'a church' may be understood as a matter of 'Christian law'[235]. The current case study has sought to explore further the merits of comparative religious law in the context of the Christian traditions. It has become clear that although this endeavour is problematic, it is not impossible. Although Christian traditions (and consequentially their laws and other regulatory instruments) have their differences, they also have much in common. A careful and nuanced approach is required. There are at least three important reasons for such an approach.

First, the comparative study of the laws of churches may provide a rich resource for ecumenical and interfaith dialogue and mutual understanding. The laws and other regulatory instruments of churches reveal in concrete form the inner character of an ecclesial community. Moreover, they illustrate the existing hurdles to unity which may be removed in practical ways by legal scholarship and law reform. Second, this analysis is of worth to public authorities, State agencies and international bodies. It may enable secular authorities at local, national and global levels to comprehend better the common pressures of belief and law which churches experience. This is especially important in current political climate. Third, this approach is beneficial in terms of scholarship. Comparative legal work allows scholars working within a single Christian tradition to contextualise their work. The category of 'Christian law' also provides a point of comparison for scholars working in the fields of Islamic, Jewish and Hindu law. Moreover, the study of the convergences and divergences between these laws may stimulate a greater understanding of the nature and role of law and of debates concerning legal pluralism. The increased sophistication of works on religious law, both in respect of interdisciplinary endeavours and comparative accounts, is thus to be welcomed but there is much more still to be done.

---

[234] N Doe, *An Anglican Covenant: Theological and Legal Considerations for a Global Debate* (London, SCM Canterbury Press, 2008); N Doe 'The Contribution of Common Principles of Canon Law to Ecclesial Communion in Anglicanism' (2008) 10(1) *Ecc LJ* 71.

[235] N Doe, 'Modern Church Law' in J Witte and F S Alexander, *Christianity and Law* (Cambridge, Cambridge University Press, 2008) 271.

LAW AND SOCIOLOGY:
TOWARD A GREATER UNDERSTANDING OF RELIGION

Russell Sandberg and Rebecca Catto

Introduction

The relationship between religion, law and society in England and Wales has changed dramatically in recent years. The long shadow of September 11th 2001 has both caused and been perpetuated in a number of moral panics concerning the wearing of religious dress, the application of discrimination laws to religious bodies and the status of religious laws. However, the scholars who have addressed these issues have largely been constrained to the confines of their own respective disciplines. Lawyers have shown little interest in approaches from the sociology of religion: despite some enthusiastic agenda-setting accounts[1], much academic work in law and religion remains doctrinal and expository in manner;[2] courts and tribunals are seldom interested in social scientific analysis[3]. This lack of interest seems to be reciprocated: a series of interviews in 2002 coordinated by the Centre for Law and Religion at Cardiff Law School indicated that 'sociologists of religion are not much interested in legal matters'[4].

This chapter contends that this academic isolation is lamentable. It begins by illustrating to lawyers the worth of the sociology of religion and illustrating to sociologists the importance of the legal dimension for their work. It contends that though each approach is separately valuable,

---

[1] Notably, N Doe, 'A Sociology of Law on Religion – Towards a New Discipline: Legal Responses to Religious Pluralism in Europe' (2004) 152 *Law and Justice* 68 and A Bradney, 'Politics and Sociology: New Research Agendas for the Study of Law and Religion' in R O'Dair and A Lewis (eds), *Law and Religion* (Oxford, Oxford University Press, 2001) 81.

[2] There have been exceptions to this rule both theoretically (e.g. W Menski, *Hindu Law: Beyond Tradition and Modernity* (Oxford, Oxford University Press, 2003)) and empirically (e.g. A Bradney and F Cownie, *Living Without Law: An Ethnography of Quaker Decision-Making Dispute Avoidance and Dispute Resolution* (Aldershot, Ashgate, 2003)).

[3] In *Eweida v British Airways* (2007) ET, Case Number 2702689/06 (December 19th 2007), for example, the Employment Tribunal narrowly interpreted material provided by the counsel as to the relationship between religion, law and society: see para 5.9.

[4] Doe, 'A Sociology of Law on Religion' 68.

it is not sufficient. In isolation, neither discipline is equipped to understand the relationship between religion, law and society: the study of law and religion may only shed light on the relationship between law and religion whilst the study of the sociology of religion may only shed light on religion as a social construct. The chapter contends that the study of the relationship between religion, law and society requires a fusion of disciplinary approaches, a 'sociology of law and religion'.

The Need for an Interdisciplinary Approach

In UK academia, it has often been argued that legal scholars should embrace insights to be found in other academic disciplines[5]. This is particularly true in the relation to the study of law and religion: the subject matter means that the work of academic lawyers has a natural connection with religious studies, theology, ecclesiology and history[6]. This is particularly true in relation to those who study religious law[7]: Andrew Huxley has noted that the comparative study of religious law was 'irrepressibly interdisciplinary'[8]; while Mark Hill has commented in his leading work on the law of the Church of England that: 'The meaning, effect and future of establishment [of the Church of England] is a complex matter of history, ecclesiology, sociology and politics'[9]. However, such work is invariably multidisciplinary rather than interdisciplinary in nature[10]: as Banaker and Travers note, while multidisciplinary work 'juxtaposes several disciplines without any attempt to integrate or synthesis aspects of their knowledge', interdisciplinary work requires 'an ambition to understand and integrate aspects of two or several disciplinary perspectives into a single approach'[11].

---

[5] See, for example, the essays published in a special edition of *Journal of Law and Society* in 1998, especially A Bradney, 'Law as a Parasitic Discipline'(1998) 25(1) *Journal of Law and Society* 71 and R Cotterrell, (1998) 25(1) 'Why Must Legal Ideas be Interpreted Sociologically?' *Journal of Law and Society* 171.

[6] The relationship between law and theology has provoked much discussion: see, for example, R Ombres 'Why then the law?' [1974] *New Blackfriars* 296 and N Doe, 'Towards a Critique of the Role of Theology in English Ecclesiastical and Canon Law' (1992) 2 *Ecc LJ* 328.

[7] As opposed to those who study 'religion law': national and international law affecting religion. See the introduction to this volume.

[8] A Huxley, *Religion, Law and Tradition: Comparative Studies in Religious Law* (Oxford, Routledge 2002) 5.

[9] M Hill, *Ecclesiastical Law* (Third edition, Oxford, Oxford University Press, 2007) 10.

[10] For a further example, see G Arthur, *Law, Liberty and the Church* (Aldershot, Ashgate, 2007).

[11] R Banaker and M Travers *Theory and Method in Socio-Legal Research* (London, Hart 2005) 5, fn11.

Moreover, few law and religion academics have recognised the value of a social scientific approach in particular. Work on religious law seldom use sociological materials[12], while work on religion law has largely constrained itself to black-letter analysis of how the law accommodates religious difference[13]: academic lawyers have 'tended not to look outside the law school for intellectual stimulation', and have seen their role as providing a 'solution to a problem' rather than 'a description of a situation'[14]. The most sophisticated account to date is that provided by Norman Doe who has contended that the merging of insights from law of religion, the sociology of religion and the sociology of law may lead to a 'sociology of law on religion' defined as the 'study of the relations between society, religion and law, and in particular, the distinctive role of law in sociology of religion: the place of law in relations between society and religion, and how the treatment of questions fundamental to the sociology of religion may be enriched by an understanding of their juridical dimension'[15].

Doe's focus upon these three sub-disciplines (rather than a broader conception of the 'sociology of law and religion' as the fusion of three disciplines, religion, law and sociology) seems appropriate since both legal and sociological work on religion has occurred away from the mainstreams of the discipline[16]. This emphasis may also maximise the potential for interdisciplinary exchange since it is very often at the boarders of disciplines where the most innovative steps are made[17]. However, Doe's agenda-setting account still calls for a merely multi-disciplinary approach: for Doe, the 'sociology of law on religion' is characterised by the juxtapositioning of claims. He notes that the study 'places law on religion in the context of the sociology of religion, and sociology of religion in the context of law'[18]. An interdisciplinary

[12] An exception can be found in W F Menski, *Hindu Law: Beyond Tradition and Modernity* (Oxford, Oxford University Press, 2003) in which Menski contends that a revival in interest in religious law can be explained by reference to sociological notions of modernity and postmodernity.

[13] That is, doctrinal analysis that 'attempts to explain law solely through the internal evidence offered by judgments and statutes': A Bradney, 'Law as a Parasitic Discipline' (1998) 25(1) *Journal of Law and Society* 71.

[14] Bradney, 'Politics and Sociology: New Research Agendas for the Study of Law and Religion' 81.

[15] Doe, 'A Sociology of Law on Religion' 68.

[16] Law and religion has only recently become an established area of study in the UK whilst the isolation between the sociology of religion and sociological mainstream is well documented: see G Davie, *The Sociology of Religion* (London, Sage, 2007).

[17] Davie, *The Sociology of Religion* 129.

[18] Doe, 'A Sociology of Law on Religion' at 92.

approach to studying the relationship between religions, laws and societies is yet to be fully realised.

The need for a Sociological Approach

Dismissing what he refers to of the 'modern myth' that a division can
be drawn between law as doctrine (studied exclusively by lawyers) and
law as behaviour (studied exclusively by sociologists), Roger Cotterrell
has contended that law and sociology are inseparable'[19]. However, this
is a controversial claim: as David Nelken has noted although there are
'lots of good reasons to encourage students and practitioners to think
about law with the help of other disciplinary perspectives', it should be
asked whether there is 'any point at which this process should stop'?[20]
Put another way, it should be asked why law and religion academics
should consult sociology as opposed to theology or politics; what is the
worth of the sociology of religion in particular?

Although there are numerous definitions of the word 'sociology'[21] and
several famous articulations of the nature of the 'sociological imagination'[22] and the sociological role[23], the precise contribution of sociology as

[19] R Cotterrell, *Law, Culture and Society* (Aldershot, Ashgate, 2006) 45.

[20] D Nelken, 'Blinding Insights? The Limits of a Reflexive Sociology of Law' (1998)
25(3) *Journal of Law and Society* 407 at 409.

[21] Literally, 'sociology' means the study of processes of companionship. The term
has two stems – the Latin *socius* (companion) and the Greek *logos* (the study of). More
technically, it may be defined as 'the analysis of the structure of social memberships as
constituted by social interaction': N Abercrombie, S Hill and B S Turner, *The Penguin
Dictionary of Sociology* (fourth edition, London Penguin books, 2000) 333.

[22] For Wright Mills, 'The sociological imagination enables its possessor to understand
the larger historical scene in terms of its meaning for the inner life and the external career
of a variety of individuals'. It enables social analysts 'who have been imaginatively aware
of the promise of their work' to ask three sorts of questions, namely questions on how
society is structured and how social organisation is possible, questions on how societies
change over time and questions on how social change affects 'human nature': C Wright
Mills, *The Sociological Imagination* (Fortieth Anniversary Edition, Oxford, Oxford University Press, 2000) 5-7. For a more recent account, see S Fuller, *The New Sociological
Imagination* (London, Sage, 2006).

[23] For Runciman, the overlapping roles of the sociologist are the gathering and presenting information gathered by different methodologies ('reportage'); the development of
hypotheses to comprehend and elucidate the data's connections, causality and correlation
('explanation''); elucidating the phenomenon by attempting to describe what it is like for
the social actors involved ('description'); and the practical application of the findings by, for
example, suggesting policy changes, for example ('evaluation'): W G Runciman, *A Treatise
on Social Theory: Volume III, Applied Social Theory* (Cambridge, Cambridge University
Press, 1997) xiv, as summarised by J Lawrence, 'The British Sense of Class' (2000) 35(2)
Journal of Contemporary History 307 at 312 and Davie, *The Sociology of Religion* 8.

an academic discipline can only be understood by reference to its historical origins. Sociology was a product of the Enlightenment, the cluster of political, philosophical, economic and social changes responsible for the advent of modern society[24]. The founding fathers of sociology who sought to explain the social effect of this shift were profoundly interested in religion[25]. Davie asserts that all of the founding fathers 'took religion seriously in their attempts to account for the changes taking place in the societies of which they were part'[26]. In their different ways, Marx, Durkheim and Weber pointed to the social effects of religion: the way in which it brought people together[27]. Moreover, all of the founding fathers accepted the enlightenment thesis that religion was in decline: the question that preoccupied them was 'how society would manage without religion'[28].

This explains why 'the era of the sociological classics was followed by a fallow period' in the sociology of religion where there was some resistance to the 'very idea of taking religious phenomena as a suitable, not to say important, topic for social scientific analysis'[29]. Beckford notes that the classic sociologists 'accounted primarily for the *decline* of religion as a social force' and were largely unconcerned with '*contemporary* religion'[30]. As Davie puts it, the particular historical context in which sociology emerged led to the development of a 'pervasive but ultimately false assumption': namely 'that the process of modernization was *necessarily*

[24] For a conventional view see, for example, G Hawthorn, *Enlightenment & Despair: A History of Social Theory* (Second edition, Cambridge, Cambridge University Press, 1987). For a different perspective, see I Craib, *Classical Social Theory* (Oxford, Oxford University Press, 1997) 19-20 and A Giddens, *Politics, Sociology and Social Theory* (Oxford, Polity Press, 1995) 5-6.

[25] M Hill, *A Sociology of Religion* (London, Heinemann, 1973) 1. 'It is a significant fact that the great "classic" theorists of general sociology ... were also major exponents of the sociology of religion': R Cipriani, *Sociology of Religion – An Historical Introduction* (New York, Walter de Gruyter, 2000) 1.

[26] Davie, *The Sociology of Religion* 4.

[27] For reflection on this point, see R Sandberg, 'Religion and Morality: A Socio-Legal Approach' (2007) *DISKUS* (online).

[28] R Robertson, 'Introduction' in R Robertson (ed) *Sociology of Religion* (London, Penguin, 1969) 12.

[29] J A Beckford, *Religion and Advanced Industrial Society* (London, Unwin, 1989) 45. See also M Hill, *A Sociology of Religion* (London, Heinemann, 1973) 1. As Hargrove comments, the sociology of religion 'seemed a dying subject', taught mainly in context of theological colleges and seen simply 'as a useful tool for the churchman who needed to know how to keep his programmes going in the face of the mounting secularism of society': B W Hargrove, *Reformation of the Holy: A Sociology of Religion* (London, F A Davis Company, 1971) 2.

[30] J A Beckford, *Religion and Advanced Industrial Society* (London, Unwin, 1989) 42.

damaging to religion'[31]. The reason why the domination of the secularisation thesis invariably resulted in the decline of the sociological study
of religion is perfectly encapsulated by Wilson's definition of secularisation as 'the process by which religious thinking, practice and institutions
lose social significance'[32]. If the social significance of religion was to be
short-lived then 'it need not trouble the mainstream'[33]. The secularisation thesis thus led to the isolation of the sociology of religion as a sub-
discipline[34].

Although the secularisation thesis defined and constrained the sociology of religion in the United Kingdom and Europe more widely[35], recent
years have witnessed a growing self-confidence in the sub-discipline.
Increased investment in the study of religion and society in the UK and
beyond[36], the recent publication of masterworks including *The Sociology
of Religion* by Grace Davie[37], (which has been of particular help in the
writing of this chapter) and *The Sage Handbook of the Sociology of Religion*[38], and the renewed attention of major social theorists to religion[39],
all demonstrate the current vibrancy and relevance of the sociology of
religion. There are several causes of this change. Global events since the
latter half of the twentieth century have undermined the assumption that

[31] Davie, *The Sociology of Religion* 2.
[32] B Wilson, *Religion in Secular Society: A Sociological Comment* (London, Penguin, 1966) xiv.
[33] Davie, *The Sociology of Religion* 4.
[34] J A Beckford, *Religion and Advanced Industrial Society* (London, London 1989) xi, 12-15; Davie, *The Sociology of Religion* 4.
[35] However, it should be recognised that the 'agenda of the sociology of religion has been shaped by a wide variety of factors': in addition to the historical construction of the sub-discipline its geographical construction is also important since 'bodies of knowledge that build up in different places embody significantly different approaches to the same subject matter, quite part from divergent interests and skills'; The sub-discipline has also not been immune from the 'the cultural turn' experienced by sociology in general: Davie, *The Sociology of Religion* 5, 9, 249.
[36] The Religion and Society Research Programme started in 2007 in the UK. It is a joint initiative of the Arts and Humanities and Economic and Social Research Councils with total funding of £12.3 million. The European Commission NORFACE Research Programme: *Re-emergence of religion as a social force in Europe?* started in 2006 providing ten transnational research projects with a maximum of 500 000 Euros each.
[37] Davie, *The Sociology of Religion*.
[38] J A Beckford and N J Demerath (ed), *The Sage Handbook of the Sociology of Religion* (London, Sage, 2007).
[39] For example, Jürgen Habermas, a famous and prolific social theorists previously paid very little attention to religion, but is regarded as having in the new millennium taken a 'post-secular turn' illustrated by his dialogue with Pope Benedict XIV, J Habermas, J Ratzinger and F Schuller *The Dialectic of Secularization: On Reason and Religion* (New York, Ignatius Press, 2007).

the process of modernization necessarily damages religion. Davie and Beyer both take 1979 as a pivotal year which highlighted that religion could not be dismissed as insignificant. In this year the Iranian and Nicaraguan Revolutions, the accession of Pope John Paul II, the beginning of the Solidarity movement in Poland, the USSR invasion of Afghanistan and the founding of Jerry Falwell's Moral Majority in the US all took place showing that religion could be a public and mainstream force[40].

The shift in the thinking of eminent American sociologist Peter L. Berger illustrates sociology of religion's change in direction. In the 1960s Berger, like many others, expected the decline of religion[41]. Yet, in 1986, he proclaimed that the non-Western world was 'as furiously religious as ever'[42] and, in 1999, edited a book entitled *The Desecularization of the World: Resurgent Religion and World Politics*[43]. Beyer places the shift in the sociology of religion in the context of a broader shift in sociology from exclusive focus on the modern, Western nation-state to a more global perspective[44], which Berger's work reflects. This new perspective has led to the positing of Europe being exceptional in its state of secularity rather than paradigmatic[45]. However, others have since contended that Europe itself cannot be conceived as secular: 'transnational religious communities in the European periphery are reintroducing religion into the center of Europe.'[46] Casanova cites the growing association of immigration and Islam as the primary cause of the present debate over how to accommodate and regulate religions in European Union states[47].

Sociological research conducted with Christian missionaries who travel from countries in the global South to evangelize Britain demonstrates that religion can be the motivation for migration in the contemporary

[40] P Beyer, 'Globalization and Glocalization' in J A Beckford and N J Demerath (ed) *The Sage Handbook of the Sociology of Religion* (London, Sage, 2007) 105.

[41] P L Berger, *The Social Reality of Religion* (London, Faber and Faber, 1969).

[42] P L Berger, 'Religion in Post-Protestant America' (1986) *Commentary* May 1986, 4.

[43] P L Berger (ed), *The Desecularization of the World: Resurgent Religion and World Politics* (Washington DC, Ethics and Public Policy Centre 1999).

[44] P Beyer, 'Globalization and Glocalization' in *The Sage Handbook of the Sociology of Religion* (London, Sage, 2007) 104.

[45] G Davie, *Europe: the Exceptional Case: Parameters of Faith in the Modern World* (Darton, Longman and Todd Ltd, 2002).

[46] P J Katzenstein, 'Multiple Modernities as Limits to Secular Europeanization?' in T A Byrnes and P J Katzenstein (ed), *Religion in an Expanding Europe* (Cambridge, Cambridge University Press, 2006) 2.

[47] J Casanova, 'Religion, European Secular Identities, and European Integration' in T A. Byrnes and PJ Katzenstein (ed), *Religion in an Expanding Europe* (Cambridge, Cambridge University Press, Cambridge 2006) 76-77.

world[48]. It also not only illustrates the point that parts of the non-Western world are as furiously religious as ever, but that religious identities still play a role within Western European borders. For the missionaries involved and the British churches and mission organizations they work with, religion is very much a social rather than simply an individual matter. They are connected in a transnational religious network and their faith inspires a range of community work in Britain and elsewhere. With the intensification of global communication and travel from the latter half of the twentieth century, religion, and its management, within and between national borders is of urgent importance[49]. The sociology of religion is enjoying a resurgence, because religion has been seen to be of continuing social significance. Yet, the sub-discipline alone cannot explore and explain such a multi-faceted phenomenon. This brings us back to the top of the chapter and the stated need for a new approach combining the sociology of religion and the study of law and religion. Thus, having elaborated the contemporary significance of religion and a sociological approach to it, now let us proceed to understand the necessity of a legal approach in combination.

The need for a Legal Approach

It is noticeable that new attitude and new approaches[50], buoyed by a trend in sociology as a whole towards bridging the gap between sociological study and the world in which we live[51], have opened the door to

---

[48] R Catto, 'From the Rest to the West: Exploring Reversal in Christian Mission in Twenty-First Century Britain' (University of Exeter, doctoral thesis, 2008).

[49] Though religion was largely ignored in initial sociological work on globalisation, its role in the process has begun to be taken seriously, R Robertson and W R Garrett (ed), *Religion and Global Order* (New York, Paragon, 1991) is a good early example of this change.

[50] An example of such a new approach is Rational Choice Theory (RCT), a product of American sociology which 'postulates that individuals are naturally religious (to be so is part of the human condition) and will achieve their religious choices, just like any other choices, in order to maximise gain (however conceptualized) and to minimize loss. RCT is a 'theory deployed by different branches of social science' and its employment by sociologists of religion consequentially results in 'a significantly greater theoretical unity amongst disciplines as diverse as economics, sociology, certain aspects of psychology, political science, moral philosophy and law': Davie, *The Sociology of Religion* 69.

[51] See, for example, Michael Burawoy's American Sociological Association presidential address 2004, published as: M Burawoy, 'For Public Sociology' (2005) 70 *American Sociological Review* 4-28. For a British reaction see C Inglis, 'Comments on Michael Burawoy's ASA Presidential Address' (2005) 56(3) *British Journal of Sociology* 383-386.

interdisciplinary collaboration and exchange in the field of the sociology of religion[52]. Given the wide number and variety of 'cognate disciplines'[53], it is not surprising, however, that much sociology of religion ignores law and politics completely[54]. This is regrettable: as Davie points out, the contributions of political scientists – 'theorists, constitutionalists, internationalists and policy-makers' – are 'vital' especially 'in terms of law and law-making, constitutional issues and questions of tolerance and human rights'[55]. Indeed, for Davie, those trained in both law and sociology are 'able to offer real insight into the debates about religious freedom (itself an ambiguous concept) and how to maintain this in rapidly changing political conditions'[56].

The moral panics of recent years have led sociologists to afford more attention to questions of religious freedom bringing their focus closer to that of the academic lawyer[57]. There is an increasing number of sociological works which analyze the subject-matter known to law and religion specialists but which use methods, theories and approaches from outside the Law School. Jean-Paul Willaime's work has used juridical notions (such as *Laicitè*) to found his sociological ideas of temperate secularism[58]. James Beckford's research on the theoretical and empirical aspects of religious organisations, new religious movements, church-State problems, civic religion, religion in prisons and religious controversies in several different countries has often included some reference

[52] This point is well-made by Grace Davie who notes that 'Sociologists do not work in isolation' and that 'cognate disciplines' may 'contribute to a better understanding of the place of religion in modern societies': Davie, *The Sociology of Religion* 128.

[53] Davie, *The Sociology of Religion* 128.

[54] S Bruce, *Politics & Religion* (Oxford, Polity Press, 2003) xi. Bruce, a Professor of Sociology, has written extensively on the nature of religion in the modern world and on the links between religion and politics, especially in Northern Ireland: S Bruce, *God Save Ulster!: Religion and Politics of Paisleyism* (Oxford, Oxford University Press, 1989); S Bruce, *Politics & Religion* (Oxford, Polity, 2003).

[55] Davie, *The Sociology of Religion* 129.

[56] Davie, *The Sociology of Religion* 129.

[57] Controversies surrounding the wearing of religious dress and symbols, blasphemy and free speech and the status of Sharia, amongst others, has engendered sociological debate about the place of religion in society. For example, the International Society for the Sociology of Religion's bi-annual conference in Leipzig in 2007 included a stream on 'Law and Religion: A Crucial Interface'.

[58] See, for example, J Willaime, *Profession, Pasteur: Sociologie de la Condition du Clerc à la fin du XXᵉ Siècle* ['Profession, Pastor-Sociology of the Condition of Clergy at end of Twentieth Century'] (Paris, Labor et Fides, 1986); J Willaime, *La Précarité Protestante: Sociologie du Protestantisme Contemporain* ['The Protestant Precariousness: Sociology of Contemporary Protestantism'] (Paris, Labor et fides 1992).

to law[59]. For example, his article entitled 'Banal discrimination: equality of respect for beliefs and worldviews in the UK'[60], used the work of Billig[61] to contend that English law was characterised by the existence of 'low-level, unthinking, but sometimes institutional discrimination' in favour of 'mainstream Christian churches and against the more marginal' religious communities and organisations. Bruce and Wright have sought to verify and explain from a sociological perspective their contention that the State's gradual abandonment of its role as arbiter or religious truth by means of piecemeal laws on religious liberty was motivated by 'necessity rather than principle'[62]. Sengers has considered how regulation affects the religious market[63], while Richardson has contended that theoretical ideas from the sociology of religion and the sociology of law may explain the factors that have given rise to and promoted the idea of religious freedom in modern human societies[64].

However, such works are exceptional. Most cross-disciplinary accounts of legal phenomena play down the distinctive role of legal analysis[65]. Some writers have even criticised the way in which lawyers 'dominate human-right studies' and have called for a 'social science of human rights'

[59] J A Beckford, 'The State and control of new religious movements' in *Acts of the 17th International Conference of the Sociology of Religion* (Paris, 1983) 115; J A Beckford, 'States, governments and the management of controversial new religious movements' in E Barker, J Beckford & K Dobbelaere (eds) *Secularization, Rationalism and Sectarianism* (Oxford, Oxford University Press, 1993) 125; J A Beckford and S Gilliat, *Religion in Prison: Equal Rights in a Multi-Faith Society* (Cambridge, Cambridge University Press, 1998); J A Beckford, 'Religion, State and Prisons' (2000) 1(1) *Religion – Staat – Gesellschaft* 61; J A Beckford and D Joly, 'Race relations and discrimination in prison: the case of Muslims in France and Britain' (2006) 4(2) *Journal of Immigrant & Refugee Studies* 1.

[60] J A Beckford, 'Banal discrimination: equality of respect for beliefs and worldviews in the UK', in D Davis and G Besier (eds) *International Perspectives on Freedom and Equality of Religious Belief* (New York, JM Dawson Institute of Church-State Studies, 2002) 25.

[61] M Billig, *Banal Nationalism* (London, Sage, 1995).

[62] S Bruce and C Wright, 'Law, Social Change and Religious Toleration (1995) 37 *Journal for Church and State* 103.

[63] E Sengers 'The Religious Market Place and its Regulation: A Sociological Perspective' (2007) 9 *Ecc LJ* 294-307.

[64] J T Richardson, 'The Sociology of Religious Freedom: A Structural and Socio-Legal Analysis' (2006) 67(3) *Sociology of Religion* 271. See also J A Beckford and J T Richardson 'Religion and Regulation' in J A Beckford and N J Demerath (ed) *The Sage Handbook of the Sociology of Religion* (London, Sage, 2007) 396.

[65] Richardson, for example, has called for a 'historically informed sociological perspective' which he deems preferable to rather than co-existent with a legal analysis: J T Richardson, 'Regulating Religion: A Sociological and Historical Introduction' in J T Richardson (ed) *Regulating Religion: Case Studies from Around the Globe* (New York, Kluwer, 2004).

which will 'put law in its place'[66]. Most non-legal writing on recent moral panics excludes or underplays the legal dimension. Even socio-legal pieces written by those based in Law Schools tend to include sociological and socio-legal materials at the expense of legal analysis. Accounts become 'law-lite'. This is misplaced: there is much to learn from traditional black-letter scholarship. Many contemporary issues which the sociology of religion seeks to focus upon, concerning the recognition, regulation and accommodation of religion, are legal issues, that can be discovered by black-letter analysis. This is true, for example, of the two case studies Davie chooses to end her book *The Sociology of Religion* with[67]: both the 'acute tension with in the Anglican Communion concerning the acceptance or otherwise of homosexuality'[68] and the 'Danish cartoons'[69] are legal issues. The same is true of questions concerning religious dress and symbols[70] and the right of religious groups to discriminate[71]. Discussion of these moral panics without reference to the legal dimension is flawed.

In *Blackstone's Tower*, William Twining provided an erudite account of how 'the study of law is in the process of being re-absorbed into the mainstream of our general intellectual life, as it was from Blackstone's time until the late nineteenth century.'[72] He notes that given the pressures upon Law Schools[73], 'the focus of legal scholarship has tended to

---

[66] For Freeman, 'excessive attention to human rights laws distorts our understanding of human rights'; 'both the theory and practice of human rights has suffered from being excessively legalistic': the use of an interdisciplinary approach reliant on the social sciences may have more to contribute than 'refined legal analysis of human rights texts': M Freeman, *Human Rights: An Interdisciplinary Approach* (Cambridge, Polity, 2002) 9, 8, 12, 177.

[67] Davie, *The Sociology of Religion* 253-256.

[68] For the legal dimension of the debate within global Anglicanism, see N Doe, *An Anglican Covenant: Theological and Legal Considerations for a Global Debate* (London, SCM Canterbury Press, 2008) and N Doe and R Sandberg, "The 'State of the Union' a Canonical Perspective: Principles of Canon Law in the Anglican Communion" (2006) 49(2) *Sewanee Theological Review* 234.

[69] For the legal dimension on the conflict between freedom of religion and freedom of expression, see J G Oliva, 'The Legal Protection of Believers and Beliefs in the United Kingdom' (2007) 9 *Ecc LJ* 66, R Sandberg, 'Religion and Morality: A Socio-Legal Approach' DISKUS (online) and Richard Clarke's contribution to this volume.

[70] See M Hill and R Sandberg, 'Is Nothing Sacred? Clashing Symbols in a Secular World' [2007] *PL* 488.

[71] See R Sandberg and N Doe, 'Religious Exemptions in Discrimination Law' (2007) 66(2) *CLJ* 302 and Pauline Roberts' contribution to this volume.

[72] W Twining, *Blackstone's Tower: The English Law School* (London, Sweet & Maxwell, 1994) xix.

[73] Law Schools are 'typically caught in a tug of war between three aspirations: to be accepted as full members of the community of higher learning; to be relatively detached, but nonetheless engaged, critics and censors of law in society; and to be service-institutions

be narrower than the scope of legal practice'[74]. This is lamentable given that 'the study of law can provide one kind of way of looking at both practical problems and social events'[75]. The question of what is unique about that way of looking is explored in depth by Twining who comments upon a 'quest for a core'[76].

Noting that 'academic law is pluralistic, involving a bewildering diversity of subject-matters, perspectives, objectives and methods', Twining declares himself sceptical of acts of mere reductionism[77]. Although he identifies a number of possible cores[78], such as the conception of law as a legal science[79], the conception of law as 'something to do with rules'[80] and the idea of the core being the negotiated body of knowledge that is prescribed by the legal profession as granting exemption from the first stage of qualification for practice[81], he concludes that these potential cores do not answer the question of 'what, if anything, is there that is unique or special about the institutionalised discipline of law?'[82]

The answer for Twining is that law provides 'local knowledge of an important area'[83]. The legal imagination has much to offer[84]. Although it is true that many of the skills of the 'legal mind' are transferable intellectual skills[85], the sources and materials lawyers draw upon are unique.

---

for a profession which is itself caught between noble ideals, lucrative service of powerful interests and unromantic cleaning up of society's messes': Twining, *Blackstone's Tower* 2.

[74] This is somewhat inevitable given that law is ubiquitous: its subject matter 'relevant to almost every aspect of public and private life'; indeed 'it is so much a part of our environment that legal education begins at birth. Everyone daily has direct experience of state law': Twining, *Blackstone's Tower* 15, 10, 17.

[75] Twining, *Blackstone's Tower* 21.

[76] See chapter 7 of Twining, *Blackstone's Tower* in particular.

[77] Twining, *Blackstone's Tower* 123. He noted that it is a task easy pilloried: 'it is tempting to dismiss questions about the core or essence of a discipline as misguided or plain silly, to be treated no more seriously than the quest for a non-existent Holy Grail or where the rainbow ends': 153-154.

[78] Since 'the theme is sufficiently persistent and there is enough at stake to make it worth looking at some salient examples of attempts to define the core': Twining, *Blackstone's Tower* 153.

[79] On the basis that academic law embodies' the idea of systematic, objective neutral exposition of the law as it is': Twining, *Blackstone's Tower* 155.

[80] Twining, *Blackstone's Tower* 174-177.

[81] Twining, *Blackstone's Tower* 156-166.

[82] Twining, *Blackstone's Tower* 154, 177.

[83] Twining, *Blackstone's Tower* 181.

[84] J Boyd White, *The Legal Imagination* (Chicago, Chicago University Press, 1985).

[85] 'Thinking like a lawyer' requires the qualities that are commonly valued as intellectual skills. However, these skills – such as the ability to express oneself clearly in orally and in writing, ability to construct an argument, ability to identify key issues – are not unique to law. The claim is simply that the 'subject-matter of the discipline is potentially

The Law Library epitomises law's distinctiveness[86]: journals and periodicals are shunned in favour of volumes of statute books and law
reports[87]. Finding and interpreting such elusive data requires 'study, experience and local knowledge'[88]. Law is constantly in flux and is 'a partic-
ipant-orientated discipline': law students are constantly reminded of the
practical impact of their subject and are forced to make decisions[89]. The
nature and importance of the particular contribution of law must not be
forgotten: as Twining put it, 'in carrying controversy and enquiry from
one discipline into the territory of another it is important to have some
local knowledge of the terrain'[90].

The need for a 'Sociology of Law and Religion'

It is imperative that a sociological approach to law and religion builds
upon the distinctive strengths and insights offered by both law and sociology. Both legal and sociological materials need to be contextualised
separately employing the rigorous use of methods and approaches that
are common within each discipline, they then need to be not simply jux-
taposed but synthesized[91]. A sociology of law and religion should not
merely be a conversation between lawyers and sociologists about points

an excellent vehicle for developing such general intellectual skills': Twining, *Blackstone's
Tower* 180.

[86] This is well-shown in the way in which the Law Library serves as the law student's
laboratory: 'In law library one consults and uses rather than reads books – it is primarily
a place of reference'. Moreover, unlike the libraries of other disciplines, the Law Library
is often a distinct place. It 'excludes people': 'There is probably no branch of the humanities and social sciences that at first sight seems less user-friendly to the non-specialist':
Twining, *Blackstone's Tower* 93-95.

[87] Law reports constitute 'a vast anthology of stories, each one of which raised a moral
or social dilemma or problem. In order to be included in the anthology the problem
was such that people genuinely disagreed about the best solution. In addition to each story
closing with an ending, denouement or other resolution, it also contained a sub-plot in
which arguments for and against competing endings were advanced and then one or more
wise persons announced their solution and reasons for adopting it': Twining, *Blackstone's
Tower* 102-103.

[88] 'Demystifying the law is as much as anything a matter of confidence. ... Learning
how to read, interpret, and use different kinds of legal texts efficiently and intelligently is
a complex art which, in the eyes of many, is central to a good legal education': Twining,
Blackstone's Tower 96.

[89] 'The culture of academic law seems to be markedly different form that of history or
philosophy or anthology': Twining, *Blackstone's Tower* 130.

[90] Twining, *Blackstone's Tower* 184.

[91] This goes beyond the conception offered by Doe, though interestingly some of the
examples he gives of possible areas of work also seem to go further than his multidisciplinary conception of the field: N Doe, 'A Sociology of Law on Religion'.

of contact. It should seek to unlock the sociological dimensions of law and the legal dimensions of social reality. As Cotterrell has noted 'law and sociology share a fundamentally similar subject matter'[92]: they 'are concerned with the whole range of significant forms of social relationships' and both require the abstract to be applied to the concrete[93]. Legal change is both a cause and a product of social change: legal invention makes a real contribution to social life, [94] and social life shapes legal development[95]. The relationship between religion and society cannot be understood without reference to law and the relationship between religion and law cannot be understood without reference to sociology. A sociology of law and religion is concerned with how social forces shape the legal regulation of religion and how law is used to affect religion and its social expression. It seeks to shed further light upon the complex relationship between religion, law and society.

The need for a sociology of law and religion may be demonstrated by reference to the question of the definition of religion[96]. This vexed question is an appropriate area of study for a sociology of law and religion since although both lawyers and sociologists have devoted much ink to the definition issue, few have sought to combine insights from both disciplines. Moreover, legal definitions of religion have sociological effects and the content of legal definitions may be informed by sociological analysis. It is for these reasons that the question of defining religion requires a sociology of law and religion in particular:

---

[92] Both disciplines derive 'from the same cultural assumptions or conceptions of policy relevance' and 'typically seek to view these phenomena as part of, or potentially part of, an integrated social structure': R Cotterrell, *The Sociology of Law* (Second edition, London, Butterworths, 1992) 5.

[93] See K Patchett, 'The Role of Law in the Development Process' (1987) 48 *Commonwealth Legal Education Association Newsletter* 36.

[94] 'Law viewed as technology has long history of inventions, devices, concepts and solutions to problems' ranging from the constitution of the United State to the trust: Twining, *Blackstone's Tower* 179.

[95] Take, for example, changing societal attitudes to homosexuality which has resulted in a major legal changes culminating in the Civil Partnership Act 2004. On which, see Mark Hill's contribution to this volume.

[96] See further, R Sandberg, 'Defining Religion: An Interdisciplinary Approach' in Revista General de Derecho Canonico y D Derecho Ecclesiastico del Estado (forthcoming) and R Sandberg, 'Religion, Society and Law: An Analysis of the Interface between the Law on Religion and the Sociology of Religion' (Cardiff University, doctoral thesis, forthcoming).

Legal definitions of religion have sociological effects

Sociologists of religion recognise that defining religion is 'an exercise of power' which can have serious repercussions[97]. Legal systems seek to define religion to determine which individuals and groups should be bestowed by legal advantages (such as charitable status or relief from generally applicable rules) by virtue of the fact that they are 'religious'. For example, as Bradney points out, 'the law of charities distinguishes between those religions which it finds acceptable and those it does not'[98]. The definition of religion in English charity law requiring 'faith in a god and worship of that god'[99], has been used to refuse the Church of Scientology charitable status[100] while Buddhist charities were not refused despite being outside the letter of the law[101]. This use of the definition of religion as a means of inclusion and exclusion has sociological effects and is sociologically informed[102].

Both lawyers and sociologists recognise that the meaning of religion is not fixed but changes over time, across societies and within societies[103]. Reference to law may aid the sociological understanding of religion as a social construction since changes to meanings can be brought about or marked by legal mechanisms: as Beckford notes, 'boundary disputes' may 'erupt' formally in legislatures and courts of law[104].

Indeed, Beckford has criticised the way in which some social theorists have framed religion 'in unhelpful ways' by treating it as 'a relatively

[97] E.g J Beckford, *Social Theory & Religion* (Cambridge, Cambridge University Press, 2003) 23.

[98] See A Bradney, *Religions, Rights and Laws* (Leicester, Leicester University Press, 1993) 122.

[99] *Re South Place Ethical Society* [1980] 1 WLR 1565.

[100] In 1999, the Charity Commissioners held that the Church of Scientology would not be registered as a charity: it was not an organisation established for the charitable purpose of the advancement of religion because although the 'core practices of Scientology, being auditing and training, do not constitute worship as they do not display the essential characteristic of reverence or veneration for a supreme being': See: <http://www.charity-commission.gov.uk/Library/registration/pdfs/cosfulldoc.pdf>

[101] On the basis that Buddhist belief is multivariate and generally not in a single god (R F Gombrich, *Theravāda Buddhism: A Social History from Ancient Benares to Modern Colombo* (London, Routledge, 2006). Section 2(3)(a) of the Charities Act 2006 now states that belief in no god and belief in more than one god are now included. See Peter Luxton's contribution to this volume.

[102] For example, Susan J Palmer shows how the classification of 172 religious minorities in France as '*sectes*' has had a considerable impact upon these groups' (S J Palmer, 'France's Anti-Sect Wars' (2002) 69(1) *Nova Religio* 174.

[103] Its meaning is negotiated – 'contested, rejected, modified or confirmed'– through social interaction: Beckford, *Social Theory & Religion* 13.

[104] Beckford, *Social Theory & Religion* 13.

unproblematic unitary and homogenous phenomenon'; he has questioned 'whether it is helpful to theorise about "religion", as if it were a generic object' and has called for an analysis of 'the various situations in which religious meaning is constructed, attributed or challenged'[105]. Reference to law may help overcome these problems by providing case studies of this process. A sociology of law and religion may shed light upon State perceptions of religion and religious communities. It may reveal the inherent biases found in the administration rather than the letter of the law (which may be seen as being a clear example of the 'banal discrimination' identified by Beckford)[106] and may illustrate how laws are being distorted to justify socially-held views about certain groups, suggesting the need for law reform.

The content of legal definitions may be informed by sociological analysis

Legal definitions do not exist in societal isolation: legal definitions must conform to the meaning of language in society at large[107]. Sociological change may force a change in the content of legal definitions[108]. Moreover, the content of legal definitions can be understood sociologically. The application of sociological classifications to legal definitions of religion may lead to an appreciation of the social dimensions of religion. For instance, sociologists frequently distinguish between substantive definitions which identify religion for what *it is* and functional definitions which identify religion for what *it does*[109]. This classification may be

[105] Beckford, *Social Theory & Religion* 15-16. Beckford contends that there is a need 'to abandon the search for, and the assumption that there are, generic qualities of religion'.

[106] J A Beckford, 'Banal Discrimination: Equality of Respect for Belief and Worldviews in the UK' in Davis and Besier (eds) *International Perspectives on Freedom and Equality of Religious Belief* (J M Dawson Institute of Church-State Studies, Baylor University 2002).

[107] V C R A C Crabbe, *Legislative Drafting* (London, Cavendish Publishing, 1993) 115. This means that the influence of a dictionary definition is likely to still be felt regardless of the 'legal' meaning that is 'expressly attached to a term'.

[108] Most famously in House of Lords decisions in *R v R* [1991] 3 WLR 767 where the House held that the marital exemption to rape was no longer a rule of law. It was no longer applicable in modern times when marriage was viewed as a partnership of equals (see M Giles, 'Judicial Law-Making in the Criminal Courts: The Case of Marital Rape' [1992] *Crim LR* 407). Note particularly, Lord Keith's judgment stressing that the common law able to evolve in light of changing social, economic and cultural developments. Less dramatically, judges may find it 'impossible to cancel the ingrained emotion of a word' merely by its displacement by legal announcement: F A R Bennion, *Statutory Interpretation: A Code* (Fourth edition, London, Butterworths, 2002) 480.

[109] Examples of substantive definitions in sociology include Tylor's "minimum definition" of religion as: 'the belief in Spiritual Beings' (E B Tylor, *Primitive Culture* (Volume I,

applied to legal definitions. The definition of religion in English charity law requiring faith and worship of a God is a substantive definition[110], while section 57 of the Equality Act 2006 includes a functional definition of religion specifying that the purpose or function of an 'organisation relating to religion or belief' and thus, by implication, a religion itself, is to practice, advance and teach the principles of that religion, to enable persons of the religion to receive benefits and engage in activities and to improve relations between religious groups. These definitions can be understood sociologically: for instance, the definition in the Equality Act 2006 can be understood as underlining the sociality of religion as a key definitional attribute of religious groups. These definitions can also be critiqued sociologically: for example, the cumbersome drafting in the Charities Act 2006 which seeks to remove any doubt as to the inclusion of polytheistic religions and atheism could have been avoided if law-yers had followed sociological literature advocating the use of the term 'Supreme Being' as opposed to 'God'[111]. The drafting of the Act may be criticised as still presenting such beliefs as exceptional.

Other sociological works providing dysfunctional definitions of religion as capable of playing a negative role in people's lives[112] may also shed light upon implicit legal definitions. Whilst English law does not follow the leading Australian case, *Church of the New Faith v Commissioner for Payroll Tax*[113] in explicitly stating that if a religion has such dysfunctions then it should lose all legal privileges commonly given to religions[114], it

---

London, John Murray, 1920) 424) and Steve Bruce's list that religion 'consists of beliefs, actions and institutions which assume the existence of supernatural entities' (S Bruce, *Religion in Modern Britain* (Oxford, Oxford University Press, 1995) ix). The most famous functional definition in sociology is that provided by Durkheim who defines religion as 'a *unified* set of beliefs and practices': for Durkheim religion is 'something eminently collective', it links people together in communities providing 'social solidarity' (E Durkheim, *The Elementary Forms of Religious Life* (Oxford, Oxford University Press, 2001) 46.)

[110] *Re South Place Ethical Society* [1980] 1 WLR 1565.

[111] Which, interestingly, was the language used by the Charity Commissioners in 1999 in their deliberations over the Church of Scientology.

[112] For example, Simmel wrote that the function of religion was division – he defined 'religion' as 'the hostile demarcation from other groups' (G Simmel, *Essays on Religion* (Yale, Yale University Press, 1997). As is well known, for Marx and Engels, the function of religion was that of compensation for exploitation: 'Religion is the sigh of the oppressed creature, the heart of a heartless world, just as it is the spirit of a spiritless situation. It is the opium of the people.' K Marx, *Contribution to the Critique of Hegel's Philosophy of Right*, republished in K Marx and F Engels, *On Religion* (New York, Fredonia Books, 2002) 42.

[113] (1983) 57 ALJR 785.

[114] 'for the purposes of the law, the criteria of religion are twofold: first, belief in a supernatural Being, Thing or Principle; and second, the acceptance of canons of conduct

nevertheless includes implicitly the notion that the legal definition of religion requires the religion not to offend public morality. It was confirmed in *Thornton v Howe*[115] that charity law would not recognise gifts to religions whose doctrines are subversive of all morality[116]. It is recognised where an otherwise religious activity is socially dysfunctional, it consequentially does not benefit from legal recognition. This implies that the State generally thinks that recognised religion is a good thing.

The application of sociological notions to legal definitions of religion may lead to an appreciation of the collective and individual dimensions of religion[117]. The move towards protecting religion as a human right may reveal a perception that religion is primarily an individual rather than a collective affair[118]. Article 9 of the European Convention of Human Rights does not protect the right of religious collectives: the right to manifest religion or belief is an individual right which may be exercised individually ('alone') or collectively ('in community with others'). Although the European Court of Human Rights has heard cases brought by religious groups[119], when such cases are brought it is actually the individual members who are exercising their individual rights collectively[120]. Moreover, there is legal evidence to suggest that legal mechanisms increasingly view religion as a private affair[121]: courts are reluctant to intervene in religious disputes[122] and have classified much religious activity as akin to

---

in order to give effect to that belief, though canons or conduct which offend against the ordinary laws are outside the area of any immunity, privilege or right conferred on the ground of religion'.

[115] (1862) 31 Beavan 14.

[116] 'It may be that the tenets of a particular sect inculcate doctrines adverse to the very foundations of all religion, and that they are subversive of all morality. In such a case, if it should arise, the Court will not assist the execution of the bequest, but will declare it to be void.'

[117] See further, R Sandberg, 'Religion and the Individual: A Socio-Legal Perspective' in A Day (ed) *Religion and the Individual* (Aldershot, Ashgate, 2008).

[118] See, most notably, the comments of Lord Nicholls in *R v Secretary of State for Education ex parte Williamson* [2005] UKHL 15: 'Religious and other beliefs and convictions are part of the humanity of every individual. They are an integral part of his personality and individuality'.

[119] E.g *X and the Church of Scientology v Sweden* [1979]16 D&R 68 and *ISKCON V United Kingdom* [1994] 90 D&R 90.

[120] R Sandberg, 'Religion and the Individual: A Socio-Legal Perspective' in A Day (ed) *Religion and the Individual* (Aldershot, Ashgate, 2008).

[121] As a matter of legal fact, matters formerly under ecclesiastical jurisdiction (such as the enforcement of contracts, defamation proceedings and matrimonial causes) have been rendered to the State.

[122] See M Hill 'Judicial Review of Ecclesiastical Courts' in N Doe, M Hill and R Ombres, *English Canon Law* (Cardiff, University of Wales Press, 1998). It is also

a leisure activity[123]. However, a sociological approach (*pace* Durkheim) stresses religion is more than an individual activity. Recent research within the sociology of religion has reinforced the fact that religion cannot be considered exclusively a private affair[124].

Indeed, there are a number of laws in England and Wales which protect religion as a collective phenomenon by extending legal protection to religious groups. This is particularly true of the numerous exemptions under discrimination law and the recently created criminal offences[125]. This seems to indicate that English law recognises that religion is both an individual and collective phenomenon: the House of Lords, for example, has recognised that worship may be communal or personal[126]. However, the dominance of human rights thinking, the furore surrounding the refusal to specifically exempt Roman Catholic adoption agencies from laws forbidding discrimination on grounds of sexual orientation[127], coupled with the long-standing unease regarding faith schools may suggests that increasingly religious groups are treated with some hostility[128]. A sociologically informed perspective could provide a more nuanced and contextualised approach to defining and regulating religion by means of law.

Aside from the question of defining religion, there are a number of contributions that a sociology of law and religion may make. In addition to shedding light on religion law, it may also shed light on religious law.

notable that Parliamentary statute has been used to 'privatise' certain churches: e.g Welsh Church Act 1914 disestablished the Church of England in Wales and rendered the Church in Wales a voluntary association.

[123] See, for instance, the comments of Hoffmann LJ (as he then was) that 'the attitude of the English legislator to racing is much more akin to his attitude to religion...it is something to be encouraged but not the business of government': *R. v Disciplinary Committee of the Jockey Club ex parte Aga Khan* [1993] 1WLR 909 at 932.

[124] For example, J Casanova *Public Religions in the Modern World* (Chicago, University of Chicago Press, 1994); P Chambers 'Public Religion and Political Change in Wales' (2005) 39(1) *Sociology* 29-46; Ş Şahin 'The Rise of Alevism as a Public Religion' (2005) 53(3) *Current Sociology* 465-485.

[125] See Pauline Roberts' and Richard Clarke's contributions to this volume respectively.

[126] *R v Secretary of State for Education ex parte Williamson* [2005] UKHL 15.

[127] The Equality Act (Sexual Orientation) Regulations 2007 (SI 1263) includes an exemption for 'organisations relating to religion or belief' but this exemption is lost if organisation makes provision with and 'on behalf of a public authority under the terms of a contract': see R Sandberg and N Doe, 'Religious Exemptions in Discrimination Law' (2007) 66(2) *CLJ* 302.

[128] 'Despite the statutory requirements of s 13 [of the Human Rights Act 1998], the state sees religious groups and the doctrines which govern their behaviour with a degree of caution': M Hill and R Sandberg, 'Is Nothing Sacred? Clashing Symbols in a Secular World' [2007] *PL* 488, 506.

For example, a sociologically informed approach may demonstrate how religious communities are influenced by the State and secular trends. Religious laws reveal a shift towards wider participation and democratisation[129], and an emphasis upon choice[130]. Religion law reveals an increased expectation that religious communities will conform to secular standards[131]: most notably there has been a shift towards recognising that clergy are entitled to secular employment rights[132]. Similarly, a sociological perspective may interpret proposals in global Anglicanism for an 'Anglican Covenant'[133] to strengthen existing non-juridical 'bonds of affection' between the forty-four member churches of the Anglican Communion as a sign of globalisation[134]. Thus it can be seen that changes in religious law reflect broader social change. Beckford and Richardson referring to religious law as 'self regulation', note that the phenomenon 'is particularly interesting from a sociological perspective for what it reveals about the variety of ways in which religions seek to control their practices and their practitioners.'[135] However, such an appreciation of religious law is otherwise largely absent from the literature within

[129] For example in relation to the Church of England, the Church of England Assembly (Powers) Act 1919 and the Synodical Government Measure 1969 gave increased power to what is now the General Synod. Church rules increasingly require decision-makers to consult, to give reasons and to be accountable.

[130] In Episcopal churches, recent innovations enable the exercise of choice through: alternative episcopal oversight; the rise of team and group and a focus on subsidiarity (and local need) in church government.

[131] The twentieth century saw a profound increase in State law across the spectrum of churches, expressing a growth both in state interest in religion and the complexities of institutional religious life, including provisions on religious aspects of: abortion, child welfare, adoption, education, Sunday trading, heritage, and religious freedom, data protection and religious discrimination.

[132] See *Percy v Church of Scotland Board of National Mission* [2005] UKHL 73 and *New Testament Church of God v Stewart* [2004] EWCA Civ 1004. See J Duddington, 'Ministers of Religion and Discrimination Law: A Story from the Glens of Angus' (2006) 156 *Law and Justice* 59 and J Duddington, 'God, Caesar and the Employment Rights of Ministers of Religion' (2007) 159 *Law and Justice* 129.

[133] On which see N Doe, *An Anglican Covenant: Theological and Legal Considerations for a Global Debate* (London, SCM Canterbury Press, 2008).

[134] The relationship between the churches of the Anglican Communion has been historically characterised by autonomy within communion. Whilst offices and institutions exist at the global level of the Anglican Communion, there is no body at this level competent to make decisions binding on individual churches: see generally N Doe, *Canon Law in the Anglican Communion* (Oxford, Oxford University Press, 1998).

[135] J A Beckford and J T Richardson 'Religion and Regulation' in J A Beckford and N J Demerath (eds) *The Sage Handbook of the Sociology of Religion* (London, Sage, 2007) 396-418, 398.

the sociology of religion. This is regrettable since religious law would provide a concrete focus for sociological research into religious development.

A sociology of law and religion may also provide methodological advantages. As the Archbishop of Canterbury has recognised, fear of sham claims means that those invoking religious rights cannot be afforded a 'blank cheque'[136]. However, courts have struggled with the matter of excluding bogus claims. Although the House of Lords in *Williamson* emphasized that courts should not be concerned whether the religious belief professed is a good faith in terms of judging the validity of that faith and that it is not the case that 'that a perceived obligation is a prerequisite to manifestation of a belief in practice'[137], lower courts have excluded claims on the basis that the religious observance was not mandatory according to that religion. In *R (on the Application of Playfoot (A Child) v Millais School Governing Body[138]*, for example[139], the High Court rejected an application for judicial review on behalf of a year-old school girl who had wanted to wear a 'purity' ring at school as a symbol of her religiously-motivated commitment to celibacy before marriage on the basis that the claimant was under no obligation, by reason of her faith, to wear the ring[140]. This approach seems confused in that while Courts may be concerned with whether the claim of religious belief was made *in* good faith, they are not concerned with whether the religious belief professed is *a* good faith in terms of judging the validity of that faith.

In this respect, law may have much to learn from the debate in the sociology of religion concerning the extent religion can be subjected to scholarly analysis[141]. In particular, much may be learnt from the notion

[136] R Williams, 'Civil and Religious Law in England – A Religious Perspective' Available at <http://www.archbishopofcanterbury.org/1575>.

[137] *R v Secretary of State for Education and Employment and others ex parte Williamson* [2005] UKHL 15 at para 32-33.

[138] [2007] EWHC Admin 1698.

[139] See also the Employment Tribunal decision in *Eweida v British Airways* (2007) ET, Case Number 2702689/06 (December 19th 2007) concerning the visible wearing of a cross by a uniformed employee in breach of what was then the policy of British Airways.

[140] See R Sandberg, 'Controversial Recent Claims to Religious Liberty' (2008) 124 *LQR* 213.

[141] Two opposite views may be identified: (1) the '*sui generis* thesis': that the impossibility of a valueless understanding of religion necessitates the conclusion that religion must be treated as a phenomenon in its own right, understandable and explainable only on its own terms; and (2) the 'reductionist thesis': which seeks to explain religion by subjecting it exclusively into the explanatory frameworks of other subjects.

of 'methodological agnosticism'[142]: as Simmel pointed out, a distinction can be drawn between the 'metaphysical event that is readily capable of implying or forming the basis of religion' and 'the subjective attitude of human beings'[143]. Methodological agnosticism requires drawing this distinction and bracketing aside the question of the status of religious claims[144]. Critical perspective is not abandoned but is limited in terms of ambit by excluding the determination of theological truths. As Simmel put it, religion is considered simply as a 'human process'. Methodological agnosticism, as a principle, may inform the interest in religion taken by both lawyers and sociologists.

This reference to methodological agnosticism relates to the very strong tradition within the sociology of religion of studying the object empirically. Sociologists investigate religion both quantitatively and qualitatively facilitating a comparison between the macro and the micro level. As Gernstein writes: 'It is essential to recognize that social action is inherently and inseparably dual in nature: quantitative and qualitative. ... In Weber's famous duofold, an account of social action must strive for interpretive adequacy at the level of statistics and the level of meaning.'[145] Given that lawyers tend to focus exclusively upon the means of regulating religion ignoring the effects[146], they may have much to learn from the sociological tradition of both quantitative and qualitative empirical investigation.

An example of where reference to social scientific investigation could enhance legal understanding is in relation to the religion question(s) posed in the 2001 UK Census[147]. The high proportion of the British population regarding themselves as Christian (71.6%) provoked much comment. However, legal texts often omit important nuances that a sociological perspective can offer. For example, the academic lawyer David McClean in his account of Church and State in the United Kingdom commented only that the figure 'was greeted with some surprise, as many commentators had expected a lower figure' and concluded that 'All this

---

[142] M Hamilton, *The Sociology of Religion: Theoretical and Comparative Perspectives* Oxford, Routledge, 2001) 5.

[143] G Simmel, 'Contributions to the Epistemology of Religion' in G Simmel, *Essays on Religion* (Yale, Yale University Press, 1997) 121.

[144] M Hamilton, *The Sociology of Religion: Theoretical and Comparative Perspectives* (Oxford, Routledge, 2001) 5.

[145] D R Gerstein 'To Unpack Micro and Macro: Link Small with Large and Part with Whole' in C Alexander *et al* (ed) *The Micro-Macro Link* (California University of California Press, 1987) 87.

[146] R Sandberg and N Doe, 'Church-State Relations in Europe' (2007) 1(5) *Religion Compass* 561.

[147] <http://www.statistics.gov.uk/census2001/>.

points to a large number of nominal, or inactive, or lapsed members who still identify themselves not only with Christianity but with a particular expression of it: as it is sometimes said, they know which church it is they do not attend.'[148] Sociological analysis may shed further light on such contentions. There has been much sociological reflection on and criticism of the question on religion included in the Census and the process leading up to its inclusion[149]. The sociologist of religion Abby Day, for example, has provided in depth qualitative work exploring the disjunction between the numbers proclaiming Christian affiliation and the numbers regularly attending places of worship[150]. This research illustrates the complexity of the relationship between belief and practise and ethnic, religious and national identities which must be taken into account when studying religion. Lawyers should surely refer to such research in their elucidation of census statistics: by triangulating quantitative and qualitative approaches, it is possible to dig deeper behind the data[151]. However, a sociology of law and religion requires more than mere cross-referencing. Lawyers have much to gain from sociological research methods. Sociologists give much consideration as to how the researcher's background, values and beliefs affect fieldwork, particularly in relation to religion[152]. By contrast, academic lawyers pay less attention to how their own values and beliefs shape their own interpretation of the law. A sociology of law and religion could help redress this.

Conclusion

Law relating to religion does not exist in isolation from societal trends. The moral panics of recent years show that there is an urgent need to understand the relationship between law and social trends. That is why it is vital that critical attention is paid not only to individual legal developments but also to their collective effect[153]. The fusion of disciplinary approaches,

---

[148] D McClean, 'Church and State in the United Kingdom' in G Robbers (ed) State and Church in the European Union (Second edition, Baden Baden, Nomos 2005) 554, 556.

[149] J R Southworth '"Religion" in the 2001 Census for England and Wales' (2005) 11 *Population, Space and Place* 75.

[150] A Day, 'Belief in Britain' [2006] *Anthropology News* October edition, 58. Day is also on the Academic Advisory Group for the 2011 Census Questionnaire Development, Office for National Statistics.

[151] B Hanson, 'Wither Qualitative or Quantitative? Grounds for Methodological Convergence' [2008] 42(1) *Quality and Quantity* 97.

[152] J Landres, B McGuire and J Spickard *Personal Knowledge and Beyond: Reshaping the Ethnography of Religion* (New York University Press, New York, 2002).

[153] M Hill and R Sandberg, 'Is Nothing Sacred? Clashing Symbols in a Secular World' [2007] *PL* 488, 506.

as advocated by Doe and Davie, may help us to understand the immense legal and sociological changes that have occurred in relation to religion over the last decade in light of one another.

A sociology of law and religion is advantageous for both lawyers and social scientists. For sociologists, reference to law may provide definite examples of how religion is constructed, attributed or challenged and the practical effect this has. The sociological dimension would be enhanced by more attention to the legal framework in which religious groups act and which religious groups create, providing a more grounded focus for research. For lawyers, acknowledgment of sociological problems and awareness of the sociological effects may well inform the drafting, interpretation and implementation of law. Consideration by lawyers of sociological approaches could contribute many methodological benefits.

Both law and sociology have their strengths and weaknesses. Moreover, each discipline's weaknesses can be mitigated by an interdisciplinary approach. Whilst law and religion academics have, understandably, focussed on legal change, sociology of law and religion may help contextualise legal change in the context of wider social change. Whilst sociologists of religion have theorised and sought to explain social changes concerning religion, a sociology of law and religion may provide specific and concrete legal examples of these changes. A key point of contact between law and religion and the sociology of religion is the contentious relationship between theory and practice. Sociology has been criticised for its inability to engage with government and affect policy development[154], whereas lawyers often focus solely on the means of regulation rather than its effects. There is a clear need for the more nuanced, contextualised and integrated approach which a sociology of law and religion provides, especially given the current age of uncertainty.

This chapter has illustrated how such an interdisciplinary advance might proceed. Although it draws upon examples from England and Wales, the approach demonstrated extends beyond this context: sociological analysis and local, technical, legal knowledge of religion may be combined in differing national contexts. Together, building upon the strengths of each discipline, a sociology of law and religion may shed light upon the bigger picture, indicating the current relationship between religion, law and society and perhaps suggesting its likely future direction.

---

[154] N McLaughlin and K Turcotte 'The Trouble with Burawoy: An Analytic, Synthetic Alternative' (2007) 45(1) *British Journal of Sociology* 813.

SOME SCEPTICAL THOUGHTS ABOUT THE ACADEMIC ANALYSIS OF LAW AND RELIGION IN THE UNITED KINGDOM

Anthony Bradney

Introduction

The last part of the twentieth century and the first few years of the twenty-first century have seen a considerable change in the fortunes of the academic analysis of the intersection of law and religion in the United Kingdom[1]. Before this era such work was an occasional part of the law school's agenda. Little attention was given to it in law schools and where individuals did take an interest it was, with the exception of some work on canon law, only a small part what they did. Academics were experts in land law, contract law or whatever and, even if they did write an article or essay on law and religion, they did not see themselves as thereby becoming experts in law and religion[2]. Now this has radically changed. The study of law and religion in the United Kingdom has acquired that panoply of specialist conferences, collections of essays, monographs and even a journal and a centre that characterise an academic sub-discipline[3]. Much of the writing in this area has been either explicitly or implicitly

---

[1] For a more detailed argument about the change in the place of the analysis of law and religion in the law school's agenda see A Bradney, 'Politics and Sociology: New Research Agendas for the Study of law and Religion' in R O'Dair and A Lewis (eds) *Law and Religion* (Oxford, Oxford University Press, 2001) 65 at 65-75.

[2] This is not something that is unique to the study of law and religion. Thus, for example, Treitel's essay on the law in Austen's novels 'Jane Austen and the Law' ((1984) 100 *LQR* 549) did not make him an expert on law and literature, another area of study that has now become part of the law school's agenda.

[3] Becher and Trowler have surveyed the literature on the nature of academic disciplines (T Becher and P Trowler, *Academic Tribes and Territories* (Second edition, Buckingham, The Society for Research into Higher Education and Open University Press, 2001) chapter 3. The study of law and religion does not fully match the necessary characteristics for status as a discipline that they describe. For example, Becher and Trowler identify a separate space in the structural framework of the university as being significant (41-43) but there are no separate departments of law and religion in United Kingdom universities. However, this is also true for other long-established specialist areas in law. For this reason I would characterise the study of law and religion as a sub-discipline like criminal law or family law rather than a discipline. For a more detailed argument about sub-disciplines and disciplines see A Bradney, 'The Rise and Rise of Legal Education' (1997) 4 *Web Journal of Current Legal Issues* <http://webjcli.ncl.ac.uk/>.

policy-orientated in its nature, seeking to either to ameliorate the position of religious believers in society or to establish the proper limits of religion and religious belief[4]. As such it is susceptible to the general criticism that can be levied at research in law schools; that it fails to address the central thrust of the university's focus, the search for knowledge, and thus, inevitably, places itself at the periphery of the university[5]. However, it is not this problem that I wish to address in this chapter. Instead I want to look at the obstacles to success for such policy-oriented work on law and religion; obstacles that I will argue are, in some instances, a severe limitation on what can be done in this field and even on what should be done.

The Archbishop of Canterbury and Sharia Law

A starting point for this chapter is the reaction to the Archbishop of Canterbury's, Rowan Williams, lecture in the Royal Courts of Justice on civil and religious law in England[6]. It is the reaction rather than the lecture itself that is the centre of my analysis. However, in order to assess that reaction, it is necessary first to note briefly the main themes that Williams developed in his lecture.

In his lecture Williams argued for the need to give more attention to the 'level of public or legal recognition, if any, [which] might be allowed to the legal provisions of a religious group'. This issue is hardly one that is unknown or strange to scholars of the intersection between religion and law whether in the United Kingdom or elsewhere. Indeed Williams explicitly drew on a range of previous academic writing in the field in his lecture. The lecture gave no prescriptions as to what should be done but instead identified three central issues that needed to be discussed in more detail; first how 'vexatious appeals to religious scruple' could be avoided, secondly whether the recognition of the legal provisions of a religious group might involve recognising repressive forces and, thirdly,

---

[4] Not all work takes this form. See, for example, Gardner's essay 'Law as a Leap of Faith' (J Gardner, 'Law as a Leap of Faith' in P Oliver, S Douglas Scott and V Tadros (ed) *Faith in Law: Essays in Legal Theory* (Oxford, Hart publishing, 2000) 19-31.

[5] On this see further A Bradney, *Conversations, Chances and Choices: The Liberal Law School in the Twenty-First Century* (Oxford, Hart Publishing, 2003)

[6] R Williams, 'Civil and Religious Law in England – A Religious Perspective'. The lecture was delivered on 7th February 2008. It is to be found on the Archbishop's web-site at <http://www.archbishopofcanterbury.org/1575>. In part the reaction was also a reaction to a radio interview that the Archbishop gave on the same date. This interview is to be found at the same place.

whether 'it [is] not both theoretically and practically mistaken to qualify our commitment to legal monopoly'[7]. In the conclusion to his lecture, which largely focussed on the example of Islam and sharia law, Williams noted the need to engage in 'a fair amount of "deconstruction" of crude oppositions and mythologies, whether of the nature of *sharia* or the nature the Enlightenment'. The tone of Williams' lecture was nuanced and cautious, arguing the need for more detailed and prolonged discussion of an area of concern that had already been identified by other commentators.

The immediate reaction to the lecture, particularly the immediate reaction from politicians, was neither nuanced nor cautious; crude oppositions and mythologies were to the fore. The dominant themes in comments from politicians published in the media immediately after the lecture were a categorical rejection of Williams' lecture and an insistence on the need for everyone to live under a common legal code with same legal rules being applied to everyone[8]. What is important in this reaction is the intellectual level of the debate. It seems unlikely that many, if any, of the politicians who were willing publicly to respond to Williams' lecture had had the chance to listen to it or read it. Few, if any, had any legal training or any obvious reason for being knowledgeable about the areas that Williams' was discussing. Nevertheless, in the main, they were happy to reject Williams' arguments without even hearing them[9]. Moreover, the bedrock for their rejection of Williams' lecture was a basic misunderstanding of the nature of the legal systems in the United Kingdom as they are now and as they have been for several centuries[10]. The notion that in the United Kingdom there is simply one law for everyone and that the law never seeks to accommodate religious difference is one that

[7] The last issue was perhaps put rather inelegantly since, at best, it is questionable whether we start from a point a point of 'legal monopoly'. Williams himself is clearly aware of this. In the radio interview that Williams gave to the BBC on the same day as his lecture Williams observed that 'as a matter of fact certain provision[s] of Sharia [are] in certain circumstances recognised in our society and under our law' and later in the same interview that in relation to abortion 'there are perfectly proper ways in which the law of the land pays respect to customs and community'.

[8] See, for example, a series of comments published in the Telegraph available on the Telegraph's website at <http://www.telegraph.co.uk/news/index.jhtml>.

[9] I am not suggesting that there is necessarily anything particularly unusual in this. It may well be the case that political debate is usually couched in unsophisticated terms. If this is so, one of the things that concerns me in this essay is the implications that this possible general truth has for the work of scholars in the field of law and religion.

[10] Implicit in the reaction is also the inaccurate belief that Williams is alone in raising the concerns that are central to his lecture.

is incapable of sensible defence[11]. Despite this a wide range of political figures were quoted as saying things such as 'there's one law in this country and it's the democratically determined law' (Jacqui Smith, the Home Secretary), '[w]e cannot have a situation where there is one law for one person and different laws for another' (Nick Clegg, leader of the Liberal Democrats) or '[a]ll British citizens must be subject to British laws developed through Parliament and the courts' (Baroness Warsi, the shadow minister for community cohesion and social action)[12].

Two possibilities need to be considered when analysing the political reaction to Williams' lecture. First, the argument that might be being made by these various politicians, albeit in crude terms, could be the simple one that, in the final analysis, it is State law that determines what is and what is not legally recognised by the state and that in the United Kingdom this is a system of law whose content is largely determined through a process of Parliamentary democracy. If this is so the retort would be that this basic picture in no way contradicts the arguments that Williams sought to develop in his lecture. The question is what further accommodations should Parliament make to religious sensibilities in addition to those that it has already made? The second possibility is that what the media reports and that which has actually been said may be different things. Even if this true a problem for scholars in the area of law and religion whose work is policy oriented is still raised. If public debate takes places at such a low level and is ridden with basic errors what possibility is there to affect change through serious scholarship? However, whether there is any great difference between what is being said by politicians and what is being reported is, at least in this area of public debate, open to doubt. In the same *Telegraph* source that provided the above quotations Ten Downing Street was quoted as saying that:

> Our general position is that Sharia law cannot be used as a justification for committing breaches of English law, nor should the principles of Sharia law be included in a civil court for resolving contractual disputes. In general terms, if there are specific instances that can be looked at on a case-by-case basis, that is something we can look at. But the Prime Minister believes British law should apply in this country, based on British values.

---

[11] The argument that this should be the case is another matter. Barry, for example, has put forward just such an argument: B Barry, *Culture and Equality: An Egalitarian Critique of Multiculturalism* (Cambridge, Polity Press, 2001) 44-50.
[12] These comments are all taken from Telegraph website noted above.

A press briefing on 11th February 2005, available via the Prime Minister's website, is much more detailed than the report in the Telegraph but the basic argument that is developed is the same[13]. On the one hand the argument is that 'British laws must be based on British values and that religious law... should be subservient to British criminal and civil law'. At the same time,

[t]here had been particular circumstances where it had been possible to accommodate the concerns of particular groups [citing the case of sharia law and stamp duty], but that was a different proposition from what this debate was about which was the relationship between British law and religious law.

In reality, of course, precisely what is at issue is the possibility of accommodating the concerns of particular groups. The political responses misread the debate and the responses, whether shortly reported in the media or developed at more length in a full briefing and no matter which major political party is involved, are largely the same.

Politicians, however influential they are, do not hold a monopoly on the development of public policy. However, when one looks at the response of others to Williams' arguments in his lecture the same message of ignorance and simplification comes across. The response to Williams' lecture in a press release issued by the Chairman of the Equality and Human Rights Commission, Trevor Phillips, begins by saying that:

[t]he Archbishop's thinking here is muddled and unhelpful. As far as I am aware no serious body of Muslim opinion supports the idea of special treatment, or exemption from the law of the land based on some vague 'conscientious objection'[14].

In fact calls for the introduction of personal law systems in the United Kingdom go back at least as far as the 1970s[15]. The press release then goes on to accept that there should be debate about how religious faiths have their practices recognised by the law but then goes on to argue that:

his [Williams'] implication that British courts should treat people differently based on their faith is divisive and dangerous. It risks removing the protection afforded by law, for example, to children in custody cases or women in divorce proceedings.

---

[13] The website is to be found at <http://www.number10.gov.uk/output/Page1.asp>.
[14] This press release is to be found on the Equality and Human Rights Commission website at <http://www.equalityhumanrights.com/en/newsandcomment/Pages/sharialaw.aspx>.
[15] I Yilmaz, *Muslim Laws, Politics and Society in Modern Nation States: Dynamic Legal Pluralisms in England, Turkey and Pakistan* (Aldershot, Ashgate, 2005) 59.

As we have seen above, Williams' lecture specifically identified the possibility that religious laws might be repressive as one of the three major concerns that needs to be looked at in debate about this issue. Moreover, more generally, if it is right, as Phillips suggests, that British law should look to see how it can recognise the practices of religious faiths how can British courts, on occasion, avoid treating people differently because of their faith? 'Muddled' is a word that seems to be more accurately applied to Phillips' response to Williams' lecture than to the lecture itself.

The hostile reaction to Williams' lecture and the low level of debate that accompanied it should come as no surprise given what has previously happened when another common-law country, Canada, was forced to address the issue of the interrelationship between religious law and State law. In 2003 a Muslim group announced its intention to use the Ontario law of arbitration to help resolve disputes about matters relating to inheritance and to the family. Under the proposed scheme, the disputes would be settled according to religious sharia law but then enforced by the state as an arbitration decision, something that the Jewish Beth Din (in Canada termed the Beis Din) and Christian groups had previously been doing for some years. The resulting public furore culminated in the setting up of a special inquiry[16]. Despite a largely positive report regarding the Muslim proposals and despite some support in the academic literature the Ontario legislature passed the Family Statute Law Amendment Act 2006 which, amongst other things, amended section 1(1) of the Arbitration Act 1991 so as to ensure that all arbitrations are carried out under 'the law of Ontario or another Canadian jurisdiction'[17].

The lesson of both the experience of Canada and the reaction to Williams' lecture is that policy oriented-work in relation to religion and law is done in a context that is unpropitious both intellectually and politically. There is a low level of general knowledge surrounding the area and the issues involved are highly charged. Reactions to proposals that seem to give religion a more prominent place are frequently immediate and emotive. Given this the prospects of academic arguments actually being properly heard and debated seem limited.

---

[16] The resultant report was published as M Boyd, *Dispute Resolution in Family Law: Protecting Choice, Promoting Inclusion* (Toronto, Ministry of the Attorney-General, 2004).

[17] See, for example, A Emon, 'Conceiving Islamic Law in a Pluralist Society: History, Politics and Multicultural Jurisprudence' (2006) 2 *Singapore Journal of Legal Studies* 331-355.

Judges and Religious Belief

The second problem for policy oriented work on law and religion that I want to raise is the prevalent attitude of the senior British judiciary towards some forms of religious belief[18]. An illustrative example of this attitude is to be found in dicta in *Re P (Medical Treatment)*[19]. The case concerned a Jehovah's Witness child aged 16 years and 10 months who objected to blood transfusions. The court ruled that:

> [t]o overrule the wishes of John seems to me to be an order that I should be (as indeed I am) reluctant to make...
>
> Nonetheless, looking at the interests of John in the widest possible sense – medical, religious, social whatever these may be – my decision is that John's best interests will be met if I make an order in the terms sought by the NHS Trust [that would allow the use of blood transfusions].

For the court religious belief is part of a range of things that need to be considered in determining what is best for John. It is not that religious beliefs are to be ignored; however religious beliefs have to be balanced against other matters when arriving at a decision about what is to be done. It seems unlikely that John would have agreed with this analysis.

Beckford, in his account of Jehovah's Witnesses, observes that 'the vast majority of British Jehovah's witnesses accept and internalize the Watch Tower Society's ideology'[20]. Belief is usually neither contrived nor forced: 'What is sociologically interesting about Jehovah's Witnesses is that they derive psychological satisfaction from perceiving a coherent pattern in their beliefs'[21]. For believers such as these there is no gap between religion and other interests; there is no balance that can be achieved; their religion maps the world for them and therefore maps the course of their lives[22]. There is thus a wide gap between what was

---

[18] By the 'senior British judiciary' I mean those judges whose judgments can be reported in the law reports. The attitude of judges in the lower courts that are not reported is also important for the work of scholars interested in law and religion. It is, after all, these courts that hear the majority of cases even if their judgments create no precedents. However, since we have little information on the views of these judges, we have no way of knowing whether or not they have the same attitude towards religious belief as the one that seems dominant amongst the senior British judiciary.

[19] [2003] EWHC 2327 at paras 11-12.

[20] J Beckford, *The Trumpet of Prophecy: A Sociological Study of Jehovah's Witnesses* (Oxford, Basil Blackwell, 1975) 196.

[21] Beckford *The Trumpet of Prophecy* at 120.

[22] To some degree this might be said of the place of any religion in a believer's life. However what is different here is the strength of belief and the degree to which belief penetrates every decision in the believer's quotidian life.

probably John's view of the world and the view that the court took. This attitude towards religion is not of course something that is unique to Jehovah's Witnesses. A similar stance is seen, for example, in Hewer's comment on the nature of Islamic education, '[w]hen a Muslim teacher comes to devise a curriculum unit, the starting point will be "what has the Qur'an to say on this subject?"'[23]. Once again a religion provides a non-negotiable direction as to action. However the senior judiciary seem resistant to the notion that a religion can frequently give clear directions to what a believer should do and that those directions should automatically take precedence over anything else.

The argument here is not that the courts regard religious belief as being unimportant. On the contrary we find Mr Justice Munby arguing in an extra-judicial article that '[r]eligion – whatever the particular believer's faith – is no doubt something to be encouraged'[24]. More than that there is a range of judicial *dicta* which emphasise the validity and even value of religious views that the judiciary do not themselves subscribe to. Thus Lord Donaldson notes in *Re W*:

> I personally regard religious or other beliefs which bar any medical treatment or treatment of particular kinds as irrational, but that does not make minors who hold those beliefs any less *Gillick* competent [to make decisions about medical treatment][25].

Equally, Scarman LJ, as he then was, argued that, in relation to the Jehovah's Witness way of life,

> it was not necessarily wrong or contrary to the welfare of children, that they should be brought up in a narrower sphere of life and subject to stricter religious discipline than that enjoyed by most people[26].

However in practice the courts consistently find religious belief that gives an absolute priority to religious precepts over other things troubling. Despite the sentiments expressed by Scarman LJ in *Re T* the Jehovah's Witness mother in the case was only allowed to retain care and control of her children when she gave undertakings that the children would spend Christmas, Easter and their birthdays with their non-Jehovah's Witness

---

[23] C Hewer, 'Schools for Muslims' (2001) 27 *Oxford Review of Education* 515 at 523.

[24] Mr Justice Munby, 'Families Old and New – The Family and Article 8' (2005) 17 *Child and Family Law Quarterly* 487 at 504.

[25] *Re W* [1993] Fam 64 at 80.

[26] *Re T (Minors) (Custody: Religious Upbringing)* (1981) 2 FLR 239 at 245.

father, that she would permit blood transfusions to be used and that the younger child would not be taken to meetings for worship in the Jehovah's Witness Kingdom Hall[27].

Re ST (A Minor) is a case that concerned a child who was living with his mother in a community that was part of the religious group, The Family[28]. Ward LJ in his judgement noted that the mother's

> closing words to me were to plead with me not to denigrate the Law of Love [The Family's central tenet of faith]. It was an extraordinary observation from her. I would have expected her to plead with me not to remove her son... But NT did not. It was as if the integrity of the Law of Love was more important to her than S [her son]. Where is her sense of priorities?

It seems possible and even probable that in fact NT did not, in Ward LJ's terms, put her child before her loyalty to the Law of Love. Abraham, after all, did not put Isaac before his loyalty to what he understood to be God's wishes[29]. Nevertheless, when Ward LJ made an order permitting NT to retain care and control of her son, like the court in *Re T (A Minor)*, he did so subject to a number of conditions, one being that NT was required to say that she put the welfare of her son before her commitment to The Family.

In *Re W* Balcombe LJ quoted with approval Ward J's observation in the unreported case of *Re E*, a case concerning a Jehovah's Witness minor who wished to refuse blood transfusions, that 'this court ... should be very slow to allow an infant to martyr himself'.[30] It seems unlikely

---

[27] Christmas, Easter and birthdays are not things celebrated by Jehovah's Witnesses. The result of the judgement is to allow the mother to keep care and control of the child but not bring it up in the Jehovah's Witness faith. It should be noted that these conditions were offered by the mother and not imposed on her (at 249-250). However there seems to be little doubt that she would have not retained care and control of the children if she had not made these concessions.

[28] This case is not reported. My analysis is based on a copy of the judgement given to me by members of The Family. For a more detailed analysis of this judgement see A Bradney, 'Faced by Faith' in P Oliver, S Douglas Scott and V Tadros (eds) *Faith in Law: Essays in Legal Theory* (Oxford, Hart Publishing, 2000) 89 at 96-98. This judgement is of particular interest because of its length and the degree of attention that Ward LJ gives to the question of religion. The full judgement is 278 A4 pages long and has a further 22 pages that were added later. In the judgement Ward LJ says that the hearing took 75 days and that he took nearly a year to write the judgment. Again according to Ward LJ's judgment, there were over 10,000 pages of typed written evidence whilst he made 2000 pages of notes from the oral evidence. 7 expert witnesses were heard and their evidence is summarised in Ward LJ's judgment.

[29] Genesis 22: 10.

[30] *Re W* [1992] Fam 64 at 88.

that E would have seen his death as martyrdom[31]. Martyrdom, according to the Oxford English Dictionary, is something that occurs when death is the penalty for refusing to renounce one's faith[32]. The notion of martyrdom carries with it a connotation of evangelising for one's faith. The deaths of the early Christian martyrs were public events[33]. It is difficult to see that a contemporary Jehovah's Witness decision to refuse blood transfusions is of the same order of things. Death may be made more likely by such a refusal but will rarely be made absolutely certain. The medical literature is replete with material about alternative treatments, albeit medically less satisfactory treatments, that are available for Jehovah's Witnesses[34]. Where death does occur, it is a largely private matter that is of consequence only to the Witness themselves, their family and friends. Moreover, in the context of the faith, the decision to refuse transfusions does not seem unreasonable. Given the notions that transfusions are divinely forbidden and that our behaviour in this world will have an impact on what happens to us in that which is to come after death, refusing transfusions seems a rational choice. Yet, despite all of this, the term 'martyrdom' does seem an apt characterisation of how the judiciary see some manifestations of faith.

For the senior British judiciary some religions fall outside the pale of acceptable, moderate faiths. This does not usually lead to them to treat these religions with hostility[35]. However, it does put in question the ability of the judges to fully comprehend the people who are appearing before the court[36]. Acknowledging the importance of faith is one thing; understanding how it works in the lives of those who are very different from you is another. If this is so the policy imperatives noted above that

---

[31] In *Re P* [2003] EWHC 2327 at para 8 Mr Justice Johnson notes that when E reached the age of majority and was able to insist on his views about medical treatment being respected he did in fact die.

[32] Oxford English Dictionary <http://www.oed.com/>.

[33] See, for example, W Frend, *Martyrdom and Persecution in the Early Church* (Oxford, Basil Blackwell, 1965).

[34] See, for example, J Marsh and D Bevan 'Haematological Care of the Jehovah's Witness Patient'(2002) 119 *Journal of Haematology* 25-37. Jehovah's Witnesses also stress the medical advantages of avoiding the medical risks that accompany blood transfusions (see, for example the Watchtower, Official Web Site of Jehovah's Witnesses, http://www.watchtower.org/).

[35] Latey J's description of Scientology as being 'immoral and socially obnoxious' and 'corrupt, sinister and dangerous' is unusual in this respect (*Re B and G* [1985] FLR 134 at 157).

[36] It is, for example, unlikely that the judiciary have the 'anguished feelings' about the future, world peace or the stability of important social institutions that Beckford describes as being typical for Jehovah's Witnesses (Beckford *The Trumpet of Prophecy* at 165).

lies behind much work in the area of law and religion could be impeded in its application by the inability of the senior judiciary to empathise with some forms of religion within United Kingdom society.

Respecting Religions

The scepticism that I have expressed so far concerns the climate within which arguments about the relationship between religion and law will be received. For the final doubt that I have about the possibilities for any easy success in the analysis of law and religion if that work is policy oriented I want to return to Williams' lecture on the recognition of religious laws and religions by the state.

In his lecture Williams argued against a society where:

> certain kinds of affiliation are marginalised or privatised to the extent that what is produced is a ghettoised pattern of social life in which particular sorts of interests and of reasoning are tolerated as private matters but never granted legitimacy in public as part of a continuing debate about shared goods and priorities.

In the conclusion to the same lecture Williams developed this theme, observing that,

> a universalist Enlightenment system has to weigh the possible consequences of ghettoising and effectively disenfranchising a minority, at a real cost to overall social cohesion and creativity[37].

The general arguments that religions as a whole and some religions in particular see themselves as having only a peripheral place in contemporary society and that this is both wrong in principle and damaging to society are familiar ones that have a number of different intellectual sources.

Figures as diverse as Raz and Taylor have argued for the need for both a wider and deeper recognition of cultural groups (which could include religious groups) within society. Thus Taylor writes that we should 'all *recognize* the equal value of different cultures, that we not only let them survive, but acknowledge their *worth*'[38]. Raz makes a somewhat different argument, suggesting that 'it is in the interest of every person to be fully integrated in a cultural group' since '[o]nly through being socialized in

---

[37] Williams, 'Civil and Religious Law in England – A Religious Perspective'
[38] C Taylor, 'The Politics of Recognition' in A Gutmann (ed), *Multiculturalism: Examining the Politics of Recognition*, (Princeton, Princeton University, 2004) 64.

a culture can one tap the options that which give life meaning'[39]. For Raz, in a multicultural society, affirmation of different cultures has greater value than either mere toleration or non-discrimination[40]. From another perspective a liberal society, given Mills' market-place of ideas, is seen to gain the more contributions that are made to public discourse and loses if the width of that discourse is limited or some ideas are treated as incontrovertible[41].

All of the above points would have attractions for at least some commentators working on policy oriented analyses in the field of law and religion. For many of them either religions themselves or having religions in society are seen as being valuable; for such commentators their aim is to achieve the widest possible pursuit of religious freedom in terms of both belief and practice[42]. There are, however, limitations of both politics and sociology on the one hand and ethical principle on the other that would indicate both that some, and perhaps all, religions will, to a greater or lesser degree, feel themselves marginalised in contemporary British society and that some religions should be marginalised if this is to be a liberal society.

The websites of two religions that are the focus of some of the cases discussed above, Jehovah's Witnesses and The Family, contain material about the prospect of an imminent end to the world[43]. Although in both instances discussion about these matters is linked to observations of natural phenomena such as earthquakes the analysis is not grounded on such evidence. Instead the discussion focuses on theological arguments about relatively immediate dramatic future events on earth. Neither the predictions nor the theology that provides the foundation for these predictions will appear attractive to the vast majority in contemporary society. Public discourse is couched in terms that at least attempt to be, in the main, secular and rational. A liberal state demands that we offer 'public reasons' in debate. To:

---

[39] J Raz, 'Multiculturalism: A Liberal Perspective' in *Ethics in the Public Domain: Essays on the Morality of Law and Politics* (Oxford, Clarendon Press, 1994) 177.

[40] Raz, 'Multiculturalism: A Liberal Perspective' at 174-175.

[41] The truth, validity or even inherent value of each of these ideas is irrelevant because we gain both from seeing why ideas are false and from seeing why they are true (J S Mill, 'On Liberty' in J S Mill *Utilitarianism, On Liberty and Considerations on Representative Government* (London, JM Dent, 1972) 78-113.

[42] I would include myself in this group but with the qualification that follows in this essay.

[43] <http://www.watchtower.org/e/20060915/article_02.htm>; <http://www.thefamily.org/endtime/>.

offer fellow citizens "public reasons"... is to undertake two burdens. The first is the requirement that the reasons offered be justificatory: that is, they should be reasons which justify the proposals that they are offered to support.... Second these reasons should also be candidates for free assent by those citizens who will be bound by the proposal. If an argument could not win the assent of others then it cannot be a public reason[44].

Arguments in this discourse are just that; arguments, not statements of apodictic certainty sustained by an appeal to spiritual authority. *Pace* Williams, in contemporary British society certain forms of reasoning, like references to imminent apocalypses predicted in scriptural sources, are tolerated as matters done in private but are not accepted as legitimate in public discourse.

The limitations on what is and what is not acceptable in public discourse are well understood by those religions that engage in reasoning of the sort described above. The Jehovah's Witness website's discussion of issues relating to blood transfusions begins with arguments about healthcare issues in relation to the use of blood transfusions; scriptural arguments against the use of blood transfusions are found much deeper in the website[45]. In reality however, for religions such as the Jehovah's Witnesses or The Family, the rational arguments they raise are irrelevant. Jehovah's Witnesses would refuse blood transfusions even if there were no health risks involved; their reading of biblical sources tells that this is what they must do. In such circumstances some feeling of marginality, to a greater or lesser extent, is inevitable. The form of language they use, the arguments they would like to present and the conclusions they reach are dismissed without serious consideration by the majority of the population. If they are to take part in conversations within society or with the state they must largely use a vocabulary that reflects neither their values nor their commitments. Such religions feel themselves to be marginal in British society because in fact they are marginal to public, political discourse.

Religions such as those that I have described above represent an extreme, albeit significant, example of the place of religions in contemporary British society. More mainstream religions may seem to be more comfortable with the nature of public discourse. However even these religions tend to avoid specifically religious arguments when engaging in public debate.

---

[44] M Festenstein, 'Toleration and Deliberative Politics' in J Horton and S Mendus (eds), *Toleration, Identity and Difference* (London, Palgrave Macmillan, 1999) 148.

[45] <http://www.watchtower.org/e/hb/article_02.htm>.

Thus, for example, although the churches were heavily involved in attempts to oppose the liberalisation of the Sunday trading laws the arguments that they used related to issues such as potential harm to family life rather than references to Biblical prohibitions about what could be done on the Sabbath[46]. A peer who took part in the debates that resulted in the religious education and collective worship provisions of the Education Reform Act 1988 justified his decision to use secular arguments, even though he described himself as being a 'convinced Christian', by referring to the 'secular audience' that there was for his remarks[47]. In a similar fashion, notwithstanding his position as Archbishop of Canterbury, Williams' lecture about the place of religion within the legal system is couched in rational, liberal terms; there are some references to theology but there is almost no theological discussion[48].

Religions that are more comfortable with the demand for rational arguments found in a liberal society suffer less marginalisation. Nevertheless, to the extent that these religions root themselves in faith based on authority, they are separated from the majority in British society who are either overtly secular or merely have a loosely held individual religiosity[49]. In response to this we have seen that Taylor would argue that we should realise that all cultures have value whilst Raz would argue for the affirmation of all cultures. The difficulty with this is that for some and perhaps for many it is precisely the case that, because of their own secularity or individual religiosity, they see no value in religions *qua* religions and that they thus have no wish to affirm them. Toleration, non-discrimination and the right of the believer to practice their own religious belief are one thing; an acceptance of the value of that religion, except as a false idea in the marketplace of ideas, is another matter.

The confusion that can occur when there is an attempt to overstate the place of religion in contemporary British society is exemplified by the Racial and Religious Hatred Act 2006. By making the incitement of religious hatred a specific criminal offence the Act can be seen as an

---

[46] *The Shops Act: Late-Night and Sunday Opening: Report of the Committee of Inquiry into Proposals to Amend the Shops Act (Auld Committee)* (Cmnd 9376, 1984) para 11.

[47] J McHugh, 'The Lords' Will be Done: Interviewing the Powerful in Education' in G Walford (ed), *Researching the Powerful in Education* (London, UCL Press, 1994) 61.

[48] The exception is one brief passage that refers to the place of 'the human as such' in Christianity in particular and the Abrahamic faiths in general.

[49] There is extensive debate about the history of secularisation in Great Britain, its precise nature at present and its likely future. However none of the sources cited in this essay seem to doubt that public debate is largely secular in tone.

attempt to reassure religions about their place within society. In doing
this, it might be argued, the State is seeking to counter any feelings of
marginalisation that religions may have by addressing their specific interests. However closer examination of the terms of the 2006 Act suggests
that in fact the very reverse is more likely to be the result of the application of the Act.

Given the range of existing criminal offences before the passage of the
2006 Act, a number of writers have noted the limited ambit of any new
protection afforded by the Act[50]. However what is more important in the
context of the arguments presented here is what the Act clearly does still
permit. As a result of the 2006 Act a new section 29J of the Public Order
Act 1986 holds that:

> [n]othing in this Part [relating to incitement to religious hatred] shall be read
> or given effect in a way which prohibits or restricts discussion, criticism or
> expressions of antipathy, dislike, ridicule, insult or abuse of particular reli-
> gions or the beliefs or practices of their adherents, or of any other belief
> system or the beliefs or practices of its adherents, or proselytising or urging
> adherents of a different religion or belief system to cease practising their
> religion or belief system.

In so doing the Act emphasises the dominance of secular, liberal discourse in society. Religions can be ridiculed, insulted or abused because
of the centrality that is afforded to debate in liberal societies. Once again
the specifically religious claims of religions are disregarded.

The limitations of the 2006 Act from the perspective of some religions
is very clear. Slaughter, in his analysis of the events that followed the
publication of *The Satanic Verses*, notes both the width of notions of honour in Islamic communities and the importance that is attached to these
ideas in such communities[51]. Similarly Kunzru observes that in some faith
communities 'offending against religion is viewed as a kind of public violence against the believer'[52]. However the 2006 Act does not just fail to
take account of the specific notions of insult and honour that are to be
found in some faith communities; it rejects entirely the notion that there
should be a legal right to protect religions or believers from insult. Being
insulted is part of the possibilities of debate, particularly where that debate

[50] See, for example, K Goodhall 'Incitement to Religious Hatred: All Talk and No
Substance?' (2007) 70 *MLR* 89 at 91 and Richard Clarke's contribution to this volume.
[51] M Slaughter, 'The Salman Rushdie Affair: Apostasy, Honor and Freedom of Speech'
(1993) 79 *Virginia Law Review* 153 at 193-200.
[52] H Kunzru, 'Respecting Authority, Taking Offence' in L Appignaneri (ed) *Free
Expression is No Offence* (London, Penguin Books, 2005) 123.

occurs in a cosmopolitan society where the very nature of what counts as an insult is part of that debate.

Martin argues that '[r]eligion is a mode of activity deploying its own grammar'[53]. However recognising this grammar is precisely what the liberal State cannot do:

> [For the liberal State] [t]o acknowledge higher antecedent [religious] rights is simply to revisit the very foundations of liberal democracy and to gainsay the longstanding secular basis to the State. That debate is over, the Enlightenment happened and religion lost[54].

Conclusion

The doubts described above are doubts about how successful attempts to improve the position of some religious believers will be and doubts about how far those attempts should go. They are not, however, doubts about whether there should be work in this area. The body of academic work that has accumulated over the last few decades has made it clear that there is discrimination against some believers both in British society in general and in the legal system in particular. Some of that discrimination may be unwitting and much is indefensible in principle. In both these instances there should be an attempt to reform the position[55]. However such work is likely to be slow and it should not over-estimate what it can do. In the end '[i]t is not possible for secular politics to address fully the religious needs of individuals or groups for a sense of unconditional acceptance'[56].

[53] D Martin, *Secularization: Towards a Revised Theory* (Aldershot, Ashgate, 2005) 171.

[54] R Ahdar, *Worlds Colliding: Conservative Christians and the Law* (Aldershot, Ashgate) 283.

[55] Who should do this is another matter. To say that academic work is policy-oriented is, of itself, simply to say that it has policy implications. The degree to which academics are or should be concerned with trying to see that those policy implications find a place in actual policy outcomes is another matter. For debate about why and how academics should try to have an impact on policy in the context of geography see R Martin, 'Geography and Public Policy: The Case of the Missing Agenda' (2001) 25 *Progress in Human Geography* 189 and P Dorling and M Shaw 'Geographies of the Agenda: Public Policy, the Discipline and its (Re)"turns"' (2002) 26 *Progress in Human Geography* 629.

[56] S Rockefeller, 'Comment' in A Gutmann (ed), *Multiculturalism: Examining the Politics of Recognition* (Princetoon, Princeton University Press, 1994) 97.

CONCLUSION: NEW HORIZONS

Norman Doe and Russell Sandberg

Introduction

It was not meant to be like this. It was widely anticipated that the effect of the Enlightenment was the decline of religion. Although the Judeo-Christian tradition had been a crucial element in the historical evolution of Europe as a whole, in modern Britain religion was said to have lost its social significance[1]. As Steve Bruce has written 'Individualism threatened the communal basis of religious belief and behaviour, while rationality removed many of the purposes of religion and rendered away many of its beliefs implausible'[2]. Religious activity was seen to have retreated to the private sphere and to have become akin to any other leisure activity. The role of the law was to be minimal, as Hoffmann J commented in 1993, 'the attitude of the English legislator to racing is much more akin to his attitude to religion...it is something to be encouraged but not the business of government'[3]. Simon Brown J made an even more far reaching comment in 1992 observing that there existed a 'well-recognised divide between church and state'.[4] However, these comments by the English judiciary seem rebutted by the plethora of laws concerning religion enacted, interpreted and administered in the early years of the twenty-first century[5].

There has been a step change in England and Wales from passive accommodation to prescriptive regulation[6]. Whether this transformation is desirable is an open question. Although sociological research suggests

---

[1] B Wilson, *Religion in Secular Society* (Middlesex, Penguin 1966) 14; B Wilson, *Religion in Sociological Perspective* (Oxford, Oxford University Press, 1982) 149.

[2] S Bruce, *Religion in the Modern World: From Cathedrals to Cults* (Oxford, Oxford University Press, 1996) 230.

[3] *R v Disciplinary Committee of the Jockey Club ex parte Aga Khan* [1993] 1 WLR 909 at 932.

[4] *R v Chief Rabbi, ex parte Wachmann* [1992] 1 WLR 1036 at 1043.

[5] Indeed, these statements were questionable before recent developments.

[6] M Hill and R Sandberg, 'Is Nothing Sacred? Clashing Symbols in a Secular World' [2007] *PL* 488 at 490; R Sandberg, 'Religion, Society and Law: An Analysis of the Interface between the Law on Religion and the Sociology of Religion' (Cardiff University, doctoral thesis, forthcoming).

that religious vitality 'is likely to be higher in societies where agencies of the state do not significantly regulate the markets for religion', this needs to be weighed against 'the assertion that deregulation leads to abuses of religion, threats to the freedom of thought and attacks on the cohesiveness of society'[7]. Regardless of the view taken, however, analysis of the exact line drawn by the law remains important. Moreover, these wide-ranging changes of the early years of the twenty-first century – both legal and extra-legal – have played a considerable role in causing an expansion in academic interest which has fostered the growth of law and religion as a distinct academic discipline in England and Wales. This is to be welcomed. However, the major changes of recent years have also curtailed scholarship. The pace of change has meant that most attention has been afforded to the content and effect of specific changes whilst the effect upon the larger canvas both in terms of law and in terms of scholarship has been neglected. This collection has sought to redress these two omissions in the existing literature, by providing an analysis of the collective effect of the jurisprudential evolution and an evaluation of the ambit and scope of law and religion as an academic discipline. This concluding reflection therefore seeks to synthesize some of the conclusions made in previous chapters to reflect upon the new horizons for the study of law and religion in England and Wales.

The Legal Step Change

The first theme of this collection is that there has been a step change in the way in which English law regulates religion and that this has, in part, caused the development of law and religion as an area of study. However, a degree of caution is required. As Anthony Giddens has contended, every academic discipline has a 'constructed history':

> Every recognized intellectual discipline has gone through a process of self-legitimization not unlike that involved in the founding of nations. All disciplines have their fictive histories, all are imagined communities which invoke myths of the past as a means of both charting their own internal development and unity, and also drawing boundaries between themselves and other neighbouring disciplines[8].

---

[7] J A Beckford and J T Richardson 'Religion and Regulation' in J A Beckford and N J Demerath (eds), *The Sage Handbook of the Sociology of Religion* (London, Sage, 2007) 396 at 411-412.

[8] A Giddens, *Politics, Sociology and Social Theory* (Cambridge, Polity Press, 1995) 5.

This reminder is important in the context of the study of law and religion in England and Wales. It is tempting to construct a history of law and religion which sees its origins firmly in the Human Rights Act 1998 and the plethora of laws which followed it, most notably the extension of discrimination law to cover religion or belief[9]. However, as Augur Pearce's opening chapter reminds us, this would be a gross over-simplification. Even the most cursory examination of English law illustrates the complex ways in which law and religion interacted in English law long before the advent of the European Convention on Human Rights. Clerical fingerprints on much of English law have faded rather than disappeared.

For instance, although it is clear that the Church of England has lost its monopoly as a vehicle for rites of passage, and that the powers of the ecclesiastical courts have declined, these trends should not be over-exaggerated. In addition to its profound legacy upon the substantive laws and procedures of modern English law, ecclesiastical law remains part of the law of the land and English law continues to recognise various rights for all who are resident in parishes of the Church of England in relation to marriage and burial[10]. Moreover, although there has been a move towards self-governance and autonomy on the part of the established church in England[11], the link between Church and State remains strong: as Bradney has noted although it is often said that there has been a trend towards 'a separation of church and state, religion and law..., allowing a multi-religious country to maintain social stability... [d]etailed enquiry suggests that this separation is in fact far from complete'[12].

This does not mean, however, that the Human Rights Act 1998 should not be seen as a watershed in the legal regulation of religion in England and Wales. In a similar manner as toleration marked a substantial shift from post-Reformation discrimination, the Human Rights Act 1998 encapsulated a considerable shift from passive toleration to the active promotion of religious liberty as a right[13]. Whilst it is true that prior to the

[9] Employment Equality (Religion or Belief) Regulations 2003 SI 2003/1660; Equality Act 2006.

[10] It is commonly understood that parishioners have the right to be married in the parish church (*Argar v Holdsworth* (1758) 2 Lee 515, subject to the individual cleric's conscience (Matrimonial Causes Act 1965. Parishioners also have a right to burial, dependent upon space (*Kemp v Wickes* (1809) 3 Phil Ecc 26; Burial Law Amendments Act 1880).

[11] Church of England Assembly (Powers) Act 1919; see also Welsh Church Act 1914.

[12] A Bradney, 'Faced by Faith' in P Oliver *et al* (ed), *Faith in Law* (Oxford, Hart, 2000) 89.

[13] For a fuller reflection see M Hill and R Sandberg, 'Is Nothing Sacred?'

Human Rights Act 1998, Parliament legislated in an *ad hoc* manner to provide partial rights, duties and obligations such rights did not amount to a general positive right to religious liberty. Recognition of conscientious objections to military service[14], oath taking[15], and abortion[16], and exemptions from generally applicable rules concerned with the wearing of protective headgear[17] and rules on slaughter[18], operated within the structure of a fundamentally restrictive law on religion[19]. The general position remained that Britain was 'not a country where everything is forbidden except what is expressly permitted' but was rather 'a country where everything is permitted except what is expressly forbidden';[20] the law's starting point was that 'every citizen has a right to do what he likes, unless restrained by the common law ... or by statute'[21]. At common law, in the absence of a legal prohibition people were permitted to do as they wished[22]. The legislature and judiciary generally adopted a stance of passive accommodation as opposed to prescriptive regulation[23].

The Human Rights Act 1998 introduced into domestic law the notion of religious freedom as a human right. It gave '*further effect* to the rights and freedoms guaranteed under the European Convention on Human Rights'[24]: whereas previously the ECHR had only the status of an international Treaty (albeit with a right to individual petition to Strasbourg vested in the individual against their State), the 1998 Act provided domestic courts with the 'jurisdiction directly to enforce the rights and freedoms under the Convention'[25]. As Charlotte Smith's chapter explains, there is an inherent culture clash between the organic common law approach and the codification of rights embodied in the ECHR. The different approach required by the Human Rights Act 1998 in terms of

---

[14] Military Service Act 1916, s2.

[15] Promissory Oaths Act 1868; Oaths Act 1978.

[16] Abortion Act 1967, s4.

[17] Employment Act 1989, s11; Motorcycle Crash Helmets Religious Exemption Act 1976, now see Road Traffic Act 1988 s16.

[18] Welfare of Animals (Slaughter or Killing) Regulations 1995 (SI 1995/731) Reg 2.

[19] N Doe, 'National Identity, the Constitutional Tradition and the Structures of Law on Religion in the United Kingdom' in Proceedings of the European Consortium of Church and State Research, *Religions in European Union Law* (Luxembourg, Guiffre Editore, 1997) 109.

[20] *Malone v Metropolitan Police Commissioner* [1979] Ch 344.

[21] *AG v Guardian Newspapers Ltd (No 2)* [1990] 1 A.C 109.

[22] See S Poulter, *Asian Traditions and English Law* (Trentham Books Stoke-on-Trent 1990) 1.

[23] M Hill and R Sandberg, 'Is Nothing Sacred?' at 490.

[24] Long title. Emphasis added.

[25] *Waddington v Miah (Otherwise Ullah)* [1974] 2 All ER 377.

interpretation is well expressed by the Court of Appeal in *Aston Cantlow Parochial Church Council v Wallbank*[26]:

> Our task is not to cast around in the European Human Rights Reports like black-letter lawyers seeking clues. In the light of s 2(1) of the Human Rights Act 1998 it is to draw out the broad principles which animate the Convention[27].

The predictions of many commentators in relation to the Act seem to have been fulfilled. For instance, Anthony Bradney forecast a dramatic 'increase in litigation about rights' which would make the gap between religious beliefs and modern legal discourse 'ever clearer'[28], while Mark Hill foresaw that courts would 'find themselves looking at perennial questions but with new eyes' and would find themselves brought 'more clearly into the political arena where policy arguments [would] be of greater significance'[29]. The two major House of Lords decisions on Article 9 to date, *Williamson* and *Begum*[30], suggest that although the incorporation of a positive right to religious freedom into domestic law by the Human Rights Act 1998 may not have yet affected the actual decisions reached by the judiciary, it has affected the reasoning[31]. Although early domestic cases followed a Strasbourg-complaint approach in focussing upon the question of whether the interference with the right was justified under Article 9(2), later cases have diverged from the Strasbourg jurisprudence to focus quite unnecessarily upon the question of whether there was interference with the right under Article 9(1).

The reasoning of the House of Lords in *Begum* provided the tipping point. Their lordships gave general effect to the 'filtering device' used at Strasbourg which may be styled the 'specific situation rule'[32]. This rule states that where the claimant has voluntary submitted to a voluntary system of rules, this 'specific situation' may limit the right they would otherwise enjoy under Article 9. Although Strasbourg institutions used this rule

---

[26] [2001] 2 All ER 363. This Court of Appeal judgment was later overturned on each and every substantive issue by the House of Lords: [2003] UKHL 37, [2004] 1 A.C 546.

[27] Per Morritt V-C at para 44.

[28] A Bradney, 'Faced by Faith' in P Oliver *et al* (ed) *Faith in Law* (Oxford, Hart, 2000) 104-105.

[29] M Hill 'A New Dawn for Freedom of Religion' in M Hill (ed) *Religious Liberty and Human Rights* (University of Wales Press, Cardiff, 2002) 13.

[30] *R v Secretary of State for Education and Employment and others ex parte Williamson* [2005] UKHL 15, and *R (on the application of Begum) v Headteacher and Governors of Denbigh High School* [2006] UKHL 15.

[31] M Hill and R Sandberg, 'Is Nothing Sacred?'; R Sandberg, 'Controversial Recent Claims to Religious Liberty' (2008) 124 *LQR* 213.

[32] See further, ibid.

restrictively, applying it only in relation to cases where there were contractual relations (such as those involving employees and university students)[33], the House of Lords in *Begum* went noticeably further, applying the rule to the case of a school child without questioning whether she had voluntarily submitted to her situation and noting in broad terms that:

> The Strasbourg institutions have not been at all ready to find an interference with the right to manifest religious belief in practice or observance where a person has voluntarily accepted an employment or role which does not accommodate that practice or observance and there are other means open to the person to practise or observe his or her religion without undue hardship or inconvenience. ...
>
> Even if it be accepted that the Strasbourg institutions have erred on the side of strictness in rejecting complaints of interference, there remains a coherent and remarkably consistent body of authority which our domestic courts must take into account and which shows that interference is not easily established[34].

Subsequent lower court decisions concerning Article 9 have borne out these words: numerous claims have failed on the grounds of no interference[35]. The long-standing notion that the 'right to resign' is the 'ultimate protection' of religious freedom in the workplace[36] has been extended to the education sphere and beyond. Criticisms in relation to employment that relying solely on this 'somewhat drastic remedy may be to fail to provide adequate protection to religious interests'[37] are multiplied outside that context. Simply ruling that a prohibition on wearing religious dress or symbols in school does not affect a pupil's religious freedom because they can move school seems harsh. The current case law suggests that the reasoning of *Begum* this has bred uncertainty and constrained the Article 9 right[38].

It is not, however, only the interpretation of Article 9 that has led to uncertainty. The Human Rights Act (and culture) has inspired, in part,

---

[33] See e.g. *Ahmad v United Kingdom* (1981) 4 EHRR 126; *Karaduman v Turkey* (1993) 74 DR 93.

[34] *R (on the application of Begum) v Headteacher and Governors of Denbigh High School* [2006] UKHL 15, *Per* Lord Bingham, paras 23-24.

[35] Eg. *R (on the application of X) v Y School* [2006] EWHC (Admin) 298; *R (on the Application of Playfoot (A Child) v Millais School Governing Body* [2007] EWHC Admin 1698.

[36] See L Vickers, *Religious Freedom, Religious Discrimination and the Workplace* (Oxford, Hart, 2008) 45.

[37] Ibid 46.

[38] R Sandberg, 'Controversial Recent Claims to Religious Liberty' at 217.

other legislative developments that have transformed the face of religion law. The most significant of these changes are explored in the chapters by Mark Hill, Pauline Roberts, Peter Luxton and Richard Clarke. Mark Hill's chapter on the Civil Partnership Act 2004 refers to a development which like the Human Rights Act 1998 has had significant impact upon the established Church. The Civil Partnership Act 2004 in creating a new legally recognised human relationship for same-sex couples marks a major departure in English law and the thin line the Act takes to creating a status with 'virtually identical legal consequences to marriage'[39] whilst 'at the same time, demonstrating support for the long established institution of marriage'[40] will doubtless keep the courts and commentators occupied for some time. This includes religious groups and believers. Although the Act itself only mentions religion to exclude it, this does not mean that the Act will have no effect on religious bodies. Regardless of their own doctrines, religious bodies have to accept the legal rights of civil partners; indeed, for those bodies who are opposed to homosexual practice rather than homosexuality *per se*, the question of whether their ministers and other employees can enter into civil partnerships raises interesting questions. Those questions may also shed light upon the broader question of what the definitive element of a civil partnership is and how it precisely relates to marriage.

The Civil Partnership Act 2004 also highlights the potential conflict between prohibiting discrimination on grounds of sexual orientation and the freedom of religion. This conflict comes to the fore again in Pauline Roberts' chapter which explores recent developments in discrimination law, prohibiting discrimination on grounds of religion or belief[41] and sexual orientation[42]. The substantive law and the exemptions afforded have already produced an abundance of case law, especially at the level of employment tribunals[43]. Further litigation in respect of the more recent laws extending the law to goods and services is also to be expected. The case law to-date in relation to religious discrimination reveals that although some indirect discrimination claims about

---

[39] *Secretary of State for Work and Pensions v M* [2006] 1 FCR 497 at para 99.

[40] *Wilkinson v Kitzinger* [2006] EWHC (Fam) 2022 at para 50.

[41] Employment Equality (Religion or Belief) Regulations 2003 SI 2003/1660; Equality Act 2006, part 2

[42] Employment Equality (Sexual Orientation) Regulations 2003 SI 2003/1661; Equality Act (Sexual Orientation) Regulations 2007.

[43] See R Sandberg, 'Flags, Beards and Pilgrimages: A Review of the Early Cases on Religious Discrimination' (2007) 9 *Ecc LJ* 87.

working hours and holy days have been successful[44], a number of claims
have failed on the basis of lack of evidence[45]. This may suggest that
although the new law has resulted in much litigation, it has not substantially increased religious freedom. In relation to the religious exemptions, it is noteworthy that in relation to both religion or belief[46] and
sexual orientation[47] discrimination, the narrowness of religious exemptions has been stressed[48].

The extension of equality law to prohibit both discrimination on
grounds of religion and sexual orientation has been replicated in the
criminal law by new laws prohibiting stirring up hatred on grounds of
religion[49] and sexual orientation[50]. Richard Clarke's chapter exploring
the balancing of freedom of religion and freedom of expression examines
not only the Racial and Religious Hatred Act 2006 but also the abolition
of the blasphemy laws[51]. It is a sign of the pace and extent of change in
religion law that one of the few laws on religion that are commonly
known no longer exists and that in their place there is a plethora of little-
known laws. In addition to a number of statutory provisions, enacted in
the nineteenth and early twentieth centuries[52], numerous public order
offences have been used in the context of religion: prosecutions have

---

[44] See, eg. *Khan v G & S Spencer Group* ET, Case Number 1803250/2004 (12 January
2005); *Williams-Drabble v Pathway Care Solutions* ET, Case Number: 2601718/2004
(2 December 2004); *Fugler v MacMillan – London Hairstudios Limited* ET, Case Number:
2205090/2004 (21-23 June 2005).

[45] *Williams v South Central Limited* ET, Case Number: 2306989/2003 (16 June 2004);
Baggs v Fudge ET, Case Number: 1400114/2005 (23 March 2005); *Devine v Home
Office* ET, Case Number 2302061/2004 (9 August 2004); *Ferri v Key Languages Limited*
ET, Case Number: 2302172/2004 (12 July 2004); *Mohamed v Virgin Trains* ET, Case
Number: 2201814/2004 (12-14 October 2004; 20 May 2005); *Eweida v British Airways*
E T Case Number: 2702689/06 (19 December 2007); *Harris v NKL Automotive Ltd &
Anor* [2007] UKEAT/0134/07/DM; 2007 WL 2817981 (3 October 2007); *McClintock v
Department of Constitutional Affairs* [2007] UKEAT/0223/07/CEA; 2007 WL 3130902
(31 October 2007).

[46] *Hender v Prospects for People with Learning Disabilities*, ET Case Number:
2902090/2006 (12th May 2008); *Sheridan v Prospects for People with Learning Disabilities*, ET Case Number: 2901366/06 (12th May 2008)

[47] *R (Amicus MSF Section) v Secretary of State for Trade and Industry* [2004] EWHC
860; *Reaney v Hereford Diocesan Board of Finance* [2007] ET Case Number 1602844/2006
(17 July 2007).

[48] See, generally, R Sandberg and N Doe, 'Religious Exemptions in Discrimination
Law' (2007) 66(2) *CLJ* 302.

[49] Racial and Religious Hatred Act 2006.

[50] Criminal Justice and Immigration Act 2008 s74.

[51] Criminal Justice and Immigration Act 2008 s79.

[52] Such as the Ecclesiastical Courts Jurisdiction Act 1860, section 36 of the Offences
against the Persons Act 1861 and section 7 of the Burial Laws Amendment Act 1880.

been made under the Public Order Act 1986,[53] under the Protection from the Harassment Act 1997[54] and the common law offence of breach of the peace[55]. Moreover, since 2001, the criminal law has recognised that the sentence for specific crimes may be increased if that crime is racially or religiously aggravated[56].

The law on religious charitable trusts, the other area of religion law which is most commonly known (largely since it is usually taught as part of a core subject on undergraduate syllabuses), has also changed. Although the Charities Act 2006, like the Racial and Religious Hatred Act 2006, had a long legislative history, this did not result in legal certainty when the Act finally reached the statute books. As Peter Luxton's chapter elucidates, the provisions of the Charities Act 2006 concerning religion are far from clear and this seems to be exacerbated rather than clarified by the interpretation offered by the Charity Commission. In addition to concerns about public benefit, the definition of religion provided by the Act is also controversial. For instance, whilst the Charities Act 2006 speaks in terms of 'a god', the Commission in its decision on the Church of Scientology spoke in terms of a 'supreme being'[57], and their most recent literature speaks of 'a divine or transcendental being, entity or principle'[58]. At the very least, this spreads confusion. Definitional confusion seems to be a recurring concern in the new body of religion law[59], especially since the different legal definitions of religion intended to 'reflect, to some extent, the different purposes that

[53] See, e g *Horseferry Road Metropolitan Stipendiary Magistrate ex parte Siadatan* [1991] 1 QB 260; *Percy v DPP* [2001] EWHC Admin 1125; *Norwood v DDP* [2003] EWHC Admin 1564; *Hammond v DDP* [2004] EWHC Admin 69; *Dehal v CPS* [2005] EWHC Admin 2154.

[54] See, e g *Christ of Latter Day Saints v Price* [2004] EWHC Admin 325; *Singh v Bhaker* [2006] Fam Law 1026.

[55] See, e g *Wise v Dunning* [1902] 1 KB 167.

[56] The Crime and Disorder Act 1998 created a new category of 'racially aggravated criminal offences'. Under section 39 of the Anti-Terrorism, Crime and Security Act 2001 (post 9-11), this category becomes 'racially or religiously aggravated criminal offences'. This applies to the law on assault, criminal damage, public order offences and offences under the Protection from Harassment Act 1997.

[57] <http://www.charity-commission.gov.uk/Library/registration/pdfs/cosfulldoc.pdf>

[58] Charity Commission, *Public Benefit and the Advancement of Religion: draft supplementary guidance for consultation*, February 2008, at 13; and see Charity Commission, *Analysis of the law underpinning* Public Benefit and the Advancement of Religion, February 2008, para 2.21-2.24.

[59] R Sandberg, 'Religion, Society and Law: An Analysis of the Interface between the Law on Religion and the Sociology of Religion' (Cardiff University, doctoral thesis, forthcoming). See, in relation to discrimination law, P Griffith, 'Protecting the Absence of Religious Belief? The New Definition of Religion or Belief in Equality Legislation' (2007) (2) 3 *Religion & Human Rights* 149.

the laws are intended to have'[60], do not refer to one another. It seems that the purposive definition found in section 57 of the Equality Act 2006, for example, may be beneficial when assessing whether the purpose of a charity or trust is religious.

This failure to understand the connections between different parts of religion law is also a problem for academics since reference to specific developments in isolation undermines claim that law and religion exists as a discipline: it supports the view that law and religion is simply a Frankenstein-like combination of other legal disciplines and that law and religion should be subject to criticisms similar to that made of family law lacking 'a clear set of organising principles'[61]. It is therefore imperative that scholarly attention be paid to the collective effect of the rights-driven protection of religious liberty ushered in by the Human Rights Act 1998 and subsequent developments. As Frank Cranmer's chapter from a Quaker's perspective shows, by examining human rights, the Human Rights Act 1998 and recent calls for a new British Bill of Rights and Responsibilities, there has been 'a decisive shift in public policy-making from Judaeo-Christian ethics to a common moral paradigm'. Moreover, religious perspectives on human rights may be helpful in understanding rights as co-existing with duties and subsisting together in the same person, as two sides of the same coin[62].

Given the calls to move beyond the Human Rights Act examined by Cranmer and reforms in discrimination law towards a single Equality Bill[63], it is also vital to recognise that the development of religion law is on-going. David Harte's chapter, employing a model of pluralism to evaluate the current position of English law, suggests that further developments are to be welcomed since a thoroughly plural system has yet to be achieved. A comparison with the law relating to sexual orientation may be telling in this respect[64]. As Glennon has noted[65], it is possible to

---

[60] House of Lords debate, 13 July 2005 col 1107-1108.

[61] G Douglas, *An Introduction to Family Law* (Oxford, Claredon Press, 2004) vii.

[62] For further reflection, see e.g, N Doe, 'Canonical Approaches to Human Rights in Anglican Churches' in M Hill (ed), *Religious Liberty & Human Rights* (Cardiff, University of Wales Press, 2002) 185.

[63] Labour Party Manifesto 2005, *Britain Forward Not Back*, 112. Legislation is expected shortly.

[64] The same process from legal prohibition through legal tolerance to legal promotion has occurred in relation to sexual orientation, albeit that tolerance came much later in respect of the latter.

[65] L Glennon, 'Displacing the "Conjugal Family" in Legal Policy – A Progressive Move?' (2005) 17 *Child and Family Law Quarterly* 244; L Glennon, 'Strategizing for the Future Through the Civil Partnership Act' (2006) 33 *Journal for Law and Society* 244.

identify a journey which several countries have taken in relation to same sex couples[66]: first, the law removes criminal offences prohibiting same-sex activity; second, it bestows upon same-sex couples a growing number of rights; third, it creates a status equivalent to but different than marriage for homosexual couples; and fourth, it permits them the right to marry. English law has currently reached the third stage in relation to both sexual orientation and religion. In relation to the latter, religions other than the established Church have experienced a move from legal sanction through legal disinterest to legal promotion but the establishment of the Church of England means that there is not complete equality. However, it may well be that the utopian final stage is not obtainable or even that it is not advisable. Law reform does not offer a magic wand that operates within a legal vacuum. Existing imperfections and compromises may serve religious liberty better than codified specific rights which lack flexibility subtlety and nuance. A contextual understanding of the effect of recent changes in religion law may provide an important starting point for examining future reform proposals.

It is vital, however, that the study of law and religion in England and Wales does not become too domestic in outlook. Many of the changes addressed in this volume were motivated or inspired by supra-national bodies. The European Court of Human Rights and other international bodies, at both a global and a regional level, have clearly influenced the growth of religion law in England and Wales. The case law of the European Court of Human Rights has regarded Article 9 as one of the foundations of a 'democratic society' and 'one of the most vital elements that go to make up the identity of believers and their conception of life, but it is also a precious asset for atheists, agnostics, sceptics and the unconcerned'[67]. Indeed, more recent cases show a new-found confidence on the part of Strasbourg with the Court, for example, taking 'a broader view of what amounts to an interference' in relation to Article 9[68], which contrasts sharply with the domestic interpretation post-*Begum*. Moreover, the Grand Chamber in *Refah Partisi v Turkey*[69] made it clear that States are required to facilitate religious freedom:

---

[66] J Herring, *Family Law* (Third edition, Essex, Pearson, 2007) 66.

[67] *Kokkinakis v Greece* (1994) 17 EHRR 397, at para 31.

[68] S Knights, *Freedom of Religion, Minorities and the Law* (Oxford, Oxford University Press, 2007) 44. See, eg. *Thlimmenos v Greece* (2001) 31 EHRR 15; *Sahin v Turkey* (2005) 41 EHRR 8.

[69] (2003) 37 EHRR 1.

in democratic societies, in which several religions coexist within one and the same population, it may be necessary to place restrictions on this freedom in order to reconcile the interests of the various groups and ensure that everyone's beliefs are respected. The Court has frequently emphasised the State's role as the neutral and impartial organiser of the exercise of various religions, faiths and beliefs, and stated that this role is conducive to public order, religious harmony and tolerance in a democratic society. It also considers that the State's duty of neutrality and impartiality is incompatible with any power on the State's part to assess the legitimacy of religious beliefs and that it requires the State to ensure mutual tolerance between opposing groups[70].

In addition to developments in the Council of Europe, the impact of the European Union should not be forgotten. Membership of the EU entails acceptance of religious diversity[71] and the prohibition of discrimination on grounds of religion[72]. Indeed, it has been suggested that it is possible to speak of a 'common law on religion in the European Union'[73]. As Alexandra Pimor's chapter explains, it is possible to talk about a religious citizenship and a spiritual dimension to EU citizenship.

Moreover, in addition to pressure on the State from 'above', there is also increasingly pressure from 'below' as the chapter by Javier Oliva and David Lambert makes clear. Decentralisation of political power means that laws on religion may be made at sub-State levels. Religion laws may differ within one State. The existence of regional 'ecclesiastical law' (in a continental European sense) adds a further dimension of complexity in relation to understanding religion law. Changes in religion law thus need to be understood not only in their national context but in a supra- and sub- national context. The increasing complexity and level of regulation provides much for law and religion academics to study[74] but it is vital that in addition to the study of individual developments, attention is also afforded to general trends.

---

[70] Para 91.

[71] See, e.g., Treaty of Amsterdam, Appendix: Declaration on the Status of Churches and Non-confessional Organisations.

[72] See Council Directive 2000/78/EC.

[73] N Doe, 'Towards a Common Law on Religion in the European Union (2009) 37 (H2) *Religion, State and Society* (147).

[74] Indeed, there are important areas of religion law that space has prevented this volume from analysing such as developments in education, immigration and employment law.

The Challenges for Scholarship

The second major theme of this collection is how the step change in the regulation of religion affects its study. This theme is implicit in the chapters describing various aspects of the new religion law. The pace of change poses clear challenges: the major legislative reforms of recent years have led to and will most probably continue to lead to an overabundance of litigation. This coupled with further changes on the horizon means that there will in all probability be much to occupy scholars in this field. A key theme of this collection is that such work should not become too isolated and piecemeal since developments in one part of religion law may have much to learn from developments in other parts. Reinventing the wheel should be avoided. Further, the chapters discussed above have clear implications for academics engaged in studies of law and religion however narrowly or broadly those studies are defined. For instance, Oliva and Lambert's chapter on 'regional ecclesiastical law' has clear ramifications for writers in this field, questioning the last part of the problematic phrase 'Church and State'[75].

Before focussing on some of the opportunities and challenges for scholars, however, it is worth recognising that the changes elucidated also have clear consequences for religious groups themselves (and for individuals be they religious or not). For instance, as Oliva and Lambert explain, the ramifications of 'regional ecclesiastical law' in terms of lobbying and dialogue render it vital that religious bodies know the appropriate government level to communicate with. The question of how the law affects and is affected by specific religious groups is a key theme of the chapters that follow. Norman Doe's chapter illustrates the importance of the laws and regulatory instruments created by religious groups themselves. The content, interpretation and enforcement of religious law reflect communal religious identity. Moreover, as Doe's chapter makes plain, religious law can serve as an ecumenical and interfaith tool for mutual understanding and collaboration and, therefore, perhaps for the harmonisation that religion laws seek within society.

These chapters are also important in terms of scholarship. Although Doe's chapter is not the only one in this collection that touches upon religious law, the overwhelming focus of this volume on religion law is

---

[75] The reference to the word 'Church' is problematic in an age of religious diversity. The use of the term by the judiciary proved problematic, for example, when it was applied uncritically to Islamic religious practice in *Ibrahim Esmael v Abdool Carrim Peermamode* [1908] AC 526 at 535.

symptomatic of the discipline of law and religion as a whole in England and Wales. Indeed, this emphasis is to be expected given the pace of secular legal change. However, the significant attention afforded to the lecture by the Archbishop of Canterbury, Rowan Williams, on 'Civil and Religious Law in England'[76], which many chapters comment upon, means that it may well be the case that interest and scholarship on religious law in England and Wales may blossom. Indeed, as the first three chapters of this collection make clear, the establishment of the Church of England renders any precise distinction between religion law and religious law impossible. Thus, answering the question of how far English law does and does not (and should and should not) accommodate religious difference *necessarily* requires reference to religious law.

Doe's chapter illustrates, with reference to the laws and regulatory instruments of Christian churches, the value of comparative religious law in terms of scholarship: in addition to enabling writers within a single tradition to contextualise their work, the category of 'Christian law' also provides a point of comparison for those working in the fields of Islamic, Jewish and Hindu law[77]. Moreover, the study of religious law may shed light upon the meaning and nature of law itself. It is unsurprising therefore but significant that many of the moves towards interdisciplinary study, theoretically[78] and empirically[79], have occurred in relation to the study of religious law. The need for an interdisciplinary approach, particularly the value of a sociological approach, is the theme of the chapter by Russell Sandberg and Rebecca Catto.

Sandberg and Catto's chapter returns to one of the main themes of this collection: lamenting academic isolationism[80]. In this context, it is the gulf between law and religion and the sociology of religion which is focussed upon and the chapter explains the need for a genuinely interdisciplinary approach to the relationship between religion, law and society.

---

[76] R Williams, 'Civil and Religious Law in England – A Religious Perspective' Available at <http://www.archbishopofcanterbury.org/1575>. The lecture has subsequently been published see: (2008) 10(3) ECC LJ 262.

[77] See further, N Doe, 'Modern Church Law' in J Witte and F S Alexander, *Christianity and Law* (Cambridge, Cambridge University Press, 2008) 271.

[78] E.g A Huxley, *Religion, Law and Tradition: Comparative Studies in Religious Law* (Oxford, Routledge, 2002)

[79] E.g A Bradney and F Cownie, *Living Without Law: An Ethnography of Quaker Decision-Making Dispute Avoidance and Dispute Resolution* (Aldershot, Ashgate, 2000); W Menski, *Hindu Law: Beyond Tradition and Modernity* (Oxford, Oxford University Press, 2003); G Arthur, *Law, Liberty and Church* (Aldershot, Ashgate, 2006).

[80] On which see, more broadly, A Bradney, 'Law as a Parasitic Discipline' (1998) 25(1) *Journal of Law and Society* 71 at 80.

However, a considerable degree of caution is required: over-reliance on sociology results in work which is 'law-lite'; over-reliance on law risks prostituting the sociological imagination to do law's bidding. It follows that there remains a need for black-letter legal analysis. Interdisciplinary work should build upon rather than replace local, technical, legal knowledge of religion. This is not to say, of course, that insights from another discipline may not challenge legal conclusions. A sociological approach may be valuable in this respect providing methodological insights, highlighting the social effects of regulation and contextualising legal change in the context of wider social change. Also important, though, is the contribution that law and religion can make outside the Law School, not least by the simple reminder that most of the religious stories found in news headlines have a legal dimension.

As Anthony Bradney's chapter examines, law and religion scholarship can also make a contribution outside the university in terms of work that has policy implications and work that is policy-orientated[81]. However, as Bradney notes, there are a number of obstacles to this endeavour. These relate largely to issues of understanding. He notes that the public debate takes place at such a low level and is ridden with basic errors, that the senior judiciary seem unable to empathise with some forms of religion and that the State has problems in recognising the 'grammar' of some religious groups. Given the number of complexities, ambiguities, and, sometimes, contradictions found in English religion law and the pace of legal change, a lack of knowledge is perhaps unsurprising. It is often linked to what Rowan Williams referred to as need to avoid 'vexatious appeals to religious scruple'. The fear of the sham claim or the 'obdurate believer'[82] prompts authorities to rely on 'filtering devices' to exclude claims from the outset. This seems to be the motive for the expansion of the 'specific situation' rule in *Begum* and for the increased willingness of courts (and it seems the Charities Commission) to confuse the appropriate question of whether the claimant is acting *in* good faith with the inappropriate question of whether their belief *is a* good faith[83].

---

[81] As he notes, in many cases this has been the explicit or implicit aim of law and religion scholarship and Bradney has warned elsewhere that this is problematic, suggesting that law and religion writers need to seek 'not a solution to a problem, but, rather, a description of a situation': A Bradney, 'Politics and Sociology: New Research Agendas for the Study of law and Religion' in R O'Dair and A Lewis (eds) *Law and Religion* (Oxford, Oxford University Press, 2001) 65 at 81.

[82] For a discussion of obdurate believers see A Bradney, 'Faced by Faith' in P Oliver *et al* (ed), *Faith in Law* (Oxford, Hart, 2000) 89.

[83] On which see R Sandberg, 'Controversial Recent Claims to Religious Liberty'.

The obstacles elucidated by Bradney, together with other challenges to scholarship expressed throughout this volume, present a challenge to the blossoming law and religion academic community which should be faced. There is, of course, no one simple answer but a way forward may be achieved by the fostering of the law and religion community. A conversation needs to begin between law and religion scholars themselves. The study of particular developments needs to be understood in the broader context of religion law. The study of religion law needs to take into account religious law. The national study of law and religion needs to be understood in light of supra- and sub-State developments. This conversation then needs to broaden within the academy: law and religion has much to gain from and much to contribute within an interdisciplinary climate. At least part of the solution is that the law and religion conversation becomes more outward-facing. The conversation needs to move beyond the Law School to bring in insights from other parts of the academy and beyond. A key variable in overcoming the obstacles identified is the building up of relationships between the academic community and those who form, create, interpret, adjudicate and use the law, be they policy-makers, legislators, judges and practitioners. Those interested in law and religion need not only be aware of the new horizons but also need to be looking outwards. These are exciting but challenging times.

Conclusions

It is hoped that this volume illustrates the range and importance of the work of law and religion scholars in England and Wales. For those interested in the study of law and religion in the British context, it is hoped that the studies included will help to contextualise their own work both in terms of the changing legal framework and also in terms of their position within the blossoming academic community. For those whose work focuses on the interaction between law and religion in other jurisdictions, it is hoped that this collection has shown the some of the detail and some of the nuances of the English experience which are invariably lacking from comparative accounts that simply focus on Church-State relations in the form of models based on constitutional provisions[84]. As we have argued elsewhere, saying that England is a country with a State church

---

[84] R Sandberg and N Doe, 'Church-State Relations in Europe' (2007) 1(5) *Religion Compass* 561; R Sandberg, 'Church-State Relations in Europe: From Legal Models to an Interdisciplinary Approach' [2008] 13 *Journal of Religion in Europe* 329.

says very little about the legal regulation of religion in England[85]. It is hoped that this collection says a little more.

In particular, the following fifteen broad conclusions may be ventured:

i. The increase in interest in the study of law and religion in England and Wales is in part attributable to a step change from passive accommodation to prescriptive regulation.

ii. However, the study of law and religion did not begin in 1998. A historical dimension is vital, especially to appreciate the difference between the established Church of England and other voluntary religious bodies.

iii. Yet, the Human Rights Act 1998 was a watershed. In a similar way as toleration marked a substantial shift from post-Reformation discrimination, the Human Rights Act 1998 encapsulated a considerable shift from passive accommodation to the active promotion of religious liberty as a right.

iv. The codified rights found in Human Rights Act 1998 and the different rules of interpretation clashed with the English constitutional heritage, bringing judges more clearly into the political arena and leading to greater litigation. The case law in relation to religion under the Human Rights Act 1998 may not have yet affected the actual decisions reached by the judiciary, but has affected the reasoning. The reasoning of the House of Lords in *Begum* has constrained the Article 9 right.

v. Further legislative developments followed the Human Rights Act 1998. The effects of Civil Partnership Act 2004 are not yet fully understood, especially in relation to the Church of England.

vi. Developments in discrimination law have led to an increase in litigation that seems to overshadow any increase in the protection of religious freedom. The narrowness of religious exemptions to these laws is increasingly stressed.

vii. Developments in criminal law have seen the abolition of the blasphemy laws but the advent of a plethora of statutory offences, the ambit of which is currently unknown.

viii. Similarly, the provisions of the Charities Act 2006 concerning religion are far from clear and this seems to be exasperated rather than clarified by the interpretation offered by the Charity Commission.

---

[85] Ibid.

   ix. Further developments in religion law are to be expected. In addition to the ever-going body of case law, there have been calls to move beyond the Human Rights Act and reforms in discrimination law point towards a single Equality Act.

   x. Religion law is increasingly affected by supra- and sub-national authorities. An increased focus on religion by the Council of Europe and the European Union, in particular, has led to the internationalisation of religion law. Moreover, increasingly it is possible to speak of a 'regional ecclesiastical law' in many jurisdictions.

   xi. The pace of change is challenging in terms of scholarship. It is imperative that specific developments are understood in the wider context of religion law. Developments in one part of religion law may have much to learn from developments in other parts

   xii. The study of law and religion, moreover, includes the study of religious law as well as religion law. The study of the two is invariably intertwined, as the law of the Church of England makes clear.

  xiii. The study of religious law may shed light upon the meaning and nature of law itself. The comparative study of religious law enables those who work within a single tradition to contextualise their work. The category of 'Christian law' provides a point of comparison for those working in the fields of Islamic, Jewish and Hindu law.

  xiv. The study of the relationship between religion, law and society requires an interdisciplinary approach, fusing legal and social scientific insights. However, such work needs to build upon rather than replace local, technical, legal analysis. Law and religion academics have much to gain but also much to give to other parts of the academy.

  xv. Law and religion scholarship can also make a contribution outside the university in terms of work that has policy implications and work that is policy-orientated. However, low levels of understanding provide an obstacle to this work. This is likely to be overcome the more law and religion becomes an outward facing discipline.

The study of law and religion in England and Wales is a fast-growing area of study. Although less entrenched in North America and many continental European countries, the study of law and religion has now moved beyond the embryonic stage. For those who work in this field, these are exhilarating but challenging times. It is hoped that the essays in this collection illustrate this excitement, inspiring and stimulating further work on law and religion and its new horizons.